COME BACK TO ME MY LANGUAGE

J. EDWARD CHAMBERLIN

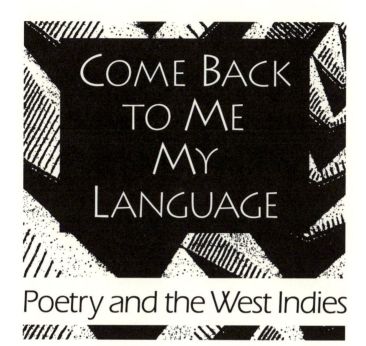

COME BACK TO ME MY LANGUAGE

Poetry and the West Indies

UNIVERSITY OF ILLINOIS PRESS
Urbana and Chicago

© 1993 by the Board of Trustees of the University of Illinois
Manufactured in the United States of America
1 2 3 4 5 C P 5 4 3 2 1

This book is printed on acid-free paper.

Library of Congress Cataloging-in-Publication Data

Chamberlin, J. Edward. 1943–
    Come back to me my language : poetry and the West Indies / J.
Edward Chamberlin.
        p. cm.
    Includes bibliographical references and index.
    ISBN 0-252-01973-3 (alk. paper). -- ISBN 0-252-06297-3 (pbk. : alk. paper)
    1. West Indian poetry—History and criticism. 2. West Indies—
Intellectual life. 3. West Indies—Languages. I. Title.
PN849.C3C48 1993
809.1'099729—dc20   92-21910
                                                              CIP

For
Sarah, Geoffrey, and Megan

Contents

Acknowledgments ix

1 "A black apostrophe to pain" 1

2 "Where then is the nigger's home?" 30

3 "Come back to me my language" 67

4 "To court the language of my people" 109

5 "Loose now the salt cords binding our tongues" 153

6 "i a tell no tale" 217

Epilogue 271

Notes 275

Selected Bibliography 295

Acknowledgments

This book began in 1985 with the generous support of the John Simon Guggenheim Memorial Foundation and continued with assistance from many friends and colleagues. Like the book, they took turns. I am especially grateful to those who read the mansucript at various stages and gave generous encouragement and advice: Edward Baugh, Hugh Brody, Stewart Brown, Sander Gilman, Linda Hutcheon, Michael Kirkham, Mark McWatt, Anne Michaels, Mervyn Morris, Rex Nettleford, Stephen Regan, Jon Stallworthy and Robert Welch. Many others provided help and hospitality and the opportunity to try out my ideas throughout the project. Listing some, I hope I acknowledge them all: Tom Adamowski, Anne Adams, Kay Baxter, Tom Berger, Frank Birbalsingh, Dionne Brand, Kamau Brathwaite, Ron Bryden, Fred Case, Victor Chang, Michael Cooke, Carolyn Cooper, Hans de Groot, Nadi Edwards, Rob Finley, Honor Ford-Smith, Jack Foster, Lorna Goodison, Wilson Harris, Gary Holthaus, Jim Howard, Zhongwen Huang, Mary Kancewick, Janet Lambert, Ann Lancashire, John Lavery, Michael Levin, John Lynen, Dorik Mechau, Karen Mulhallen, Ossie Murray, Peter Nesselroth, Mary Nyquist, John O'Brian, Mary O'Connor, Molara Ogundipe-Leslie, Michael Ondaatje, Rob Prichard, Gordon Rohlehr, Ann Saddlemyer, Bruce St. John, Roydon Salick, Jose San-Pedro, Patrick Saul, Olive Senior, Carolyn Servid, Philip Sherlock, Adam Shoemaker, Makeda Silvera, Jean Smith, Linda Spalding, Ricardo Sternberg, Paddy Stewart, John Stubbs, Patrick Taylor, Hidde Van Duym, Derek Walcott, Dwight Whyllie, Jane Widdicombe and Geoffrey Williams. At the University of Illinois Press, Karen Hewitt and Rita D. Disroe have been especially helpful.

Acknowledgments

I owe many thanks to Jane Chamberlin for her patience and support. And I have three other special acknowledgments. Ramsay Derry threw a line to me just as I was going under, pulled me to shore, helped me put my craft back together ... and then, being the best of editors, pushed me off on my own again. I owe him this book. Frederick Morgan brought the encouragement and support he has given me over the past twenty years to bear on this project, and showed the way through. And Janet Turnbull Irving ... who believed in this book, and in its author, and in poetry. She is an agent like no other; and her friendship has been a blessing.

1

"A black apostrophe to pain"

Slavery shaped the West Indies. It was expensive and inconvenient, and presented considerable problems of governance; but nobody came up with an alternative, especially for the production of sugar. The desires and the anxieties of the European colonizers in turn shaped slavery, through the institutions that developed for establishing civil and religious order in the region and for promoting its economic prosperity.

During the 350 years of slavery in the West Indies, Africans with a rich and ancient inheritance were transported with brutal force thousands of miles from home to strange islands in the middle of a strange sea. They were separated from their families and friends and from others who spoke their language, and put to work in conditions in which their very humanity was only barely acknowledged and their traditions broken up and denounced. They were visibly different from the people among whom they now lived, and this difference became a mark of dispossession and contempt. The slaves who came to the West Indies were scorned and feared and mocked by the Europeans who brought them; and they were far from a home to which they could not return. They were cast out and closed in, and burdened by doubt and disbelief about who they were and where they belonged.

For 500 years, this has been the legacy of slavery, even though slavery itself was abolished between 100 and 150 years ago throughout the West Indies. But it lives on in the memories of West Indians. It has produced testaments not only to cynicism and despair but also to the hope and possibility that have emerged out of those dark and haunted nights. These testaments, like those dark nights, are a legacy we all share, whoever we are and wherever we live.

With its grim and ghastly images of colonial history, slavery still inspires West Indian dreams of individual freedom and collective independence. It also haunts their nightmares. Slavery's past is part of the present life of the West Indies; and it finds eloquent expression in West Indian poetry. Here is an epitaph to that inheritance, by the Jamaican Dennis Scott.

> They hanged him on a clement morning, swung
> between the falling sunlight and the women's
> breathing, like a black apostrophe to pain.
> All morning while the children hushed
> their hopscotch joy and the cane kept growing
> he hung there sweet and low.
> > At least that's how
> they tell it. It was long ago
> and what can we recall of a dead slave or two
> except that when we punctuate our island tale
> they swing like sighs across the brutal
> sentences, and anger pauses
> till they pass away.[1]

The heritage is all here, in a catalog of West Indian experience. The legacy of sugar, bitter rather than sweet for those enslaved to work the plantations that for so long provided the main economic resource for the West Indies. The juxtaposition of brutality and beauty ("they hanged him on a clement morning"), and the ironies of a familiar sentimentality ("sweet and low"). The wonder of human beings in the presence of something immeasurably larger than themselves, whether the awful power of the slave system or the hushed loveliness of life, renewed every morning and sustained by the gaiety of children. The mix of spoken and written languages, punctuated by silence and suffering and the stark image of the hanged man ("a black apostrophe to pain"). The experience of West Indian women, whose place has often been obscured but who both literally and figuratively have given breath to their people, and whose bravery has deep roots in this heritage. And the uncertainties of all such accounts ("at least that's how they tell it"), underwritten as they are by fear and hope as well as by rage and resignation, and signifying a humanity that paradoxically defies both hanging and history.

Slavery was not just the beginning, the first cause, of West Indian colonization. It was also its end, its final cause and purpose. Because of this, it continues to inform the imaginations of West Indian writers and artists, just as it continues to influence the realities of West Indian life. Many of the most powerful accounts of these realities are in poems written by West Indians, and contemporary West Indian poetry provides a unique chronicle not only of the inheritance of slavery but also of the changes that have taken place over the past fifty years as the islands have moved to political independence, and as their people have come to new terms with their past. In new ways. And new languages.

This inheritance is forcefully recalled in a poem by the Guyanese writer Martin Carter, published while he was imprisoned in Georgetown in the 1950s for his resistance to continuing colonial rule in British Guiana. The poem conveys an intensely personal suffering, and the opening words confirm both the difference of this experience from anything that many of us have been through and the language that is part of that difference.

> I come from the nigger yard of yesterday
> leaping from the oppressors' hate
> and the scorn of myself;
> from the agony of the dark hut in the shadow
> and the hurt of things;
> from the long days of cruelty and the long nights of pain
> down to the wide streets of to-morrow, of the next day
> leaping I come, who cannot see will hear.[2]

In one of the central paradoxes of literature, poetic voices that are genuinely different, as Carter's is, make us newly conscious of what is shared by all poets and by their readers in different times and places. In one sense, this should not be all that surprising. Poets, even those who have lived through such experiences, are in many ways much like the rest of us. And even their experiences are often quite close to ours. When they are at home they get restless, and when they are away they get homesick. They fall in love. And they talk about these things. *That's* where the significant difference comes in. And that's why we read them. Robert Burns, writing for an eighteenth-century British audience, said "my love is like a red, red rose," opening everyone's eyes to love . . . and to roses. And while his metaphor holds our attention still, William Carlos Williams, in industrialized America in the twentieth century, needed something new. So he said, "my love is like a green-glass insulator against a blue sky," and recovered something of the freshness—or outrageousness—which Burns's image must once have had, and which we associate with being in love. The Guyanese poet John Agard, writing for British and West Indian readers in the 1970s—and like Burns and Williams, for himself too—brings something new again, something different into the language of literature and of love.

> If I be the rain
> you the earth
> let love be the seed . . .
> If I be a tree
> clinging to parch earth
> this time you be the rain
> and love the wind . . .
> and love go spread wings
> love go spread wings.[3]

The local language used here, in conjunction with the literary phrasing and imagery of the poem, underlines the difference. But difference often takes a more complex form, as in a poem called "Guinea Woman" by the Jamaican writer Lorna Goodison. It tells of love and loss in the specific terms of that heritage of slavery which is the central legacy of West Indians. In so doing, it also shifts the poetic paradigms of love.

> Great grandmother
> was a guinea woman
> wide eyes turning
> the corners of her face
> could see behind her . . .
>
> It seems her fate was anchored
> in the unfathomable sea
> for great grandmother caught the eye of a sailor
> whose ship sailed without him from Lucea harbour.
> Great grandmother's royal scent of
> cinnamon and escallions
> drew the sailor up the straits of Africa,
> the evidence my blue-eyed grandmother
> the first Mulatta
> taken into backra's household
> and covered with his name.
> They forbade great grandmother's
> guinea woman presence
> they washed away her scent of
> cinnamon and escallions

controlled the child's antelope walk
and called her uprisings rebellions.

But, great grandmother
I see your features blood dark
appearing
in the children of each new
breeding
the high yellow brown
is darkening down.
Listen, children
it's great grandmother's turn.[4]

C. S. Lewis used to say that the Romance of the Rose would not ring true if rewritten as the Romance of the Onion. What he should have said was, not in Europe. A romance of the rose would ring very false indeed as the figure for this West African/West Indian romance; while a romance of the onion, or of cinnamon and escallions, might be just right.

The St. Lucian poet and playwright Derek Walcott brings this into even wider perspective in his poem *Omeros*, a story of European and African adventure with a chorus of characters both from the Homeric epics and from the brutal history of contact with the aboriginal peoples of the Americas—a history too of broken words and dislocated peoples, just like the story of slavery; and no account of the Americas can ignore the connection between them. Walcott makes the passage from the old world to the new with a seafarer's sense of similarities and a poet's sense of differences. Land is land, and love is love; but always with a difference. Achilles and Hector and Helen play their parts; but they do so differently in the West Indies . . . just as the Mediterranean is different from the Caribbean, with different conventions of life and literature. And yet similar, too. The poem opens with a fisherman from St. Lucia named Philoctete. He has been wounded in the leg by a rusted anchor, is in pain from the swelling that "he believed . . . came from the chained ankles of his grandfathers,"[5] and is finally cured by the healing power of grandmothers. And like the aboriginal inhabitants of the West Indies, he smiles for the tourists "who try taking his soul with their cameras."[6] The image of dispossession merges with the distortions of those first tourists, beginning with Columbus, whose ways of seeing and saying—and of taking—started the shadowy story of the West Indies and the mistaken naming of Indians throughout the Americas. (The use of the terms West Indies and West Indians throughout this book reflects the ironies of colonial representation, and the ways in which both classical names and European languages have been appropriated into the everyday life of the region.)

Omeros is the Greek word for Homer and a pun on the English word for home; and at the end of the poem Walcott comes full circle, back to the ways in which literature embodies the differences and the similarities between experiences, especially the experiences of departure and homecoming, of loss and love. A local fisherman named Achille recalls Hector his rival (who died driving his taxi cab Comet); and then he puts a wedge of dolphin aside for Helen, who in Walcott's poem is both a black St. Lucian woman of extraordinary beauty and the island of St. Lucia itself—which in a familiar imperial script was "discovered," named Helen, and fought over by European rivals. In this final moment of grace and love "a full moon shone like a slice of raw onion."[7] A Romance of the Onion after all.

Which brings us right back to the earliest accounts of the West Indies by European adventurers, taking souls and souvenirs. Making memories. Those who sailed west across the Atlantic on their voyages of discovery brought little with them, not even slaves at first. But two things they did bring made all the difference: their ways of seeing, uniquely European and centered in their stubborn sense of themselves; and their ways of talking about what they had seen, ordered according to a strict set of European habits and desires.

In some respects they were wonderfully straightforward. They certainly recognized land when they saw it, and they wrote about their landings with adventurous naiveté. But they missed some other things, or construed them in ways that were blatantly convenient. They did not see, for example, that the new world to which they had come was as old as their own. And they chose to see the aboriginal societies as primitive and haphazard, rather than as civilizations organized much like their own into tribal units and confederations, within a complex network of sacred and secular affiliations.

Invention became part of discovery. Reality reflected their imaginations. Columbus based his description of his first encounter with native people more upon his fancy than upon any accurate observation. "They all go naked as their mothers bore them," he wrote, "and the women also, although I saw only one very young girl."[8] If Columbus had founded his navigation on that kind of fanciful generalization about the women of the new world, he would have ended up in Tierra del Fuego or Constantinople. Nothing encourages a sailor's imagination like being on dry land.

Distortions and deceptions were part of the settlement of the new world from the very beginning. Slavery followed soon after. It came naturally to Columbus, who had moved from Genoa to Lisbon twenty years earlier, just as the Portuguese city was developing not only as a leading center of navigation and cartography but also as the base for the recently established trade in African slaves. So slavery was on his mind, along with speculation about savages and their salvation. "They should be good servants," he said of the native people he encountered. "And I believe that they would easily be made Christians, for it appeared to me that they had no creed." Slaves by nature; Christians by nurture.

Europeans brought their hopes with them and imitated in the new world all that they prized in the world they left behind. Mostly they prized order and opportunity. They brought with them their fears as well. For European colonists, the choice seemed stark. The alternative to a civil society was a barbaric one. And with their old-world eyes they saw barbaric ways all around them in the new world. The simple meaning of barbarism was—and still is—what other people do, those who are different, Them who are not like Us. The word barbarian originally meant "one who does not speak Greek" . . . to the Greeks, of course. But it soon came to mean all those people out there, beyond the walls of the city.

The ravaging of the aboriginal societies of the new world by the representatives of European civilization is closely related to the story of slavery and to the brutal dispossession and despair that are its legacy. Five hundred years later, we are still trying to come to terms with its causes and effects; but there is widening agreement that the presumptions and preoccupations that conditioned first contact with aboriginal peoples also determined the circumstances of slavery and settlement. This is a prominent theme in contemporary poetry, and indeed in all contemporary literature, in the West Indies; and it has a lot to do with the repossession of its languages. To set the stage, we will begin with a very brief account of the origins of these attitudes, which shaped West Indian society and fostered its legacy of slavery.

The early settlers in the new world had their eyes peeled for barbarians. At first they saw in the aboriginal people only the social instincts of a more or less advanced herd of animals. But then some doubts were raised, a heightened consciousness of how modes of perception and representation are as much the product of fashion as modes of anything else. This is, of course, itself a fashionable insight right now, especially with regard to representations of race and gender and class. But it had a first run shortly after contact. Maybe they were not seeing what was right before their eyes, suggested some settlers. Maybe the aboriginal societies were rather different than they first appeared.

Maybe order and good government were there, though in a different form. A celebrated disagreement broke out among the early Spanish colonists and their imperial mandarins about all of this. The matter was not merely metaphysical, for it involved the fundamental question of whether the new-world peoples, misnamed Indians, were to be considered human; and whether their dispossession and enslavement were justifiable. The dispute culminated in a formal debate held in Valladolid in Spain between 1550 and 1551.

It is not so much the debate itself that is of continuing interest, as the set of questions it raised about the authority of ideals and about representations of difference. Many of these same questions are at the heart of this book, which is about the ways in which representations and ideals, especially those sustained by the authority of language and its particular expressions of difference, can underwrite or undermine a people's sense of who they are and where they belong. It is about relationships between relative and absolute standards, and the notions of naturalness and artifice we use to validate these standards. And it is about how strangeness and familiarity condition these judgments. These questions were asked five hundred years ago; and they still preoccupy contemporary West Indian literature and contemporary West Indian life.

On the one side in the debate at Valladolid, there was Juan Gines de Sepulveda, a distinguished translator of Aristotle and the official historian for the Spanish court. He argued that there was just cause in the Spanish conquest of the aboriginal inhabitants of the new world. The Indians were incapable of orderly living, being disobedient by nature, and they should therefore be subjected to rule, including enslavement.

On the other side was Bartoleme de Las Casas, whose father had sailed with Columbus on his second voyage and brought back with him to Seville an Arawak Indian slave, whom he gave to his son as a personal attendant. When his father returned to the newly established Spanish settlement in Hispaniola (now the Dominican Republic and Haiti), Bartoleme joined him, and for the next few years was part of the process of colonization of the Caribbean as the Spanish expanded their settlements to Cuba, Jamaica, and Puerto Rico. He was ordained as a priest in 1510.

At first, Las Casas had no difficulty reconciling Christian ideals with the realities of enslaving Indians to work the plantation estates. The case against the treatment of Indians under Spanish authority in the West Indies was in fact first put not by Las Casas but by other members of the Dominican order, most notably by Fray Antonio de Montesinos in a memorable sermon on the Sunday before Christmas in 1511 to the wealthy landowners of Hispaniola. "You are in mortal sin," he told them, "for the cruelty and tyranny you use in dealing with these innocent people. Tell me, by what right and justice do you keep these Indians in such cruel and humble servitude? . . . Are these not men? Are you not bound to love them as you love yourselves? Be certain that in such a state as this you can no more be saved than the Moors or Turks."[9] It was not a popular sentiment, and it certainly must have spoiled Christmas that year. For a time, the Dominicans were in some danger in Hispaniola. Montesinos went to Spain to argue the case, and the king set up a commission to consider the whole issue.

It was not until a couple of years later that Las Casas saw the light. But when he did he was tireless in his efforts to change the system, even though as a remedy for the labor shortage the liberation of Indians would create he at first proposed that licenses be given for the importation of black slaves from Africa, on the logic that they had been enslaved by their rulers with a just title. The distinction between just and unjust title, familiar to Spanish advocates of "natural reason," was based not on racial difference but on religious classification and on whether the slaves were won in a "just" war or "properly" purchased. But in coming to realize the injustice of the methods by which the majority of Africans were being enslaved, Las Casas had also come to realize the fallibility of this kind of logic. The cruelty and horror of the slave trade imprinted themselves on Las Casas's mind and confirmed his opposition to all forms of slavery.

More was at stake in the debate than the economic viability of the Spanish land grant system. The argument was about how Christian Europeans viewed strange (that is, non-European, non-Christian) people and about the relationships between Christian European ideals and those held by others, in other places. Must the relationships be hierarchical, with ideals other than European by definition being subservient; or could they be reciprocal, with respect for the differences? Las Casas argued that the Indians of the new world were human and rational, and that their societies were highly developed, internally coherent, and continuously sustained by a set of habits and values to which all members of the society adhered. Their enslavement, therefore, was unjustifiable, and unjust.

Las Casas proposed that the justice of actions affecting other peoples such as the Indians of the new world should be determined by acknowledging the contingent authority of all systems, not on the basis of the absolute authority of one set of doctrines. Las Casas would probably be accused of "political correctness" these days, for he argued that we must recognize relativities of meaning and value. Of course, his argument was conditioned by his own European and Catholic values and intellectual habits. But he had an instinct for the pernicious effect of narrow doctrinal logic and its sometimes extraordinary persistence over long periods of time. And he was right, on that last count at least. The institution of slavery, and the logic of absolutes that sustained it and that Las Casas found so offensive, had the doctrinal approval of the Catholic church for fourteen hundred years, until officially changed by the Second Vatican Council in 1965.

The admirable feature of the debate was that it took place, and that the Spanish obsession with theoretical questions focused on an issue of such immense practical importance to the new world. The sad fact, however, was that national and international pressures overtook the disputants, and the debate never came to a clear conclusion; or, more precisely, that it never came to Las Casas's conclusion. The race for power and profit in the new world was on, and black slaves from Africa were necessary for the agricultural and industrial prosperity of the colonies. Other European nations challenged Spain's power in the West Indies, and new possibilities opened up for the exploitation of the region and the importation of slaves to do the work.

These possibilities depended upon three things: land, labor, and laws to regulate them. Land was there for the taking, at least once the European powers had played their military and diplomatic cards, devastated the aboriginal inhabitants, and divided up the territories. Secular laws were provided by the Spanish, British, French, and Dutch legal and administrative systems, imported along with other commodities to make life resemble European society as closely as possible, while spiritual laws came from on high, via the agents of the Catholic and Protestant regimes that accompanied European colonization. For a labor supply, the settlers turned first to the aboriginal people—the Arawaks and the Caribs—but their brutal exploitation produced neither a sufficient nor a reliable supply of workers. The expansion of ranching and sugar production, as well as the energetic exploitation of mineral resources and the establishing of towns and roads and all the paraphernalia of settlement, required a more certain and less complicated labor force.

To supply this, the colonists and their European imperial governments turned to the trade in West African slave labor which had been established by the Portuguese. By the 1450s, slaves were being traded in Lisbon, and once settlement in the new world developed this trade quickly expanded to the Caribbean and to South, Central, and North America. Slaves were a commodity that almost everyone in the colonization business wanted and needed. A multinational trade in slaves developed, and traffic in slaves became the base of a triangle, with the other sides transporting raw materials to Europe and manufactured products to Africa. The Middle Passage, as the route from West Africa to the Caribbean came to be called, served the convenience of both European and African imperial powers, evil empires all to the extent that they conspired in the slave trade. The trade thoroughly corrupted the economic, social, and political life of the West African nations; though in some measure it did the same to the European countries. But when the demand failed, the supplier suffered most.

The Europeans who established colonies in the West Indies put in place laws designed to justify and administer the institution of slavery by controlling the land and the labor upon which the colonial venture depended. Colonists, being notoriously resistant to anything that interfered with their ability to do whatever they wanted, needed to have their own whims and fancies restricted. The scum as well as the cream floated to the top in colonial society, and imperial authorities living several thousand miles away could not count on being able to tell the difference. So laws applying not only to slaves and servants but also to their military and political masters were crucial for the orderly governance and continuing prosperity of the colonies. The ideals upon which these laws were based were sometimes high-minded, after a fashion. The fashion was inevitably European.

Ideals are *always* more or less fashionable, conditioned by specific attitudes and expectations. They take shape in particular times and places and among particular peoples; and the meanings and values they embody shape all the discourses of a society, including its history, laws, and literature. In these discursive forms, such ideals have extraordinary authority, shaping representations of self and society; though the discourses themselves often mask questions about whether that authority is grounded in reality or in the imagination, and about whether it should be judged according to standards of objective truth or standards of coherence, consistency and utility. This is most obviously true with regard to the discourses of history and literature; but the slave laws put in place in the early days of settlement embodied this ambivalence too, delineating both the realities of the situation and the imaginations of the colonists.

The Spanish imposed a system of laws in the West Indies that went back to the thirteenth century and were called the *Siete Partidas*.[10] The French legal system that regulated slavery was developed in the seventeenth century and called the *Code Noir*. The British, in characteristic fashion, did not codify their laws but instead incorporated specific slave laws into the general framework of colonial law. The most chilling thing about all the slave laws is that they were brought into being and kept in place because the imperial societies were reasonably comfortable with the notion that people could be enslaved.

The laws enforcing slavery embodied the contradictions of a European tradition that on the one hand respected the artifice of civilization, and on the other, coveted a natural order. The Spanish enthusiasm for intellectual consistency prevailed in their essentially European medieval code, which displayed a facility with these kinds of contradictions. It defined slavery in the context of its opposite, liberty; and it described slavery as "something which men naturally abhor" and "contrary to natural reason" but yet "an agreement and regulation" of ancient origin and of legal status. Liberty, according to the *Siete Partidas*, is the good that "all creatures in the world love and desire, and much more do men, who have intelligence superior to that of others." The code deemed the slave to be a person rather than property, and while it confirmed the rights of the owner, it also prescribed humane duties. There is something very disturbing about the notional humanity of the Spanish code, since it defined such an inhumane practice. But if it is any comfort to those who look for coherence in such matters, it does not appear that the Spanish principles were ever taken all that seriously or strictly in the West Indies. As with the slave laws of the other imperial governments, Spanish slave laws were primarily in place to ensure public order.

The British system of slave laws reflected the fact that Great Britain itself did not bring to the West Indies a set of regulations developed at home, for slavery and serfdom had disappeared from the British isles long before they did in Spain. Also, the British tradition of representative government tended to give to the local colonial authorities (which in practical terms meant the slaveowners) the responsibility for designing these laws; though the principles of government involved here should not be exaggerated, for in other situations where the British imperial government decided it had a vested interest in local laws, as in Indian affairs in British North America, it was quite ready to insist on sole authority.

One clear distinction from the Spanish code was that under British law slaves were looked upon not so much as persons but as property, albeit of a special kind for which the owner had particular responsibilities. Most of the laws governing these responsibilities were essentially police laws, and were directed toward maintaining order and respect for private property. As the sophisticated and remarkably candid planter and slaveowner Bryan Edwards put it, "in countries where slavery is established, the leading principle on which the government is supported is fear: or a sense of that absolute coercive necessity which, leaving no choice of action, supercedes all questions of right."[11]

Protection for slaves was meager. All slaves, both men and women, were arbitrarily subject to the same range of penalties, of which flogging was the most common and by all accounts one of the most brutal. In the British West Indian colonies, the normal remedies available in common law were not usually available to slaves, mainly because local interests found them inconvenient and even subversive. Especially following the American revolutionary wars, despite some consternation in England about the plight of slaves, there was considerable resistance to any interference from London with what were claimed as local prerogatives. The Jamaica Assembly, for example, refused to accept a modestly progressive report in 1788, which proposed that "the negroes in this island are under the protection of the common law, with the rest of His Majesty's subjects residing in this island, except in cases where it has been found necessary to enact limitations; which limitations do not extend further than the public good requires, and are consistent with the preservation and welfare of the said negroes themselves." Instead, the Assembly put in place an amendment "that negroes in this island are under the protection of lenient and salutary laws, suited to their situation and circumstances."[12]

In the French West Indies, too, a slave was first of all deemed to be a thing rather than a person, though there was more room in the French code for considering a slave a person as well so that, for example, slave families were not supposed to be broken up when individual slaves were sold, and slaves were not to be forced to marry without consent (though they were certainly not allowed to marry *except* with the consent of their master). However, the concern for public order was predominant, especially as the numbers of slaves grew, so that by the middle of the eighteenth century the French government was of the view that "while the Slaves should be maintained and favourably treated by their Masters, the necessary precautions should also be taken to contain them within the bounds of their duty, and to prevent all that might be feared from them." A few years later, the government was even blunter. "It is only by leaving to the masters a power that is nearly absolute, that it will be possible to keep so large a number of men in that state of submission which is made necessary by their numerical superiority over the whites. If some masters abuse their power, they must be reproved in secret, so that the slaves may always be kept in the belief that the master can do no wrong in his dealings with them."[13]

The Dutch colonies and the Danish territories under company rule had laws that were fairly similar to those in the French territories, partly because both had their origins in Roman law. And both regimes maintained a stern sense of the place of slaves in the scheme of things. About the same time as the French government was sending the instruction quoted above to one of its colonial governors, the Dutch governor of Surinam was told by his fellow colonists on the Surinam Police Court that "although an owner should never presume the right of life and death over the slave, it is imperative that the slave continues to believe that his master has that right, as it would be impossible to control them if they were aware that their masters were liable to punishment or the death penalty for beating a slave to death."[14]

European settlement and African slavery in the West Indies became the rage early in the sixteenth century, when the British, French, Dutch, and Danish governments realized that Spain was onto a good thing in the new world; and that this good thing was helping finance Spain's military campaigns against them. So they all moved into the arena and took up imperial positions. Over the next two hundred years, there were settlements and skirmishes and in due course new settlements and new skirmishes throughout the region as islands were brought into or taken out of the control of one or another of these powers. The story of imperial enterprise is a story with familiar names—Hawkins and Drake and Raleigh among the English, for example—and the names represent the association of European military and mercantile adventure with the colonization of the West Indies.

By 1763, with the Treaty of Paris ending the Seven Years' War between England and France and Spain, the distribution of West Indian territory along European lines—and in European languages—was fairly well established. Some of the islands, such as Tobago, St. Lucia, St. Vincent, and Dominica, were not in the hands of any European power in the years leading to the Seven Years' War, though there were French settlers on the first two, while St. Vincent and Dominica were basically in the hands of the Caribs. The Treaty of Paris mapped out the political and linguistic contours of the West Indies. The British, who had first established colonies in the early seventeenth century, maintained by far the largest group of islands, including Jamaica, Barbados, Trinidad, Tobago, St. Vincent, Grenada, St. Kitts, Nevis, Montserrat, Antigua, and Dominica; while despite the protestations of hawkish British politicians such as William Pitt, the French kept St. Domingue (Haiti) and St. Lucia (which had changed hands a number of times already, and would again), and regained Martinique and Guadeloupe (basically in exchange for Canada). Cuba, along with Santo Domingo and Puerto Rico, stayed in Spanish hands. The Dutch were in Surinam, in the provinces of Essequibo, Demerara, and Berbice (which together became British Guiana in 1831), as well as in Curacao, the southern part of St. Martin, and Aruba. The Danish remained in possession of St. Thomas, St. John, and St. Croix (which were purchased by the United States in 1917 and renamed the United States Virgin Islands).

As settlement developed, so did the great sugar plantations, which took over from the diversified agricultural economy of coffee, tobacco, indigo, and cattle to become the most important commercial enterprise in the West Indies. (Gold and silver and salt were important too, but found mostly on the mainland.) These sugar plantations required large numbers of workers, which for the first 350 years were mainly slaves from West Africa. One planter estimated the "stock" required to keep three hundred acres in sugar production as 250 negroes, 80 steers, and 60 mules. Advertisements such as the following, from a Barbadian newspaper around 1770, were common. "For sale: two mules, three goats, a sow with eight pigs and a fine healthy woman with four children."[15]

During the eighteenth century alone, over 3 million slaves were imported to the West Indies to supply this stock. Sugar production went on for several months in the spring of the year, day and night, in field and "factory," cutting the cane and milling and boiling to make the sugar; while during the other months, slaves were put to work cultivating, replanting, and weeding in the fields, and at the never-ending chores of rural and domestic life. Women routinely worked at the same tasks, for the same number of hours in the field, as men. The life of all slaves was all too similar everywhere, though there were certainly differences among the islands and between plantations. Mirroring the European society of which it was a warped image, the institution of slavery encouraged the masters in everything from grotesque violence to petty tyranny, with some kindness too, albeit often condescending or capricious. Most of all, and despite the slave laws, it encouraged a brutal arbitrariness, which left a slave's well-being almost entirely in the hands of overseers and bookkeepers and drivers in the fields.

A plantation owner's largest capital investment was not in land but in labor—which is to say, in slaves; and therefore most planters, though often themselves absent, put priority on providing adequate food and shelter for their slaves. Slave huts were usually built by the slaves themselves, of materials grown on the estate. Clothes—normally two suits a year, of coarse linen—were provided by the owners. Food varied considerably. In some areas, such as Jamaica and St. Domingue, marginal land in the foothills or mountains was set aside for slaves to grow vegetables, with surplus being sold at Sunday markets. On other islands the planters' regular cropland was used for this purpose, the enterprise being much more highly organized with crews of old men, nursing women, and children doing the fieldwork. Elsewhere, nearly all the food for slaves was imported. And every area depended on some imports, which meant that interruption of supply (in times of war, for example) could bring widespread starvation. Efforts were constantly made to introduce new food plants. During the period of the American revolutionary wars at the end of the eighteenth century, both the ackee tree and the mango were brought over to the West Indies from Africa, and breadfruit from the south Pacific.

As more and more slaves were imported, a simple but significant change took place. West Indian society became black rather than white. And slowly, surely, especially in the nineteenth century, the islands became more and more distinctly West Indian. Different from the African homelands of most West Indians. Different from Europe, along whose lines the island settlements were modeled. Different from the aboriginal communities which had been dislocated or destroyed. And different too from the settlements that were developing in South and Central America, and from the newly independent colonies in the United States, to which blacks were also being brought as slaves.

This difference is a stubborn fact—not always recognized on the mainland—and an enduring legacy. It was not until the early nineteenth century that slavery became a central element of social, economic, and political life in the United States, with the expanded production of sugar, cotton, and tobacco. Sugar cane gave Louisiana (acquired by the United States in 1803) an economic base; the cultivation of tobacco by slave labor transformed Virginia, Kentucky, and Tennessee; and in less than twenty-five years, between 1800 and 1825, the United States took over most of the share of the British market for cotton, which had formerly belonged to the West Indies.

By this time, too, the campaign against the European slave trade was in full swing, led by powerful activists such as William Wilberforce in England. At the time Britain abolished the trade in 1808, over half the market in slaves was in British hands. The United States abolished the trade in the same year, but this was before the southern states had become dependent on cotton production. As cotton became king in the United States, trading in slaves came back into currency, though by then in other, mainly illegal, hands. France abolished its trade in 1818, and Spain in 1820; but trading continued openly for a number of years in ships sailing out of French and Spanish ports, as long as the demand lasted. In the West Indies, Cuba imported slaves up until 1865.

Abolishing the slave trade was one thing. Emancipating slaves was quite another, and came much more slowly. After several decades of encouraging local West Indian legislatures to better the conditions of slaves, the British government eventually passed an Abolition Act, which came into effect on August 1, 1834, and was binding on all its colonies. It immediately freed all children under six, but provided for others a period of apprenticeship varying from four to six years. In 1838, all slaves in British colonies were formally freed of this bond as well.

Slavery had been abolished in French colonies during the French Revolution, but it was reestablished by Napoleon. Beginning in 1830, France moved cautiously toward an emancipation act, which was finally passed and applied to its colonies in 1848. The Dutch moved even more slowly, and did not free all slaves in their colonies until 1873. Slaves in the Spanish island of Puerto Rico were freed in the same year; while slaves in Cuba saw the possibility of freedom only with the passing of an act in 1880 for their gradual emancipation, completed in 1886.

During this period, some of the labor force that had been provided in the West Indies by slavery was replaced by immigration, usually under contract or indenture arrangements. By far the greatest number of these workers came from India, so that by the 1880s more than a quarter of the population of British Guiana was East Indian, and one-third of the population of Trinidad.

The dates of emancipation do not mean a lot. Like the slave laws, the laws freeing slaves were one thing in theory, quite another in practice. And while it would trivialize slavery to say that freedom meant little during the years following emancipation, it is probably true that for many it meant full freedom to participate in the economic and social collapse of the society and little freedom to take part in its political affairs. But as West Indian historians Philip Sherlock and John Parry tell the tale, it was still a time of possibilities.

> The cassia tree, which grows throughout the West Indies, is a symbol of alternating despair and hope. Most West Indian trees are evergreen; but the cassia loses its leaves, and the bark peels from its grey-white trunk, as from a dead stick. Then suddenly, overnight, the tree becomes a cascade of golden flowers, as short-lived as it is lovely.
>
> The period in West Indian history which followed emancipation was like the death and rebirth of the cassia tree. It was the best and the worst of times. One disaster followed another; bankruptcy and financial chaos

in the eighteen-forties, droughts and epidemics in the eighteen fifties, rioting and bloodshed in the eighteen sixties. Yet in these disastrous years the initiative and courage of newly emancipated people were creating an independent peasantry. Radical constitutional changes were made in some territories, while the abolition of imperial preferences completed the destruction of the old plantation system. A rigid slave society marked by division and dominated by fear disintegrated and conditions were created for the growth, however slowly, of a new and dynamic society.[16]

Still, the legacy of slavery continued to shape this society, long after slavery was abolished. Among other things, those who had imported slaves had done a great deal to break up whatever social coherence and continuity might have been possible among the African blacks they brought over. The main reason for this was practical. Those who were confused and disoriented were less likely to rise up and resist. There were undoubtedly some advantages to encouraging certain patterns of community development. But the strategy of sustaining only a minimal level of social organization among slaves, and only a necessary level of literacy, was widely accepted and played to the prejudice that black society was fundamentally uncivilized. By the time the slaves were freed, the apparent simplicity of their social structure was routinely associated with their lack of progress and with the presumed backwardness of each member of it. According to the most advanced natural and social sciences in the nineteenth century, complexity was the signature of progress, and its absence was an indication of either immaturity or degeneracy. Slave societies were, willy nilly, shaped by their masters to satisfy this model; just as later Europe shaped Africa to satisfy its expectations of primitiveness and underdevelopment.

One of the consequences of this European self-interest was to frustrate—or more precisely, to fragment—the development in the West Indies of those accounts of origin and purpose by means of which people give significance to their societies and to themselves. Quite apart from the determined assault on individuals, the discontinuities of their collective lives made it very difficult but also very important for the slaves to develop a narrative of shaping forces, causes and effects, actions and reactions; just as the absence of some fundamental coherences—of family life, for instance—both impaired their ability and gave urgency to their need to provide a logic of goals and ideals according to which they could confirm and celebrate their collective identities. The development in the West Indies of an extraordinarily rich tradition of imaginative expression drawing deeply on African inheritances, especially in such conditions of relative discontinuity and incoherence, provides a good indication of the significance of imaginative traditions generally, and suggests one of the central functions of literature and the arts in all societies. Most of all, it is a tribute to the indomitable spirit of the people themselves.

There is another aspect of this situation that has had a continuing effect on West Indian life: by breaking up groups of slaves taken from the same place and separating those who spoke the same language, the colonists effectively imposed on the slaves a European language. Although African languages were routinely spoken on the plantations, they were systematically discounted in a West Indian society dominated by Europeans, and were at least officially replaced by European languages and culture and history. Behind the brutally practical reasons for depriving slaves of the use of their mother tongue and replacing it with a European language—a kind of accustoming of cattle ("two-legged cattle" was the Greek word for slaves) to their new corral—was an attitude shared by colonial officials and by the local governments that followed them in various parts of the world. Put simply, European colonizers believed that their languages were civilized, and others were not. Along with the privileged artifice of civilization that their languages exemplified, they thought that these languages enjoyed a kind of natural superiority as well. This dichotomy between naturalness and artifice continues to inform even our most sophisticated views of language and literature, generating a set of issues and ironies that will provide one of the themes of this book.

The colonizers held their European traditions in high esteem, sending their children back to Europe to school and usually living there themselves as much as possible. And so a great deal of room was left for slaves to develop new and distinctly West Indian forms of social and cultural expression. Various facts of slave life, such as a range of domestic chores that were done together, contributed to this process. The stubborn durability of African social and cultural traditions and forms of religious expression also helped create solidarity among blacks both during the period of slavery and in the years after, as their shared experiences in the West Indies gave them a sense of belonging both to this new place and to each other. In all of this, a common language was crucial, and ironically became one of the most powerful instruments of collective action.

This positive aspect, of course, does not diminish the grim consequences of imposing a second language on those who were brought as slaves from Africa to the West Indies. For them and for their children, being denied the full use of their own language must initially have been almost as brutal as the Middle Passage itself. Eventually, however, they turned it to advantage; for as they were thrown together with others, English or French or Dutch or Spanish became a bond rather than a barrier, and European languages were integrated with elements of their own African languages. Pronunciation and grammar and vocabulary changed, and forms developed that differed substantially from European dialects and gave West Indians a distinct linguistic identity and unique possibilities for literary expression.

There are about 34 million people throughout the West Indies. In both its history and its present habitation, the Caribbean is mainly a Hispanic Sea, for 65 percent of the people have Spanish as their mother tongue. Another 20 percent speak French or a French creole. There is something to be learned from comparative accounts of what happened in each area of European imperial enterprise, with the heritage of slavery being the common bond for all West Indians, in all parts of the West Indies. But there is also good reason to focus on regions that share a common language and with it a common set of relationships to a European linguistic and literary heritage. This book is about the English-speaking Caribbean. Its population is not large, but its substantial geographical as well as social, economic, and political diversity provides some good illustrations of a history and a heritage belonging to all West Indians. And some powerful images of a future, and a literature, which are uniquely West Indian, and which have their roots in slavery.

The practice of slavery in the West Indian colonies created a fundamental contradiction. Slaves were central to the economic and social well-being of the colonies, but they were marginal to colonial society and to its perception of itself as a civilized enterprise. Slaves were everywhere to be seen, and yet in another way they were not seen at all by the Europeans who looked out over their elegant lawns and gardens from the Great Houses of their plantation estates.

They were invisible partly because they were deemed items of property, things one took for granted rather than persons one noticed. But their invisibility went beyond this. Even when acknowledged as persons, slaves were often denied personalities, and generalized and caricatured in a devastatingly impersonal way. Occasionally, as the diaries of overseers demonstrate, relations between slaves and their masters were characterized by bonds of affection, serving the mutual needs of both. But whatever the situation, slaves were all but unnoticeable to the laws that protected the personal rights of other people, white people.

As property, slaves were just part of the landscape or the furnishings. As persons, they were typically so as well. Blacks in the West

Indies continued to be viewed in this way long past the period of slavery, for Europeans ordered their lives there to create the illusion not simply that it was a white world they lived in, but that the world was somehow not the West Indies. They spent their leisure time dreaming their way out of the country, reading poems about hosts of golden daffodils in a land where these were seldom to be seen, and ignoring the presence of the blacks, who were everywhere.

For blacks, invisibility has long been a powerful image of the dispossession and loss that were part of their history in the new world. This image becomes more compelling in the light of the simple fact that blacks were undeniably—and in the eyes of the whites, ostentatiously—a visible part of the West Indian world from the time they arrived. For along with a kind of invisibility went an equally exaggerated—and equally irrational—visibility. White colonists, when they did open their eyes to the world around them and saw the West Indies for the African diaspora they had made it, drew attention to the menace of blackness in an overwrought way that reflected their fears about the social and economic order of the colonies. Although they sustained the economic system and conditioned the social arrangements of the islands, slaves were also seen as the main threat to colonial peace and prosperity.

But there was more to it. The preoccupation of European whites with African blacks and blackness, evident in almost all the writings about the West Indies by residents and visitors alike, flowed from a dog's breakfast of neurotic and psychotic obsessions about "others" that Europeans brought with them along with their manners and moralities. From Sambo to Satan, the black was caricatured as idle or simple or savage or diabolical, in all instances representing a state of being that observers either feared or fancied somewhere deep in their white souls. We structure our worlds with stereotypes, or at least the worlds of difference we perceive between ourselves and other people and things. These typologies are designed to give us a measure of comfort in the midst of our anxieties, while preserving—with that perversity of human psychology—the fear and fascination that we associate with difference. Because they are so intimately related to our own identity and to perceived threats to its integrity, stereotypes involve systems of representation that are both projections and rejections of elements in ourselves, especially those over which we have no fundamental control; and not surprisingly, they often focus on the categories of sexuality and race and disease. The fictions that were developed to justify the situation of African slaves and their European masters read like a circus of stereotypes.

The nineteenth century was especially industrious in the production of typologies, mostly because they seemed to be a necessary part of the colonial enterprise and the ideology of European racial and national superiority upon which it depended. (The obsession with racial purity, which had implications beyond the construction of stereotypes, was transformed in due course into a wide range of other ideals of purity, especially regarding language.) The civilian drew paranoid assurance from the occasional admiring glance of the barbarian whom he (or she) professed to despise, while the overall ideology of superiority was grounded in depressingly consistent pronouncements from some of the major European philosophers and scientists about the innate inferiority of blacks. As so often with racist ideologies, this was reinforced by a self-interested sort of realism. As mercantilism took over from militarism in the business of colonization, European nations began to identify their economic welfare with a favorable balance of trade, which depended substantially upon their colonies. And so when slavery ceased, the productivity of black labor—or the lack of it—became a matter of urgent concern, and of caricature. Blacks could no longer be taken for granted, and their foolish or fiendish predispositions therefore became matters of general interest. Much depended upon the industriousness of blacks, and their supposed idleness preoccupied the colonizers, frustrating their imperial appetite for profit and feeding their desire for continued control of the lands and coercion of its laborers, according to widely accepted principles of international law that deemed idle use of land justification for exercising European domination to bring such lands into production.

These attitudes were not confined to those whose interests were directly involved in the economic prosperity of the colonies. They shaped conventional commentary, which in turn reinforced colonial policy. The English novelist Anthony Trollope provides a good example, writing in 1859 after a trip to the West Indies. Trollope was the author of over fifty novels, the best known of which are the "Barsetshire Chronicles," beginning with *Barchester Towers*. His visit to the West Indies was on a business trip for the Post Office, in which he worked for thirty years. He traveled widely, read voraciously, and wrote regularly. His background was cosmopolitan: his father was a lawyer who dabbled in literary activity; and after his father turned disastrously to farming, his mother maintained the family by her writing, including an acid-tongued book (after a sojourn in the United States) called *Domestic Manners of the Americans* and a variety of travel books and fiction. So Trollope's comments are typical of a reasonably well educated, reasonably well disposed observer. Writing of what he saw as the representative black worker, Trollope suggested that "he is idle, unambitious as to worldly position, sensual, and content with little. . . . The negro's idea of emancipation was and is emancipation not from slavery but from work. To lie in the sun and eat breadfruit and yams is his idea of being free."[17] Moving to another topic, Trollope expanded on his theme. "Intellectually," he proposed, a black man

> is apparently capable of but little sustained effort; but, singularly enough, here he is ambitious. He burns to be regarded as a scholar, puzzles himself with fine words, addicts himself to religion for the sake of appearance, and delights in aping the little graces of civilization. He despises himself thoroughly, and would probably be content to starve for a month if he could appear as a white man for a day; but yet he delights in signs of respect paid to him, black as he is, and is always thinking of his own dignity. If you want to win his heart for an hour, call him a gentleman; but if you want to reduce him to a despairing obedience, tell him he is a filthy nigger, assure him that his father and mother had tails like monkeys, and forbid him to think that he can have a soul like a white man.[18]

The scorn of self to which Martin Carter referred, the self so deeply divided that it has neither lamp nor mirror by which to confirm its dignity, is starkly cast in this brutal prescription. "These people," Trollope concluded, "are a servile race, fitted by nature for the hardest physical work, and apparently at present fitted for little else."[19] And yet, he said elsewhere with more than a little exasperation, "Sambo has learned to have his own way. . . . 'No, massa, me weak in me belly; me no workee today; me no like workee just 'em little moment' . . . This is all bad—bad nearly as bad can be—bad perhaps as anything short of slavery. . . . As matters are, one cannot wonder that the black man will not work. The question stands thus: cannot he be made to do so? Can it not be contrived that he shall be free, free as is the Englishman, to eat his bread in the sweat of his brow?"[20]

Like many other British observers who wrote about the condition of the West Indies in the nineteenth century, Trollope was acutely conscious of what was referred to as the "condition of England": the endemic poverty and despair that afflicted large parts of the population as a result of the severe dislocation generated by the industrial revolution and, ironically, the costs of running a large empire. The notion that indolent blacks in a British colony might be better off—better fed, and in better health—than industrious whites at home in Great Britain was deeply disturbing.

The historian Thomas Carlyle was one of the most offended British commentators during this period, and one of the most offensive. His comments convey a familiar attitude, however, and a familiar logic of imperial responsibility and colonial policy that included a hierarchy of human beings going from black at the bottom to white at the top. In his "Occasional Discourse on the Nigger Question," written in 1849, he argued that

> with regard to the West Indies, it may be laid down as a principle . . . that no Black man who will not work according to what ability the gods have given him for working, has the smallest right to eat pumpkin, or to any fraction of land that will grow pumpkin, however plentiful such land may be; but has an indisputable and perpetual *right* to be compelled, by the real proprietors of said land, to do competent work for his living. . . . Induce him, if you can: yes, sure enough, by all means try what induce-ment will do; and indeed every coachman and carman knows that secret, without our preaching, and applies it to his very horses as the true method:—but if your Nigger will not be induced? In that case, it is full certain, he must be compelled. . . . No; the gods wish besides pumpkins, that spices and other valuable products be grown in their West Indies; thus much so they have declared in so making the West Indies:—infi-nitely more they wish, that manful industrious men occupy their West Indies, not indolent two-legged cattle, however "happy" over their abun-dant pumpkins.[21]

The caricature of blacks was not the stuff of tabloids and trashy novels, but rather was handed down from the serious chroniclers of the thoughts and feelings of the age. These remarks reflect not only the pathological condition of European consciousness at the time but also the great concerns of the imperial enterprise in the West Indies: land and labor and their productive use in the service of the empire. This perception of the West Indies and West Indians as a place and a people serving interests essentially located elsewhere continues to the present day in the economic, social, and political assumptions of international trade and tourism, and the geopolitical determinism of the World Bank, the International Monetary Fund, and other national and multinational authorities. It also underlies some familiar attitudes toward West Indian language and literature.

The troubles in Jamaica that broke out in 1865 provide an instance of how questions of land, labor, and the laws regulating them con-verged, and how these questions concentrated the anxieties of those in authority. Times were difficult in Jamaica in the 1850s and 1860s. Pro-longed drought, bad crops, and commodity prices that were inflated due to the American Civil War, had intensified the insecurity and injus-tice that plagued black laborers. Many of them were anxious to gain a measure of independence as small farmers.

In a familiar way, the blame for much of the difficulty was put on the blacks themselves, who were described by E. J. Eyre, the colonial Governor in Jamaica, as idle, improvident, and vicious, "in a low state of civilization and being under the influence of superstitious feelings."[22] Just the sort of people from whom one could expect trouble.

The British had uprisings on their mind anyway, because of the Indian Mutiny abroad, and closer to home discontent in the north of England and in Ireland. And so Eyre, who represented their concerns, was unsympathetic to the anxieties of West Indian blacks. But he was not entirely insensitive. He sensed trouble. And it came.

Some of the peasants in one district appealed to the Queen for land they might cultivate cooperatively. (As an indication of the predicament of laborers in the region during this period, one of the most reliable contemporary accounts—written by W. G. Sewell as a series of letters in the *New York Times*—was entitled *The Ordeal of Free Labour in the West Indies (1862)*). The Colonial Office in London, on behalf of Her Majesty, rejected the appeal in the following terms, arguing

> that the prosperity of the labouring classes, as well as of all other classes, depends, in Jamaica, and in other countries, upon their working for wages, not uncertainly, or capriciously, but steadily and continuously, at the times when their labour is wanted, and for so long as it is wanted; and that if they would use this industry, and thereby render the plantations productive, they would enable the planters to pay them higher wages for the same hours of work that are received by the best field labourers in this country; and, as the cost of the necessaries of life is much less in Jamaica than it is here, they would be enabled, by adding prudence to industry, to lay by an ample provision for seasons of drought and dearth; and they may be assured, that it is from their own industry and prudence, in availing themselves of the means of prospering that are before them, and not from any such schemes as have been suggested to them, that they must look for an improvement in their conditions.[23]

Industry and thrift, but no land. It was the Colonial Office's favorite prescription for progress to all of their non-white subjects, all over the world. It was medicine that many West Indian blacks were unwilling to take. To reinforce its authority, Eyre instructed that the "Queen's Advice," as it was called, be read from the pulpit of all Anglican churches in Jamaica.

The Anglican church was also known as the Established church. In its role as the official custodian of state opinion on religious matters, it was occasionally used to express opinions more secular than sacred. Church congregations that over the years parted ways with the Established church were called "dissenters" or "nonconformist" or "free

churches." They stand in relation to the Established churches somewhat as those who speak dialect do to those who speak a "standard"
or established language.

The nonconformist churches in the English-speaking world have
routinely opposed close connections between the comfortably established church and the comfortably established state, both of them (in
the view of the dissenters) conspiring to protect privilege and resist
change. In Jamaica, as in many parts of the West Indies, nonconformist
churches were (as they still are) powerful instruments of dissent, conveying distinctly local views in distinctly local voices. And so it should
have been no surprise that in 1865 the nonconformist churches refused
to read out the "Queen's Advice."

One of the most eloquent proponents of change, a fierce opponent
of Eyre's, and a committed nonconformist churchman, was George William Gordon. He was a landowner and a "free colored" member of the
legislative assembly. His mother had been a slave, his father a lawyer
and estate owner, and he knew the country and its people well. For
several years, he had protested loudly against both Eyre's actions and
his inactions. As an expression of distress and discontent at the Queen's
Advice, a black Baptist preacher named Paul Bogle, whom Gordon had
in fact ordained, led a group of his followers to a parish meeting in
Morant Bay in October 1865. There was a clash with authorities, and
rioting broke out. Twenty-one white and colored persons and seven
blacks were killed, and some property destroyed.

Eyre reacted savagely. He declared a state of emergency in the area,
and ordered that Gordon, who with no proof was suspected of com-
plicity in the outbreak of violence, be taken from Kingston (where he
had been at the time and which was still under ordinary law) to Morant
Bay, where under martial law he was quickly court-martialed and
hanged. Bogle too was hanged. In the ensuing exercise of law and
order, 580 men and women were killed, 600 flogged, and 1000 homes
destroyed.

This event is well remembered in contemporary Jamaica, along with
the legacy of brutality of which it is part. In a poem called "Name
Change: Morant Bay Uprising," Lorna Goodison tells of how some
people who were called Bogle changed their names after the uprising;
and she tells it in language that represents a change to which we will
be turning in the rest of this book, a change to a view and a voice of
West Indian life that is unmistakably West Indian.

>   After the trouble
>   some with the name Bogle

catch fraid like sickness
and take panic for the cure.

For it was going to be hard to survive
if identified with the hung figure
revolving in the wind
from the yard arm of the Wolverine.

So some took bush for it,
and swallow cerasee to cleanse
deacon Paul blessed name
from blood and memory.

Or some with the help of bamboo root
bent the truth into Bogie, or Boggis
or Buddle, or some come out of that
alphabet all together.

Some would answer to no name on earth.
Sometimes after man see hanging
as example, preach like Paul,
your words will fall on stony ground.[24]

The past leads up to the present. The heritage of slavery flourished after emancipation with the legacy of caricature and intimidation of blacks that was widespread in the nineteenth century. It continues still, and this is why a shuttling between despair and hope continues to be part of West Indian consciousness and its expression in West Indian literature. The Jamaican poet and critic Edward Baugh brings things sharply up to date with a poem incorporating his anger and his need to transform it into something more than the momentary outrage—and the momentary laughter—which West Indian history sometimes invites. Holding humor and heroism in balance, with neither subverting nor overwhelming the other, is one of the most remarkable achievements of contemporary West Indian literature, and indeed of contemporary West Indian life. The poem is called "Nigger Sweat," and it begins with a sign.

"Please have your passport and all documents out and ready for your interview. Kindly keep them dry." (Notice in the waiting-room of the U.S. Embassy, Visa Section, Kingston, 1982.)

No disrespect, mi boss,
just honest nigger sweat . . .
And I know that you know it

as good as me,
this river running through history,
this historical fact, this sweat
that put the aroma
in your choice Virginia
that sweeten the cane
and make the cotton shine;
and sometimes I dream a nightmare dream
that the river rising, rising
and swelling the sea and I see
you choking and drowning
in a sea of black man sweat
and I wake up shaking
with shame and remorse
for my mother did teach me,
Child, don't study revenge.[25]

Blacks in the West Indies are not the only people with a history of oppression. But theirs is a special history, bringing with it a grim inheritance of someone else's images of difference and disdain, images that for five hundred years have conditioned their special and sometimes desperate need to determine for themselves who they are and where they belong. It is a need that in some way we all share, which is why the witness of West Indians is an important part of all our lives. And it is why West Indian poets, like all good poets, see their role as the traditional one of helping people—their own people, and all people—to live their lives.

And so the heritage of West Indians involves much more than a sequence of events in the history of slavery, and the gaining of freedom from bondage. It involves contradictions and caricatures; it involves the determinisms of representation and of language, and the freedoms of these too, complicated by the perennial tensions between individual and collective claims. But for West Indians, first of all it involves coming to terms with what has been taken away or taken over, in order to determine where to find it and how to get it back.

Loss and dispossession have been transformed into migration and exile to Europe and North America for many West Indians, as they reverse Columbus's voyages of discovery and invention in a quest for a place called home, both the beginning and the end of their story. The unknowns that haunt the West Indian imagination all converge in a single question, framed by the Barbadian poet, historian, and critic Edward Kamau Brathwaite in his book *Rights of Passage*.

Where then is the nigger's
home?

In Paris Brixton Kingston
Rome?

Here?
Or in Heaven?[26]

2

"Where then is the nigger's home?"

 Behind the desperation of Brathwaite's question—where then is the nigger's home?—is the shadow of a hopeless answer. Niggers are nobodies; and if they are West Indians, they are living nowhere. A little later in the poem, Brathwaite muses on the reasons for this bewitching and bewildering condition.

> For we
> who have cre-
>
> ated nothing,
> must exist
>
> on nothing.[1]

In order to understand this paralyzing despair, we need to go a little deeper into the darkness. The voice of Brathwaite's poem reflects another voice, that of the Trinidadian V. S. Naipaul. Naipaul is a formidable figure in the international literary world and a troublesome one in the West Indies. He has published over twenty books of fiction and nonfiction, and has had a significant influence on other West Indian writers. His chronicles of the West Indies are undoubtedly perceptive, though he often seems to work like an engraver using acid to etch the copper plate of Caribbean colonial consciousness. "Old Misery" he is called by some; less complimentary names by others. His family heritage is East Indian rather than African, but he knows well the common heritage shared by all West Indians; and he writes about it with bitter irony and regret.

For nearly forty years, Naipaul has lived mainly in England, though he has stayed from time to time in other countries; and he has returned to the islands occasionally. Whatever or wherever his refuge, much of his writing is concerned with the West Indies, or with being a West Indian, or with experiences West Indians have in common with each other and with other colonial people—concerns epitomized by Paul Theroux's remark that for Naipaul, "the awkward questions are 'where are you going' and 'where are you from.' "[2] Naipaul's work has ranged across continents and topics and literary forms; but his subject has always been the search for meaning and value and a language to bear witness. His presence—or more precisely his absence—casts a shadow on many West Indian writers not because of his achievements, which are greeted with about the same mixture of admiration and envy as those of other great writers, but because of a single statement. It was made in a book titled *The Middle Passage* (begun in 1960, published in 1962) about British, French, and Dutch colonial society in Trinidad, British Guiana (now Guyana), Jamaica, Martinique, and Surinam.

The Middle Passage, a travel book of personal remarks and reminiscences, was Naipaul's first book of nonfiction after four successful novels (the best known of which is *A House for Mr. Biswas* [1961]). Its unnerving combination of comedy and condescension makes it typical of many travelogues, which depend for their effect upon the assumed superiority of the observer. But Naipaul's book is unique in the power of its occasional descriptions of his central subject—the decay of the place and its people. Writing of Coronie in Surinam, he tells of its reputation for having the idlest people in the country—*de luie neger van Coronie,* "the lazy Negroes of Coronie"—and of his visit to the one East Indian family in the region, whose life he merges with the lives of all the others in the country, and especially the blacks who predominate. Strangers in a strange land, helpless and homeless. "A derelict man in a derelict land; a man discovering himself, with surprise and resignation, lost in a landscape which had never ceased to be unreal because the scene of an enforced and always temporary residence; the slaves kidnapped from one continent and abandoned on the unprofitable plantations of another, from which there could never more be escape: I was glad to leave Coronie, for, more than lazy Negroes, it held the full desolation that came to those who made the middle passage."[3]

The statement of his that stunned so many West Indians and that has echoed through the literature and history of the past three decades had to do with what he called "the history of this West Indian futility."

It was a statement about the way West Indians see themselves and talk about their heritage. Naipaul put it this way. "The history of the islands can never be satisfactorily told. Brutality is not the only difficulty. History is built around achievement and creation; and nothing was created in the West Indies."[4]

For Naipaul, the West Indies was a cheap imitiation, like all colonies. He wanted the real imperial thing. But in wanting something else so badly, he missed something that was there all the time, part of the colonial heritage he shared with other West Indians and which began with the story of oppression and uprising that was the central history of the West Indies. The history of creating a place to call home.

This history had been recognized by others for what it was, a history of courage and achievement as well as of brutality and stupidity. But making this history reflect the experiences and the aspirations of West Indians was not simply a matter of choosing between the right and the wrong accounts. Terms of historical recognition and representation are always problematic, depending in part on whether we view history as a discovery of order or an invention of it, a natural science or a work of art. From whichever perspective, these terms are conditioned by very definite, and sometimes very different, categories and criteria. Especially when the historical discourse is unchallenged, the prescriptive nature of its perspectives and representations often remains unrecognized. But occasionally, it is explicitly identified, and sometimes even celebrated. When Walt Whitman announced (in 1860, at the beginning of *Leaves of Grass*) that he was now going to "report all heroism from an American point of view,"[5] he was inaugurating a very powerful, and in its general format a very familiar, project of collective self-representation, a rewriting of history (and to some extent of personality) with new standards of creation and achievement.

This kind of project creates a double bind, of particular significance in West Indian cultural and historical representation. On the one hand, nobody wants to live enthralled by images of accomplishment certified elsewhere, and by others; and so people create their own images, empowering their lives by the force of their imaginations. On the other hand, this may do nothing more than confine them in images of their own devising, no less disabling and much less diverse. Furthermore, in either case individuals may find that their freedom to create models of achievement is constrained by the imperious authority of the community. We may recognize noble ambitions in Whitman's call. But these ambitions can also be menacing: in Whitman's day, for the women and the blacks and the aboriginal people who were not fully included in his concept either of the American or of the heroic; and in our time for those who are not Americans, for example, or for whom American heroism has become yet another imperial intimidation. Territorial determinisms along lines of race, gender, and class are usually part and parcel of these sorts of national redefinitions and representations. The task of negotiating between determinisms has been the central challenge of West Indian literature, and of West Indian life. We are possessed as well as sustained by what belongs to us, and this includes our imaginative traditions and modes of representation.

Notionally "universal" models, such as those provided by European humanism, are sometimes appealing, though they are no less arbitrarily centered in particular concepts of individual and collective accomplishment. Nonetheless, the revolutionary period of the late eighteenth and early nineteenth centuries, when humanism held sway over a large empire of imaginations, did produce some encouraging acknowledgments of West Indian achievement. In 1802, the English poet William Wordsworth celebrated one of its heroes, the former slave Toussaint L'Ouverture, who had led the blacks of Haiti toward independence and who was at that moment imprisoned in Paris. The final line of Wordsworth's poem praising "man's unconquerable mind" became one of the rallying calls of nineteenth century European progress.

> Toussaint . . . Thou hast left behind
> Powers that will work for thee; air, earth, and skies;
> There's not a breathing of the common wind
> That will forget thee; thou hast great allies;
> Thy friends are exultations, agonies,
> And love, and man's unconquerable mind.[6]

In the early 1790s, Toussaint had been inspired by the French revolutionary ideals of liberty, equality, and fraternity, which were in such stark contrast to the realities in his country. He recognized the opportunities in this period of European turmoil for taking the West Indies out of imperial hands and led a revolt in what was then St. Domingue. The rebellion of the Black Jacobins, as the revolutionary West Indian leaders of this time were called, is a tangled tale of military and political power exercised in economic and social confusion. It is also a tale of great leadership, which inspired similar (though ultimately less successful) uprisings in Martinique and Guadeloupe, Grenada and St. Vincent.

In Jamaica, it was the Maroons who rose up, in protest against some specific actions of the local authorities. The Maroons were originally slaves who ran away from the Spaniards in the middle of the seventeenth century when the English came to Jamaica—the word comes from the Spanish, *cimarron,* meaning wild. The term came to refer to wide-ranging resistance, with one of the major strongholds in the hemisphere being at Palmares in Brazil. In Jamaica, the Maroon warriors were legendary, and leaders such as Cudjoe and Nanny became part of a noble West Indian heritage. Over the years the Jamaican Maroons, like those elsewhere, were joined by other runaways, and became a formidable presence in the mountain areas where they lived and held sway.

One of these areas was the Cockpit Country, a forbidding region of Jamaica with limestone formations of steep-sided valleys and cone-shaped hills dotted with sinkholes and caves. The valley bottoms of the Cockpit Country have been used by farmers for many years, with much of the area now given over to growing marijuana and guarded with a new kind of brutal determination. It was a Maroon stronghold in the eighteenth century; and the southern section, still called the "Land of Look Behind" from the time of the Maroon wars, is described by the Jamaican poet and historian Philip Sherlock.

> The chase stopped here
> at this harsh border-line
> where tangled undergrowth and green-fringed
> parapets of rock define
> a freedom-fortress place,
> the Land of Look Behind. . . .
> These brooding jagged rocks, these trees,
> the bitter damsel and wild tamarind
> with scarlet twisted pod,
> the Cassia with pointed leaves
> the green heart and the bulletwood,
> these are our revelation-place,
> from each, as once in Ghana far away
> the spirits speak.[7]

This heritage of resistance and recovery is celebrated by many contemporary West Indian poets; and we have already seen reference to the Land of Look Behind in Lorna Goodison's description of her great grandmother's "wide eyes turning / the corners of her face / could see behind her."

The idea of a freedom-fortress place has also shaped the tradition of language in the West Indies. The Maroons communicated, especially in times of trouble, by means of the "abeng," or cow's horn, as well as by drumming; and they spoke a language understood only by themselves, in which words of African origin predominated. "Dread talk," or the particular language of Rastafarians, which we will be discussing later and which has developed as part of that community's retreat from an oppressive society, also has many of the characteristics of a "secret" language. Indeed, these characteristics are in some measure shared by every discourse, for *all* language has codes that function both to facilitate communication within the given circle and to frustrate communication beyond. (A recent account of the language of blacks in London, for example, talked about a "breach in the linguistic barrier" when police were given a phrase book.[8]) In its resistance to appropriation by the center, especially in circumstances where communities feel themselves under seige, local language often paradoxically confirms the marginality against which it is a protest. Images of solidarity and betrayal also become indispensable to the ideology of language in these situations, so that terms like "nation language,"[9] which Kamau Brathwaite (among others) has proposed to represent the authority of local languages (though not necessarily along national lines), carries with it the same political logic of loyalty and treason that we associate with nationality.

This tradition of resistance and solidarity, with its ambivalent elements of inclusion and exclusion and its different levels of communication, takes many forms in the contemporary West Indies. Some of them are derived from the years of widespread nationalist uprising in the early nineteenth century. The story of Haitian independence includes all the elements of bravery, brutality and betrayal that characterize most chronicles of creation and achievement. After a series of brilliant military campaigns, Toussaint achieved a measure of control in St. Domingue, and appointed himself ruler for life. He was then deceived by the republican French, captured and taken to France, where he later died in prison. He was succeeded, during another period of brutal conflict, by the African-born Dessalines, and then by Henri Christophe, both ex-slaves. On the last day of December in 1803, the leaders formally declared St. Domingue independent, and returned its old Indian name Haiti.

Haiti was the first among the European colonies in the West Indies to be free of imperial authority. And while some of its contradictions— the shady hierarchies of color in the development of social, economic and political life, for example; or the proposal to introduce the English language as a radical agent of change and national unification[10]— reflected a persistent tension in West Indian history, the Haitian revolution is one of the touchstones of West Indian independence. In both official and colloquial accounts of the movement from slavery to freedom it figures largely. It turns the heritage of slavery into an image of

that unconquerable mind which Wordsworth celebrated. It is an image
sustained by the possibilities of freedom which the Haitian revolution
confirmed, and ironically also by the innumerable incidents of brutality
and intimidation which slavery either demanded or encouraged, and
which all too often have been replicated in the grim events of postcolonialism. This heritage of brutality has not yet been laid to rest.

"Duppy Conqueror," a song by the great Jamaican reggae musician
Bob Marley, begins "Yes, me friend, me friend, him set me free again."
It is about breaking free from the power of a duppy, a ghost or spirit
of the dead whose burial rites have been incomplete. The spirit wanders
homeless, ready to be captured by others with evil on their minds.
Instead of being an ancestral protector the duppy becomes an evil presence, performing the will of the obeah-men, who in the rhetoric of
Marley's song are the politicians and judges who represent the corrupt
society of contemporary Babylon.

The song conveys a warning about the price we all pay, one way or
another, for failing to come to terms with our past, for failing to bury
our dead. Some years ago, on television from Tehran, the Ayatollah
Khalkhali paraded the corpses of dead American soldiers, the ones who
had come to rescue the hostages being held by Iran. It was an appalling
scene, and made those who watched from afar feel helpless, baffled,
and outraged. But anyone who was able to recollect the story of Achilles during the siege of Troy might have seen in the incident a certain
sort of meaning. At the very end of Homer's *Iliad,* there is a scene in
which Achilles drags the corpse of Hector in the dust behind his horses
to the funeral pyre of his friend Patroclus, whom Hector has killed; and
Achilles leaves Hector there in the open to be eaten by dogs and birds.
But the goddess Aphrodite annoints Hector's body with ambroisia, and
Apollo keeps the sun away to save it from rotting, until finally on
Zeus's command (and the payment of a large ransom) Achilles delivers
up the body to Hector's father.

"Thus they held funeral for Hector, tamer of horses." These are the
final words of Homer's *Iliad,* and they give hope of dignity in the face
of death and desolation. It is impossible now to bury those slaves who
died at sea on the Middle Passage, or to assuage the suffering and
humiliation that was waiting for those who made it across. But contemporary West Indian poets and artists have done their best to bear witness to their passing and to their unconquerable heroism. This is one
of the ambitions of Derek Walcott's epic *Omeros,* Homeric in so many
ways. And of Kamau Brathwaite's poems of recollection and recognition. But it is also the achievement of many others in that West Indian
tradition of poets as duppy conquerors, setting the spirits free and giv-

ing their people the ability to forget, as well as remember. In a poem called "Sometimes in the Middle of the Story," Edward Baugh balances the inspiring story of Toussaint with one of the most routinely horrifying incidents of the Middle Passage, when slavers would throw slaves overboard to lighten their load during heavy weather at sea. (Insurance regulations encouraged this, for slaves were considered property and like other cargo could under certain circumstances be jettisoned as ballast and the loss recovered from the insurers. There was sometimes a suspicion that owners would dispose of sick slaves this way if there were an opportunity, for they could not recover insurance on slaves that died on board.) Baugh's poem also refers to Toussaint's horse Bel Argent, on whom he was reputed to cover great distances at night in his legendary accomplishments as military leader. The poem brings together a collective memory shared by West Indians with a very personal expression of the experience of being black and being West Indian, and it does so in language that hovers ironically between West Indian speech and a poetic discourse inherited from the British right along with slavery.

> Sometimes in the middle of the story something
> move outside the house, like
> it could be the wind, but is not the wind
> and the story-teller hesitate so slight
> you hardly notice it, and the children
> hold their breath and look at one another.
> The old people say is Toussaint passing
> on his grey horse Bel-Argent, moving
> faster than backra-massa timepiece
> know to measure . . .
> But also that sound had something in it
> of deep water, salt water, had ocean
> the sleep-sigh of a drowned African
> turning in his sleep on the ocean floor
> and Toussaint horse was coming from far
> his tail trailing the swish of the sea
> from secret rendezvous, from councils of war
> with those who never completed the journey,
> and we below deck heard only the muffled
> thud of scuffling feet, could only
> guess the quick, fierce tussle, the
> stifled gasp, the barrel-chests bursting
> the bubbles rising and breaking, the blue

closing over. But their souls shuttle
still the forest paths of ocean
connecting us still the current unbroken
the circuits kept open . . .[11]

In *The Middle Passage*, Naipaul recognized only the negative side of
the heritage of slavery and bluntly denied both the achievement of
those who survived and the humanity of those who perished. As the
epigraph to his book he quoted from a nineteenth-century imperial
enthusiast, the historian James Anthony Froude, author of a popular
twelve-volume *History of England* (1865–70). English readers eventually
forgot about Froude, but his remarks made a deep impression on the
West Indies, a measure of how vulnerable people are to the condescension of others, especially when the others come from elsewhere, as
authority so often seems to. Naipaul took as his motto a comment
Froude made in his book *The English in the West Indies; or, The Bow of
Ulysses*, published in 1888.

> [The West Indies] were valued only for the wealth which they yielded,
> and society there has never assumed any particularly noble aspect. There
> has been splendour and luxurious living, and there have been crimes and
> horrors, and revolts and massacres. There has been romance, but it has
> been the romance of pirates and outlaws. The natural graces of life do
> not show themselves under such conditions. There has been no saint in
> the West Indies since Las Casas, no hero unless philonegro enthusiasm
> can make one out of Toussaint. There are no people there in the true
> sense of the word, with a character and purpose of their own.[12]

Froude's reference to "people in the true sense of the word" recalls
the question that preoccupied Las Casas and Sepulveda. It also reveals
Froude's brutally ethnocentric ignorance, the kind of ignorance that
earlier had construed the aboriginal societies of the new world as something less than human, and that indeed has never confined itself to
comments about people of aboriginal or African heritage. It was this
kind of ignorance, for example, that was fond of distinguishing
between what Froude's fellow traveler Charles Wentworth Dilke liked
to call the "dear races" and the "cheap races." Froude himself became
notorious at home for his anti-Celtic bias, arguing that since the Irish
were by nature weak, they should willingly submit to rule.

These were fashionable points of view in the nineteenth century. The
historian Edward A. Freeman expressed perhaps the most contemptible version during a visit to the United States in 1881. "This would be
a grand land," he remarked, "if only every Irishman would kill a negro,
and be hanged for it."[13] Even as intelligent a commentator as Samuel

Taylor Coleridge, though inclined to nothing like this kind of remark, displayed his frankly biased perspective in an open letter early in the century condemning the United Irishmen for their "delusive and pernicious sublimation of local predilection and clannish pride into a sentiment and principle of nationality." But these were precisely the sentiments and principles Coleridge so admired in the English, for he commented in the same letter that "I hold the *amor natalis Soli* of priceless value, for its kindly influence on the virtues and amities of private life, and more especially as the preparatory school and the almost indispensable condition of patriotism."[14]

There were other views, especially about the virtues of patriotism of *any* kind. One eminent English historian in the nineteenth century who distrusted all affirmations of nationality was Lord Acton. He argued that "a state which is incompetent to satisfy different races condemns itself; a state which labours to neutralize, to absorb, or to expel them, destroys its own vitality; a state which does not include them is destitute of the chief basis of self-government. The theory of nationality . . . is a retrograde step in history."[15] Instead of the artifice of nationality, Acton believed in a kind of natural progress, whose achievement or failure it was the business of historians to reveal.

Most historians, however, saw progress revealed along national lines, and viewed race, gender, and class, for example, primarily from that perspective. In this regard, Froude's assertion that "there are no people there in the true sense of the word" has ironic relevance in a period such as ours, which sometimes celebrates its postcolonial superiority. The United Nations is routinely involved in the designation of "peoples." The aboriginal peoples of the Americas have long struggled for this recognition, with fierce opposition from governments whose national ideals and territorial imperatives are challenged by these affirmations. Although primarily of economic and political significance, the presumptions (and the assumptions of power) involved in this process are closely related to the ways in which literature exercises its territorial prerogatives, acknowledging (or denying) the character and purpose of people with imperial aplomb along national, linguistic, and chronological lines, or more recently along lines of gender and race. These can be just as prescriptive, and just as political, as any other designations of collective identity, especially for communities determined to recognize "character and purpose" on their own terms, shaped by their own perceptions of "the natural graces of life" and the forms (from romance to rap) in which these will be celebrated.

Froude wrote with imperial style, and imperial stupidity. Had he been open-minded on his visit to the West Indies, he would have seen something of how man's unconquerable mind had indeed prevailed through the agony of slavery—patiently sometimes, and sometimes by seizing political power as Toussaint did. But then again, perhaps through his imperial eyes this is precisely what Froude did see, and what outraged him in what he called the "nigger warrens"[16] of the West Indies. He was writing within a racist and absolutist tradition, which presumed, in the words of one contemporary (C. S. Salmon, who was in fact attacking it), that "mankind is divided into two distinct sections; those made to rule, and those made to be ruled."[17] And he was pre-occupied with what he saw as the menace of self-government. "Give them independence," he cautioned—"them" being blacks in the West Indies—"and in a few generations they will peel off such civilization as they have learnt as easily and as willingly as their coats and trousers."[18] Once again, naturalness and artifice jostle each other, as the idea of societies growing naturally toward self-government is contradicted by the idea of government as a cultivated refinement. Reconciling the two is as difficult as accomodating sugar lumps in a silver bowl with sugar cane in the field. In Froude's scheme, what comes naturally is the falling back of savage blacks into degeneracy, threatening the accomplishments of culture.

Froude's views fell into line with the likes of Sir William Hooker, the renowned botanist and director of Kew Gardens in London, whose opinion about blacks was repeated by supporters of Governor Eyre during the troubles in Jamaica in the 1860s: "That the Negro in Jamaica . . . is pestilential, I have no hesitation in declaring; nor that he is a most dangerous savage at the best. . . . When his blood is up, very cruel acts are his first acts, and these in great number. . . . I consider him a savage, and a most dangerous savage too."[19]

Like many of his British contemporaries, Froude was bothered less by brutality than he was by an anarchy in which British ideals of civilization would be replaced by barbaric habits. Matthew Arnold wrote of the dangers of letting barbarians and philistines prevail over civilized sweetness and light in his book *Culture and Anarchy*, published in 1867. And while Arnold's concern was for Great Britain, in which social divisions and economic distress were taking a terrible toll, many saw the choice between civilization or barbarism as especially applicable to the empire.

Froude was particularly obsessed by the laws in Haiti which, at the time he was writing, prohibited whites from owning land. To Froude, these laws exemplified the breakdown of civil order. Of the blacks in Grenada, he commented (in a manner that eerily foreshadows the logic behind the American invasion of Grenada in 1983) that "if left entirely to themselves, they would in a generation or two relapse into savages; there were but two alternatives before not only Grenada, but all the English West Indies—either an English administration pure and simple, like the East Indian, or a falling eventually into a state like that of Haiti, where they eat the babies, and no white man can own a yard of land."[20] It is not clear which practice Froude despised more. And lest any of us becomes too comfortable, it is worth reflecting that the two alternatives Froude describes—civility or savagery—are mirrored in contemporary attitudes toward the West Indies: as idyllic and peaceful on the one hand, a place of easy times and easy profits; and on the other as violent and unstable, a place of unreason and unrest.

It is a nice testament to the minds and spirits of West Indians that one of the most powerful voices of dissent against Froude came from a Trinidadian, John Jacob Thomas. Born of African parents in the West Indies in 1840, two years after slavery was abolished, Thomas spent most of his life in the civil service, dedicated (like Arnold in another world) to improving public education. He was one of the first to condemn the inappropriateness of what then passed for a curriculum, with its imitation of English models of ambition and achievement. In particular, Thomas argued for the teaching of West Indian history and geography and of Spanish and French as languages of commerce in the West Indies. Languages were his special interest, and he was the author of a significant early study of West Indian dialect titled *The Theory and Practice of Creole Grammar* (1869).

Froude's book offended Thomas, as it offends West Indians a century later. For his part Thomas wrote a book called *Froudacity: West Indian Fables by James Anthony Froude, Explained by John Jacob Thomas* (1889), which took Froude to task for his blinkered account. What Froude missed, in Thomas's view, were the possibilities for racial equality and political independence in the West Indies, possibilities founded on principles derived from its own distinctive history rather than from the imitation of European traditions. For Thomas, a true account must begin with the heritage of slavery, and with an understanding of how demands for collective power and individual self-respect emerge together out of its remembered humiliations, generated by deeply human desires for freedom and dignity.

Over the past fifty years, West Indian literature has brought a new consciousness of these demands. But the confidence that sustains the best contemporary West Indian writing has been hard won, especially in the period of colonial independence following the Second World War when a chasm of doubt opened up between the dreams and desires of colonial people and the realities of their lives. This condition was not confined to the West Indies, of course, but was endemic in India and, of course, Africa and in other areas where former colonies were charting an independent course for themselves under the condescending eyes of their old imperial masters. And it was notably apparent as new nations sought to express their visions of the future in literature, which ultimately is one of the most powerful ways in which a society negotiates its identity but which is also especially vulnerable to crises of faith, often centered around the perennial question of whether literature thrives by being engaged with the life (and the language) of its time and place, or whether its strength derives from its distance, its detachment. The answers to this question are relative to a whole set of other factors, some of them easily misconstrued; and although it is true to say that poetry is always intimately involved with the conditions of its language, we tend to forget that this language may be either local *or* literary, and that each has characteristics and politics of its own.

This is all part of an old story, about the relative merits of what are sometimes called particulars and universals: ideas and things rooted in place and time, on the one hand; and those that transcend time and place. The argument about particulars and universals goes back a long way—in the relatively short memory of European civilization, back to Boethius, in prison near Milan in the year 525 A.D. in the dark-end days of the Roman empire, writing a book called *The Consolation of Philosophy* . . . which became a medieval best-seller for nearly a thousand years. But this is not some dusty old question, this issue of particulars and universals. It is around us constantly: in the arguments about local and literary language; about standards determined here or elsewhere; about advice coming from those directly involved or those distant and detached, about practice and theory. It is there in the contradictions between individual and collective rights; and between local laws and those of supposedly higher standing, derived from the notional universality of either natural reason or revealed religion, and transcending local particularities. Civil disobedience rests its case upon this distinction; and it received eloquent expression in Martin Luther King's famous Letter from Birmingham Jail, when he answered the charges that his actions were untimely, that he was an outsider, and that he was disobeying a particular law of the land with an appeal to the universals of justice and freedom. And it is there, this tension between particulars and universals, in the continuing argument about whether literature is centered in the yard or the tower, whether it should be rooted in everyday experiences or set above and beyond them, whether it is generated at home—in *this* place—or away, in some *other*, separate place. At the still point, or in the turning world.

In eighteenth-century Europe, with demographic shifts of extraordinary proportions, a changing international consciousness (brought about in part by the industrial revolution), and the emergence of many new artistic forms, it was common to hear poets argue for the separation of poetic language from the idiosyncracies of everyday local speech in order to achieve a measure of universality. "The language of the age is never the language of poetry,"[21] said Thomas Gray—the author, it is worth noting, of perhaps the most popular poem in the English language, the "Elegy Written in a Country Churchyard." But times change. By the nineteenth century, in an era of nationalist ideology, there was considerable support for the idea that poetry should be closer to the people, though (as with all such ideas) this one too was shadowed by doubt. When American literature was emerging as an expression of the aspirations of American nationality, and despite the extraordinary confidence of its revolutionary heritage, there was a clutch of anxieties—about whether the American language was sufficiently different to shape a distinctive style, and whether American literature could be sufficiently distinctive to make a difference. Ralph Waldo Emerson and Walt Whitman and the other writers of the so-called American Renaissance, for all their enthusiasm, were not at all sure they were witnessing the birth of an American literary consciousness. They viewed literature as a central instrument of cultural definition. They recognized that British literary traditions reflected old-world ideologies; and they resisted their involuntary translation into the new world. But they wondered whether the particulars of American life and the American language could generate a literature that embodied universals of human experience and expression. Doubt was still very much a part of their literary lives and their national dreams.

Doubt is part of all our lives. In a paradoxical way, it is necessary for belief; and sometimes it is much in fashion even when belief is not. But when doubt threatens to undermine the confidence of people in themselves and replace it with an expectation that they be someone or something else, or be caricatures of what others want them to be, then it is debilitating and dangerous, often causing them to seek proof of identity in increasingly desperate and increasingly violent affirmations that preempt any negotiation between particulars and universals. And so it is too when modes of achievement are imported or imposed from outside rather than developed from within. This was the immediate menace in the West Indies in the years leading up to independence, and the form it took had much to do with language and literature.

People need images of themselves that reflect the possibilities of their own lives, rather than possibilities imitated from elsewhere. And they need a language and a literature of their own devising. The Guyanese writer A. J. Seymour addressed this in 1952 in a notable editorial in the influential journal *Kyk-Over-Al,* which he founded. (The name comes from a fort at the confluence of two rivers by Georgetown. It was one of the most important journals to come out of this period of literary and political liberation.) Seymour quoted from the introduction to the Canadian poet and critic A. J. M. Smith's recent anthology of Canadian poetry, which was one of the first anthologies from the British Commonwealth (then still called the British Empire) to break free from models of imperial achievement. Smith castigated what he referred to as the colonial attitude of mind, "a spirit that gratefully accepts a place of subordination, that looks elsewhere for its standards of excellence. . . . [It] sets the great good place not in its future but somewhere outside its own borders, somewhere beyond its possiblities."[22]

This attitude of mind takes hold in private before it becomes public, which is why literary forms such as autobiography or lyric have been so important in chronicling the predicament in which West Indian writers found themselves during the 1940s and 1950s. In an early prose version of what eventually became his autobiographical poem *Another Life,* Derek Walcott caught the pathos of living the kind of pathological disability that this colonial habit of mind creates. "I was sure, until very late, that the texture of my hair and my complexion were a profound mistake, and that one morning I would rise and find the joke over."[23] The words of an old Jamaican proverb tell another, older version of the same tale. "Every John Crow tink him pickney white."

Naipaul's blunt rejection in *The Middle Passage* of any West Indian achievement set in motion a series of troubled reactions. If "nothing was created in the West Indies," then West Indians must be nobodies, just like in the days of slavery. Nothing was created . . . and nothing has changed. In *Rights of Passage,* Kamau Brathwaite posed his grim question. "Where then is the nigger's home?" Walcott proposed one answer in a poem called "The Schooner *Flight,*" which when it was published in *The Star-Apple Kingdom,* in 1979, announced a new awareness of the possibilities of West Indian identity. The narrator is the mulatto Shabine, and the poem begins with his colonial bewilderment as he leaves Trinidad on his wanderings.

> If loving these islands must be my load,
> out of corruption my soul takes wings.
> But they had started to poison my soul
> with their big house, big car, big-time bohbohl,

> coolie, nigger, Syrian, and French Creole,
> so I leave it for them and their carnival—
> I taking a sea bath, I gone down the road.
> I know these islands from Monos to Nassau,
> a rusty headed sailor with sea-green eyes
> that they nickname Shabine, the patois for
> any red nigger, and I, Shabine, saw
> when these slums of empire was paradise.
> I'm just a red nigger who love the sea,
> I had a sound colonial education,
> I have Dutch, nigger, and English in me,
> and either I'm nobody, or I'm a nation.[24]

The voice in this poem is Shabine's, whose ancestry is the same as Walcott's: English, Dutch, and African. (The fact that the specifics of his African ancestry are so uncertain and that he denigrates this inheritance by the word *nigger* is of course part of the point. It is also to the point that my word *denigrate* and Shabine's *nigger* come from the same root, to blacken.) The voice of Walcott the poet is also here, in a dialogue with the character Shabine that displays an engagement both of languages and of logics. There's another kind of dialogue going on here as well, between the two alternatives that Shabine portrays for himself: "either I'm nobody or I'm a nation." The dichotomy is not nearly as simple as it seems. One ("I'm nobody") parodies a colonial condition; the other ("I'm a nation") mimics imperial categories. Slave or master. Walcott is much too subtle to let this dichotomy rest . . . but also too much imbued with the heritage of slavery not to try out its temptations.

Just as the image of nobody recalls black invisibility, as well as Naipaul's specter of West Indian nothingness, so the idea of a "nation" raises another issue, having to do with competing theories of human society and of human personality. These two theories are very much part of the continuing dialogue of West Indian literature. Any society is made up of constituent individual parts, which contribute to the whole in a complex way. Without them, the whole would obviously not exist; with them, it becomes something different from and greater than the sum of its parts. Many people, steeped in the ideological premises of liberal individualism, see the constituent part rather than the whole as the focus of their moral and political attitudes—though feminism, and movements such as black power and the collective affirmation of aboriginal rights, have modified nineteenth-century liberalism somewhat. So have various regionalisms and nationalisms. But many people continue to view the state or social group as a necessary convenience, the embodiment of a contract or the fulfilment of a design, essentially existing to serve and protect individual interests.

If we shift our viewpoint, however, and assume that the larger social entity is not one to which we (however theoretically) elect to belong but within which we find ourselves, willy nilly, then we view it as a natural organic form rather than the product of ingenious artifice. That is to say, we *either* look upon the individual as prior to the community and giving *to* the community (or the place, or the moment in history) its signficance; *or* we perceive the individual as receiving life and meaning *from* the community, much as a branch does from the tree. If we accept the former scheme, we value our individuality above all else and the community insofar as it enhances this. The latter attitude, on the other hand, implies that our individuality derives from and depends upon our belonging to a group or being custodians of a place or citizens of a political unit. It emphasizes the group as a natural and inevitable family of interests rather than an artificial or convenient one.

The tradition of liberal democracy has established the general expectation that collective authority is valuable only insofar as it nourishes and protects individual rights. The parallel tradition has insisted that there is a higher authority in certain institutional arrangements and collective allegiances that reflects profound and persistent human needs and desires, or values that transcend individual concerns. The nation is the most significant political manifestation of this, an idea, as it were, beyond politics; and the local community or the collectivity of shared interests or heritage or experience is the most immediate, as an entity that in being greater than the sum of its parts is also less menacing than a simple aggregate of human wills.

Insofar as literature created by individuals is associated with these collectivities, it shares this general ambivalence, and it offers us one or other of these alternative relationships to it. Furthermore, literature often brings into the foreground the way—or more precisely, the different ways—in which we derive a sense of being from a sense of belonging, and it illuminates how these determine our cultural and political identities. These different ways have considerable influence on the uses of and attitudes toward local and literary language in poetry, and on the relationships between West Indian literature and West Indian national life. Walcott identifies these from a different perspective a little later in the poem when Shabine wittily says "I had no nation now but the imagination,"[25] underlining both the artifice of nationality (it is the product of the imagination) and its naturalness (the imagination transcends arbitrary boundaries and reflects deeply human wants and needs).

In 1962, the year in which by a nice irony Naipaul's book appeared, Great Britain opened the way for the independence of individual English-speaking island nations. Jamaica, despite strong domestic disagreement on the issue, eliminated the possibilites for a Federation of the West Indies (which had emerged out of discussions that began in 1947 to provide a broad framework for representative government in the anglophone Caribbean) by pulling out, prompting Eric Williams of Trinidad to remark that 1 from 10 leaves 0, and to call for his people to break free from Mother Africa and Mother England and take their identity from Mother Trinidad and Tobago. Jamaica and Trinidad and Tobago became independent in 1962, Barbados and the mainland territory of Guyana in 1966, and the other islands of the English-speaking Caribbean over the following decades. But Naipaul's scepticism remained. In a note to a later edition of *The Middle Passage* published in 1969, he said that had he realized the extent to which he was writing about what one reviewer had called "a client culture and a client economy," his book "might have been less romantic about the healing power, in such a culture, of political or racial assertion."[26]

The healing power that Naipaul dismisses was not the fiction of nationalist romance, but the product of a view of West Indian history that saw independence as the inevitable end of the process of decolonization—inevitable both because the forces of change were on any reading of events bound to produce this result and because such a destiny was implicit in the realization of collective identity. This healing power was the prophetic power of seeing what will be, not of dreaming about what might be. It was also the power to shape history. The nineteenth-century historian Ernest Renan once said that because national unity is usually achieved by force, it is as important to forget as to remember certain things about the past.[27] We might phrase it differently and talk about revisiting, revising, and rewriting. But we would have healing as much as history in mind. Naipaul's view, on the other hand, was that West Indians were caught up in a mirage, sustained by mistaken readings of both history and destiny, and that they were so mesmerized by their fear of the past and their fascination with the future that it was impossible for them to balance the two ideals that they held so dearly: a longstanding desire for self-government, looking forward; and looking back, a shared history of colonial exploitation. Freedom and slavery. This, for him, was a disabling dichotomy.

He was correct in one sense: the relationship between racial and political assertiveness had shifted over the years in ways that were not always acknowledged. During the 350 years of slavery, racial identity all but defined the experience of oppression, and a consciousness of being black was one of the key elements of resistance and rebellion. During the century and a half since slavery was abolished, assertions of political power by West Indians have moved beyond the exclusiveness of racial solidarity. But still, racial solidarity and regional self-government are intimately related in the history of the West Indies, as all of the eighteenth- and nineteenth- century imperial chroniclers recognized. At the end of the twentieth century, citizens of African heritage are still the overwhelming majority in most West Indian nations. Trinidad and Guyana are notable exceptions, where those of East Indian descent are a substantial presence; and Naipaul's upbringing in Trinidad made him acutely conscious of the dynamics of politics and race.

Race and region are therefore not exactly congruent categories in the West Indies these days. Nor are they in most places around the world, though the convergence of ethnicity and nationality is increasingly obvious. (Over the long run, in fact, the history of European, Asian, and African political life suggests that ethnic solidarity and national identity have been linked only in exceptional circumstances, with marginality and pluralism being the norm.[28]) But despite the diversity of West Indian society, and in line with Naipaul's own conflation of African and Indian inheritances in *The Middle Passage,* the most powerful expressions of political coherence and cultural continuity in the West Indies have generally been images of a heritage that belongs to blacks first of all, and is shared with others insofar as they identify with the experience of dislocation and dispossession which that heritage represents—whether they came from Africa by way of the Middle Passage; or from India across the *kala pani,* the black water; or in the other ways that people came to the new world to satisfy old-world wants and needs. The process of West Indian independence started as a struggle for the souls of black people, which is to say of all those who in Naipaul's words share "the full desolation that came to those who made the middle passage." A struggle for black power.

This struggle took many forms, beginning with the resentment and resistance of the first slaves to set foot in the West Indies. The assertion of black power came into prominence with the rebellions of Toussaint and others from the late eighteenth century on. Often this resistance was first of all personal. Perhaps it always began there. Samuel Smith, an Antiguan born in 1877 who grew up in the aftermath of slavery, gives a moving account of how imitating imperial models was one sure way to sustain colonial dependence. "Them force us to have manners. I personally had too much, but somebody with no manners, somebody unruly was gibbetted. Bakkra always say, 'Manners maketh the man.'

Well, let me tell you, not in Antigua, maybe somewhere else, I don't know. It maketh us slaves instead."[29]

Collective action finally made the difference in the move toward independence in the English-speaking West Indies, as labor unrest and political nationalism converged with the formation of trade unions and agricultural producer associations in the 1930s and 1940s. Later, during the 1960s, the black power movement in the United States also had an important influence on West Indian social consciousness and political development, though the situations were significantly different. Among other things, blacks were in the majority in the West Indies. American black power scared many West Indians, who (despite the fact that some American leaders such as Stokely Carmichael were West Indian born) saw in it either a new imperialism, which threatened the distinctive cultural and political development of the West Indies, or a challenge to newly established West Indian national authorities. Those who wanted to protect their political interests recalled for the benefit of the masses that "we believe in only one power and that is the power of people working for the benefit of the country as a whole and for the stability of the nation."[30] Those who wanted to protect their cultural independence chose to forget that American black power had its roots not only in the heritage of slavery shared by blacks in the United States and the West Indies, but also in a heritage of preaching and politics— and of poetry—that found eloquent expression in the lives and works of several prominent West Indians earlier in the century.

It was the Martiniquan poet Aimé Césaire who gave the advocates of a renewed black consciousness one of their most powerful images. During the 1930s, while living in France, Césaire became aware of the way in which many black people were caught between an attachment to their African heritage and an urge to distance themselves from this heritage because of the sense of "barbaric" inferiority to their colonial masters that it often conveyed. To regain for himself the strength of his own heritage and the capacity to resist intimidation by European traditions, Césaire began writing a long poem entitled "Cahier d'un retour au pays natal" ("Notebook of a Return to the Native Land"). In it, he coined the term *negritude* to describe a heritage that all blacks shared, an ancient heritage of one homeland and of a time and place in which there was no need to ask Brathwaite's question. It was also, for Césaire, a heritage of the dislocation and dispossession that black people experienced, wherever they were.

Negritude was only an idea; and it had all the limitations of essentialist ideologies, rendering a large range of meanings and values and identities in a single category. Structurally, it was a mirror image of the paradigm of Them and Us to which it was a reaction. But it had great appeal, satisfying a deep need in the individual and social psychology of blacks. Césaire described negritude as "the simple recognition of the fact of being black, and the acceptance of this fact, of our destiny as black people, of our history, and our culture."[31] Others, such as Léon Damas from French Guiana and the Senegalese writer and politician Léopold Senghor, picked up the idea and translated it into a political logic to generate black African nationalism, drawing as well upon the concept of black identity elaborated by W. E. B. DuBois in *The Souls of Black Folk* (1903). The universality of the idea was the key to its power. It encouraged blacks everywhere to think of their African heritage, their origin and purpose. And it encouraged whites to think of the part played by European imperialism in making this a heritage of slavery outside Africa and of colonial exploitation within (highlighted by the Berlin Conference of 1885, which divided up Africa along European lines). It also encouraged both blacks and whites to recognize that Africa had its own history, which needed to be told from an African perspective.

Soon, the idea of negritude was blended with European ideologies to generate a new consciousness of colonialism and new calls for freedom. Though many of its early advocates were French-speaking, they had considerable influence on English-speaking blacks in Africa and the West Indies. And so did some European commentators. The French writer Jean-Paul Sartre articulated his sense of negritude as a historical phenomenon in *Black Orpheus* (1948), a text (which first appeared as the introduction to an anthology edited by Senghor) that had very wide currency. Sartre prescribed the idea of negritude as a necessary part of the process of black liberation and described how the predicament of blacks was being given a powerful voice by the new generation of black writers. And since European politics in the broadest sense had created the wretched situation of blacks, Sartre proposed that European political ideologies, both capitalist and socialist, could be important instruments for understanding how this had happened.

Only fairly recently, especially with the publication of the Senegalese scholar Cheikh Anta Diop's *Civilization or Barbarism* (1981; trans. 1991), have African ideologies been used to reshape what are still essentially European categories of history, philosophy, and science; though West Indian writers such as Kamau Brathwaite and the Guyanese poet, novelist, and critic Wilson Harris have long argued for different historical structures in the Caribbean—structures and styles that accomodate the full range of West Indian experience, including aboriginal, African, Asian, and European. Sometimes, this agenda has been dismissed as merely the expedient delusion of black historians who are determined to ignore facts. But we should recall that since the nineteenth century facts have been losing their grip on *all* historians and have been recognized first of all (in line with their etymology) as things made by human agency. Artifacts; like history itself. Even Matthew Arnold acknowledged the inevitable conflation of ideas and things, and many of his contemporaries drew attention to different ways of seeing and saying and to the complex relationship between fictions and facts.

Sartre's central concern was with the connection between political power and the power of imaginative expression, especially the power of writing and speaking. This connection was routinely subverted, according to Sartre, by the inheritance of European languages. Black writers, he suggested, "have no language common to them all; to incite the oppressed to unite they must have recourse to the words of the oppressor. . . . Only through it can they communicate; like the scholars of the 16th century who understood each other only in Latin, the blacks rediscover themselves only on the terrain full of traps which white men have set for them. The colonist rises between the colonials to be the eternal mediator; he is there, always there, even though absent, in the most secret councils."[32]

So the issue becomes one of power. For Sartre, it was first of all the power of language. A power that could enslave, or liberate. For Césaire, it was that power, to be sure, as well as the power of ideas—and particularly the idea of negritude—to light the way toward freedom. For his fellow Martiniquan Frantz Fanon, the issue was powerlessness, and the desperate struggle that must take place if the powerless were to regain power. Freedom was not something to be given by others, but something to be taken, whether out of desire or destiny.

Fanon described the racism he encountered as a black in France; and he told of the grotesque ironies of postcolonial independence in North Africa, where the violence of colonialism had left such a terrible legacy. Fanon saw violence as the only effective way to counter violence and create change, by generating first of all an awareness of the brutality that blacks had suffered for centuries and then by forcing the conditions for freedom. In advocating this difficult road to black liberation, Fanon inspired others in the 1950s and 1960s to develop the ideology and politics of the movement that became known as black power.

Césaire and Sartre and Fanon had no monopoly on black power, nor on the idea that an affirmative black consciousness would bring pride and purpose to black people. But they helped to give the notion currency and to create the recognition that changes which might be achieved by black people *any*where would encourage solidarity among oppressed people *every*where. During the 1950s the notion of a *third world* was proposed, first in 1952 by the French geographer Alfred Sauvy, emphasizing that this "other" world had something to say and its own way of saying it. "We speak all too willingly of two worlds and their possible wars, their coexistence, etc, often forgetting that there exists a third, more important world, one which, in terms of chronology, comes first. . . . This Third World, ignored, scorned, exploited, as was the Third Estate, also wants to say something."[33] (The Third Estate was the name given to the common people of France who in 1789 rebelled against the privilege and power of the nobility and the clergy, the other two "estates" in what was then called the "estates-general" of the French nation). The term *third world* was picked up at the Bandung Conference in Indonesia in 1955, a gathering of nonaligned nations organized by Prime Minister Nehru of India.

Decolonization of the British empire after the Second World War began in 1947 with Indian independence, and undoubtedly this act encouraged other colonies of Great Britain to think about political freedom. Still, there was scepticism about the trendy application of some of these notions. Many scorned catch phrases such as *negritude* and *third world* as nothing more than the latest metropolitan fashion. James Baldwin and Richard Wright expressed scepticism about the idea of negritude as expounded by Cesaire and Senghor during the First International Congress of Black Writers and Artists in Paris in 1956. The Nigerian writer Wole Soyinka suggested that there was something unnatural and unnecessary about the celebration of negritude; after all, he said, "the duiker (a small African antelope) does not proclaim its duikritude. You know it by its elegant leap."[34] It was not the self-consciousness so much as the homogenizing effect of terms like *negritude* and *third world* that bothered Régis Debray, a Frenchman who fought with Che Guevara in Cuba and South America. He called the notion of the *third world* "a shapeless sack into which one could simply dump peoples, classes, races, civilizations and continents so that they might more easily disappear."[35] Others saw the idea of negritude as an intellectual indulgence. And still others, including Césaire, called with unnerving prescience for blacks to beware of a new American imperialism masking as anticolonialism. "Aid to the less fortunate countries," declared Truman. "The old colonialism is over." Interpret this, said Césaire, as "the time is ripe for American big business to raid all the countries of the world."

But on the whole, the 1940s and 1950s produced an awareness of some common things to look for in the lives that blacks shared, and some common things to say that might lead toward a recovery of what blacks had lost, and a finding of new freedoms. Many turned to their local traditions to recover a sense of coherence and continuity by recalling the history of black resistance over the years, including go-slows on the plantations as well as the major slave uprisings and the rebellions of anonymous individual men and women. Attention was paid to those who had celebrated these traditions, such as the Spanish-speaking writers José Martí, Alejo Carpentier, and Nicolás Guillén from Cuba. Names that had long been part of a local heritage came to take their rightful place. As for the names of the lost, their loss was recollected and properly mourned.

In the West Indies, the labor force (both during slavery and much later in the 1930s when trade unions were being organized) and religious movements were the main focus of agitation for social and political change, though individual leaders emerged from time to time in all walks of life. Expressions of black consciousness did not come to the West Indies solely as an invention of the 1940s and 1950s, or simply by way of Césaire and Sartre and Fanon. These writers certainly influenced the political and cultural life of the time. But the call for black power came from much further back in West Indian history. It arose out of the suffering and deprivation that blacks had suffered during slavery and out of the determination of West Indian men and women to find freedom in their new world while maintaining links to their old.

One of the most important modern figures in this call for freedom was Marcus Mosiah Garvey, born in Jamaica in 1887. Garvey became involved at an early age in activities to improve the situation of blacks. After traveling to Central and South America and spending some time in England, he returned to Jamaica and founded the Universal Negro Improvement Association in 1916, with an ambition "to unite all the Negro peoples of the world into one great body to establish a country and a government exclusively their own." Inspired by the great black American writer and educator Booker T. Washington, Garvey soon left for the United States, where his idealism caught on and he became the center of a large movement directed toward black independence, with membership in the millions. Reaching beyond his ambitions for a black country and a black government, Garvey's influence on black artistic and cultural development is an enduring part of his legacy.

In immediate practical terms, he was not so successful. Some of his schemes were dramatic failures, such as the Black Star Steamship Line to facilitate trade between black nations and to involve blacks in the world of international commerce. He was convicted of mail fraud in connection with the Black Star Line and served a prison sentence in the United States. He was then deported back to Jamaica, where his ideas and personality captured the imagination of many West Indians, though the colonial authorities in place at the time were not so enthusiastic. Garvey has remained a figure of vision and inspiration to later generations of black power advocates, and to all who hold hope for a future in which the dispossessed will recover their inheritance and those who are caught up in a Babylonian captivity of poverty and powerlessness will be free. As Philip Sherlock said, "he challenged us to smash the old stereotype, to put self-esteem in the place of self-contempt, to put self-confidence and self-reliance in the place of dependence and distrust. . . . Most of those who had position and power rejected him. But the common people never did. . . . The work of self-liberation had begun."[36]

The black power movement in its most familiar form was American, and it emerged in the 1960s during the agitation for civil rights. The black power slogan itself became a rallying cry for blacks during a march from Memphis, Tennessee, to Jackson, Mississippi, in the summer of 1966. James Meredith led the march, which was designed to encourage blacks to register to vote. He had gained prominence in 1962 as the first black to attend the University of Mississippi. Meredith was one of those people whose lives were not given over to politics but whose actions made an extraordinary difference in the life of the nation; one of those people like Rosa Parks, whose refusal to move and make room for a white man on a bus in Montgomery, Alabama, on December 1, 1955, started the long walk toward equal rights for blacks in the United States.

The leaders of the black power movement in the United States included Stokely Carmichael, H. Rap Brown (who succeeded him as chairman of the militant Student Nonviolent Coordinating Committee), and Malcolm X (a prominent figure in the Black Muslims and founder of the Black Nationalists, who was assassinated by rivals in 1965). Along with the call for black power came a more general appeal for power to be returned to the people—especially compelling in the West Indies, where blacks remained in the majority—and an implicit warning against betrayal by new elites. The black power movement included not only counsels of violence—which Brown once called "as American as cherry pie"—but also calls out of the ghettos for equality and justice and peace, Martin Luther King's dream of a nation living out the full meaning of its creed, with all its people finally able to say "free at last, Great God Almighty, we are free at last."

West Indian poets were watching and listening during these years. In the late 1940s and 1950s, while they were finishing school in Barbados and St. Lucia and moving out into the larger world, Brathwaite and Walcott came to realize the forceful presence of a West Indian and African heritage in their lives and in their literature. And in the 1960s, poets such as Goodison became conscious of the ways in which blacks everywhere were shaping a legacy of hope out of the depths of despair in which they found themselves. The sense of possibility, which was part of the 1960s and the early 1970s, inspired Goodison's generation of West Indian poets, just as the questioning that led up to that decade prompted Brathwaite and Walcott and their contemporaries. For all of them, in each generation, there was a renewed awareness that harrowing the land was eventually followed by harvest. At the same time, there was a profound ambivalence. Power might not grow naturally, but might have to be forged by hand.

Behind the advocates of black power, whether in the United States or the West Indies, and whether advocating violent revolution or visionary redemption, was the voice of Garvey proposing that "power is the only argument that satisfies man. Except the individual, the race or the nation has power that is exclusive, it means that that individual, race or nation will be bound by the will of the other who possesses this great qualification. . . . Hence it is advisable for the Negro to get power of every kind. Power in education, science, industry, politics and higher government. That kind of power that will stand out signally, so that other races and nations can see and if they will not see, feel."[37]

For Garvey, as for his successors, the seizing of power by force was the only choice left when saying what you see does not convince, indeed does not even interest, those who see and say things differently. That is precisely why the saying can be so important. For people who have nothing left to lose, it is the only alternative to violence. It is this alternative that has led to a new perception of the relationships between poetry and politics and the consciousness of being black in the exercise of power in the West Indies. For ultimately it was not a counsel of violence but a vision of a promised land—and even more the particular way in which he talked about it—that made Garvey such an influential figure in developing black consciousness in the West Indies. The words of Marcus Garvey, like those of many other great leaders, became his empowering legacy. This legacy was taken up most prominently by the Rastafarians, who combined the idea of redemption of blacks from their Babylonian exile in the lands of new-world slavery with a revelation of God incarnate in the person of one Ras Tafari, who became Haile Selassie I, the Conquering Lion of Judah, on his coronation as Emperor of Ethiopia in 1930.

Over the past several decades, Rastafarianism has been a major force in West Indian life, incorporating a visionary idealism with a sternly

realistic attention to the conditions of poverty and suffering that so
many West Indian blacks endure. Its influence on the consciousness of
West Indians has also been profound, involving new ways of seeing
the place and its people, and a new sense of language. It may represent
the only genuine myth to emerge from the experience of European,
African, and Asian dislocation in the new world.

Rastafarianism began in the 1930s and came to the fore in the 1950s,
first of all in Jamaica. It combined a legacy of black rage and frustration
in the new world with an Old Testament revelation of an African homeland. Inspiration for this interpretation came from several sources: from
Garvey, with his ambition to found a black state in Africa and his call
to "Look to Africa, when a black king shall be crowned, for the day of
deliverance is near"; and from a messianic Baptist preacher named
Alexander Bedward, who founded a ministry in August Town near
Kingston, Jamaica, in the 1890s, which drew large numbers of blacks
together. In 1895 Bedward told his followers that "Hell will be your
portion if you do not rise up and crush the white man . . . there is a
white wall and a black wall and the white wall has been closing around
the black wall but now the black wall is becoming bigger than the white
and they must knock the white wall down."[38] For these words, Bedward was declared insane by the British authorities and committed,
but others intervened on his behalf and he was quickly freed. He continued his ministry with increasing zeal, until in 1920 he announced
that he was ready to fly to Heaven on New Year's Eve. He was taking
literally a figure of speech commonly used during revival worship
about "flying" or traveling quickly from place to place, a figure best
understood in the context of Myalism, a religion that developed in
Jamaica during the period of slavery with a core of beliefs inherited
from Africa and influenced by Christianity.[39] And Bedward was giving
one kind of answer to Brathwaite's question—"Where then is the nigger's home? Here? Or in Heaven?"

Thousands came from the other islands of the Caribbean and from
Central America to witness Bedward's miracle . . . which was post-
poned. After a period of waiting for the right moment, a frustrated
Bedward led a march to Kingston to purge the evil town. He was
arrested, committed once again to an asylum, and died there.

For many, Bedward's prophetic voice was evidence of the importance of messianic revelation. In due course, scriptural texts were inter-
preted in a way that identified Haile Selassie I as the new Messiah.
These texts also indicated the need to return to Africa as the true source
of spiritual strength and material purification.

The Rastafarian dream of a home in Africa is a West Indian version of the place of peace and prosperity for which European imaginations have found so many images, especially in times of trouble and discontent. The new world itself was one, the product of both imaginative artifice and blunt realism. And the Bible provides many others. The home of which Rastafarians dream is Ethiopia, the Africa of their imaginings. In one sense, it is an ideal place, not to be found on any map. But in another sense, as Ishmael said in *Moby Dick*, "true places never are."[40] The Rastafarian dream of home is shaped by both desire and despair, and it is a powerful reality in the life and literary imagination of West Indians.

Rastafarianism extended its influence in a variety of directions. Some of them included extremes of political activism, with the Nyabingi brethren, for example, advocating death to white oppressors. But at the center of Rastafarianism was a cooperative ideal that committed Rastafarians not to activism but to a retreat from the materialistic and competitive society of the contemporary West Indies. There is much in Rastafarianism that is receptive to traditions other than those exclusive to blacks and much that derives from customs indigenous to the West Indies. The use of marijuana, which (along with the growing of long matted and braided hair—"locks" or "dreadlocks") is for many people the most familiar association with Rastafarianism, goes back a long way in Jamaican history. Some claim its use in the West Indies has African origins. It is known for certain that indentured laborers from India brought marijuana with them in the 1840s; and the word *ganja*, which is the commonly used term for marijuana in Jamaica, is itself a Hindi word. Ganja tea was used in Jamaica for medicinal purpose for generations before Rastafarianism. The association of marijuana with states of heightened spiritual awareness is familiar from Hindu practice. It is also consistent with traditions of African as well as aboriginal meditation. Which is to say that, like assertions of black power, it is not simply the product of the 1950s or 1960s; just as the spiritualism with which it has links has deep roots in the traditions of African peoples and in their contact with European religious customs.[41]

Rastafarianism has contributed much to a sense of solidarity among blacks in the West Indies. During the 1950s and 1960s, when social and economic stresses were severe, this was no small thing. And the contribution of Rastafarianism continues. In a song called "Caribbean Man," played at Carnival in 1979, the Trinidadian calypsonian Black Stalin (Leroy Calliste) set the influence of Rastafarianism alongside some recent economic and social initiatives, and then suggested that there was really no comparison. Rastafarianism makes a lasting differ-

ence to the people, sang Black Stalin; novelties such as Carifta (the
Caribbean Free Trade Area established in 1968 to provide some of the
economic solidarity that the collapse of political federation made
increasingly necessary in the region) make none at all. The final line,
with characteristically calypsonian humor, prescribes ganja for the
health and wealth of the West Indies.

> Dem is one race—De Caribbean Man
> From de same place—De Caribbean Man
> Dat make de same trip—De Caribbean Man
> On de same ship—De Caribbean Man
> So we must push one common intention
> Is for a better life in de region . . .
> A man who don't know his history can't form no unity
> How could a man who don't know his history form his own ideology
> If the rastafari movement spreading and Carifta dying slow
> Den is something dem rastas on dat dem politicians don't know.[42]

For the authorities, there were troublesome features about Rastafarianism. The popular identification of some Rastafarian groups with
violence generated considerable political reaction in the West Indies in
the 1950s. The rhetoric of the movement encouraged it, and the genuine
desperation of many who could see no alternative made it easy to confuse the call for change with a call to violent action. In 1960, in the
context of widespread concern about the social and political goals of
Rastafarianism in Jamaica, a report on the movement was prepared by
Rex Nettleford, Roy Augier, and Michael G. Smith from the University
of the West Indies. One of the points made in the report was that the
question of violence was inseparable from the question of language.
"The language of the movement is violent . . . because it is the language
of the Bible, and especially of the Old Testament. It is apocalyptic language, in which sinners are consumed with fire, sheep are separated
from goats, oppressors are smitten and kings and empires are over-
thrown. All Christians use this violent language, in their religious serv-
ices and elsewhere. The use of such language does not mean that they
are ready to fight in the streets. It does, on the other hand, mean that
the concepts of revolution are neither frightening nor unfamiliar."[43]

Music, especially reggae, has provided one of the most widely recognized expressions of Rastafarianism. During the 1950s, and particularly in Jamaica, various popular musical forms developed. Influences
included the traditional slow drumming of the Rastafarians and the
music of religious revivalism, with its mixture of European and African

traditions, as well as elements of American jazz and rhythm and blues in which these traditions also converged. One of the earliest West Indian forms was called "ska", which combined a strong drum beat with wind instruments—especially the trombone. Eventually, ska slowed down its pace to a style that became known as rock steady, which soon evolved into the familiar, persistent rhythms of reggae— what one practitioner called "a waxy beat—like you stepping in glue" with "a different bass, a rebel bass."[44] Linton Kwesi Johnson, a Jamaican dub poet who for the past thirty years has lived in England, describes it in his poem "Reggae Sounds" as "Shock-black bubble-doun-beat bouncing / rock-wise tumble-doun sound music."[45] But what was most important about reggae was its combination of a new instrumental sound with lyrics of social protest, picking up the tradition of the hard-hitting lyrics of revivalist hymns and having the same kind of popular appeal as the Woodstock era singers and musicians in the United States, and some later rock musicians. And having also their belief that music, like other forms of art, can change the world.

Reggae's first superstar was Bob Marley, who with his group The Wailers achieved international recognition for songs created out of a deep belief in Rastafarian ideals. In a song called "Chant Down Babylon," Marley brings together the possibilities of both destructive and redemptive change, of political violence and poetic power. The fundamental belief that shines through is a belief in the transforming power of the imagination, chanting down Babylon, burning down Babylon.

> Come we go burn down Babylon
> One more time.
> Come we go chant down Babylon
> One more time.[46]

Change was an unsettling fact of life during the 1950s and 1960s. Along with the emergence of a fragile political independence in the West Indies came troubles in Jamaica and Trinidad and several other places, and a sturdy political reaction on the part of the new authorities, who with leaders such as Alexander Bustamante in Jamaica and Grantley Adams in Barbados represented an older generation of political activism. Economic troubles were intensified by severe local inequities, and black power advocates generated widespread political anxiety. As always, language—in this case, the language of revolutionary change— played a central role. Books were banned. Outspoken individuals were banned, too. The Guyanese sociologist Walter Rodney, for example, who taught at the University of the West Indies, was refused reentry to Jamaica on his return from a black writer's conference in Montreal in 1968. The decision precipitated a demonstration at the university and widespread disturbances in which several people were killed in downtown Kingston. The focus was not so much on Rodney himself (whose gifted career ended brutally with his murder in 1980 in Georgetown) as on the general predicament of blacks in the West Indies, and on the place of black power in West Indian politics. A couple of years later, black power advocates mounted a serious political challenge to the government of Eric Williams in Trinidad, and during this time Stokely Carmichael was denied permission to return to his native land.

One of the most significant West Indian institutions to develop during this period was in fact the University of the West Indies. Established in 1948, first of all as a College of the University of London, it has since then played an important role in forging a West Indian consciousness and sense of identity. Over the past forty years, the University has expanded to include not only the original campus in Jamaica at Mona, a hillside suburb of Kingston, but also campuses in Trinidad at St. Augustine near Port of Spain and in Barbados at Cave Hill near Bridgetown. It also has an extensive extramural program, which serves students on the other islands; and its three campuses bring students from all the islands together. The University of the West Indies became an independent—and necessarily an international—degree-granting institution in 1962. During the next decade it nourished a tradition of indigenous scholarship and teaching and established itself as a center for the analysis of West Indian social, economic, and political conditions, exemplifying the spirit of intellectual inquiry and passionate dispute to which universities have often, but not always, aspired. It also became the target of considerable criticism—sometimes because of its engagement with controversial issues, and sometimes for exactly the opposite reason, because its commitment to conventional academic structures and standards was seen to represent an unconscionable detachment from the realities of West Indian life. In a poem ironically titled "Book So Deep," Brother Resistance, a performance poet from Trinidad and one of its graduates, expressed his Rastafarian protest

> against
> de miseducation
> brain squeezer
> foreign
> indoctrinator
> brain slave dealer
> and tho' de book so deep

> no hill too steep
> for we to climb
> in we push
> to shake down
> dis prison of progress[47]

But most of all, and through all these challenges, the University of the West Indies became a place where there was lively discussion, during often troubled times, of issues fundamentally important to the future of the region and its people.[48]

The Barbadian poet Bruce St. John has a short poem about this time, and incidentally about Stokely Carmichael, called "West Indian Litany." It is structured according to the call-and-response ritual of fundamentalist churches in the West Indies and uses local dialect to convey an uneasy recognition of the place—and the power—of black solidarity in West Indian affairs.

Stokely like he mad!	Da is true
He outah touch wid de West Indies.	Da is true
He ain' even discreet!	Da is true
He can' be 'pon we side.	Da is true
He mussy wukkin' fuh de whites!	Da is true
Dem thrives 'pon we division.	Da is true
So dey won' leh 'e talk!	Wuh da?
Suppose he right though?	Da is true
Suppose he right though?	Da is true[49]

Though the language is relatively uniform, the voices in dialogue here define the range of attitudes and expectations that characterized this period, sustaining its tensions and shaping its opportunities ... some of which (in the familiar ways of both speech and writing) are not stated but are there in the gaps and silences.

St. John's poem first appeared in 1971 in a special issue of the magazine *Savacou* (named after a mythical Carib Indian war bird). It was published by the Caribbean Artists' Movement, originally a London-based group begun by the Trinidadian writer, publisher, and activist John La Rose, the Jamaican Andrew Salkey, and Edward Kamau Brathwaite to raise the profile of Caribbean imaginative expression. As Brathwaite recalled the time, Carmichael

> visited London and magnetized a whole set of splintered feelings that had for a long time been seeking a node. He enunciated a way of seeing the Black West Indian that seemed to make sense of the entire history of

slavery and colonial suppression, of the African diaspora into the New
World. And he gave it a name. Links of sympathy, perhaps for the first
time, were set up between labouring immigrant, artist / intellectual, and
student. Sharing, as he saw it, a common history, Carmichael produced
images of shared communal values. A black International was possible.
West Indians denied history, denied heroes by their imposed education,
responded. From London (and Black America) the flame spread to the
University campuses of the archipelago. It found echoes among the urban
restless of the growing island cities. Rastafari art, 'primitive' art, dialect
and protest suddenly had a new urgency, took on significance.[50]

By this time in the West Indies, literary and artistic expression often
had a very strong political dimension. Almost everyone recognized that
the social and economic challenges of independence could only be met
by drawing on a sense of collective aspiration and achievement. But
very few were anxious for state sponsored art. This left many writers
in a paradoxical situation. On the one hand, they were raised in English
literary traditions that were based on the authority—or at the least on
the myth of authority—of the individual imagination. On the other,
they were convinced that imaginative freedom from the pernicious
effects of over four hundred years of colonial conditioning, in which
they were trained to see themselves as inferior, could only be achieved
by some sort of collective enterprise. Celebrating the simple fact of
being West Indian was not so simple.

The literature in which this celebration was taking place made obvious its collective resistance to compromise; and it made obvious the
need for a criticism that would do justice both to the new literary tradition that was developing and to the individual writers, some of
whom were following very independent lines. In fact, the ambivalent
allegiances of writers to tradition and to their individual talent provided an image of the dilemma facing the entire West Indian society.
European democracy was the last imperial legacy to the West Indies.
It encouraged competing national visions and the energetic expression
of conflicting individual priorities. But during this time of transition
from colonial status to nationhood, the West Indies needed cooperation
between individuals at the very least, and collective solidarity at best.
Writers were therefore under pressure to make common cause in shaping a collective vision. Inevitably, there was considerable controversy
about exactly what this involved. And the perennial tension between
tradition and individual talent had this additional twist in the West
Indies, with writers sometimes being expected to surrender their imaginative autonomy to unwelcome communal prerogatives on the one
hand, and to uncongenial literary conventions on the other. This is a

familiar condition of literary creativity and craft, of course, but it took an intense turn during this period. As Ovid says, in Derek Walcott's poem "The Hotel Normandie Pool," "Romans . . . will mock your slavish rhyme, the slaves your love of Roman structures." [51]

Savacou appeared at the same time as another anthology, entitled *Breaklight*. It was edited by Andrew Salkey and included only poetry, whereas *Savacou* had poems and both fiction and nonfiction prose. *Breaklight* was divided into sections, whose titles describe the development of West Indian consciousness that was chronicled in the anthology: The Concealed Spark, The Heat of Identity, The Fire of Involvement, The Blaze of the Struggle, Breaklight. In his introduction, Salkey argued that "something familiar has been abandoned, and something strange and bright, a sharp light slicing its way through the Caribbean, is being grasped, and shaped with inventiveness and daring by a few poets there. . . . The promise now is one of spiritual and social redefinition." [52]

It was a justifiable claim, for the poems in *Breaklight* demonstrated a new sense of confidence and a renewed determination not to be intimidated by a past that was shaped by somebody else. They also illuminated some of the relationships between familiarity and strangeness upon which all literature depends and which has been one of the most challenging features of contemporary West Indian poetry. But it was *Savacou* that got the most attention and generated the most antagonism.

The reason was simple. While Salkey's introduction and his selection of texts left room for a variety of attitudes and ambitions, Brathwaite cornered all those who might have a different perspective. In his introduction, which he called "Forward," he made it clear that he conceived the anthology as a challenge to conventional notions of literary enterprise. He drew attention to the "revolutionary questioning" of the poems and stories and praised the "dream of wholeness" that he saw as the dominant imaginative element, a healing remedy for "the divided islands of ourselves." "Art-revolution-society," in his view, were "a continuum of imagination, a seamless garment of expression," and the language of literary expression had to reflect this.

For Brathwaite, a truly West Indian literature must represent the central heritage of slavery shared by black West Indians, not because everyone who mattered in the West Indies was black, but because blackness as an image of slavery defined the dispossession and exploitation, which to anyone looking around the West Indies was clearly not over. The language of blacks—the local dialects and the newly coined Rastafarian words and so forth—incorporated the historical and contemporary consciousness of West Indians in a special way, embodying a recapitulation of the past and a signal of a new West Indian awareness of what Brathwaite called "not you and me, but us. Not what is happening there, but *here*."[53] And this language had to be part of the literature.

One of the poems in the *Savacou* anthology was by a Rastafarian called Bongo Jerry (formerly Robin Small), whose revolutionary polemic infuriated some critics. The name "Bongo" begins the polemic, for (in association with the Bongo dance and its accompanying songs, which for a long while were prohibited in the colonial West Indies) it came to mean ugly, stupid, barbaric, "African." A number of Rastafarians had taken the name in an ironic gesture of indifference to those who would use it, or any other word, in a derogatory way to describe blacks. They were affirming new freedoms within the old determinisms of slavery. The name Bongo was also used to identify members of Convince, the oldest surviving form of Myalism and a direct link to African spiritualism. (This kind of referential complexity, especially when it involves a form of "insider" irony, underlines the importance of recognizing the context, or framing, of these West Indian texts.)

Bongo Jerry's poem is called "Mabrak," a Rastafarian word meaning "black lightning," recalling both the biblical creation of the world out of nothing, the divine Word in the beginning, and the final apocalyptic vision of a new heaven and a new earth, with illumination and revelation being associated here with blackness instead of whiteness. There are clever moments, with SAR (the demeaning "Sir") mirroring RAS (an elevating Rastafarian prefix); and the sometime fashion of artificially straightening African hair to conform to European ideals of beauty becoming an image for imitating the "correctness" of English speech by bringing the deviations of the local language into line, straightening the tongue. The achievement of the poem is mostly limited to its rhetorical energy, with its first effect being its strongest; though we need to recognize the special limitation, which we will be discussing later, of reading instead of hearing such a text. But however we come to it, that initial effect is considerable, and draws attention not only to the frustration and resentment of the poet but also to the arbitrariness and intimidation of language.

Lightning
is the future brightening
for last year man learn
how to use black eyes.
(wise!)

Mabrak:
NEWSFLASH!
"Babylon plans crash"
Thunder interrupt their programme to
announce:
BLACK ELECTRIC STORM
IS HERE
How long you feel "fair to fine
(WHITE)" would last?

How long calm in darkness
    when out of BLACK
        come forth LIGHT? . . .

MABRAK,
Enlightening is BLACK
hands writing the words of
black message
for black hearts to feel.

MABRAK is righting the wrongs and brain whitening—HOW?
Not just by washing out the straightening and wearing dashiki t'ing:

MOSTOFTHESTRAIGHTENINGISINTHETONGUE—SO HOW?

Save the YOUNG
from the language that MEN teach,
the doctrine Pope preach
skin bleach.

HOW ELSE . . . MAN must use MEN language
            to carry dis message:

SILENCE BABEL TONGUES; recall and
recollect BLACK SPEECH.

Cramp all double meaning
                an' all that hiding behind language bar,

for that crossword speaking
                when expressing feeling

is just English language contribution to increase confusion in
                Babel-land tower—

delusion, name changing, word rearranging
                ringing rings of roses, pocket full of poses:

"SAR" instead of "RAS"

left us in a situation
                    where education
mek plenty African afraid, ashamed, unable to choose
                        (and use)

BLACK POWA. (Strange Tongue)

NOT AGAIN!
Never be the same!
Never again shame![54]

The *Savacou* anthology brought language into the center of West Indian political consciousness. And it brought a consciousness of language and politics into the center of West Indian poetry. The language of black power was strange, in a way; but what was particularly strange was hearing that language in poetry. "Mabrak" signaled that poetry could be about power—black power, the power to make things different (Never be the same!), the power to create a new world (Never again shame!). Some of this power, of course, might be destructive—the power to burn down / chant down Babylon. And while many critics argued that this kind of "bawling for a bloodbath" needed to be understood in the context of Rastafarian language and symbolism,[55] others worried that invitations of this sort cannot always be held in control by literary forms. If poems do indeed make something happen, then poets have a great responsibility. But here, at least, the violence of the poem and the violence that is done in the poem to the familiar proprieties of poetry were an inseparable part of the process of illuminating and empowering the language in the light of a renewed consciousness of the central heritage of West Indians. The heritage of slavery.

3

"Come back to me my language"

 "Nothing will always be created in the West Indies for quite a long time, because whatever will come out of there is like nothing one has ever seen before," wrote Derek Walcott in 1973,[1] in answer to Vidia Naipaul. First of all, Walcott had in mind that West Indians whose ancestors came from Africa by way of the Middle Passage look different from European migrants to the new world. Walcott also knew that for a poet, this difference went deeper. For West Indians also *sound* different, different from speakers of European languages anywhere else. This too is the legacy of the West Indies. And it is central to the development of its literature. As Kamau Brathwaite proposed in his history of the development of creole society in Jamaica, "it was in language that the slave was perhaps most successfully imprisoned by his master, and it was in his (mis-)use of it that he perhaps most effectively rebelled."[2]

This "misuse" is of course a matter of perspective, like the misuse of freedom by blacks who demanded racial equality and political power. The story of contemporary West Indian poetry is the story of a better perspective and of more power. The English language no longer belongs to the English, just as West Indian blacks no longer belong to their white masters. But colonial habits are hard to break, especially habits of mind that maintain a distinction between the authority of civilized standards and the rebelliousness of local (which is to say, barbaric) practices. Differences, to this way of thinking, are deviant or decadent or dangerous. John Agard's poem "Listen Mr. Oxford don" takes up this theme.

I ent have no gun
I ent have no knife
but mugging de Queen's English
is the story of my life . . .

Dem accuse me of assault
on de Oxford dictionary
imagine a concise peaceful man like me
dem want me serve time
for inciting rhyme to riot . . .

So mek dem send one big word after me
i ent serving no jail sentence
I slashing suffix in self-defence
I bashing future wit present tense
and if necessary

I making de Queen's English accessory
to my offence[3]

Although few of the whites who came to the West Indies from Great Britain during the seventeenth or eighteenth century spoke what would have been considered cultivated English, there was still a consciousness of the difference between the regional British dialects spoken by the white owners and bookkeepers and overseers and the English spoken by slaves. By the nineteenth century, when there was a heightened awareness of the distinction between imperial standards and colonial habits, this difference troubled those who were in authority. "There is scarcely a black in the country who speaks pure English," remarked one observer, "and the white people take no pains to correct them. Sometimes they even adopt the barbarous idiom of the negro, thinking to make themselves understood. The consequence is, their pronunciation is abominable, and the rising generation, notwithstanding the pains taken to educate them, retain the villainous *patois* of their parents."[4] In this description, the language of the West Indies is strange and barbaric, like its blacks. The prescription is obvious. Civilize them.

The campaign to civilize the West Indies began in earnest about a hundred years ago. But it had been underway from the fifteenth century. In 1492, when Queen Isabella was proudly presented with the first grammar of Spanish ever written, she asked impatiently, "What is it for?" The answer she got from the Bishop of Seville must have appealed to the woman who sponsored Columbus. "Language is the perfect instrument of empire."[5]

From the beginning of European settlement in the new world, language was the most popular instrument for turning barbarians into civilians. At the heart of the endeavor was a sort of secular evangelism, a preaching of the gospel of intellectual and emotional progress. It was assumed that European thought and feeling were superior, and that these superiorities were embodied in its languages. It was therefore hoped that savage feelings might be changed into civilized thoughts by instruction in one of these languages.

Planters had a narrower ambition with their slaves, to be sure, though slaves who were in domestic service needed to be reasonably competent in massa's tongue. But mostly, slaves were to be kept down, not lifted up. It was somewhat different with the aboriginal people of the new world. As they were driven off their land, the Indian tribes that survived the brutal process were welcomed into the arms of those who wanted to civilize and convert them. A tough task, it was realized, but just the kind of thing to engage the enterprise of the energetic newcomers. "The Indian tongue is the great obstacle to the civilization of the Indians and the sooner it is removed the better," said one impatient civilizer.[6] This attitude did not die with the seventeenth or eighteenth or nineteenth centuries. Until quite recently in Canada and the United States, relentless efforts were made to obliterate Indian languages and to create what turned out to be tragic discontinuities beween generations of aboriginal people. Children were discouraged from speaking their mother tongue and from participating in their family and tribal life, for these were viewed as regressive and pernicious. Instructed in English in school, children were beaten for speaking their native languages, even in recess or in the residences away from home in which they often lived while they were at school. As George Manuel, an Indian chief from the northwest coast, once remarked, "three things stand out in my mind from my school years: hunger; speaking English; and being called a heathen because of my grandfather."[7]

Images of coercion are surprisingly common in discussions about language, though they are usually muted by the niceties of linguistic jargon. They derive from one of two basic premises: that language determines thought, or that language conveys thought. The latter view, in its simplest form, holds that language was invented for the purpose of communicating, and that language use is to be judged accordingly, as in Alexander Pope's famous commendation of "what oft was thought but ne'er so well expressed." This was the most familiar eighteenth-century attitude toward language, with debate centering around whether linguistic invention was what we might call semantic or pragmatic; that is, whether it involved the revelation of meaning or the production of "effects" (which is to say, thoughts in the minds of listeners) through speech acts and other signs and gestures.

In the nineteenth century, there was considerable discussion about the alternative view, in which language in some sense precedes, creates or conditions thought and shapes our perception of the world. Early in the twentieth century, the American linguist Benjamin Lee Whorf argued persuasively (mostly by reference to what he called Standard Average European languages and those of aboriginal Americans, especially the Hopi) that differences in behavior and thought, including differences in concepts of space and time and matter, are a function of differences in language.[8] Language, that is to say, represents an attitude toward reality, and toward others. This view in turn influenced arguments about how language (and of course literature) encodes not only perspectives but also privileges. As Ludwig Wittgenstein proposed, with characteristic ambiguity, the limits of our world are the limits of our language.

This notion of linguistic relativity became very popular, informing accounts such as Samuel Hayakawa's *Language in Action,* which was widely read as a Book-of-the-Month Club selection in the United States during the 1940s. But Whorf's ideas, which drew on a tradition of linguistic speculation stretching from Wilhelm von Humboldt in the 1830s to Franz Boas and Edward Sapir a century later, also came under considerable attack. In its radical form, the proposition that language determines thought and culture implied the impossibility of communicating from one particular linguistic community to another—the essential untranslatability of languages, and ultimately of experiences. Anthropologists in particular were very troubled by this; and many linguists, too, some of whom turned instead to a search for universals, especially universal grammars. One argument to discredit Whorf ran this way: if linguistic determinism is true, it should be impossible for anyone to break free from the categories of his or her native language to understand the categories of another; and yet this is precisely what Whorf claimed to have done in demonstrating the *difference* in Hopi. Whorf's response was that there were still a wide range of possibilities for communication and understanding across languages and cultures, but that we need to be aware of the limitations before we can truly understand the possibilities. To use Brathwaite's image, we need to recognize that we are imprisoned before we feel the need to break out. This is especially true, Whorf and others argued, of what Friedrich Nietzsche called "the prison-house of language."[9] This has a positive side, of course, which we see in Brathwaite's account of the development of creole languages and a creole society and in Frantz Fanon's comment that "every dialect is a way of thinking."[10]

The discussion of linguistic differences stimulated by Whorf coincided with the development of another kind of analysis, also focusing on the structure of language. This analysis centered around the idea that language, and especially poetic language, operates along two axes: metaphoric ("this is that"); and metonymic ("this is put for that"). (The elements of difference and displacement that are such important features of West Indian literature are, it turns out, mirror images of the similarity and contiguity that define metaphor and metonymy; and these figurative structures also provide the most common framework for representations of identity and authority). Developed from many directions, anthropological as well as linguistic, it drew upon two venerable notions of language: as magic, on the one hand; and as communication, on the other. Roman Jakobson, a linguist whose work began in Moscow just before the Revolution and continued in Prague from the 1920s through the 1950s, made the most significant contribution.

Jakobson's analysis was prompted by his study of linguistic disorders, specifically aphasia. He pointed out that among the features of unsuccessful communication, the most fundamental are the inability to use the structure of a language as well as its words, and an indifference to the relationships between them. The study of those whose communicative abilities were impaired provided Jakobson with new insights into what linguists call "code-switching," and into a variety of the relationships between "private" languages (or idiolects, an individual's way of speaking at a particular time) and public languages (or sociolects). Most forms of communication depend on these relationships, which also determine some of the effects of literature. Because Jakobson's analysis was concerned with boundaries between structure and substance, and between the personal or particular and the public or universal, it also provided ways of understanding linguistic interactions in terms of the dynamics of knowledge and power. Poets, who routinely court disruptions and discontinuities that are not unrelated to these pathologies, operate on the same boundaries of language that Jakobson studied; and his investigations provided new perspectives on poetic language.

Another set of insights about the language of poetry with obvious relevance for West Indian literature emerged around the same time from a different direction, through the study of discursive relationships between different varieties of languages (in situations of what is sometimes called "heteroglossia") as well as between distinctly different languages (or situations of "polyglossia"). The Russian linguist Mikhail Bakhtin was the most widely acknowledged exponent of this analysis; and his work focused on the circumstances of what he called "utterance" (written or oral), where words are perceived as events or enactments rather than as things or signifiers of things. The relationships between communication and performance in language, and between language as an "equivalent" (metaphorically identified with or metonymically standing in place of something) and language as a speech act, are central to the function of all literary texts. Our response to literature shuttles between these alternative models, and many of the most significant features of poetry derive from the ambivalence this generates. And so Bakhtin's work, like Jakobson's and Whorf's, has prompted considerable interest.

Theoretical discussions of this sort sometimes seem merely ostentatious; but I hope that they will suggest some of the broader significance of the central themes of this book, and some of the challenges of contemporary West Indian literature. The ideas involved here have deeply affected arguments about standards and difference that have shaped postcolonial ideologies of language and literature and the liberation of peoples, with local languages and local forms of cultural expression acknowledged as embodying whole—and wholly different—worlds of thought and feeling. These ideas have also provided new ways of understanding how the languages of classification and typology routinely use metaphors and metonymys as if they were realities, and how literature depends on these uses . . . for instance with the word *nigger*, to take just one grim example whose effect is by no means always conveniently ironic.

These twentieth-century speculations also provide a useful context for reviewing ideas about language and literature that took shape in the nineteenth century. The development of West Indian cultural identity was profoundly influenced by these earlier discussions, which illustrated tensions that have been central to the development both of an independent literary tradition in the West Indies and of contemporary theories of language—tensions between the real and the imagined, discovery and invention, familiarity and strangeness, naturalness and artifice, self and other, individual freedom and collective or institutional determinism, and the barbaric and the civilized.

And this highlights another dimension in the nineteenth-century discussions that also links them to contemporary literary and linguistic concerns; for while the debate about language was intense, the anxieties about civil order were even more so. Whether language shaped or served thought was an interesting point, but it seemed irrelevant to those who felt that their values were under seige from the barbaric hordes. The challenge was to bring everyone into line, and to order everyone's minds along similar lines. Language was the straight edge, set to rule behavior as well as thought. Whether it created or imposed the right stuff was not uninteresting, but was essentially immaterial.

In the West Indies after emancipation, colonial experience and imperial ambition converged in a determination to turn blacks into whites, or Africans into Europeans. To many European listeners, the absence of articulate language—or more precisely the presence of what was construed as the inarticulate babble of African languages (with the transfer of some of their intonations into West Indian speech)—was inevitably associated with the absence of coherent thought and civilized feeling. Even enlightened nineteenth-century reformers believed that racial and political equality would only come about when blacks started behaving like whites. And speaking like whites. And learning about white achievements. This is how a colonial education officer in Trinidad in 1934 described the importance of British history for West Indians. "History:—This subject has not found favour in many schools. This is to be regretted; for when Empire Day comes round, it must be difficult for teachers to impress their pupils sufficiently, when the latter know nothing of the growth of Empire, the glorious deeds of Britain down the centuries, the lives of her greatest heroes and statesmen, the main turning points of British history, and the results of the British occupation of the colonies."[11]

Reporting heroism from a West Indian point of view was obviously not yet on the agenda. Lorna Goodison gives an account of her own schooling that underlines how even the most obvious models of self-representation were distorted by these traditions. "I was at primary school, about 7 or 8, and sad to say in those days Jamaican children used to do drawings and painting of people and they were all white people. I remember doing this painting of a lady sitting down, reading a book or something. I remember mixing red and yellow and black together and I painted this lady a very dark brown. The children laughed and they said, 'You've painted an African lady'. And the teacher said to them, 'But you know . . . a lot of you look like that lady.' She put the painting up, and it was up there for a long time."[12]

In her novel *Crick Crack, Monkey*, published in 1970, the Trinidadian writer Merle Hodge gives a nice example of how racial and religious issues get bound up together in language, that instrument of empire. The main character, called Tee, describes how education insinuates itself into all aspects of life—which perhaps should not be all that surprising, since this is precisely what we usually hope education will do.

Or at least one of the things, since behind the educational ambitions of this system, the product of nineteenth-century liberal individualism, was a simple premise: that human personalities (and human societies) can be changed, which is to say "improved"; and that education can accomplish this improvement. (The reformers of the early twentieth century—Maria Montessori, Rudolf Steiner, and others—were much more conservative in their assumptions and much more committed to the notion that differences are immutable and should be nourished rather than annihilated. And of course they did not find much of a place in the European colonial educational systems of the time.) Here is Tee's account.

> Various kindly and elderly folk had long since asssured me that my mother had gone to Glory. And now at school I had come to learn that Glory and The Mother Country and Up-There and Over-There had all one and the same geographical location. It made perfect sense that the place where my mother had gone, Glory, should also be known as The Mother Country. And then there was "Land of Hope and Glory / Mother of the Free. . . ." Every Sunday at Sunday-school we were given a little card with a picture and a Bible verse —pictures of children with yellow hair standing around Jesus in fields of sickly flowers, and with yellow rays emanating stiffly from all these personages, or the children with yellow hair kneeling with their hands clapsed and their faces upturned towards some kind of sun that had one fat ray coming down at them. Thus it was that I had a pretty good idea of what kind of a place Glory must be, and of what happened to you there; for also at Sunday-school we sang:
>
> > Till I cross the wide, wide water, Lord
> > My black sin washed from me,
> > Till I come to Glory, Glory, Lord
> > And cleansed stand beside Thee,
> > White and shining stand beside Thee, Lord,
> > Among Thy blessed children.[13]

Christianity seemed to depend on having a correct set of ideals, European ideals. Civilization, on the other hand, seemed to depend on speaking and writing properly, as Europeans did. Once again, there was a paradox: civilization and the language that exemplified it were construed on the one hand as natural growths, and on the other as the products of ingenious artifice. In both models, however, the notion of a correct language was closely associated with the idea of a civil society, with incorrectness supposedly encouraging incivility . . . and ultimately the kind of degeneration that causes the fall of civilizations and the rise of the barbarian hordes. If letters to the editors of countless newspapers over the past couple of centuries are any indication, law and order seem to be jeopardized more by sloppy vocabulary than by almost anything else. Strong armies save the world. Weak grammar may lose it all again. As one anxious observer in the nineteenth century noted, "there is no surer or more fatal sign of the decay of a language than in the interpolation of barbarous terms and foreign words. . . . A corrupt and decaying language is an infallible sign of a corrupt and decaying civilization. It is one of the gates by which barbarism may invade and overpower the traditions of a great race."[14] He added that "as an index and a school of national character the importance of poetry can hardly be exaggerated." Another commentator predicted "public calamity, perplexity, war, and revolution"[15] if things continued to decline, and if dialect words—which Thomas Hardy once called "those terrible marks of the beast to the truly genteel"[16]—continued to insinuate themselves into literature, and thereby into common currency among the civilized.

The nineteenth century was the heyday of this sort of apocalyptic anxiety. The European imperial powers, confident of their civilized superiority, were increasingly putting themselves in the company of lesser folk, the barbarians of the East and West Indies, Africa, China. And they were convinced that if language was the instrument of empire, education was the instrument of language. Furthermore, since literature was presumed to be the most eloquent expression of language, it must be a central element of education.

For several hundred years, after having concluded their arguments over the relative merits of ancient and modern languages, European nations had been celebrating their achievements in their own languages, and their own literatures. Often, as in Spain, this involved imposing one language and its literature on others, with Castilian taking precedence not only over other Spanish dialects such as Andalusian but also over other non-Spanish languages such as Basque and Catalan. In Great Britain, too, the English language prevailed over the Gaelic spoken by many Scots and Irish (though speakers of Irish Gaelic in the Middle Ages, when the English language was just developing a distinctive identity, used to refer to it as "excremental"). And English literature became the token of British achievements. Before we get overly indignant, we should recall that this attitude toward literature is still in many ways our own, perhaps in our colonial imitation of imperial habits of mind. But whatever its origins, it undoubtedly informs our commonly held view that black literature, or women's literature, or any other literature that is in some sense construed as the product of a particular community is accordingly taken as an expression of its collective identity, signaling and certifying its achievements.

During the great imperial reign of Queen Victoria, it was common to associate the glory of the earlier great period of national enterprise in the sixteenth and seventeenth centuries under Queen Elizabeth I with the great literature—and specifically the glorious language—of Shakespeare and Milton, and the King James translation of the Bible. As a corollary, the novels and poetry—and certainly for the Queen herself, the drama—of Victorian England were taken to represent a new period of national greatness. And with the celebration of this national greatness came a celebration of the civilizing influence of the language and literature in which it was embodied. In the words of one nineteenth-century commentator, it was vitally important

> that here, in the seat and cradle of our race, under the tutelary sanction of our public schools and universities, with a highly educated class of men engaged in the liberal professions and in public life, and in the very centre of the literary activity of the nation, we should endeavour, as far as possible, to fix and determine the correct meaning and value of those words which are destined to pass current throughout the world, and to express the manifold inflections and varieties of thought, feeling and perception, in so many myriads of men. The greater the extension of the language, the more important does it become to throw around it all the lustre of literary authority, and to preserve it as far as possible from the innovations which tend to vulgarize and degrade it.[17]

Behind all of this was something much more serious than snobbery. The logic that identified national character with national literature, and the language of literature as a superior language, dictated that places and people without national status—colonial places and people—would only develop what Froude called "a character and purpose of their own" if they first embraced the national literature and language of their imperial masters. It was assumed that education in the mysteries of European languages and the marvels of European literatures would generate both an allegiance to European ideals and an ambition to emulate European achievements. Naipaul had the logic ready for the West Indies a century later. Why reduce everyone to the lowest common denominator when the highest is at hand? Why try to make something out of nothing, when great things are there to be copied?

One of the most infamous expressions of this attitude in the nineteenth century was the historian Lord Macaulay's memorandum in 1835 on the question of education in the British East Indies. It was a crucial time in the development of attitudes toward the West Indies. Slavery in the British colonies had just been abolished, and saving the world for civilization was the latest imperial fashion. Macaulay made all the imperial assumptions, including the assumption of responsibility. "I will never consent," he said, "to keep (Indians) ignorant in order to keep them manageable."[18] For Macaulay, ignorance was the natural condition of non-European peoples, and there was not a lot of help close by. Literature in the languages of Asia seemed to him trivial, and essentially uncivilized. "I have never found anyone who could deny that a single shelf of a good European library was worth the whole native literature of India and Arabia. . . . When we pass from works of imagination to works in which facts are recorded and general principles investigated the superiority of the Europeans becomes absolutely immeasurable. . . . The question now before us is simply whether, when it is in our power to teach the English language, we shall teach languages in which by universal confession there are no books on any subject which deserve to be compared to our own."[19]

Macaulay's relentlessly ethnocentric view of the world had widespread currency among those who controlled British imperial enterprise. Colonial education in the nineteenth century celebrated intellectual and social attainments prized in England, and created an admiration for the language in which they were chronicled.

In the first few decades after the abolition of slavery, not much public money was spent on education in the West Indies. Partly, this was because there was not much there to spend; and partly because there lingered an opinion that the laboring class, which was to say the freed slaves (and in due course immigrant workers such as those brought from India beginning in 1838 as indentured laborers), should be taught what was euphemistically called "a love of employment"—which meant they should be taught to work rather than to think. Even in the best schools and to the brightest students, and even until very recently, little attention was given to such fundamentals as West Indian history (and certainly not from a West Indian perspective), or West Indian traditions of imaginative expression. Learning their place had only one meaning for West Indians in this educational system. Imitation of European models was the ideal, with no acknowledgement even of Africa or Asia, the other great old-world heritages for West Indians. And local dialects were routinely scorned.

Although it has a different function, higher education also figures in this story, for it was from the University of the West Indies that the new materials in history and the social sciences and a new sense of literary achievement first began to emerge in a way that influenced primary and secondary education. By way of comparison between the various settler societies in the Americas and their different attitudes

toward the significance of indigenous educational institutions, Philip
Sherlock provides the following image to chronicle the establishment
of universities in the Caribbean.

> Three and a quarter centuries after St. Kitts and Barbados were settled
> (by the first British colonists in the West Indies) . . . the University College
> of the West Indies was founded. We can highlight the time-lag by (imag-
> ining) a film whose showing-time of five hours corresponds to the five
> centuries since Columbus, each century being allowed one hour. We see
> Spanish colonists settling in Hispaniola and friars founding three uni-
> versities within half-an-hour of their arrival. After an hour and twenty
> minutes of showing we see the Pilgrim Fathers landing and other British
> colonists settling in the eastern Caribbean. We see the Puritans founding
> Harvard College ten minutes after their arrival. Three and a half hours
> later, just fifteen minutes before the film ends, we witness the founding
> of the University College of the West Indies.[20]

When we see what influence this university has had on the developing consciousness of the English-speaking West Indies, especially in
the reconstitution of West Indian history, we can understand the special
significance of its absence for so long. In "The Lesson," the Grenadian
poet Merle Collins displays how names of local places and people were
left out of the colonial curriculum and replaced by a litany of events
and personalities, which in its unreality had a kind of spectacular hold
on the imagination, like some list of eternal presences and powers. In
a turn of the tables, Collins demands our attention in this poem with
the familiar assurance of any good storyteller, taking her time, pausing
for breath, refusing to be rushed, listing the names at a deliberate pace,
maintaining the authority of what she says by the precise way in which
she says it.

> You tink
> was a easy lesson?
> Was a
> deep lesson
> A well-taught
> lesson
> A
> carefully-learnt
> lesson
>
> I
> could remember
> Great Grand-Mammy
> Brain tired

And wandering
Walkin' an' talkin'
Mind emptied and filled
Bright
Retaining
And skilfully twisted
By a sin
Unequalled by Eve's
Great Grand-Mammy
Living proof
Of de power
of de word
Talked knowingly
Of William de conqueror
Who was de fourth son
Of de Duke of Normandy
He married Matilda
His children were
Robert
Richard
Henry
William and
Adella . . .

Grannie
Din remember
No Carib Chief
No Asante king
For Grannie
Fedon never existed
Toussaint
Was a
Whispered curse
Her heroes
Were in Europe
Not
In the Caribbean
Not
In Africa
None
In Grenada

Her geography
Was

Of de Arctic Ocean
An' de Mediterranean
She spoke of
Novasembla
Francis-Joseph Land
And Spitbergin
In de Arctic Ocean
Of Ireland
And de
pharoah islands
belong to Denmark
Spoke
Parrot-like
Of
Corsica
Sardinia
Sicily
Malta . . .

Collins ends her poem by telling how she and her people

Understanding all dat
And a little more
Will cherish
Grannie's memory
And beckon William across
To meet and revere
Our martyrs
Fedon
And Toussaint
And Marryshow
And Tubal Uriah Buzz
Butler
And the countries
And principles
They fought for . . .

Kay sala se sa'w
Esta es
su casa
This is
your home![21]

"Kay sala se sa'w esta es su casa" means "this is your home" in the speech of many older Grenadians, the expression of their history in a language that reflects their own inheritance and the European imperial presence on the island over the centuries. In the absence of any recognition of these languages or these histories, and without any celebration (with all its attendant hazards) of their heroes, it is small wonder that Brathwaite's question—"where then is the nigger's home?"—has haunted West Indians for the past 150 years of colonial education, and God knows with what terrible intensity during the preceding 350 years of slavery.

These colonial lessons produced a people alienated from themselves, dislocated in their notions of who they were and where they belonged, with neither facts nor fictions to make their world make sense. There were a few words here and there, but they didn't connect. The great good place, to use A. J. M. Smith's phrase, was firmly beyond their possibilities. And so, in another sense, was the place they lived, for they were taught that the things closest to their hearts and homes put them furthest from prestige and power.

The Guyanese poet and editor A. J. Seymour, who quoted Smith in *Kyk-Over-Al*, described the colonial intimidation he experienced as a youth in the early years of the century. "I sometimes got the feeling from the educated and well placed individuals around me that it was positively indecent that a young Guyanese should want to write poetry. That sort of activity was for a person born in another country. You should read about it happening in England or America but in a colony it meant that you were young and conceited and so should be taken down a peg or two."[22]

The educational system, with its celebration of European literary accomplishments, kept those it taught firmly on the margins. It did so by the simplest means, drawing attention to the things that made them different. Their color. And their speech, their languages. Only the most gifted mimic among West Indians could set aside a West Indian dialect, a West Indian's mother tongue, and speak exactly like someone from the Mother Country. The rest would always sound different. Just as they would always look different. Picturesque, perhaps, but not proper. As an Irish critic remarked about the function of British stereotypes of his people, "if the Celts stay quaint they will also stay put."[23] Difference may be the root of metaphor, but it is also the formula for marginalization.

Some of the ironies involved when those on the margins seek acceptance from the center are represented in a touching scene from the Trinidadian Samuel Selvon's novel *The Lonely Londoners* (1956). Galahad, a West Indian immigrant who has been living in England for some time, tries to strike up a conversation with a white Englishwoman and her child (who has just said "Mummy, look at that black man!"). He puts on "the old English accent" and says "what a sweet child! What's your name?"

> But the child mother uneasy as they stand up there on the pavement with so many white people around: if they was alone she might have talked a little, and ask Galahad what part of the world he come from, but instead she pull the child along and she look at Galahad and give a sickly sort of smile, and the old Galahad, knowing how it is, smile back and walk on.[24]

The mother tongue for the vast majority of the earliest migrants to the West Indies was African. Most slaves during the seventeenth and eighteenth centuries were brought to the West Indies from the coastal areas stretching from modern Senegal to Nigeria, where the Mande and Kwa language groups dominate. (Twi is a prominent language within the latter group.) A European language was imposed or acquired as the need arose, and its forms developed in ways that reflected the speaker's African mother tongue and the circumstances of second language learning, which might in some situations (such as St. Lucia) be complicated by the fact that two European languages vied for power over a number of years.[25]

Going back to the early days of settlement, pidgin languages developed. Pidgins are marginal languages in a special sense, being the product of commercial or colonial contact between people who have no common language and who have need for communication of a fairly limited sort. A pidgin is a language for doing business, and not normally ever the native language of any of its speakers. Pidgins are routinely looked upon as inferior or degenerate by those who claim a lineage to superior (usually European) languages, and often claim superiority on other grounds as well. Yiddish, for example, was looked upon as a pidgin long after it had developed its own linguistic integrity. "Inferiority made half-articulate" was the description as recently as 1953 of Neo-Melanesian, the English-based pidgin of Papua New Guinea.[26]

Creole languages develop from pidgins either when people are permamently in a multilingual situation and need to expand the pidgin to include a much wider range of human experience than the pidgin allows, or when the pidgin becomes so useful or so prestigious among people sharing it as a common tongue that it takes over as the preferred language and in due course becomes the first language children learn.

The first situation prevailed over several centuries in the West Indies, and the second is occuring right now in parts of Papua New Guinea, where Neo-Melanesian is looked upon as a ticket to progress.

The distinction between pidgins and creoles is not a precise one, and considerable disagreement remains over whether creoles are to be considered separate languages. There *is* general agreement that creoles provide an indispensable vehicle for expressing the deepest thoughts and feelings of people for whom they are the common language. When Edward Kamau Brathwaite uses the term *creolization* to describe the interaction between languages and between peoples, he is underlining its literary and political as well as its linguistic integrity.

There are several dialects of English spoken in the West Indies, along a spectrum that includes forms very similar in syntax, vocabulary, and pronunciation to standard English, and forms that are sufficiently different both from the standard and from each other that they seem like separate languages. Some forms, such as Jamaican, are grammatically distinct, and this distinctiveness has given Jamaican English an early prominence in West Indian literature. Other forms, of which Barbadian is the clearest example, are characterized by distinct pronunciation. The distinctiveness of some local speech makes it clearly identifiable—as Jamaican or Barbadian or Tridindadian or Guyanese, for instance. In other regions, the speech is recognizably different but less easily attached to a specific island, though still unmistakably West Indian. Furthermore, there is both standard and nonstandard speech in each area, a fact often ignored by those who assume that a sense of linguistic decorum is the monopoly of English speech from somewhere in southern England, with everything else being simply improper.

Bruce St. John once quoted an authoritative text on pronunciation, commonly used in the West Indies, which insisted that "a mistake among students of English is to the place the stress (in words of three syllables) on the suffix."[27] But as St. John pointed out, for Barbadian speakers to make this "mistake" is to speak correctly: for example, pronouncing educate, demonstrate, multiply, telephone, dialect with the stress on the last syllable. Anything else would be nonstandard in Barbadian speech. There is a nice irony here, in that Barbadian pronunciation may in fact be closer than any other contemporary form of English to what is usually taken as the prototype of the language, late sixteenth-century and early seventeenth-century English speech. Whatever the case, it is important to keep the differences in mind, for it is often said that West Indian poetry does not conform to standard metrical schemes. Sometimes indeed it does not. At other times, it does; but non–West Indians who comment upon the text hear it differently and do not recognize its conformity. At still other times, it deliberately hovers between its allegiances to West Indian and non–West Indian practice.

The idea of a standard form of the language is a powerful fiction, which among other things represents a hierarchy of prestige and power. And a presumption of familiarity, for the strange is by definition nonstandard. The "difference" of poetic language—the difference from standard, from speech, from any common currency—is one of the most difficult issues in any discussion of poetry. It involves not only the categories of familiarity and strangeness and of naturalness and artifice but also some less easily handled notions of engagement and disengagement, of the popular and the elite, and of power. Does the language of poetry, by virtue of its separateness as well as its status, become the language of power? How does it maintain its immunity from the corruptions of power while at the same time aspiring to power of its own? Are there different kinds of power? Is there such a thing as a purified power here below; or a purified language, as the modernists liked to believe?

Standard language tends to have *some* corner on power. And it does generate resistance, uprisings against the government of the tongue,[28] which may ultimately be its most valuable function. As one critic said of James Joyce's prose, "it is perhaps the last development of the Irishman's habit of inventing new languages which *shall not be English.*"[29] That ambition *not* to be standard, that sense of the need to decenter oneself, is both a fundamentally poetic instinct and a venerable strategy for those who are determined to get out from under the shadow of imperial governments, linguistic or otherwise. And while it is in a sense true that standard English is a language never spoken by anyone— Thomas Hardy referred to it as "the governess-tongue of no country at all"[30]—this ubiquitous governess seems to have shuttled about the new world with formidable Brittanic zeal over the past couple of centuries, waving a grammar book and talking like the Queen.

Of course, distinctions between "central" and "marginal" language varieties, like those between poetic and ordinary language, are essentially arbitrary, being contingent on the specific social and cultural as well as linguistic situation. There are consequently good linguistic (as well as political) reasons to view *all* language use as in some sense marginal, or else to forego these terms altogether and focus on other elements in these relationships. Also, we need to keep in mind that there are two distinct models of the relationship between notional standard, or central, languages and local, or marginal, varieties. One, a continuum model, construes them as points on a linguistic spectrum.

The other sees them as always in some sense discontinuous, interacting with each other in more or less dynamic ways.

The nineteenth century was a great period for imperial waving and talking and writing. It was also a great period for the study of languages, and alongside those who called for rigid standards of correctness stood many others who recognized that languages either change in changing times and places, or they die away. Max Muller, one of the best known of nineteenth-century linguists, used this organic model of language in describing how "what are commonly called classical languages pay for their temporary greatness by inevitable decay. They are like stagnant lakes at the side of great rivers." Then, venturing into the wider fields of social and historical circumstances, Muller continued. "It is during times when the higher classes are either crushed in religious and social struggles, or mix again with the lower classes to repel foreign invasion; when literary occupations are discouraged, palaces burnt, monasteries pillaged, and seats of learning destroyed; it is then that the popular or, as they are called, the vulgar dialects which had formed a kind of under current, rise beneath the crystal surface of the literary language, and sweep away, like the waters in spring, the cumbrous formation of a bygone age."[31]

What Muller envisaged was hardly inclined to thrill the custodians either of language or of empire. But its rejection of the permanent authority of literary language inspired James Murray, the editor of the greatest national linguistic enterprise of the period, the *Oxford English Dictionary*.[32] The issue facing Murray was whether standards of language should be derived from speech or from writing. Samuel Johnson, Murray's great eighteenth-century predecessor, had put together a canonical list of language based exclusively on literary usage, drawing on texts that he called "the wells of English undefiled," though "with no testimony of living authors." Later lexicographers were inclined to be a bit more daring and include words used by contemporary writers. But Murray decided not only to incorporate current literary references and terms used in journals and newspapers but also the language of texts that represented varieties of common speech, some of it (in Murray's words) "English to some Englishmen, and undreamt of by others," including the slang that one reviewer of the dictionary described as "formerly confined to tramps, gipsies, and thieves" but which "has in our day invaded the educated and semi-educated classes."[33] Murray's *Oxford English Dictionary* confirmed enough power in the heightened discourse of literature that the faithful did not rush out of the gates. But they worried a lot, reflecting an attitude still widely held:

books are high and talk is low. This attitude, of course, paradoxically nourished the ambition to bring local languages into literature.

Dictionaries were deemed the treasuries of the language, the places where the gold that backed the currency was kept safe. And literature embodied national character and purpose, and had great symbolic as well as substantive importance. Therefore any barbarian invasion that threatened to overcome these strongholds was a frightening menace. Unless, of course, you happened to be a barbarian; as, for example, the nineteenth-century Americans were in the eyes of the British, from whom they had recently and rudely revolted. West Indian efforts to give legitimacy to their own standards of speech and writing have a precedent in the determination of many Americans in the early years of postcolonial independence to underwrite their political autonomy by insisting on the authority of their own distinctive way of speaking. The best-known proponent of this was Noah Webster, whose *American Dictionary of the English Language* appeared in 1828. Nearly forty years earlier, Webster had laid out his plan in terms that apply nicely to the ambitions and achievements of West Indians over the past fifty years.

> As an independent nation, our honour requires us to have a system of our own, in language as well as government. Great Britain, whose children we are, and whose language we speak, should no longer be *our* standard; for the taste of her writers is already corrupted, and her language is on the decline. But if it were not so, she is at too great a distance to be our model, and to instruct us in the principles of our own tongue. . . . Several circumstances render a future separation of the American tongue from the English necessary and unavoidable. . . . Numerous local causes, such as a new country, new associations of people, new combinations of ideas in arts and sciences, and some intercourse with tribes wholly unknown in Europe, will introduce new words into the American tongue. These causes will produce, in a course of time, a language in North America as different from the future language of England as the modern Dutch, Danish and Swedish are from the German, or from one another. . . . We have therefore the fairest opportunity of establishing a national language and of giving it uniformity and perspicuity, in North America, that ever presented itself to mankind. Now is the time to begin the plan.[34]

This proposal infuriated some observers, especially those with their eyes peeled for barbarians. One reviewer said that if Webster "considers the retaining of the English language as a badge of slavery, let him not give us a Babylonish dialect in its stead, but adopt, at once, the language of the aborigines."[35]

A national language was one thing. A national literature was quite another. It was also in significant ways quite distinct, for literature typically has its own "standards," only some of which are the standards that appeal to linguists and lexicographers. Among other things, literary standards—or more particularly standards of language in literature—are determined by the ways in which literature frames itself. This "framing" is a matter of constant interest in all the arts, and of continuing entertainment. Playwrights, for example, play with our inclination to confuse the stage with the street; sculptors present us with "found objects"; painters draw a fine line between life and art, or redraw it; and poets court the illusion of conversation, whether with others or themselves. Some years ago, *The New Yorker* featured a cartoon of a dog in an art gallery looking needily at a painting of a tree. Where language is concerned, there is a wide range of possibilities for representational confusions and for transgressions—or at least testings—of the limits of the form.

As part of the framing of its discourse, new literary traditions underwrite new standards of language. In the case of the new United States in the mid-nineteenth century, it was the poet Walt Whitman who used the language that Webster described to determine a new literature, and who demonstrated the power of poetry to shape (as well as to reflect) the language of national consciousness. Edgar Allan Poe was also part of this process, but in such radically different ways that non-English speakers seem to have been the first—indeed for a long while the only—ones to recognize what he was doing. When T. S. Eliot wrote (in "Little Gidding") about purifying the dialect of the tribe, he was writing (by way of Stephane Mallarmé, who coined the phrase) about Poe. Whitman, on the other hand, knew and said precisely what he was doing, and for the special attention of the custodians of civilization he described his language as a "barbaric yawp"—D. H. Lawrence approvingly referred to him as "the first white aboriginal."[36] Whitman called his long poem *Leaves of Grass;* and he promoted it as "a language experiment—an attempt to give the spirit, the body, the man, new words, new potentialities of speech—an American range of self-expression. The new world, the new times, the new peoples, the new vistas need a tongue . . . yes, what is more, will have such a tongue."[37]

Whitman called for a new independence in this poetic language to satisfy the "appetite of the people of these states for unhemmed latitude, coarseness, directness, live epithets, expletives, words of opprobium, resistance." And he drew attention to the "ten thousand idiomatic native words [that] are growing, are today already grown, out of which vast numbers could be used by American writers, with meaning and effect—words that would be welcomed by the nation, being of the national blood—words that would give that taste of identity and locality which is so dear in literature."³⁸

It is dear, we should remind ourselves, in *some* traditions of literature. In others it is disdained. There has been a long dispute, in European literature at least, between literature that derives its power from real places, including the language of those places, and literature that locates itself on Parnassus, which is to say in an ideal place well away from the here and now. These are never clear distinctions, for attachment to place often becomes a literary formula. And we can see the relationship between these traditions, and between the artifice and naturalness they court, in the Greek and Latin words for poet—the one a maker, whose imagination shapes the poem; and the other a diviner, locating sources of inspiration in the everyday.

Twentieth-century literature has been an arena of special conflict in this regard, privileging the universality of literature in some quarters and its particularity in others. Obviously, language is a central issue here. Contemporary West Indian literature, along with some other literary traditions over the past fifty years, has actively nourished a poetry of place, celebrating the sacredness of ordinary things and the authenticity and authority of vernaculars; and it has cherished a belief that washing a guest's feet is as precious as having a meal with the gods—and usually much more interesting. As Derek Walcott has said, it is important to walk barefoot in order to get the proper sense of scale.

There is a special complication for West Indians—their profound uncertainty about one particular place, the place called home. In Brathwaite's phrase, is it here or in heaven? Real or imagined? There are other difficulties, too. Regional differences often work against the idea of an even relatively homogeneous West Indian literature in English, and of a coherent literary tradition committed to the geographical and political particularities of place. At the same time, these differences are surprisingly similar to those that were part of Whitman's America, and in which he took such refreshing delight.

But the challenge still centers around the use of *any* West Indian vernacular. For a long while, the spoken language of West Indians was separated by a gulf as wide as the Atlantic from the written language of literature, with any expression of national character and purpose being conditioned by ideals located elsewhere. The colonial habit of mind was represented in an admiration for language that was beyond the possibilities of local speech and for literature that embodied the inaccessibility of that language. Only recently has this gulf been bridged. Louise Bennett, who since the 1940s has been writing and performing stories and verse in "Jamaica talk," tells of someone in the audience calling out as she finished one of her early performances of dialect verse "is dat yuh modder sen yuh a school fa?"[39] The dog in *The New Yorker* cartoon is not the only one who gets confused.

But around that time, the late 1940s, attitudes began to change, though there had been earlier encouragements in periodicals such as *The Beacon,* published in the early 1930s in Trinidad. Among the most important influences were the various collections of local proverbs and stories that appeared in the 1950s and 1960s. In the Barbadian magazine *Bim,* which along with *Kyk-Over-Al* in Guyana and *Focus* in Jamaica was one of the main outlets for literary and cultural expression, the editor Frank Collymore began a glossary of words and phrases in Barbadian dialect, which was followed by a list of Barbadian proverbs collected by Margot Blackman. Around the same time, *Kyk-Over-Al* published several articles on West Indian dialect. The *Caribbean Voices* radio program, which originated in London, gave West Indian writers a chance to have the speech of their islands heard by a wide audience within and outside the Caribbean. *Tamarack Review* in Canada and the *London Magazine* published special West Indian issues, a development noted in *Bim.* In the early 1960s *Caribbean Quarterly,* edited by Rex Nettleford, began publishing out of the Department of Extra-Mural studies at the University of the West Indies, providing another outlet for the discussion of language.

And there were other voices calling for a renewed attention to dialect and to its place in the range of spoken and written expression. In Jamaica, Frederic Cassidy published a lively and detailed account of Jamaican creole in 1961 in his book *Jamaica Talk,* which is significantly subtitled *Three Hundred Years of Jamaican English.* (In many ways, it is comparable to H. L. Mencken's great book on *The American Language,* which first appeared in 1919.) Then in 1967, Cassidy and R. B. LePage brought out a *Dictionary of Jamaican English,* which began for Jamaican creole what Webster had started for the American language. (In a nice continuation of this tradition, Cassidy is now the supervising editor of the *Dictionary of American Regional English,* which draws on spoken as well as written sources from an extraordinarily wide range.) More recently, and in their own distinctive ways, writers such as Edward Kamau Brathwaite (*History of the Voice: The Development of Nation Language in Anglophone Caribbean Poetry* [1984]), Hubert Devonish (*Language and Liberation: Creole Language Politics in the Caribbean* [1986]), and Peter Roberts (*West Indians and their Language* [1988]) have illuminated the character and the challenge of West Indian languages and their place in West Indian life and literature.

As with Webster in the United States, Cassidy and Collymore and the others in the West Indies during the 1950s and 1960s were part of a collective enterprise in which literature played an important part. Not that poets and playwrights and novelists spent their evenings poring over the new glossaries and dictionaries. But they may have spent their days listening more carefully than they had before to what was being spoken around them. Nobody—except auctioneers and travel agents—is enthusiastic about everything that has a local flavor about it. But everyone seemed to be paying a new kind of attention to things that had previously been taken for granted. And this brought home to the writers a responsiblity that literature had always cherished, and a challenge it could not ignore. A consciousness of some new possibilities for expression was beginning to emerge, and this expression would be, to pick up Walcott's phrase, like nothing anyone had ever heard before.

But with this came also a consciousness of the risks. Some West Indian writers felt that they had enough elements of risk in their lives without surrendering their identity to a local language customarily used for daily business or gossip. In the 1950s and 1960s, as their island nations moved toward independence and all West Indians were encouraged to see themselves as forging a new national as well as personal identity, writers were tempted to turn to a language that had shown it could do the job, the language of English literature, the tried and true language of national character and purpose. Furthermore, education in the proprieties of speech and writing held the key to a heightened social and economic status for many West Indians. So it was not always obvious that their local language, the language in which they carried out their daily affairs, was capable of giving them a clear sense of being West Indian and a clear vision of the West Indies. Or else, while it might be clear enough, it would be depressingly common.

But slowly, West Indian writers became aware of two things: how European literatures had for centuries been taking up precisely the challenge that now faced them, of bringing local languages into the center of literary currency; and how the long tradition of African literatures demonstrated the arbitrariness of many European literary conventions. A rich African-based oral tradition of story and song was part of life for many West Indians and, though no less stylized than any other tradition of imaginative expression, it had always included lively proverbial sayings and figurative language derived from local speech. And the use of spoken language had long been part of the development of European literature too. Dante made a new tradition of poetry out of his vernacular language; and from Chaucer and the anonymous poet of *Sir Gawain and the Green Knight* onward, local language has had a place in English poetry.

Again, a number of linguistic issues come into play here, identified nearly a century ago by the Swiss linguist Frederick de Saussure, who distinguished between the system of a language (which he referred to as *la langue*) and language as a speech act (*la parole*). It is a distinction that has sometimes been redefined as one between "rules" and "behavior"; or between "competence" in the laws of a language on the one hand, and "performance," which uses (or abuses) these laws for special purposes on the other; and it has led to an interest in the various factors in literary texts that condition performances (speech acts or behavioral gestures); and in the relationships between different linguistic structures and situations, and between different genres.

Different genres, of course, offer distinct possibilities for the confluence or conflict of language varieties and of language use. Theater often employs local speech, in a European tradition from the medieval mystery plays through the great period of Renaissance drama to the nineteenth and twentieth centuries. It was natural for West Indians to embrace this tradition, especially when it was blended with elements of performance that were distinctly local. During the 1950s and 1960s, Derek Walcott, his brother Roderick, Barry Reckord, Errol Hill, and Trevor Rhone produced important plays that drew on the literary possibilities of local language. In 1959, Walcott established the Trinidad Theatre Workshop, where many of his plays were produced over the next twenty years; and other theater companies and theater spaces had already established a lively tradition of dramatic production with groups such as the Little Theatre Movement in Jamaica and the Bridgetown Players in Barbados, along with festivals featuring the work of West Indian playwrights, actors, directors, and designers. As well, the Little Carib Theatre in Trinidad and the National Dance Theatre Company in Jamaica brought the folk traditions of West Indians, including the language of their songs, onto center stage.

There has been a longstanding practice in English literature of using dialect in fiction, especially in periods when it is proclaiming its realism. Throughout the nineteenth century, a number of novelists such as Walter Scott, Emily Brontë, Charles Dickens, and Thomas Hardy represented the spoken language of some of their characters. It was not until the end of the century, however, that it became common to make these characters the central figures of the story and to represent their speech according to a logic of literary naturalism, which prescribed that their different languages convey the different reality of their lives. This became an accepted convention in American fiction, which during the nineteenth century had developed an ear for the distinctive character of American speech. Despite the continuing expressions of dismay by visitors from England about the new-world barbarisms they heard or read in the United States, and local dissent by the guardians of propriety in Boston and elsewhere, the American language was establishing a firm place in both polite speech and serious conversation, and in the literature of the land.

West Indian writers drew substantially on the realistic traditions of American fiction during the 1940s and 1950s, as they began to use dialect to tell their stories. One of the first novelists to do so was the Jamaican writer V. S. Reid in *New Day*, published in 1949. With a nice instinct for the conjunction of literary and political change, his novel tells of the time in Jamaica between the Morant Bay Rebellion in 1865 and the eventual return of constitutional government to Jamaica in 1944 (this time with a full franchise). The novel's local language (its linguistic "behavior"), which shaped the narrative, also signaled the beginning of a new literary autonomy (and new "rules"), even as it told the story of the long march toward the new rules and behavior that would characterize political independence. *New Day* managed fairly well to avoid one familiar hazard of using dialect in fiction, which is that it becomes merely an instrument of either local color or low comedy. Other writers soon extended the literary possibilities for using dialect. Roger Mais's novel *Brother Man*, published in 1954, incorporated dialect expressions and dialect intonations to convince the reader that this was the *only* way of understanding the Jamaican world that is its subject, as the novel tells the story of the contrast between Rastafarian visionary ideals and the squalid realities of life for the poor.

In 1956, Samuel Selvon published *The Lonely Londoners*, about West Indians emigrating to England during the late 1940s and 1950s. Here, we find West Indian dialect at the center, not just because it is the language of the narrator, but because it is the consciousness of the book. The language both tells the story and *is* the story. What is most interesting about the language of Selvon's novel is that it is not quite like anything anyone has ever heard before, except in this novel; that is, it is not exactly the language of anyone outside the novel. The language of the book draws attention to itself first of all as just that, the language of the book . . . and then, as the language West Indians speak in London. Somewhere between these categories, it becomes in the storytelling a language to convey the feelings and the thoughts of the characters; and it hovers between lyrical and narrative or descriptive modes, and between the artifice of literature and the naturalness of speech. In so doing, it discloses in a new way the arbitrariness of these categories, and a new frame for the "standardness" of language. Selvon invented a language for the book that is firmly grounded in the speech of West Indians, and just as firmly transformed into a language that endorses the conventions of literature. Here is the novel's closing passage.

> The old Moses, standing on the banks of the Thames. Sometimes he think he see some sort of profound realisation in his life, as if all that happen to him was experience that make him a better man, as if now he could draw apart from any hustling and just sit down and watch other people fight to live. Under the kiff-kiff laughter, behind the ballad and the episode, the what-happening, the summer-is-hearts, he could see a great aimlessness, a great restless, swaying movement that leaving you standing in the same spot. As if a forlorn shadow of doom fall on all the spades in the country. As if he could see the black faces bobbing up and down in the millions of white, strained faces, everybody hustling along the Strand, the spades jostling in the crowd, bewildered, hopeless. As if, on the surface, things don't look so bad, but when you go down a little, you bounce up a kind of misery and pathos and a frightening—what? He don't know the right word, but he have the right feeling in his heart. As if the boys laughing, but they only laughing because they fraid to cry, they only laughing because to think so much about everything would be a big calamity—like how he here now, the thoughts so heavy like he unable to move his body.
>
> Still, it had a greatness and a vastness in the way he was feeling tonight, like it was something solid after feeling everything else give way, and though he ain't getting no happiness out of the cogitations he still pondering, for is the first time that he ever find himself thinking like that.[40]

West Indian poets had also been using local language in their work from early in the century, and indeed a reading of eighteenth- and nineteenth-century poetry from the West Indies (almost exclusively by writers of British heritage) discloses a fair range of words and a few phrases that are local, though used with a high degree of "literariness" and pastoral charm. (One 1833 review of a book titled *Barbadoes and Other Poems* praised the author [one M. J. Chapman] for "writing the English language like a Gentlemen."[41]) The Jamaican writer Claude McKay, who moved to New York in 1912 when he was in his early twenties and became part of the flourishing artistic expression by blacks in the United States known as the Harlem Renaissance (which in turn had a significant influence on Aime Césaire and the early proponents of negritude), wrote poems in dialect influenced by the formidable example of Robert Burns; and although they now seem sentimental, these poems were important steps toward incorporating West

Indian languages and cultural values into European and American literary forms. Here is the beginning of his poem "Fetchin Water."

> Watch how dem touris' like fe look
> Out pon me little daughter,
> Wheneber fe her tu'n to cook
> Or fetch a pan of water:
> De sight look gay;
> Dat is one way,
> But I can tell you say,
> Nuff rock'tone in de sea, yet none
> But those pon lan' know 'bouten sun.[42]

In the 1940s and 1950s, West Indian poets began a wider range of experiment with language. At first, the use of dialect was mostly self-conscious; but occasionally—as in the following poem by the Jamaican Philip Sherlock—language and subject flow together to suggest new relationships between local speech rhythms and literary forms. Sherlock's poem is called "Pocomania." It is about the Jamaican religious cult (also known as Pukumina) that combines Christian revivalism with certain beliefs (which originally came to the West Indies with the slaves from Africa) in the coexistence of material and spiritual worlds and the possession of the living by the dead. There is a muted but clearly defined distinction between the narrator's language—in which only local pronunciation signals a difference from non–West Indian conventions—and the language of the participant in the ceremony, which displays more obvious differences of syntax and diction. But the relationship between these language varieties is sufficiently complex that the effect goes well beyond simple documentary to a subtle examination of the ways in which a conventional poetic form can accomodate a local voice bearing witness, but at a literary distance, to some deeply important aspects of local life.

> Long Mountain, rise,
> Lift you' shoulder, blot the moon.
> Black the stars, hide the skies,
> Long Mountain, rise, lift you' shoulder high . . .
>
> Black of night and white of gown,
> White of altar, black of trees
> "Swing de circle wide again
> Fall and cry me sister now
> Let de spirit come again

Fling away de flesh an' bone
Let de spirit have a home."[43]

In another, quite different, poem from the 1950s Martin Carter combines the formality of a written tradition with speech patterns that are unmistakably Guyanese. Or rather, they *are* mistakable, and it is precisely this uncertainty that is of particular interest. The opening phrase of Carter's poem reads: "is the university of hunger the wide waste. / is the pilgrimage of man the long march." What appears as an interrogative in standard English is in fact an assertion in Guyanese dialect (and well beyond, in fact, for dropping the pronoun before the verb is very common is West Indian speech. The wide currency of dialect features such as this throughout the islands reinforces the sense that West Indians share what Brathwaite calls a "nation language"). The ambivalence created by these lines depends upon the allegiances of its language *both* to the authenticity of West Indian speech and to the authority of a lyrical tradition in English literature that goes back at least to the fourteenth century. These converge, and the credibility of the poem comes to rest, in a new tradition of West Indian poetry.

is the university of hunger the wide waste.
is the pilgrimage of man the long march.
The print of hunger wanders in the land.
The green tree bends above the long forgotten.
The plains of life rise up and fall in spasms.
The huts of men are fused in misery.

They come treading in the hoofmarks of the mule
passing the ancient bridge
the grave of pride
the sudden flight
the terror and the time.

They come from the distant village of the flood
passing from middle air to middle earth
in the common hours of nakedness.
Twin bars of hunger mock their metal brows
twin seasons mock them
parching drought and flood.[44]

More than any other single writer, Louise Bennett brought local language into the foreground of West Indian cultural life. From the 1940s, when she began contributing to the annual pantomime in Jamaica, Bennett's storytelling had a substantial influence on the literary credibility of dialect. But it was not an unqualified credibility. From the beginning, Bennett was aware that language is not a simple matter and that the unfamiliar has its own appeal—especially when linked with an assumed superiority. And she dealt with the equivocation of these attitudes with relentless irony. One of her poems tells of the dismay of a mother whose son has come back from the United States with no change in his speech, no heightening of his language.

> Me glad fi see yuh come back, bwoy,
> But lawd, yuh let me dung;
> Me shame a yuh so till all a
> Me proudness drop a grung.
>
> Yuh mean yuh go dah Merica
> An spen six whole mont deh,
> An come back not a piece better
> Dan how yuh did go weh?
>
> Bwoy, yuh no shame? Is so yuh come?
> After yuh tan so lang!
> Not even lickle language, bwoy?
> Not even lickle twang? . . .
>
> No back-answer me, bwoy—yuh talk
> Too bad! Shet up yuh mout!
> An doan know how yuh an yuh puppa
> Gwine to meck it out.
>
> Ef yuh waan please him, meck him tink
> Yuh bring back someting new.
> Yuh always call him "Pa"—dis evenin
> When him come, seh "Poo."[45]

The appeal of artifice, of strangeness—the superiority that distance or difference (in the right direction) generates—are satirized here even as the poem itself relies on this appeal, for its own cleverness is implicated in the satire. In another poem, Bennett turns the tables.

> Wha wrong wid Mary dry-foot bwoy?
> Dem gal got him fi mock,
> An when me meet him tarra night
> De bwoy gi me a shock!
>
> Me tell him seh him auntie an
> Him cousin dem sen howdy

An ask him how him getting awn.
Him seh, "Oh, jolley, jolley!"

Me start fi feel so sorry fi
De po bad-lucky soul,
Me tink him come a foreign lan
Come ketch bad foreign cole! . . .

Him tan up like him stunted, den
Hear him no, "How silley!
I don't think that I really
Understand you, actually!"[46]

The acceptance of dialect in poetry, as in other forms of communication, was partly a matter of fashion. The popularity of Louise Bennett, whose work was on radio and in the newspapers as well as on stage and in books, helped create the fashion, and provided encouragement to other poets and storytellers. The Jamaican writer Evan Jones, with his very popular poem "The Song of the Banana Man" (first published in 1952), also helped bring the use of dialect into wide currency. The poem sets up a confrontation between a white tourist who disdains the local man's apparent worthlessness in language filled with superior-sounding phrases ("I suppose") and condescending names ("Boy"), and the banana man who defends his occupation with dignity and delight, and in dialect. In structure, it has some similarities to William Wordsworth's poem "Resolution and Independence" about an old leech gatherer, though Jones's poem is different in tone, and the local person (whose occupation is the subject of bewilderment in both) takes the lead in "The Song of the Banana Man" and shapes the reader's response. And although it is richer in its display of the potential of dialect than much of McKay's work, "The Song of the Banana Man" is set within a fairly melodramatic structure, with a hero and a villain and not much of the sort of subtlety that we will see in later poetry with respect to the relationships between literary and local as well as spoken and written languages. Still, it is a memorable poem, and it gave new credibility to the language of local life, including local names. Here are the first two verses.

Touris, white man, wipin his face,
Met me in Golden Grove market place.
He looked at m'ol'clothes brown wid stain,
An soaked right through wid de Portlan rain,
He cas his eye, turn up his nose,
He says, "You're a beggar man, I suppose?"

He says, "Boy, get some occupation,
Be of some value to your nation."
    I said, "By God and dis big right han
    You mus recognize a banana man."

"Up in de hills, where de streams are cool,
An mullet an janga swim in de pool,
I have ten acres of mountain side,
An a dainty-foot donkey dat I ride,
Four Gros Michel, an four Lacatan,
Some coconut trees, and some hills of yam,
An I pasture on dat very same lan
Five she-goats an a big black ram,
    Dat, by God an dis big right han
    Is de property of a banana man."[47]

Gros Michel and Lacatan are local varieties of banana, and "janga" is a local word (of African origin) for freshwater river shrimps. The use of these terms is a reminder of the situation that Derek Walcott described as particularly troubling in his early years as a poet and that gave questions of literary fashion a political as well as a poetic significance. "What I wrote had nothing to do with what I saw. While I honoured and loved them in my mind, I could not bring myself to write down the names of villages, of fruits, in the way the people spoke because it seemed too raw. . . . And I found no lines that mentioned breadfruit, guava, plantain, cassava in literature."[48]

The Barbadian poet Bruce St. John, who began writing in dialect in the 1960s, took a gently comic look at this predicament in "Education," a poem (inspired by a couple of William Wordsworth's *Lyrical Ballads*) about a conversation between two Bajans.

"Studyation beat eddication."
"Man, Archie man, what you talkin'?
'Studyation' ent even a word."

"Studyation ent even a word?
It ent a word in a damn dictionary,
But um is a good, good Bajan word.

Eddication is a lot a lot o' paper,
Studyation is 'nough 'nough brain.
A book in yuh han' an' trash bone in yuh head,
You better lef' de bloody book in de bag. . . .

> Studyation beat eddication,
> Studyation boss eddication
> Studyation plus eddication
> Is wisdom, Boysie boy, wisdom."[49]

The use of good, good St. Lucian words and the understanding of place and people that they represent is what Walcott displayed in his poem "Sainte Lucie," published in 1976. Both for Walcott and for West Indian poetry, this poem marks a turning point, bringing together a mature poet's confidence in his literary inheritance with a corresponding—and newly found—confidence in his West Indian heritage. In the poem, Walcott lists the names of the places and things of his native St. Lucia in the French and English creole that is the language of its people.

> Laborie, Choiseul, Vieuxfort, Dennery . . .

> Pomme arac,
> otaheite apple,
> pomme cythère,
> pomme granate,
> moubain,
> z'ananas
> the pineapple's
> Aztec helmet,
> pomme,
> I have forgotten
> what pomme for
> the Irish potato,
> cerise,
> the cherry,
> z'aman
> sea-almonds
> by the crisp
> sea-bursts,
> au bord de la 'ouvière.
> Come back to me
> my language.
> Come back,
> cacao,
> grigri,
> solitaire,
> ciseau
> the scissor-bird . . .

O so you is Walcott?
you is Roddy brother?
Teacher Alix son?
and the small rivers
with important names . . .

generations going,
generations gone,
moi c'est gens Ste. Lucie.
C'est la moi sorti;
is there that I born.[50]

This is where contemporary West Indian poetry begins, not so much with this poem alone as with the distinctive ambitions it represents. In listing these names, Walcott is conjuring with them, bringing them back to himself and back to life. When he calls "come back to me my language" he is asking for a return of original power: the power to bring things into being by naming them; and the power to convey their presence to others. These are the powers of language, and poets have always assumed that one of their roles is to restore that power, if only in the moment of the poem.

There is much at stake. Poets keep our spirits alive. It sounds almost trivial put that way. But there is nothing trivial about a withering away of the spirit—not just the sectarian religious spirit, though it is precious enough, but the spirit that gives each of us that sense of identity—of self and of other—without which we are lost and alone. Speaking about another kind of loss, Northrop Frye once said that "God may not be so much dead as entombed in a dead language."[51] His comment identifies something that West Indians know well, the deadening and deadly effect of language uninspired by the spirit as well as the substance of place . . . language that is not in some sense itself alive. Literary languages can of course be living languages, as can the formal languages of religious ritual. But not when they belong to someone else, or have lost their power. When Walcott says "come back to me my language" he is calling for a return of the capacity for wonder, as well as of the customary habits of home—a return of a language that is strange as well as familiar, a language that confounds as well as comforts. These are the ambitions Brathwaite signaled in his *Savacou* anthology, the ambitions of Bongo Jerry as he talked about the need to "recall and recollect black speech" in order to liberate West Indians from

... a situation
        where education
mek plenty African afraid, ashamed, unable to choose (and use)

Black Powa. (Strange Tongue).

Poets such as Walcott and Brathwaite have shown that it is possible to break the spell of imperial catalogs and orderings, the spell of what Bongo Jerry called "crossword speaking." In doing so, they have demonstrated that West Indian independence is not only a matter of political change but also of a renewed ability to express West Indian thoughts and feelings in West Indian words. A matter of making the *right* word seem like the *only* word, and of demonstrating the necessity as well as the sufficiency of local languages.

In the issue of *Savacou* in which Bongo Jerry's poem appeared and in which Brathwaite insisted on the importance of dialect, the Jamaican poet and critic Mervyn Morris had a poem titled "Valley Prince." It is about the jazz trombonist Don Drummond, who hovered on the edge of musical brilliance and of mental breakdown until in 1969 he killed his girlfriend and died under mysterious circumstances in an asylum. Morris's poem uses Drummond's language to illuminate his eccentric genius. But Drummond, like Bob Marley, caught the spirit of what it was to be West Indian, and the language of Morris's poem represents both an individual and a collective experience. It illustrates how West Indian life is inextricably bound up with its language and how both life and language are (to use Walcott's phrase) "like nothing one has ever seen before."

Morris conveys a sense that only this language, shaped in this way, could tell this story, a story that on the surface is not about black power or social unrest or economic distress or political change, but about a figure who belongs to his place and time the way William Wordsworth's Leech Gatherer did, or Evan Jones's Banana Man, or Lorna Goodison's Guinea Woman, a figure whose identity is both unique and universal, neither straight nor standard but simply and enduringly West Indian.

Me one, way out in the crowd,
I blow the sounds, the pain,
but not a soul
would come inside my world
or tell me how it true.
I love a melancholy baby,

sweet, with fire in her belly;
and like a spite
the woman turn a whore.
Cool and smooth around the beat
she wake the note inside me
and I blow me mind.

Inside here, me one
in the crowd again,
and plenty people
want me blow it straight.
But straight is not the way; my world
don' go so; that is lie.
Oonu gimme back me trombone, man:
is time to blow me mind.[52]

The poem displays a nice sense of the artifice as well as the naturalness of language, especially in phrases such as "I blow me mind," where the figurative and the literal meanings converge, as do the conventions of local speech and literary writing. Perhaps because of its achievement, it brings to center stage some questions that have been hovering in the wings so far. *Can* this kind of language, so far removed from standard English, be "an index and a school of national character," and express a new West Indian consciousness? Or is its difference, its unmistakably local character, merely a recipe for a disabling marginality? And should—or *how* should—the significant differences in West Indian speech condition differences in West Indian poetry, and determine its relationship to the older traditions of poetry in English going back five hundred years? These are the years since Chaucer, of course, and the other great poets of late middle English; but they are also the years since slavery began.

Mervyn Morris drew attention to these kinds of questions in that controversial issue of *Savacou* in another way, for right there beside "Valley Prince" was another of his poems, "The Pond." Its language (with the exception of the word *galliwasp*, which is the local word for a type of lizard) was conventionally English, and so to be sure was the tradition of lyrical expression within which it operated. Where did *this* fit? Was its effect as a poem different in kind from that of "Valley Prince"; or different for different readers? Do we need radically different critical approaches—beyond an assumed sensitivity to what each poem is about—for such different poems? Or do we let our knowledge that both poems are by the same poet prescribe a similar approach?

It is a measure of the significance of contemporary West Indian poetry that it keeps these questions alive: questions about conventions of expression and representation, and how these differ in different kinds of poems; questions about the difference between ordinary and poetic language—or more exactly between language in everyday use and language in poetic use—and about how we tell the difference, and when it matters; and questions about the appropriation of poetic voices by critical categories—of race or gender or nationality or period or structure or style or subject—and by the paradigms of one age or another, and the relationship between these particular determinisms and the freedoms of the poet on the one hand and of readers on the other. Morris's "The Pond," set alongside "Valley Prince," touches on all these questions; and the juxtaposition itself challenges some fundamental assumptions about the interpretation and evaluation of poetic texts—assumptions, that is, about the determination of meanings and the application of normative standards (by which I refer not to standards of superiority, but to the criteria according to which we assess the achievement of a text on its own terms).

There was this pond in the village
and little boys, he heard till he was sick,
were not allowed too near.
Unfathomable pool, they said,
that swallowed men and animals just so;
and in its depths, old people said,
swam galliwasps and nameless horrors;
bright boys stayed away.

Though drawn so hard by prohibitions,
the small boy, fixed in fear, kept off;
till one wet summer, grass growing lush,
paths muddy, slippery, he found himself
there at the fabled edge.

The brooding pond was dark.
Sudden, escaping cloud, the sun
came bright; and, shimmering in guilt,
he saw his own face peering from the pool.[53]

Mervyn Morris is undoubtedly a West Indian poet. In Walcott's phrase, is there that he born. And yet his poetic affiliations are not confined to the West Indies, but link him to the heritage of English literature that he shares with those born in British colonies elsewhere, as well as with those born in the British isles. At the same time, his poetry is part of—and indeed has helped shape—a literary tradition uniquely West Indian, incorporating ways of speaking and writing that reflect the heritage of those for whom "straight is not the way," the heritage of those who when they were young believed the local superstition that the bite of a galliwasp was deadly, and when they were older listened to Don Drummond playing trombone with the Skatalites.

Every poet has two allegiances: one to the facts of local experience, and the other to the formalities of literary expression. To life; and to art. Poets give expression to the literature they love, as well as to the land in which they live. In an impossibility that any poet knows, the deliberate craft, or artifice, of writing a poem is supposed to be inseparable from the unsophisticated inevitability, or naturalness, of being oneself. It should be no surprise, then, that poets feel divided. Some poets, such as Walcott, have made this feeling into a source of dramatic strength. All West Indian poets, in their best work, have used it to generate that dialogue of voices, that hovering between allegiances, which has for millenia underwritten the power of poetry. But where the tension is merely competitive, poems tend to go in two directions at once, and either fall flat or fall apart.

And so do poets. For some West Indian poets the relationships between the literary and the local, and the sometimes competing demands of universality and particularity, have been a challenge and an inspiration (as they have been for poets in different times and places). For others, they have generated extraordinary tension, in their lives as well as in their art. West Indian poets have no monopoly on this, either among poets or among people who live through changing times . . . or perhaps through any times. But they have had good reason to bring these relationships and demands to the forefront, because through their languages they are intimately associated on the one hand with the deepest thoughts and feelings of their people and the possibilities for their representation and expression, and on the other with hierarchies of privilege and power and insignia of identity and difference.

The career of the poet and critic Eric Roach, who was born in 1915 in Tobago and lived his life alternately there and in Trinidad, is a tragic illustration of the pressures on West Indians in the period since the Second World War. During the 1940s and 1950s, Roach was an advocate of the values inherent in the folk traditions of the West Indies— "the cadences of island patois, old men's goatskin drumming, young men's tin percussion," as he described them in one poem. And he lamented the distance his education created from that inheritance. "Although Cambridge school-certificated, we left school knowing

absolutely nothing of ourselves, our country, its history and circumstances. We were adolescents lost between two worlds, one to which
we belonged by birth but were educated to reject, the other we discovered in the books. We were, to coin a phrase, 'exoticized natives.' "[54]

Although Roach's poetry draws on both the formal conventions and
the language of British literature, he was no idle imitator of its conventions. He wrote passionately and persuasively about a new kind of
Caribbean, and although its language was conventional, his poetry was
deeply rooted in the sensibility of his people. And he made another
kind of commitment to the place. While others went abroad in the
exodus to England and the United States and Canada during the 1950s
and 1960s, he (along with Derek Walcott) stayed in the West Indies.

And he became increasingly worried. In a poem addressed in 1952
to the Barbadian writer George Lamming, who had temporarily moved
to England, Roach praised the way in which Lamming's "roots are
tapped into this soil, / Your song is water wizard from these rocks."
But then he described the trap into which he felt they were all falling.

> We are enslaved in the ancestral cane
> We're trapped in our inheritance of lust
> The brown boot scorns the black.
>
> Here we are architects with no tradition,
> Are hapless builders upon no foundation
> No skilled surveyors mark our forward road.[55]

When the *Savacou* anthology appeared in 1971, Roach entered the
debate about standards and skill. He insisted that for a poet to be exces-
sively preoccupied with "race, oppression and dispossession is to bury
one's head in the stinking dunghills of slavery."[56] Instead, Roach
argued, West Indians "must erect (their) own bungalow by the sea out
of the full knowledge of the architecture of English places and cot-
tages." This implied a commitment to "culture in the traditional aesthetic sense, meaning the best that has been thought, said and done."
As Matthew Arnold (whose words Roach echoed) would say, the
choice is simple: culture or anarchy.

Roach was responding more to Bongo Jerry than to Mervyn Morris
and some of the other poets in the anthology (such as Derek Walcott,
Dennis Scott, and the Trinidadian Wayne Brown); but the issues he
raised were crucial. Of course, he recognized that the English did not
have a monopoly on surveyors and architects and builders, and that as
Lamming said "English is a West Indian language," capable of its own
range of expression and—despite Naipaul's scepticism—its own

achievements. But when Lamming for example called for a language "no less immediate than the language of drums,"[57] Roach started to get anxious. After all, Matthew Arnold might be right. The alternative to transported English culture might be homemade West Indian anarchy. And a shift to local standards might merely signal a shift to a new set of cultural mandarins. Standards, like stereotypes, develop from definitions of difference. And language was still to some extent the most powerful image of difference beween culture and anarchy. Or between imperial and colonial achievements.

Arnold was the eloquent champion of a system of education that would teach "the best that has been known and said in the world," and he was a notable figure in his time. But even without sharing the racist absolutism of Carlyle and Froude, people in his time routinely knew and said that the best attitude toward those seeking a decent future for themselves in Jamaica in 1865 was embodied in the Queen's Advice to get back to work at starvation wages; that the best account of aboriginal people was embodied in legislation (like the Canadian Indian Act), which in 1876 defined "person" as "anybody other than an Indian"; and that the best approach to Africa was to get the nations of Europe together in 1885 to divide it up. It was a time that was preoccupied with questions of authority, in all estates. It was a time when people and places and the knowledge associated with them were defined, and power distributed, along what were essentially imperial lines, with colonisation (of women, for example) taking domestic as well as international forms. It was a time when much of our educational strategies and most of our intellectual disciplines were determined along lines that reflected the same knowledge, and the same attitudes.

This historical perspective is especially significant because one of those disciplines was literary studies; and our fidelity to its nineteenth-century European traditions may be at best a kind of endearing nostalgia, and at worst a continuation of invidious and intimidating habits of mind. The sort of solidarity involved here goes deeper than matters of detail, to the structure and style of literary criticism, which among other things continues to make certain heritages invisible by privileging written over oral traditions, in many cases actively discrediting the latter (and by implication those whose heritage it is). It has developed neither the theory nor the practice to take these oral traditions seriously, which is to say as something other than documents of difference. Other disciplines belong here as well. Political science, to take an example closely involved with our definitions of community, has developed in ways that presume a separation of material and spiritual values—a separation of church and state—and therefore has great difficulty accommodating the spiritual beliefs that are often so important in the expression of African and aboriginal heritages, seeing these as rhetorical, or romantic, or just plain embarrassing. Our notions of economic life, derived again from this same period in intellectual history, construe prosperity in terms of employment and access to material goods, so that small-scale farmers and fishers and those raising families or engaged in other local activities in the West Indies are classified as underemployed or unemployed, and in need of specific sorts of industrial development strategies. And economists continue to develop indices of progress such as the Gross National and the Gross Domestic Products, which discount or completely disregard the depreciation of a capital asset that occurs when we use or abuse our natural (including our human) resources.

This catalog should include history and anthropology, which, with their language and logic of discovery and their tendency to treat other peoples as objects rather than subjects, consolidate presumptions that ultimately have prescriptive as well as desriptive power, and deeply affect our attitudes toward ourselves and toward others. These comments are not intended as a gratuitous attack on these intellectual enterprises, but simply a reminder of what they are. They are in an important sense story lines, and they deserve the same serious respect. But like all stories, they need to be rooted in the circumstances of their telling. They may indeed be precious heritages. They are also in some sense imperial heritages, privileging certain kinds of knowledge and certain achievements. They are constructions of knowledge in a time and a place, and by a group of people, with particular assumptions and ambitions. And they suggest a pattern, a kind of fundamentalism that imperial enterprises often display, wherein the ultimate goal is maintaining coherence . . . which is often called maintaining standards. As with any other ideal, coherence is most often maintained by inertia. In fairness, inertia is not to be scoffed at. We depend on it for the integrity of our communities, and of our traditions. But it has its limits.

Roach knew all this well. Like the next generation of poets such as Mervyn Morris, he found ways of expressing his West Indianness in poetic forms which adhered to English models but through which his own West Indian voice came clearly, with the passion of an independent consciousness. Or more precisely, a divided consciousness, divided between hope and despair. In a poem written in the 1950s, he expressed his anguish.

> I am the archipelago hope
> Would mold into dominion; each hot green island

Buffeted, broken by the press of tides
And all the tales come mocking me
Out of the slave plantations where I grubbed
Yam and cane; where heat and hate sprawled down
Among the cane—my sister sired without
Love or law. In that gross bed was bred
The third estate of colour. And now
My language, history and my names are dead
And buried with my tribal soul. And now
I drown in the groundswell of poverty
No love will quell. I am the shanty town,
Banana, sugar cane and cotton man;
Economies are soldered with my sweat
Here, everywhere; in hate's dominion.[58]

The passage is framed by the freedoms and determinations of
dominion, and filled with the symbols of slavery: the destruction of the
languages, histories, and heritages of the slaves; the slave laws, epito-
mizing the brutality of the slave society; the relentless and brutal
exploitation borne in special measure by women, with the added burden of sexual abuse; the commodities of plantation life—people first of
all, the key commodities, and then sugar and cotton, and then after
emancipation bananas and the shanty towns and devastating poverty
of the diasporas, here, there, and everywhere; the homelessness and
helplessness of a life held together by hope, soldered by sweat, conditioned by hate; the mockery that stereotypes generate, and the
entrenchment of racism in the ideologies of postcolonialism and the
Third World. The heritage of slavery continued to take its toll.

There were ferocious pressures on all writers, on all West Indians,
during this period. Being black was a career in itself; and many failed,
at least according to standards as arbitrary as English culture. Roach
was determined that the creative imagination could make a difference.
Driven by the desperation of a divided sensibility and a single purpose,
and God only knows what else, Eric Roach committed suicide in 1974.
The issues he raised and the poems he wrote survived him, part of a
new legacy to take the West Indies beyond the horrors of slavery to a
new home.

4

"To court the language
of my people"

 "All styles yearn to be plain as life," says Derek Walcott in a poem called "The Gulf," in which he is looking out the window of an airplane flying over the Gulf of Mexico and thinking about all the gulfs that separate us from what we see and hear.[1] What he means is that a poem should seem spontaneous, inevitable, natural. He also means that it is the artifice of style that produces this effect, and makes things seem simpler, plainer, more direct. This paradox is at the center of poetry, though our sense of it changes with changing poetic fashions. Sometimes, poets write within a highly formal tradition, and cultivate a sense of style that is taken to be natural for poetry but perhaps unnatural anywhere else. Other times, they use the informal language of the streets to make the garden of verse into a public place.

This arbitrariness (what is "natural" on particular occasions, for example) is something we depend on every day, speaking differently when we talk to friends, or meet strangers, or have a conversation at the dinner table, in each case trying to speak "naturally." (Sometimes, there is an entire lexicon reserved for particular occasions: talking to one's mother-in-law, for example, for which certain words are strictly reserved if one is a member of some aboriginal tribes in Australia; or talking to anyone about children or cooking or baseball or cricket, to take just a few of life's more serious subjects.) Where formal and informal styles are fairly similar, this comes easily. And where spoken and written forms of the language are not startingly different, poets can incorporate the supposed naturalness of speech into the artifice of poetry quite fluently, though the text itself will also establish its own criteria of artifice and naturalness, as much the product of the occasion as any other instance of language use.

There is of course *always* an element of artifice in poetry; and typically poets (such as Walt Whitman) who break new ground by bringing a supposedly more "natural" language and rhythm into their poetry are accused of having no regard for standards of good form, or no ear for music, or no sense of poetic propriety. On the other hand, poets who highlight the artifice of their language are often called pretentious or insincere.

When there is a radical difference between formal and informal styles, or when (as in parts of the West Indies) there is a fundamental discontinuity between spoken and written forms, then poets have a hard time achieving a poetic style that seems plain as life unless they give their poetry entirely over to the language of everyday speech. Walcott once described the difficulty of moving between what he called "the easy applause of dialect, the 'argot' of the tribe" on the one hand, and "ceremonial speech, the 'memory' of the tribe" on the other.[2] Ceremonial speech, for Walcott, is the language of poetry; and for most English-speaking poets it is based on the venerable traditions of English literature. Dialect, however, at least to English ears, is not normally English, but is West Indian (or Irish, or Canadian, or whatever). To someone from elsewhere, West Indian speech sounds different. To a West Indian, it sounds natural. And the artifice of poetry seems to require another language. In a moving account of his own predicament, Walcott once recalled how for years as he was developing his poetic talents he became conscious of the distance between his literary and his local language. "I wrote in one language while people spoke in another."[3]

Walcott describes here what linguists call "diglossia," a situation—common in societies as different as ancient Egypt and modern Norway—in which two identifiably different varieties of a language (or sometimes two quite different languages) coincide in a speech community, each with a distinct function. Both languages typically have their own linguistic standards; but they are generally distinguished according to other criteria, with one variety (the "high" language) being used on occasions of greater formality and usually monopolizing written texts, and the "low" variety being the language of everyday intercourse and popular culture. Such distinctions commonly also reflect divisions of prestige and power.[4]

The gap in the West Indies between spoken and written forms of language, and its association with other indicators of class and control in the society, make these distinctions especially important in a poetic tradition committed to negotiating a way beyond the grim disabilities and discontinuities that are part of its heritage of slavery. One way has been to create situations in which the grounding of the language in speech and its heightening in poetry are conveyed as continuous. But more often the disjunctions between speech and writing have generated a dialogue between languages, or more specifically between linguistic discourses or varieties of language, going beyond the polarities of division to a more complex heterogeneity.

The stylizations of poetry, including those forms (such as rap) that try to maintain an illusion of continuity with the language of everyday speech, always depend upon another dividing line—between "poetic" and ordinary language. This is sometimes construed as a line between artifice and naturalness; and in written poetic forms where the idea of a speech community is foreign this line often seems to be quite precisely drawn. (This occasionally creates misunderstanding, for being plain as life can hardly have the intended effect if a reader does not know anything about either the life or the language that is the frame of reference. The words *sugar* and *wheat*, for example, may conjure up hard work or pastoral pleasure, depending on where you come from.) Poetry is located on these boundaries, walking the lines and working the gaps, which is why it is such an important form of expression in places such as the West Indies, which are characterized by very clearly defined forms of linguistic diglossia.

The difference between poetic and ordinary language, like most differences, is ultimately a matter of context and convention. Both the character and the credibility of poetic discourse is sustained (or subverted) by the expectations, or normative standards, that we bring to bear on these differences. Furthermore, different language use signals other differences, whose importance depends on attitudes and ideologies about such things as diversity (for example, whether homogeneity rather than heterogeneity is the accepted ideal in a society) and open dialogue (whether censorship and the need for highly coded forms of language exist, either to avoid the censors or to consolidate and protect distinctive communities). Accordingly, the social and political ideologies of the United States and Russia, to take two countries that have taken the lead in linguistic studies over the past several decades, do not always generate linguistic analyses that apply without qualification to other regions. This is another reason why the development of an indigenous tradition of linguistic and literary scholarship in the West Indies has been so important.

Most recent literary discussions about the dialogue between different varieties of language and the relationship between marginal and central discourses have tended to focus on prose fiction. But the conversation between language varieties in West Indian poetry discloses a unique array of stresses and of challenges, with some of the most moving poetic "statements" existing either in the dramatic tension or in the quiet space *between* languages, local and literary. This may well be a fundamental condition of all literatures. What makes West Indian poetry especially interesting is that it is also a fundamental condition of its languages.

"A Divided Child" was how Walcott described himself in his long autobiographical poem *Another Life*. A sense of divided or dual allegiance, as we have seen, is much more than a figure of speech for West Indian poets. It is a fact of life, and a feature of their languages. As in the paradox with which we began this chapter, all poetry is nourished by this kind of division. West Indian poets have found ways to break free from the spell of a debilitating schizophrenia by recognizing that it is precisely this sense of divided allegiance that unites them with other poets, and that the language of poetry in all its traditions, African as well as European, routinely includes both high and low varieties of language, as well as elements of both artifice and naturalness.

This leads to another distinction in which language is involved, the distinction between speech and writing. Poetry generates much of its interest by courting the favors of both—imitating the naturalness of the one and the artifice of the other and then suggesting that artificality and naturalness, or preciousness and plainness, are arbitrary categories anyway. As well, poetry reminds us that neither speech nor writing is intrinsically more conservative than the other and that changes in language come from both.

Poetry also takes advantage of another difference, between language that is familiar and language that seems strange. The effect of "defamiliarisation," which was emphasized by some literary critics in the 1920s and 30s, has always been central to poetry; and poets and critics have from time to time considered novelty or invention as *the* defining feature of poetic craft, occasionally going so far as to identify outrageousness with poetic originality. "Le beau est toujours bizarre," said Charles Baudelaire. Both strangeness *and* familiarity have their appeal, of course. And both can be associated with either written or spoken language. But strangeness and a sense of style are closely linked. This is what Walcott refered to when he remarked with some exasperation that "it was always the fate of the West Indian to meet himself coming back, and he would only discover the power of simplicity, the graces of his open society, after others had embraced it as a style."[5]

All of which suggests that West Indian poets are, willy nilly, at the center of a fundamental poetic issue. The tensions between naturalness and artifice, speech and writing, familiarity and strangeness are in theory sources of strength. In practice, however, they can also be sources of stress.

There are many ways of being a West Indian, and many ways of being a poet. The challenge for West Indian poets has been to ensure that neither surrenders to the authority of the other, by developing ways of saying things that become part of their life, in words that become part of their literary tradition.

Poets draw strength from both art and life. In between, as Walcott once suggested, they find their own voice. Actually, what he said was that they often lose it. He also said that poets cultivate a schizophrenic gift, trying to combine the naturalness of being themselves with the artifice of being a poet. A poet's voice is very difficult to describe. It never seems to be quite there. Listening to literary critics talk about poetic voices is like listening to nuclear physicists talk about atomic particles. First they describe them in detail, and then they tell us they've never seen them. They talk about what they saw a moment ago. Look, they say, that's where it hit something, or combined with something else, or broke up.

But like those who watch for evidence of atoms, readers of poetry are sure that there is something called for convenience (and out of long habit) a poet's voice. We are sure, as physicists are sure, because we feel its effect, the way it hits us. And as we become familiar with this particular feeling, and as we sense its consistency, we give the "voice" a name—Lorna Goodison, for example—and perhaps describe it in other ways as well—a woman's voice, a black woman's voice, a black Jamaican woman's voice, a late twentieth-century black Jamaican woman's voice. Soon we find ourselves making all kinds of other generalizations about poetic voices, and describing so-and-so as the voice of the dispossessed, or of male privilege, or of Mexican independence, or of the Puritan sensibility, or whatever.

At the same time, we recognize that poets speak not only *to* us but also *within* the literary tradition of which they are part, and that a wide array of strategies, such as using what we sometimes call masks or personae, may be part of the conventions of this different conversation. Poets are notoriously impatient about all this. The original title of T. S. Eliot's *The Waste Land* was "He Do the Police in Different Voices." But when it was suggested to Eliot that the poem, or its voices, spoke for an entire generation, he responded that it "was only the relief of a personal and wholly insignificant grouse against life . . . just a piece of rhythmical grumbling." When it was then suggested that the poem perhaps expressed a sense of disorder and despair that reflected his own intensely personal (and intensely depressing) circumstances, he turned to the French symbolists and loudly proclaimed their ideal of the impersonality of poetry. (Ironically, as Kamau Brathwaite has confirmed, Eliot's voice recordings strangely influenced a generation of West Indian poets who were trying to shape their own speech into poetry.)

The line between personality and impersonality, like the line between individual and collective identity, is a fine one. Poets typically speak in a literary voice that is identifiably their own but in a literary form that is shared. These are not disconnected categories. But they are separable, the way an individual signature is separable from the conventions of handwriting.

Perhaps to see how this works we should visit a poet in his workshop. Poets sometimes get grumpy, but at least we can try. One of the venerable poetic forms in the English literary tradition has been the sonnet. The word comes from the Italian *sonetto*, meaning a "little sound," or short poem. The sonnet originated in the thirteenth century and developed its several forms slowly, with precise demands that were sometimes intimidating. But it has been a popular and powerful vehicle for expressing personal thoughts and feelings in English literature for centuries.

Because of its association with a lyric tradition that goes back to the beginnings of English imperialism and includes buccaneers in the West Indies such as Hawkins and Raleigh and Drake—"ancestral murderers and poets," Walcott once called them[6]—and because of its reputation as the epitome of written craft, the sonnet might well be viewed as an arbitrary and capricious habit of expression for contemporary West Indian poets whose literary practices have been substantially shaped by the alternative influences of narrative and dramatic oral performance. On the other hand, its imposing presence in the literary tradition means that the sonnet form exemplifies the system, as it were, and taking it on gives poets an opportunity to demonstrate how its imperial power can be turned to colonial advantage and how West Indian voices can finally be heard on the literary equivalent of prime time.

This possibility is reinforced by the fact that for a long time the sonnet has been used prominently in English literature to express a very wide range of thoughts and feelings in very individual ways. Edmund Spenser turned the form to his own purposes back in the sixteenth century, as did John Milton and John Donne in the seventeenth century, and Geoffrey Hill and Seamus Heaney in this century. And these purposes were often defiantly political, as in William Wordsworth's great sonnet "London, 1802," with its catalogs of praise and its relatively clear, uncomplicated language.

> Milton! thou should'st be living at this hour:
> England hath need of thee: she is a fen
> Of stagnant waters: altar, sword, and pen,
> Fireside, the heroic wealth of hall and bower,
> Have forfeited their ancient English dower
> Of inward happiness. We are selfish men;
> Oh! raise us up, return to us again;
> And give us manners, virtue, freedom, power.
> Thy soul was like a Star, and dwelt apart:
> Thou hadst a voice whose sound was like the sea:
> Pure as the naked heavens, majestic, free,
> So didst thou travel on life's common way,
> In cheerful godliness; and yet thy heart
> The lowliest duties on herself did lay.[7]

Sometimes, the purposes to which the form was turned were *ironically* political, undermining the formal and informal rhetoric of enthusiasm. Along these lines, a sonnet by the American poet e. e. cummings.

> "next to of course god america i
> love you land of the pilgrims and so forth oh
> say can you see by the dawn's early my
> country 'tis of centuries come and go
> and are no more what of it we should worry
> in every language even deafanddumb
> thy sons acclaim your glorious name by gorry
> by jingo by gee by gosh by gum
> why talk of beauty what could be more beau-
> tiful than these heroic happy dead
> who rushed like lions to the roaring slaughter
> they did not stop to think they died instead
> then shall the voice of liberty be mute?"
>
> He spoke. And drank rapidly a glass of water[8]

Recently, poets have once again turned to the sonnet to show how it can be an instrument of change in poetic subject and style. Of course, they have used other forms as well. Tony Harrison, for example, has tried various ways of shifting the imperial center of gravity represented by the conventional sonnet so that it will accomodate his own experience growing up in the north of England, and speaking differently. To this end, he wrote a long poem titled *V*, set in a graveyard on Beeston Hill in Leeds in the north of England. Modeled after Thomas Gray's "Elegy Written in a Country Churchyard," it too is about love and loss, life and death, and what Gray in the 1740s called "useful toil," the everyday labors of ordinary men and women. Except that Harrison's graveyard overlooks a worked-out coal pit in the 1980s, and everyone is out of work. The words that first startle us and trouble the poet are those painted on the gravestones by vandals, and the poem moves around the ironies of decorum and the anger generated by indecency and impropriety . . . on both sides. As one of the skinheads says when the poet describes their violent acts (and violent words) as a *cri de-coeur:*

> So what's a *cri-de-coeur*, cunt? Can't you speak
> the language that yer mam spoke. Think of 'er!
> Can yer only get yer tongue round fucking Greek?
> Go and fuck yourself with *cri-de-coeu!*[9]

Harrison's most thorough exploration of these relationships between languages has been in his sonnets, where he typically sets the expectations of the poetic form (and its privileged place) against the urgencies of a voice from a different place speaking a different language. (His sonnets have sixteen lines instead of the more usual fourteen, a modification introduced by the English writer George Meredith in the nineteenth century in a sequence of sonnets he called *Modern Love;* and it has been used by others since.) In a sonnet titled "On Not Being Milton," Harrison allies himself as a northern Englishman with the struggle of West Indians to regain the power of their language, and through it the power to be independent. Aimé Césaire's poem is here, with its chronicle of dispossession, and so is the imagery of resistance and conspiracy and betrayal that we have seen so often in West Indian poetry. In a play of ironies, Harrison sets the violence done by the Luddites to the looms of the industrial revolution alongside the violence done by poets to the language of sonnets. Both represent the violence of craftsmen, threatened by the relentless powers of metropolitan standardization, trying to assert their independence and to affirm the value of their way of life and their language.

> Read and committed to the flames, I call
> these sixteen lines that go back to my roots

my *Cahier d'un retour au pays natal,*
my growing black enough to fit my boots.

The stutter of the scold out of the branks
of condescension, class and counter-class
thickens with glottals to a lumpen mass
of Ludding morphemes closing up their ranks.
Each swung cast-iron Enoch of Leeds stress
clangs a forged music on the frames of Art,
the looms of owned language smashed apart!

Three cheers for mute ingloriousness!

Articulation is the tongue-tied's fighting.
In the silence round all poetry we quote
Tidd the Cato Street conspirator who wrote:

Sir, I Ham a very Bad Hand at Righting.[10]

Of all contemporary West Indian poets, Derek Walcott's use of the sonnet is most interesting. The use of dialect did not come easily for Walcott. But it came first in a sequence of sonnets. He had of course some predecessors among West Indian poets in using dialect. As we have seen, the Jamaican Claude McKay wrote poems in dialect in the first couple of decades of this century. But McKay's *sonnets* were in conventional literary language—as, for example, "The White House."

> Your door is shut against my tightened face,
> And I am sharp as steel with discontent;
> But I possess the courage and the grace
> To bear my anger proudly and unbent.[11]

Walcott did not set out using dialect. He began his poetic career in imitation of the masters of English literature, and his early experiments in the avant-garde were very much in the style of Gerard Manley Hopkins and T. S. Eliot. Somewhere in this literary legacy, perhaps in the widespread use of the dramatic monologue in the late nineteenth and early twentieth centuries, Walcott found encouragement to build into his poetry voices that were uniquely West Indian.

In "Tales of the Islands," his sonnet sequence published in 1958 in the Barbadian literary magazine *Bim*, Walcott made his first major innovations. He explained in a letter to Frank Collymore, the editor of *Bim* and an enthusiastic champion of his work, that "what I have been trying to do with (the sonnets) over the last five years is to get a certain factual, biographical plainness about them." A style plain as life. He

added that part of his ambition was to regain for poetry the prerogative
of narrative that seemed to have been taken over by prose, and "to
dislocate the traditional idea of the sonnet as a fourteen line piece of
music. The idea is the same as in prose: dispassionate observation. Say
nothing but cut the bronze medallion and present it to the normal
reader saying, Here you are; verse was here first, and it's time we got
back what they took from it."

He was worried, though, about the effect of all this. "The pieces may
read flat," he said. "But as much selection goes into making them work
as into the traditional lyric."[12]

If he seems hesitant here, it was probably because he was not quite
sure what he was doing. This uncertainty is reflected in the first versions of these sonnets published in *Bim*, in contrast with the more confident versions that appeared ten years later in the volume *In a Green
Night*. In looking at these changes, we can see emerging a poetic style
that is distinctly Walcott's, and distinctly West Indian. The sixth sonnet
in the early 1958 text has as its epigraph "my country 'tis of thee," an
ironic nod to the English literary tradition and to e. e. cummings, as
well as to the possibilities for liberty in the sweet lands of the West
Indies, moving at the time toward independence.

> Garçon, that was a fête. . . . I mean they had
> Free whiskey and they had some fellows beating
> Steel from one of the bands in Trinidad,
> And everywhere you turn people was eating
> Or drinking and so on and I think
> They catch two guys with his wife on the beach,
> But "there will be nothing like Keats, each
> Generation has its angst, and we have none,"
> And he wouldn't let a comma in edgewise
> (Black writer, you know, one of them Oxford guys),
> And it was next day in the papers that the heart
> Of a young child was torn from it alive
> By two practitioners of the native art.
> But that was far away from all the jump and jive.[13]

There are several voices here, and the burden of witness is not on
any single one. Each operates on the boundary between its own linguistic situation and another, and the poem develops (well beyond the
effect of local color) from the tensions and compromises between them.
But there is not enough differentiation between the voices, or enough
subtlety in this differentiation, to give these relationships the complexity they need to bear the burden of the poem's theme. In this first ver-

sion, for example, the framing voices at the beginning and end, both describing local rituals of feasting and frenzy, are quite similar in their affectations. ("Garçon, that was a fête . . . that was far away from all the jump and jive.") A decade later, when the poem was published in *In a Green Night*, the epigraph was gone, the tone was changed, and the distinctions between voices were much clearer. The first framing voice is now in unself-conscious dialect, with the poem moving through varieties both of language and style (so that both the rhyming 9th and 10th lines and the final quatrain involve shifts in speech that reflect the shift in the meaning and purpose of the lines) to the muted self-consciousness of the final line. The dialect in the original 1958 text seems in retrospect mostly limited to the identification of personalities. In the later version, the use of local language becomes central to the sonnet's structure and to its subject: betrayal and violence, the burden of the past and the false promises (and sometimes false languages) of the present, with the credibility of the poetic voices becoming part of the poem's subject as well. The result is a complex interaction not only of Dionysian and Apollonian rituals but also of fear and fascination, naturalness and artifice, familiarity and strangeness, and the oral and the written. (In a nice touch carried over from the first version, Walcott balances the spoken and written qualities of the language by altering the speech idiom "wouldn't let a word in edgewise" to "wouldn't let a comma in edgewise".)

> Poopa, da' was a fête! I mean it had
> Free rum free whiskey and some fellars beating
> Pan from one of them band in Trinidad,
> And everywhere you turn was people eating
> And drinking and don't name me but I think
> They catch his wife with two tests up the beach
> While he drunk quoting Shelley with "Each
> Generation has its angst, but we has none"
> And wouldn't let a comma in edgewise.
> (Black writer chap, one of them Oxbridge guys.)
> And it was round this part once that the heart
> Of a young child was torn from it alive
> By two practitioners of native art,
> But that was long before this jump and jive.[14]

Walcott's achievement here was to establish West Indian languages within an English literary tradition. He showed how West Indians could use differences in language to illuminate their differences as West Indians and to develop sophisticated and subtle dynamics in a poetic text. This is the way that poets such as Walcott and Brathwaite and Goodison are making a poetic tradition that is both unmistakably their own and at the same time part of a wider heritage of imaginative expression in language.

They have had lots of company in this enterprise of literary naturalization. Poets in the north of England and in Ireland and Wales and Scotland as well as in Africa, Australia, India, the United States, and Canada share this determination to speak in voices that are not merely echoes of someone else, someplace else, and to use the variety of voices in their society as agents of new meaning, not just of novelty. The ironies can be very complicated. We may agree with the American poet Philip Levine that it is important "to surrender the poem for better or worse to those forces within . . . to produce writing outrageous enough to be relevant and to be American"[15]—or Canadian or Irish or West Indian. But what does this mean when it comes to language? What does it mean to say with George Lamming that English is a West Indian language?

Seamus Heaney once wrote about how he began writing with "words imposing on his tongue." One of the most memorable literary expressions of this predicament is a famous passage from James Joyce's *Portrait of the Artist as a Young Man*. It is a prototype of the colonial dilemma, and V. S. Naipaul significantly used a quotation from it as an epigraph to one of the chapters in *The Middle Passage*. Stephen Dedalus is talking with the Dean of Studies, and begins with a statement that should have a familiar cast by now.

> "One difficulty," said Stephen, "in esthetic discussion is to know whether words are being used according to the literary tradition or according to the tradition of the marketplace. I remember a sentence of Newman's in which he says of the Blessed Virgin that she was detained in the full company of the saints. The use of the word in the marketplace is quite different. *I hope I am not detaining you.*"
> "Not in the least," said the dean politely.
> "No, no," said Stephen, smiling. "I mean . . ."
> "Yes, yes; I see," said the dean quickly, "I quite catch the point: *detain.*"
> He thrust forward his underjaw and uttered a short dry cough.
> "To return to the lamp," he said, "the feeding of it is also a nice problem. You must choose the pure oil and you must be careful when you pour it in not to overflow it, not to pour in more than the funnel can hold."
> "What funnel?" asked Stephen.
> "The funnel through which you pour the oil into your lamp."

"That?" said Stephen. "Is that called a funnel? Is it not a tundish?"
"What is a tundish?"
"That. The . . . funnel."
"Is that called a tundish in Ireland?" asked the dean. "I never heard the word in my life."
"It is called a tundish in Lower Drumconda," said Stephen, laughing, "where they speak the best English."
"A tundish," said the dean reflectively. "That is a most interesting word. I must look that word up. Upon my word I must" . . .
The dean repeated the word yet again.
"Tundish! Well, now, that is interesting!"
"The question you asked me a moment ago seems to me more interesting. What is that beauty which the artist struggles to express from lumps of earth," said Stephen coldly.
The little word seemed to have turned a rapier point of his sensitiveness against this courteous and vigilant foe. He felt with a smart of dejection that the man to whom he was speaking was a countryman of Ben Jonson. He thought:
"The language in which we are speaking is his before it is mine. How different are the words *home, Christ, ale, master,* on his lips and on mine! I cannot speak or write these words without unrest of spirit. His language, so familiar and so foreign, will always be for me an acquired speech. I have not made or accepted its words. My voice holds them at bay. My soul frets in the shadow of his language."[16]

But Joyce is not finished with his chronicle of imperial insinuations into colonial households. Stephen returns to the word *tundish* at the end of the book. "That tundish has been on my mind for a long time. I looked it up and find it English and good old blunt English too. Damn the dean of studies and his funnel! What did he come here for to teach us his own language or to learn it from us. Damn him one way or the other!"[17]

The irony remains; and so does the anger. But neither anger nor irony of themselves produce good poems. Poetry that relies on resentment either "yellows into polemic or evaporates in pathos,"[18] in Walcott's words. Or as he added on another occasion, "once the New World black had tried to prove that he was as good as his master, when he should have proven not his equality but his difference. It was this distance that could command attention without pleading for respect."[19]

And so something else is called for. While poems with no dialect in them may of course still be uniquely West Indian, local language is a powerful resource for all West Indian poets as they try to achieve that liveliness and freshness that is the mark of good poetry, that sense of the rightness—and the difference—of what has been said. "The power of the dew still shakes off our dialects," said Derek Walcott, recalling what Césaire had claimed in "Cahiers d'un retour au pays natal," as the Martiniquan explored the possibilities of his West Indian language.

> Storm, I would say. River, I would command. Hurricane, I would say. I would utter "leaf." Tree. I would be drenched in all the rains, soaked in all the dews.[20]

Walcott took up Césaire's image in "The Schooner *Flight*," where the narrator Shabine asks

> You ever look up from some lonely beach
> and see a far schooner? Well, when I write
> this poem, each phrase go be soaked in salt;
> I go draw and knot every line as tight
> as ropes in this rigging; in simple speech
> my common language go be the wind,
> my pages the sails of the schooner *Flight*.[21]

This passage, with its announcement that "each phrase go be soaked in salt," comes at the end of the first section of Walcott's poem. It confirms Shabine as one who will court the language of his people, the people of the West Indies. And it confirms the confidence of Walcott that through the mask of Shabine he has found a way of speaking that will fuse literary conventions and local conditions. The poem's opening illustrates how this works . . . or in Shabine's words, "how this business begin." With Columbus; and with the Caribbean.

> In idle August, while the sea soft,
> and leaves of brown islands stick to the rim
> of this Caribbean, I blow out the light
> by the dreamless face of Maria Concepcion
> to ship as a seaman on the schooner *Flight*.
> Out in the yard turning gray in the dawn,
> I stood like a stone and nothing else move
> but the cold sea rippling like galvanize
> and the nail holes of stars in the sky roof,
> till a wind start to interfere with the trees.
> I pass me dry neighbor sweeping she yard
> as I went downhill, and I nearly said:
> "Sweep soft, you witch, 'cause she don't sleep hard,"
> but the bitch look through me like I was dead.
> A route taxi pull up, park-lights still on.

The driver size up my bags with a grin:
"This time, Shabine, like you really gone!"
I ain't answer the ass, I simply pile in
the back seat and watch the sky burn
above Laventille pink as the gown
in which the woman I left was sleeping,
and I look in the rearview and see a man
exactly like me, and the man was weeping
for the houses, the streets, that whole fucking island.[22]

First of all, this passage shows us something about poetic voices. Shabine's voice conveys an intensity, a sense of presences and powers, which seems at odds with his conversational nonchalance—until we realize that it is precisely this combination of figurative energy and everyday informality that characterizes what we recognize in other poems as Walcott's own voice. Here is the paradox again. In William Butler Yeats's words, "give the poet a mask and he will speak the truth," not because he can hide himself but because he can show himself. Also, Walcott's habit of being serious and lighthearted at the same time is something he shares with his people, whose language he uses in the poem. Here, he takes conventional images of the sky, the sunrise, the state of his soul, and makes them uniquely West Indian, uniquely Shabine's—and thereby in some sense uniquely his own. But at the same time these images are recognizably conventional, part of a tradition of literary inventiveness similar to that of Robert Burns, or William Carlos Williams, or John Agard. And although the naturalness of Shabine's speaking voice has one kind of appeal, this inventive artifice has its own additional attraction for readers familiar with the literary conventions that are being made into something new. For while Walcott's poem is certainly rich in local idiom, it is also rich in allusion, in this case (among other things) to the prologue to Langland's *Piers Plowman*, a poem from an entirely different time and place and one of the classics of English literature. "In a somer seson when soft was the sonne / I shope me in shroudes, as I a shepe were." As Seamus Heaney said of the poem,

> it is a sign of Walcott's mastery that his fidelity to West Indian speech now leads him not away from but right into the genius of English. When he wrote these opening lines, how conscious was he of another morning departure, another allegorical early-riser? The murmur of Malvern is under that writing, for surely it returns to an origin in *Piers Plowman*. . . . The whole passage could stand as an epigraph to Walcott's book in so far as it is at once speech and melody, matter-of-fact but capable of mod-

ulation to the visionary. Walcott's glamorous, voluble Caribbean har-
bours recall Langland's field full of folk. Love and anger inspire both
writers, and both manage—in Eliot's phrase—to fuse the most ancient
and the most civilized mentality.[23]

Furthermore, Walcott's entire poem, telling the story of Shabine's
journey around the Caribbean, is patterned after the epic narrative of
Homer's *Odyssey*, with Shabine as a new Odysseus and the Caribbean
as a "new Mediterranean" (a phrase that Walcott had used earlier as
the original epigraph of a sonnet in his sequence of "Tales of the
Islands"). So Walcott is taking these traditions for his own and giving
them back to his people. As he does so, he also gives them back to the
literary world they came from, but changed irrevocably.

Walcott has written a lot about how West Indian poets must find
their own voice, insisting on the need to transform their anxiety and
anger into a new expression of what it is to be West Indian, and into a
new West Indian literature. Rejecting what he calls a "literature of
recrimination and despair, a literature of revenge written by the
descendants of slaves or a literature of remorse written by the descendants of masters," Walcott celebrates "the great poets of the New
World, from Walt Whitman to Pablo Neruda." For Walcott, theirs "is
not the jaded cynicism which sees nothing new under the sun, it is an
elation which sees everything as renewed."[24] New visions, from what
Whitman called a democratic vista. These new visions needs new
voices, and that is where the poets come in. But the newness of their
voices is apparent only to the extent that older voices are too, speaking
in older forms, older rhymes. For poets, this means working within a
literary tradition. As Walcott says in *Omeros*—referring both to the
women who carried hundredweight baskets of coal on their head up
the "narrow wooden ramp built steeply into the hull of a liner tall as
a cloud" for one copper penny a load and to the traditions of "ancestral
rhyme" in which the grim heritage of "those Helens from an earlier
time" will be celebrated—

> your duty
>
> from the time you watched them from your grandmother's house
> as a child wounded by their power and beauty
> is the chance you now have, to give those feet a voice[25]

The most radical division for West Indian poets is that which separates their African and European inheritances. Whether descendants of
slaves or not, West Indian poets all share that sense of division, and it

distinguishes them from their sometime European masters. It takes a subtler form in the division between West Indian speech, with its elements of the social and linguistic inheritance of slavery, and its European counterpart, with its assumptions of superiority. West Indian poets are caught up in the tensions created by these separate inheritances, and the best of their poetry takes some of its strength from the energy this generates. But as we have seen, these tensions also create severe strains. One inheritance, the European language and its literary tradition, is an inheritance of power. And it is held responsible for the powerlessness, which, during slavery and since, has impaired the other inheritance of local imaginative expression in a local language. Prestige and power belong on one side, in this scheme; the other seems powerless, or picturesque, or pathetic.

Both inheritances belong to West Indian poets. With few exceptions, contemporary poets in the West Indies have been educated in a European tradition, and that education is part of their life and art. As Derek Walcott said in a poem from the mid 1950s titled "A Far Cry from Africa,"

> Where shall I turn, divided to the vein?
> I who have cursed
> The drunken officer of British rule, how choose
> Between this Africa and the English tongue I love?
> Betray them both, or give back what they give?[26]

This poem is all too often reduced to a simple statement of irreconcilable alternatives. In fact, it is a much more complex account of coming to terms with violence—the violence of colonial resistance (in this case, the Mau Mau uprising in Kenya) and the violence of imperial traditions. Walcott's dilemma has much in common with that of Yeats, dealing with the violence of the Easter Uprising and then of the Irish Civil War in the struggle for home rule; and with the long history of English colonialism in Ireland. Raised under British rule, in an only slightly different version of Eric Roach's dominion of hope and hate, "everything I love has come to me through English," said Yeats. "My hatred tortures me with love, my love with hate."[27] In the complex psychology of Walcott's poem, too, as of James Joyce's *Portrait of the Artist as a Young Man*, love and hate are close kin.

But Walcott's poem does not reduce itself to a matter of choice, for the alternatives—retaliation (by way of betrayal) or restoration (giving back what they give)—are not as clear as a melodramatic reading might suggest, even assuming choice would be possible. The poet is caught less in a set of alternatives than in a series of questions, each a version

of Brathwaite's "where then is the nigger's home?" And he is held by
the ambiguities of his own appeal: "Come back to me my language."
We are indeed possessed by what belongs to us. West Indian poets
who are determined not to become slaves of their European inheritance
have been conscious of the need to master it, with all of the ironies this
involves. In the words of Michael Smith, a Jamaican poet whose work
was solidly grounded in Jamaican speech and oral performance, "me
really believe seh you have fi learn the ABC of Babylon fi destroy
them."[28]

Poets are not easily intimidated. And they all struggle to reconcile
the competing claims of the natural and the artificial, speech and writing, the familiar and the strange, the local and the literary. These divisions are part of any poet's art. For some poets, who have an entirely
different language to which they can turn as an alternative to a European language, these divisions are also in another way a part of their
life. This is the case for many African poets, such as Wole Soyinka from
Nigeria, Okot p'Bitek from Uganda, or Mazisi Kunene from South
Africa, all of whom speak both their African tribal language—Yoruba,
Lwo or Zulu—and English. It is also true, for example, of some Irish
poets, who have grown up speaking Irish Gaelic. As an illustration of
how this situation can bring together poetry and the politics of national
identity, listen to the Irish poet Michael Hartnett.

> Her eyes were coins of porter and her West
> Limerick voice talked velvet in the house:
> her hair was black as the glossy fireplace
> wearing with grace her Sunday-night-dance best.
> She cut the froth from glasses with a knife
> and hammered golden whiskies on the bar
> and her mountainy body tripped the gentle
> mechanism of verse: the minute interlock
> of word and word began, the rhythm formed.
> I sunk my hands into tradition
> sifting the centuries for words. This quiet
> excitement was not new: emotion challenged me
> to make it sayable. The clichés came
> at first, like matchsticks snapping from the world
> of work: mánla, séimh, dubhfholtach, álainn, caíon:
> they came like grey slabs of slate breaking from
> an ancient quarry, mánla, séimh, dubhfholtach,
> álainn, caoin, slowly vaulting down the dark

unused escarpments, mánla, séimh, dubhfholtach,
álainn, caoin, crashing on the cogs, splinters
like axeheads damaged the wheels, clogging
the intricate machine, mánla, séimh,
dubhfholtach, álainn, caoin. Then Pegasus
pulled up, the girth broke and I was flung back
on the gravel of Anglo-Saxon.
What was I doing with these foreign words?[29]

Whatever words Hartnett is talking about here, they are not exactly foreign. Or rather, the English words *are* exactly that to Hartnett; but to English-speaking ears, it is the Irish that is unfamiliar. (Dubhfholtach means, roughly, blackhaired; álainn translates as beautiful; mánla, séimh and caoin are words whose meanings are close to the English adjectives graceful, gentle.) For Hartnett, born in Cromadh an tSubhachais (known in English as Croom, in County Limerick), these Irish words are a "final sign that we are human"; and Irish.
    They are also a reminder that

> Gaelic is the conscience of our leaders,
> the memory of a mother-rape they will
> not face, the heap of bloody rags they see
> and scream at in their boardrooms of mock oak.[30]

In this account, English is the language of colonial oppression, a foreign invader raping the mother tongue, mocking those who try to imitate its antique hardwood authority. And Hartnett is saying "A Farewell to English," the title of the poem. His choice to write henceforth only in the Irish language was made in 1975, and maintained for a decade. It confirmed a bond between him and his people, and his separation from a larger audience and the English literary tradition in which his great talents had flourished. The choice, with all its ambivalences, is not new, he insists. Poets are always making choices, though usually ones that are less extreme.

> But I will not see
> great men go down
> who walked in rags
> from town to town
> finding English a necessary sin
> the perfect language to sell pigs in.
>
> I have made my choice
> and leave with little weeping:

> I have come with meagre voice
> to court the language of my people.[31]

Hartnett's leavetaking becomes his homecoming.

For most poets, the choice is not between different languages, but between different uses of language. The way in which Hartnett combines the image of an instinctive, rhythmic interlock of word and word with the deliberate act of reaching down into tradition and sifting the centuries for words portrays the conflict that arises when uses of language that come naturally to the poet are not those he finds in the official literary word bin.

But what exactly is this thing called the language of the people? Like the notion of a standard language, it is a bit of a fiction, but a convenient and comfortable one. For a start, we can say that it is the language of common speech, since this is the form that is most distinctively public and most easily associated with a particular place. In the West Indies, it is also the most different, most like nothing one has ever heard before. This does not mean that spoken language is somehow more natural, or less contrived, than writing. Speech is as conventional as any other form of language, and as stylized, as everyday blessings and curses confirm. It is also as exclusive. It binds people together by its difference, and by the same token it sets them apart from others.

To complicate matters further, what we refer to as the language of speech is only part of what we call an oral tradition. In the West Indies, for example, this tradition includes highly refined forms of storytelling and song, as well as stylized dispute, and a kind of credit union of proverbial sayings. One particular attitude toward oral traditions holds that they are less imaginatively complex and therefore less worthy of critical attention than written expression, because the circumstances of composition and performance make the story or the song or whatever seem unsophisticated and lacking in subtlety. This is the generous view. The less-generous view is that these traditions are typical among people who have no sophistication or subtlety anyway. This is nonsense, as anyone familiar with the rich tradition of secular and sacred celebration in oral forms around the world will know. But it is stubborn nonsense.

During the nineteenth century, the priority of written over oral texts was given unusual support by Henry Maine, the author of a book called *Ancient Law* first published in 1861. By the 1870s, Oxford and Cambridge were teaching Maine and John Stuart Mill as the great modern thinkers. Maine had a lot to say about traditions, or the passing of things from one to another. "Conveyancing," lawyers call it. Commerce. (The language of property still informs our discourse about inheritance, literary or otherwise.) In its early form, according to Maine, tradition accounted for the informal ways in which certain sorts of property changed hands. Its informality was its hallmark, especially in legal or religious contexts, which is why we have a sense of traditions as things that cannot be written down, but are passed on orally or in other customary ways. There was always an alternative, the formal ceremonies according to which certain things of particular importance in society were handed over. In Roman law, such things were called *res mancipi;* and the ceremony was called a "mancipation." Among other things that fell under this procedure, the most important tended to be land, and that which was necessary for its cultivation—usually horses, oxen, and slaves. We have long since lost a precise sense of the distinction between mancipations and traditions, though the heightened significance of mancipations in some societies is retained in the strict legal and written procedures often followed, for example, in the transfer of land, the adoption of children, and the conferring of citizenship. From a European persective, Maine underlined this significance, and the corresponding priority it gave written over oral texts. Oral traditions, while undoubtedly important, were still casual, part of the scheme of things when more precise arrangements seemed to be too—well, too much trouble. The American Civil War, which was being fought just when Maine's book appeared, became eloquent testimony to the significance of written mancipations and to the way in which the term had come to refer to those conveyances about which society needed strict arrangements. One could change a thousand traditions and still not emancipate one slave, still not release a slave from the strict conditions governing his or her status as a thing to be passed along. Not, at any rate, when one part of society saw things one way, and the other saw them quite differently.

And so Henry Maine gave to written texts a kind of ethnocentric validity that has had widespread consequences, not only in literary terms. (He also completely misunderstood the significance of gift giving as part of the dynamics of material and spiritual exchange.) One of the more troublesome legacies of this, not unrelated to the distinctions we are discussing between written and oral literary traditions, has been the attitude of European settlers toward treaties with aboriginal peoples of the Americas. There is good reason to believe that these treaties were first of all oral contracts, in conformity with local traditions—when in the land of the Sioux or the Cree, do as they do—and that the written versions should be read merely as approximations. But courts in Canada and the United States and elsewhere, which are ready enough to accept oral evidence in other circumstances, have resolutely refused this interpretation. The roots of these attitudes go very deep and spread widely.

Another rather different misconception that bedevils the consideration of oral and written traditions is that written texts have lost the authenticity of speech because they lack either its supposedly realistic character or the resonant metaphorical texture that oral traditions often display. But dead metaphors abound in the clichés of speech as much as in the conventions of writing. And neither writing nor speech has any monopoly on dullness. In fact, it is precisely out of a determination to maintain vitality in their work that poets combine spoken and written language, hoping to refresh each through the resources of the other.

The traditions of speaking and writing come together in the devices of rhetoric, which include most of the ways in which speakers and writers try to please and persuade us. Rhetoric was originally based in the art and science of public speaking, and we can see traces of this in the phrase "figure of speech," used to refer to metaphors and the like. As written expression became increasingly central to European culture, rhetoric became one of the instruments of effective writing, while still keeping its place as the point of contact between written and oral expression. So when poets bring together speech and writing, they are in the simplest sense doing nothing more than taking advantage of the wide range of opportunities for rhetorical effect available to poetry; though some poets who draw in an ostentatious way on the resources of spoken language will always want to encourage the notion that speech is natural and true and closer to the people, while writing is the deceptive artifice of the privileged.[32]

There is a long history to this debate about the natural and the artificial, and about speech and writing. In the early years of this century, the poets who described themselves as Imagists called for poetry "to use the language of common speech and to employ always the exact word, not merely the decorative word." A hundred years earlier, William Wordsworth had denounced what he termed "the arbitrary and capricious habits of expression" that only "furnish food for fickle tastes and fickle appetites." He was referring to the elaborate refinements of eighteenth-century literary fashion, which seemed to him both impotent and irrelevant. Instead, he called in his 1800 preface to the *Lyrical Ballads* for "a selection of the real language of men in a state of vivid sensation," conveying "feelings and notions in simple and unelaborated expressions."[33] In a nice irony, he called for the purity of language by appealing to the impurity of speech. But he was really calling for poets to court the language of their people, and to bring back into their poetry the power of language that supposedly derives from plain speaking, rejecting the deliberate preciousness of fancy phrases and elaborate diction.

It was not a simpleminded crusade, for Wordsworth admired the poetry of many of his predecessors. His interest was in the universality and permanence of this local language, rather than its particularities— or at least, in the ways in which its particularities exemplified universal qualities; for he knew that a particular dialect, just like the literary language of a particular period, may sound out of place in another context. His own poetry, even in the *Lyrical Ballads*, displayed a respect for some of the artifices of poetry, especially rhythm, which he said "heightens and improves" its pleasure. But he sought the illusion of naturalness, and a style that, in Walcott's phrase, would seem as plain as life. He had a sense of poetry's kinship with music rather than with painting; and, preferring the awkwardnesses and extravagances of colloquial language to the precise decorums of eighteenth-century word-painting, he distrusted the tendency of his predecessors to follow the dictates of their eyes rather than their ears. Wordsworth's views in some measure reflected his own idiosyncratic assumptions about language as well as his northcountry speech; and the relationship of his poetry to the contemporary West Indies is problematic, since he provided a somewhat distant standard of poetic achievement—and a host of golden daffodils—to several generations of readers and writers. But his comments illuminate the venerable inheritance of this attitude toward local language in literature. What Wordsworth feared was the loss of contact with what a later generation would call "the soil," the loss of a language rooted in the land. What he produced was poetry with a new kind of simplicity, albeit in an old poetic form with careful iambs and clever rhymes.

> There is a thorn; it looks so old,
> In truth you'd find it hard to say,
> How it could ever have been young,
> It looks so old and grey.
> Not higher than a two-years' child,
> It stands erect this aged thorn;
> No leaves it has, no thorny points;
> It is a mass of knotted joints,
> A wretched thing forlorn.
> It stands erect, and like a stone
> With lichens it is overgrown.[34]

Wordsworth tried to write in a language "arising out of repeated experience and regular feelings." So do contemporary West Indian poets. And what, then, does all of this look and sound like in West Indian terms? Well, some of it sounds exactly like West Indian speech, though presented within a structure in which the naturalness of the language contrasts with the artifice of the form—as in "Rites," a poem by Kamau Brathwaite. This poem is about cricket, and about one particular game, between the Marylebone Cricket Club and the West Indies in 1948, in Barbados. It is also about a more general struggle between the colonial West Indies and English imperial authority for racial equality and political independence. In this excerpt, the powerful West Indian batsman Clyde Walcott is up against the subtle English bowler Wardle, with his "sweet sweet low-medium syrup." "You mean to say," says the speaker in the poem,

> THAT YOU DOAN REALLY KNOW WHA' HAPPEN
> at Kensington Oval?
>
> We was *only* playin' de MCC, man;
> M-C-C
> who come all de way out from Inglan.
>
> We was battin', you see;
> score wasn't too bad; one
> hurren an' ninety-
>
> seven fuh three.
> The openers out, Tae Worrell out,
> Everton Weekes jus' glide two fuh fifty
>
> an' jack, is de GIANT to come!
> Feller named Wardle
> was bowlin'; tossin' it up
>
> sweet sweet slow-medium syrup.
> Firs' ball . . .
> "N . . . o . . . o . . ."
>
> back down de wicket to Wardle.
> Secon' ball . . .
> "N . . . o . . . o . . ."
>
> back down de wicket to Wardle.
> Third ball comin' up
> an' we know wha' goin' happen to syrup:

Clyde back pun he back
foot an' *prax!*
is through extra cover an' four red runs all de way.

"You see dat shot?" the people was shoutin';
"Jesus Chrise, man, wunna see dat shot?"
All over de groun' fellers shakin' hands wid each other

as if was *they* wheelin' de willow
as if was *them* had the power;
one man run out pun de field wid a red fowl cock

goin' qwawk qwawk qwawk in 'e han';
would'a give it to Clyde right then 'an right there
if a police hadn't stop 'e!

An' in front o' where I was sittin',
one ball-headed sceptic snatch hat off he head
as if he did crazy

an' pointin' he finger at Wardle,
he jump up an' down
like a sun-shatter daisy an' bawl

out: "B . . . L . . . O . . . O . . . D, B . . . I . . . G B . . . O . . . Y
bring me he B . . . L . . . O . . . O . . . D"
Who would'a think that for twenty-

five years he was standin' up there
in them Post Office cages, lickin' gloy
pun de Gover'ment stamps.

If uh wasn't there to see fuh meself,
I would'a never believe it,
I would'a never believe it.[35]

For all its authenticity, and the way in which it convinces us that we would not believe it either if we did not hear it in this language and this way, the passage functions a lot like anecdote, giving us a moment of local color. But it goes well beyond that limited achievement, illustrating one of the ways in which the poetic language itself bears much of the burden of credibility by being located at the intersection not only of speech and writing but also of authority (the story, spoken or written) and authenticity (the local language).

There are other ways of combining the languages of speech and writing in West Indian poetry, ways that question rather than confirm the boundaries, as in the following poem by Lorna Goodison in which one word makes all the difference. The poem is entitled "My Will," and tells the story of the poet's bequest to her son, generous and humorous by turns, a giving away of what is not exactly hers.

> . . . for a start,
> the gift of song,
> this sweet immediate source
> of release was not given me
> so I leave it for you in the hope
> that God takes hints.
> Then the right to call
> all older than you
> Miss, mister or mistress
> in the layered love of our
> simplest ways,
> eat each day's salt and bread
> with praise,
> and may you never know hungry.[36]

Another poet might have put *hunger*. But Goodison's use of the word *hungry* from local speech, instead of the abstract *hunger*, brings into the poem a reality and a kind of urgency that suits her determination to bring her son down to earth and to keep him safe from its terrors. There is an additional element, of which Goodison herself may be unaware, but which underlines the West Indian inheritance from Africa. The "y" ending of hungry (used as a noun), which is typical of many West Indian dialect words, derives from the Twi language of West Africa, part of its legacy to West Indian speech.

Combining the conventions of written and spoken language not only blurs their differences but also creates what the American poet Wallace Stevens used to call the "sudden rightness" of the apt phrase or word or image, a mixture of custom and novelty—as with the word hungry. There may be nothing either intrinsically natural or intrinsically artificial about either *hunger* or *hungry*. But there is an effect of naturalness in the image of a Jamaican mother using the word *hungry* in speaking to her son; and there is an effect of artifice in the word appearing in a poem that in other ways is highly structured along literary lines. We might say that the voice of the poem is that of a poet and a mother. Or we might want to be more sophisticated and say that there are several voices in the poem, that of a poet and that of a mother. Or perhaps again that each of these includes two separable voices as well, speaking from perspectives that are local and particular on the one hand, and literary and universal on the other. The weaving together of these voices in the poem, then, produces both its texture and its meaning.

Combining spoken and written languages and effects of naturalness and artifice is a technique poets often use. Take a couple of examples from widely different periods and styles. First, from the seventeenth century, the great English mystic Henry Vaughan begins a poem called "The World" with phrasing that is conversationally casual, and then moves immediately into a statement of great figurative intensity: "I saw Eternity the other night / Like a great ring of pure and endless light, / All calm as it was bright."[37] It is not so much the two sides of the comparison ("Eternity," and the "great ring of pure and endless light") as the phrases "I saw Eternity the other night" and "all calm as it was bright" that exemplify the different registers of language, the latter heightened in a way that draws attention not only to its own artifice but also to the naturalness of the opening. Not that "I saw Eternity the other night" is all that natural a thing to say, of course; but it has an ordinariness of syntax and diction that provides a grounding or framing for the artifice that signals "this is a poem."

The Canadian poet Don McKay shows some other possibilities as he opens his poem "March Snow" with an unexpected statement, but expressed in plain talk; and then after expanding on the figure of speech moves to even plainer talk, which in its incongruity (in a poem) provides another dimension of surprise, generated when the naturalness of the language is set against the artifice of the poem. (The subject of the poem—spring crud, a late winter snow—as well as the language will be familiar in a special way to Canadian and some American readers.)

> The snow is sick. The pure
> page breaks and greys and
> drools around the edges, sucks
> at my snowshoe every heavy step saying
> fuck it, just
> fuck it, softly to itself.[38]

The point of these examples is to illustrate that these techniques are used by poets in different times and places. Naturalness and artifice are not the only distinctions here. There is an exotic quality about unfamiliar diction wherever it occurs, sometimes creating a different effect from the unfamiliarity of a figurative expression. Both, of course, are at the heart of how poems work. But then other issues arise. The word *galliwasp* (in Mervyn Morris's "The Pond"), for example, is not at all unfamiliar or exotic to a Jamaican reader, but only to readers from

elsewhere; just as McKay's *fuck it* has a special familiarity to Canadian
and American readers for whom this kind of cursing comes (perhaps
too) naturally. Other readers, from further away in time or place or
literary convention, might expect a phrase like "woe is me"; or for the
galliwasp, "yon miniature alligator, denizen of swamps and stone
walls, more fatal in ballad than in bite." Or something that would satisfy their expectations of unfamiliarity, of figurative expression if not
of words. Poets, of course, occasionally use words that are unfamiliar
to *all* readers, or whose unfamiliar etymology is the key to their effect.
And their figures of speech often surprise *everyone*. Making strange is
what poets do best. But what we are talking about here has to do with
the *particular* unfamiliarity of local words and the sense of artifice this
generates for readers from elsewhere . . . which of course is exactly
what we *all* are when we read texts from other periods or places, and
perhaps even other experiences of race and gender and so forth. The
Northern Irish poet Seamus Heaney tells of his delight when his short
poem "Nerthus" caught special, and not very complementary, attention:

> For beauty, say an ash-fork staked in peat,
> Its long-grains gathered to the gouged split;
>
> A seasoned, unsleeved taker of the weather,
> Where kesh and loaning finger out to heather.[39]

Kesh is a bridge over the bog, and loaning is a path; and it was these
words—"shy little parish words," Heaney later called them—which
particularly troubled one critic, who saw them as affectations, ostentatious (and unsuccessful) gestures of naturalness giving nothing more
than a cutesy sort of local color to the poem. From our perspective, they
are also the words that in their unfamiliarity give it special life and
locality, and a kind of independence. There is no doubt that poets take
risks in using such local words in this literary way; but then again,
poets always take risks with language.

One of these risks, shared by all poets, is the danger of limiting their
audience. If the poet is from a group that is marginal along geographical or political or social or sexual or racial lines, then the worry is that
this will entrench that marginality. It is a perennial issue. Poets live
with it in a variety of ways. Some embrace that marginality and the
resistance to assimilation that it represents. Others seek a universality
of language or subject or style, though no poet ever assumes a universality that completely transcends time and place, for language just does
not work that way. At their best, what poets do is make us aware of

the limits of our ability to understand meaning independent of partic-ular context, and context independent of particular meaning. And West Indian poets make us acutely aware of the ways in which language resists the enticements of "standard," not to say universal, ways of seeing and saying.

Familiarity and strangeness, then, are categories as important to the effect of poetry as naturalness and artifice, or the styles of spoken and written languages. And like the other categories, strangeness is not an absolute, any more than naturalness in language is. Language, spoken or written, is differently natural to different people. And the particular artifice of spoken and written forms in literature will work differently for different readers, depending on their familiarity both with the forms of language and with the literary forms. There are other classifications we sometimes use, in an equally arbitrary way. For example, we might say that one of the features of a word like *hungry*, used in the way Goodison does in her poem, is that it hovers between the abstract idea of hunger and the concrete reality of being hungry. And we might carry on to suggest that speech, supposedly being more natural, is also more concrete, and therefore that the artifice of written language will make it more inclined to abstraction. In certain circumstances this may be true. But these are shaky generalizations, especially regarding the lan-guage of West Indians. Abstract words are in fact very common in West Indian speech—"tribulation, sufferation, things well known by the black population"[40]—to quote the beginning of a poem by Levi Tafari, a poet of Jamaican heritage from Liverpool. (The rhyming of the "shun" sounds at the ends of the lines—and therefore the litany of abstractions—is accentuated by the West Indian speech habit of putting the stress on the last syllable).

Whatever the case, poets try to make the language they use in a poem seem natural, in the sense of making us feel that what they are saying could not be said in any other way. Natural the way a giraffe or an anteater are natural. Unusual . . . but just right for the job. And so Bongo Jerry was right when he set Black Power beside Strange Tongue. It has been the strangeness of West Indian speech to non-West Indian ears that has provided West Indian poetry with one of its most effective opportunities to assert its power and to affirm the independ-ence of a distinctly West Indian heritage centered in imaginative expression.

For a simple example of the effect of unfamiliarity, consider the beginning of a poem called "When Moon Shine" by the Trinidadian storyteller Paul Keens-Douglas.

Tim, Tim? . . . papa welcome!
Ah send an' call de doctor
An' de doctor reach before me?
Don't tell me, ah know—coconut!
Is Nanci story time on de step,
Is full moon an' everyting bright.
All little children teafin' ah "stay up,"
Playin' rounders an' catchers,
Nobody mind, not when de moon full,
Is like everybody find excuse
To leave de house.
Tanti on de porch lookin' out,
"Cover yu head, gal, yu want dew kill yu?"
But Tanti mind elsewhere like she eye.
Long time now she watchin' dem two shadow—
Two dat look like one—under de mango tree.
Other tings goin' on besides catchers tonite.
Tanti like de moon . . . she silent, but she see.[41]

The appeal of this poem begins with its imitation of a distinctively West Indian speech, with its lively expressions—"teafin' ah 'stay up,' " for example—and the nicely humorous identification of the old aunt Tanti with the moon—"she silent, but she see." The language is local, like the scene itself and some of its references—"Nanci story," for instance, refers specifically to stories whose ancestry is West African about Anancy the spider, but more generally to bedtime stories.

But this appeal varies among readers. The elements that engage a reader who is not from the islands with their surprising freshness will delight listeners from the West Indies with their well-worn familiarity. And while the naturalness of the language, for example, may be acknowledged in theory by all listeners on the basis that spoken dialects are somehow more authentic, more the "language of the people," this language still has a special kind of naturalness to those readers for whom it recalls the language spoken at home. On the other hand, the presence of this language *in a poem* may seem especially *un*natural to some West Indian readers. In a sense, this kind of poem sets up a dialogue *between* different readers, rather than *within* the poem itself. It also raises questions about the "translatability" of one language system to another, and especially of texts that are so deeply rooted in linguistic situations. Such questions, of course, are nothing new to poets, who at least in a European tradition often insist that "no other word in any other order" will do. But systemic differences between dialects complicate this venerable adage.

Poetry depends on different notions of custom and of novelty, notions that are constucted differently according to what are sometimes called positionalities—the identifiable perspectives of people with distinct experiences and interests living in particular places at particular times. If surprise is the measure of metaphor, as Aristotle claimed, then the figurative power of texts presumably will differ significantly from one place and time to another, as well as from person to person, depending on familiarity with the language of expression. We often assume that *some* poetic uses of language transcend time and place—Shakespeare's, for example, or that of the King James translation of the Bible. And yet even if this were the case, the different ways in which such language is spoken must always affect a listener's response, for the ways in which poetic language draws its authority and its energy from speech are more complicated than we sometimes assume. With West Indian poetry this is exemplified in our sense that something significant is lost if we do not have the opportunity to hear a poem read by a West Indian reader. This is especially true when the language on the page does not display in its spelling or typography or syntax the distinctive features of the West Indian language—its rhythms and intonations, for example.

Some years ago, the English critic Owen Barfield raised all of this in a book called *Poetic Diction* (1928). The quality of "strangeness" in poetic language, he argued, gives it its special appeal, indeed gives it what he called its meaning. Barfield began with the example of a line of pidgin English, from the South Pacific islands, for a three masted steam boat with two funnels: "Thlee-piecee bamboo, two-piecee puff-puff, walk-along-inside, no-can-see."[42]

He then talked about strangeness in terms of the ways in which we see things, and the ways in which we talk about them. For Barfield, the words we use shape what we see. He describes how the pidgin language opens up posibilities not envisaged by "such English words as 'mast,' 'mechanical propulsion,' 'steam,' 'coal,' 'smoke,' 'chimney for smoke to escape by,' etc., all of which are . . . fused in my own particular and habitual idea of 'steamer.' It is this idea which determines for me the quality, or meaning, of my . . . observation."[43]

If we change the language, therefore, we change the way in which we look at the steamer . . . and therefore we change what we see. This is Barfield's account of his response. "When I read the words 'thlee-piecee bamboo, two-piecee puff-puff, walk-along-inside, no-can-see,' I am for a moment transported into a totally different kind of conscious-ness. I see the steamer, not through my own eyes, but through the eyes of a primitive South-Sea Islander. His experience, his *meaning*, is quite different from mine, for it is the product of quite different concepts. This he reveals by his choice of words; and the result is that, for a moment, I shed Western civilization like an old garment and behold my steamer in a new and strange light."[44]

Two issues are involved here: the linguistic relativity that Whorf described, and that Barfield refers to as the construction of "percepts" by "concepts"; and the distinction between the situation, as well as the structure, of ordinary and poetic language. Barfield links this distinction to the question of how different uses of language appeal to the imagination in different ways. "We can hardly maintain that this particular example would be 'poetic' to the South Sea Islanders themselves. On the contrary, we may safely suppose it to be felt there as a part of the business jargon of every day. It is thus a particularly clearcut example of the fact . . . that a given group of words may be a vehicle of poetry to one individual, or group of individuals, and not to another. It may, for instance, be unpoetic to the consciousness which originates it, but poetic to the consciousness which receives or contemplates it."[45]

I think Barfield is showing his civilian colors to the barbarians here, but he raises another perennially vexing issue. It is perilous to assume that those who use lively expressions in their language are not conscious of their figurative richness. The word for a cooking pot used by roadwork crews in Jamaica when there is no woman along to do the cooking is "ooman-be-dyam" (woman-be-damned),[46] and it is hard to imagine that those who use the word are not delighted with their cleverness each time. But it is also foolish to think that its novelty does not take second place to its naturalness after a while. Poets try to restore the novelty, and retain the naturalness. That's what Walcott was doing, for instance, when he brought local names into his poetry. It is not just the novelty and the naturalness, either. Naming, according to one venerable tradition, exemplifies in its most radical form the creative possibility of language, establishing the reality of the object and its relationship to the observer, creating new meanings for both subject and object. Words in constant use, according to this account, degenerate into carriers of old meanings, becoming what Ralph Waldo Emerson once called fossil metaphors. Poets return to the language its original metaphorical freshness, both intensifying and incorporating difference; and they reestablish the creative process by which subjects and objects take form and meaning.

Barfield provides a number of other examples of poems which are more conventionally poetic than the line of pidgin English, and in which the strangeness derives from more subtle elements of rhythm and tone (though the phrase quoted certainly has its own very distinctive rhythm). But what he returns to is the change of consciousnesss generated by poetry. This is what West Indian poetry tries to achieve, a changed or intensified consciousness of what it is to be West Indian. How much of a change this is will depend on a number of factors, but in any event it will vary according to the different familiarity of different readers with its language. A line such as "may you never know hungry" intensifies a West Indian reader's sense of what it is to be West Indian, and another reader's sense of what it would be like to be West Indian.

Still, we may be forgetting that poetry depends not on some notional absolutes of what is or is not natural or familiar or conventional, or of who is or is not black or West Indian, but on the relationships *between* these categories; and that it is by establishing a coherent *pattern* of relationships that a poem provides common ground for readers, whatever their background or perspective. This pattern of relationships, then, heightens our awareness of differences that are a central part of the West Indian heritage of imaginative expression in English, and integrates these differences with conventions of poetry that are familiar to English-speaking readers well beyond the West Indies.

Probably the commonest ground for many English-speaking West Indians is the language of the seventeenth-century King James translation of the Bible, whose familiarity makes its artifice seem natural to those who have heard it all their lives, more natural than the highly figurative language of streets and seaports may appear to some people. It has something of that complex universality that is one of the ambitions of poetic language, as well as something of its simple particularities. If all styles yearn to be plain as life, in Walcott's phrase, the King James translation certainly seems to satisfy these yearnings fairly often. The famous passage in Genesis—"And God said, Let there be light: and there was light"—provides a good example.[47] Simple ... but its simplicity the product of language that is carefully, poetically contrived. The syntax of the command and of its fulfilment are almost identical (in the Hebrew, they are even closer: *jehi aur vajehi aur*); and as much as anything this straightforward similarity conveys the sense of the passage. The lines are of great theological significance, of course, but this significance is made available to us here through the poetic character of its language, plain and simple as it is. It may be the artifice of biblical language that is ultimately the basis of its authority ... but its familiarity makes it seem inevitable and uncontrived.

The language of the Bible has been the subject of study and debate for a long time, and this is not the place to review the issues. Many are remarkably similar to those we have referred to throughout this study, but one in particular has special relevance. The Bible is in every sense, both originally and in its various versions—which include many in local language—a *translated* text, interweaving both languages and situations.[48] It embodies the interconnectedness and interdependence that we see at the center of West Indian poetry, and that many would say is at the heart of *all* poetry as it tries to nourish both the particularities and the universalities of its languages. Biblical language illustrates the relativity of all linguistic virtues, including literary authority; and the use of this language or the allusion to it in contemporary poetic texts illuminates the contingencies of all the categories we have been discussing: the natural and the artificial, the familiar and the strange, the oral and the written, the abstract and the concrete.

In a famous diatribe against the corruption of language called "Politics and the English Language," George Orwell condemned what he called the "swindles and perversions" of language that is not clear and precise, but that instead conceals thought and obstructs feeling. As an example, he compared the language of a passage from Ecclesiastes with a passage translated by him into what he calls "modern English of the worst sort." First, Orwell's modern "translation."

> Objective consideration of contemporary phenomena compels the conclusion that success or failure in competitive activities exhibits no tendency to be commensurate with innate capacity, but that a considerable element of the unpredictable must invariably be taken into account.[49]

Then the language of the King James translation of the Old Testament.

> I returned and saw under the sun, that the race is not to the swift, nor the battle to the strong, neither yet bread to the wise, nor yet riches to men of understanding, nor yet favour to men of skill; but time and chance happeneth to them all. (Eccles. 9:11)

This is plain speaking, after a fashion. But there's the difficulty: the element of fashion. The style of the King James translation is distanced in time and place from us, and sounds nothing like the way most of us speak, wherever we are from. And yet it is a language with which many of us have grown up, and which has a straightforwardness that endears itself to us. Its power is something we have learned to take for granted. But it is no less imperial in its authority than the Queen's Advice to the Jamaican black laborers in 1865, enjoining them to "lay by an ample provision for seasons of drought and dearth" . . . but to forget about owning land.

The King James translators were undoubtedly gifted. They were also undoubtedly determined to establish a standard that others would follow, dismissing those they called (in the original dedication of the translation) "self-conceited brethren, who run their own ways, and give liking unto nothing but what is framed by themselves, and hammered on their own anvil." And yet the urge to frame it ourselves and hammer it on our own anvil is not limited to the self-conceited. It is the ambition of each generation and of every poet.

Oscar Wilde once said that "the creeds are believed, not because they are rational, but because they are repeated."[50] The language of the King James translation of the Bible has been repeated often enough to give it a ritual authority inseparable for many West Indians from the imperial authority of the English language. In forging a West Indian style, a style in which readers will believe, West Indian poets have drawn on this authority as part of their heritage. The relationship between the Bible and contemporary West Indian poetry is especially interesting because of the ways in which the language of the King James translation is a language of literary as well as liturgical power.

For Derek Walcott, this heritage has provided one way of coming to terms with the doubting of self that he once called a chronic malarial condition afflicting colonial people, and which Naipaul made acute with his comments about nothing being created in the West Indies. When Walcott began writing his autobiographical poem *Another Life* in 1965, he quoted a poem by the Jamaican poet George Campbell called "Holy," which had first been published in 1945 at the beginning of the development of the distinctive West Indian literary tradition in which Walcott has been such a prominent figure. The language of Campbell's poem was drawn from the Bible (and from William Blake's "The Little Black Boy"); and his subject from the experience of being black and West Indian. "Holy be the white head of a Negro," Campbell began. "Sacred be the black flax of a black child."[51] Walcott took up the Biblical language of Campbell's celebration in *Another Life*. At one point, late in his account, he sets the historical insignificance of a place he had visited for a holiday—a small fishing village on the northeast coast of Trinidad called Rampanalgas—against its spiritual importance to him. Rejecting the litany of imperial enterprises that old-world history relishes, and to which Naipaul deferred in *The Middle Passage*, Walcott has another image of

> a child without history
> . . . who puts the shell's howl to his ear,
> hears nothing, hears everything

> that the historian cannot hear, the howls
> of all the races that crossed the waters,
> the howls of grandfathers drowned
> in that intricately swivelled Babel.[52]

Here, Walcott returns us to the problematics of historical discourse with which we began, and to the particulars of West Indian history: the heritage of slavery; specters of the unburied dead, and their legacy of dispossession and loss; the arbitrary criteria of achievement, credited and discredited by turns, and the nourishing of new conditions of understanding; the alternatives of speech and silence, and the search for a language that is authentic and authoritative. He then draws on the Biblical language of the Psalms in an expression of faith in the sanctity of this local place and its simple heritage.

> my son, my sun,
>
> holy is Rampanalgas and its high-circling hawks,
> holy are the rusted, tortured, rust-caked, blind almond trees,
> your great-grandfather's, and your father's torturing limbs,
> holy the small, almond-leaf-shadowed bridge
> by the small red shop, where everything smells of salt,
> and holiest the break of the blue sea below the trees,
> and the rock that takes blows on its back
> and is more rock,
> and the tireless hoarse anger of the waters
> by which I can walk calm, a renewed, exhausted man,
> balanced at its edge by the weight of two dear daughters.[53]

For other West Indian poets, the resources of the Bible have provided a different frame of reference, and a different source of strength. The Jamaican poet Linton Kwesi Johnson, who has made England his home since the early 1960s, has a poem titled "Youtman" which draws on the New Testament parable of the tares (or weeds) of the field (told in Matthew 13) in which the wicked are cast into the furnace of fire and the righteous shine forth as the sun, and which is structured to reflect the style of the gospel. But while not only the style but also the stanza form and phrasing are part of an English literary tradition, the language and rhythm are clearly West Indian. *Site,* for example, is a phonetic spelling of the Rastafarian word *sight* meaning *understand*; and this local character of the language is intensified with the word *ovastan,* used instead of *understand,* the sound logic being that if you are in control of an idea you stand over it. This coining derives from a fundamental Rastafarian conviction that the sound should sustain the sense of

words. For example, in Rastafarian practice the word *oppression* is usually transformed into *downpression* (since if you are being pressed
down, this pressure cannot be up); and in a punning change, which by
now should ring true, *education* becomes *head-decay-shun*.[54] Naturalness
and artifice converge in these constructions, and so do the complementary functions of linguistic codes to define difference and separateness
on the one hand and to establish similarity and solidarity on the other.

    This is Johnson's poem, bringing together the languages and styles
of the Bible and the poet, and the heritages of Europe and Africa. What
Johnson also brings together are the material and the spiritual values
of his society, in language that unites the factual and the figurative . . .
a union epitomized in the words written by a Rastafarian on a building
in Surinam: "the love of Jah is like a bucket of fire."[55] Burn down, chant
down Babylon.

> youtman,
> today is your day say di time is now.
> site? ovastan. youtman.
> check out di shape yu haffe faam;
> mind who yu harm.
>
> youtdauta,
> you are di queen of di day an di nite is your mite.
> site? ovastan. youtdauta.
> check out di tide before yu jump in di watah;
> den swim, yea sing, sing youtdauta.
>
> youtrebel,
> yu know bout di flame yu livin fire.
> yu know, youtrebel, yu livin fire.
> guide di flame fram di wheat to di tares;
> watch dem burn an flee free
>
> fram yu kulcha,
> tek in di love say tek in di love.
> dont lay in di way dat will cause decay,
> an folly is di way of di fool.
> site? youtman? scene. move on.[56]

    Other West Indian poets have brought local dialect and Biblical lit-
urgy even closer together by translating passages directly into local
languages, and by locating—or perhaps dislocating—the biblical experience in words and images that are distinctly West Indian. Mervyn
Morris wrote a sequence entitled "On Holy Week," consisting of med-

itative poems on "people living through the Crucifixion." The voices
of the poems are presented as the voices of these people, even though
many of them speak formally in language close to the conventions of
Biblical witnessing. But in one sequence the two criminals who were
crucified with Christ address Him in the language of the Jamaican
streets. First, the passage in the King James version:

> And one of the malefactors which were hanged railed on him,
> saying, If thou be Christ, save thyself and us.
> But the other answering rebuked him, saying, Dost not thou fear
> God, seeing thou art in the same condemnation?
> And we indeed justly; for we receive the due reward of our
> deeds, but this man hath done nothing amiss.
> And then he said unto Jesus, Lord, remember me when thou
> comest into thy kingdom. (St. Luke 23: 39–42)

Morris presents the scene in this way:

> Malefactor (Left)
>
> So you is God?
> Den teck wi down! Tiefin doan bad
> like crucifyin!
> Wha do you, man?
> Save all a wi from dyin!
>
> Malefactor (Right)
>
> Doan bodder widdim, Master; him
> must die;
> but when you kingdom come, remember I.
> When you sail across de sea,
> O God of Judah, carry I wit dee.[57]

The voices here are those of Caribbean rather than Mediterranean
criminals, speaking of Caribbean desperations and dreams. The experience conveyed is continuous with that of the biblical characters. But
it is different, as the language is, and the difference illuminates some
things about the story itself, about being West Indian, and about being
West Indian in the 1970s when Morris wrote these poems.

In a poem called "Sam Lord," Kamau Brathwaite draws on yet
another relationship to the Bible, interspersing local—and to local people, familiar—references to Barbadian past and present life and religious experience with the language—and the different familiarity—of
the Twenty-third Psalm. The poem generates a dialogue between the
conventions of spoken and written languages, and between the artifice

of the form (exaggerated in the innovation of words like "eyevil") and the naturalness of the places and things named in the poem. This dialogue, closely resembling a call-and-response, is also between context and meaning, defining a new boundary of West Indian literary possibilities.

This poem is in a book called *Mother Poem*, about Brathwaite's native island of Barbados—"most English of West Indian islands" as he puts it, "but at the same time nearest, as the slaves fly, to Africa." The place names in the poem—Green Pond, Constitution River, Glitter Bay, Ragged Point, Oistin Town—locate the experience in Barbados. And so do the black belly sheep and the spiders, the gullyroot, limegrove, lignum vitae, breadnut, plantain, grapefruit and slave song, as well as the "bell, book and candle" of Bajan ritual, and vèvè—signs made on the floor of a place of worship to welcome the spirits. The title "Sam Lord," however, refers not to a person with any spiritual association but to an English pirate who went by that name and who enticed ships onto the reefs on the south east coast of the island by putting lanterns in the coconut trees. The "castle" he built there is now a well-known tourist resort, which may be for many readers, along with the language of the Twenty-third Psalm itself, the most familiar part of the poem.

> The lord is my shepherd
> he created my black belly sheep
>
> he maketh me to lie down in green pastures
> where the spiders sleep
>
> he leadeth me beside the still waters
> lakes, green pond, constitution river, glitter bay
>
> he leadeth me in the paths of righteousness for his name's sake
> though i am dry as a cracked sculptor's mould
>
> he restoreth my soul
>
> yea, though i walk through the valley of the shadow of death
> gullyroot, limegrove, lignum vitae
>
> i will fear no eyevil: for thou are with me
>
> ragged point at dream's morning
> oistin town dripping to dust
>
> thy rod and thy staff they comfort me
> thou preparest a table before me in the presence of mine enemies

candle, book of confectionary that i will proudly bear
bell that i will break and pour its sound in the vèvè

breadnut: casket of my mother
plaintain, mortar, slave song

and the grapefruit which is life which is love
which is death which is resurrection

skin of fire, pith of innocent air
pulp of flesh of freshest clear: gold volcano seed of earth

thou annointest my head with oil
halleluja

thy rod and thy staff no longer assault me
my cup of hands runneth over

surely goodness and mercy
francina and faith

shall follow me all the days of my life
and I will dwell in the house of the merchant for never[58]

Brathwaite is writing about how Barbados has been turned into a place owned by someone else, just as the blacks of the island were originally someone else's property. The collection of poems of which it is part goes a long way toward answering his own question—"where then is the nigger's home?" The answer is "here"; but this answer immediately raises another question—how can West Indians ensure that they do not lose their place again, and so lose themselves? Many of these poems are about this grim possibility. Taking the West Indies from the old-world powers only to turn it over to the new-world tourists and bankers is clearly not much of an improvement.

The ways in which West Indian poets have incorporated the authority of the Bible into their work illustrates how they have resisted the alternatives of being either fully assimilated with offshore imaginative power or entirely separated from it—the alternatives, false and ultimately fatal, of being drowned in the sea or marooned on an island. As a final illustration of how they are avoiding this pernicious choice, shaping language that is as old as English literature into a new literary heritage that is as plain as West Indian life, here is a poem by Lorna Goodison. It is in the tradition of biblical visionary verse, but is different in its language and location. The poem is part of a series centering around the image of a haven of peace and light that Goodison calls Heartease, and this is the title of the poem. Heartease is also a place name in Jamaica; and it represents home, the beginning and the end of the West Indian voyage of discovery—of self, of society, of salvation. It all begins for Goodison with a sign, which combines ethereal pyrotechnics with down-to-earth messages about local plants (search-me-heart and sincerity grass) and things of everyday West Indian life (wash pans and drought)

> In what looked like the black-out last week
> a meteorite burst from the breast of the sky
> smoking like a censer, it spelled out in
> incandescent calligraphy
> a message for all who had deep eyes.

> If you did not see it, I'll tell you what
> it said:
> Cultivate the search-mi-heart and
> acres of sincerity grass and turn your
> face towards Heartease.

> Set out a wash pan and catch mercy rain
> forget bout drought, catch the mercy rain . . .[59]

After this revelation comes sleep, and a vision of extraordinary immediacy—a vision of a new West Indian reality in a new language grounded in the experience of the land and its people and heightened by the imagination of the poet and her religious sensibility. The call of Marcus Garvey to look to the condition of Babylon and thence to Africa, his call to power and a place to call home, becomes transformed in this poem into the contemporary West Indian call to burn down / chant down Babylon, or to "look to the condition of your part of this yard." The poem, with its humor and its faith, becomes part of the process of West Indian independence, personal as well as political. And the process of transforming this independence into language that is true to the West Indies is similar to the process that took place in England in the sixteenth and seventeenth centuries, when during a grim period of civil division and dispute the English language was reconstituted, the Bible translated, and a powerful literature in the image of the new nation and its people established.

The language of Goodison's poem is balanced—or more exactly, enacts a kind of conversation—between what Walcott calls dialect and ceremonial speech, and it conveys the hopes and fears that are part of the reality of the contemporary West Indies, and that ultimately become either dreams or nightmares. This, we should remember, is dangerous stuff. It is why Plato wanted poets out of the republic. As Wilde said,

"society often forgives the criminal; it never forgives the dreamer."[60]
Nor should it. Dreamers obey different laws, and they sing to change
the world. Listen to Goodison.

And who hear . . . sleep in the darkened day and
dream as them sleep, how the one whose hand draw the veil,
(for it was not a black-out) the one who fling the meteor
was in a celestial vexation
saying, Imagine, how I put you here so in this most favoured place
and look how you take it and less count it.
Look how you root up my rarest blooms,
look how you take my flower bed dem turn tombs,
look how you eye red from looking over a next one yard
from envying everything him have.

Like him concrete-stressed-cast-iron-lawn
and him man-made-robot-made-by-man-to-replace-man,
you want to know how far this thing gone?
Some calling Siberia a nice open land.
At this point it look like him was too grieved to go on
him had to drink some dew water from the throat
of a glass petalled flower.
And when his wrath was dampened he spoke again:

I have many names and one is merciful . . .
So in that name I have decided that the veil I draw
will be lifted, when you look to the condition of
your part of this yard.
When you stop drawing blood cross the promise line in the
young people's palms.
When the scribes cleanse their hands and rise to write
new psalms.
When you sight up why outta the whole human race
is you of all people I choose to dwell in this place.
So who hear send me here to tell you say
we do not know bout the intentions of a next one
but we catching mercy rain in zinc and tub pan
and in addition
to the search-mi-heart
the sincerity seeds
and the pilgrimage to Heartease
we planting some one-love

undivided everliving healing trees
and next week if you want to come, welcome
for we goin to set up again
to extend the singing rosary of our ancestors' names
till the veil is rent from the eyes of the sky
of everyone
forever and ever
illumination.

Goodison's final lines recall the ending of the Lord's Prayer—"for thine is the kingdom, the power and the glory, For ever and ever. Amen." She renews her faith in a West Indian idiom by recollecting "the singing rosary of our ancestor's names" and by the simple generosity of her welcome and her blessing to "everyone forever and ever illumination." The differences between familiarity and strangeness, artifice and naturalness, writing and speech, and between dialect and ceremonial speech, become part of the negotiation in this poem between the imagination and reality, dreaming and waking; and these differences establish the lines of the poem's allegiance to art and to life, from both of which the language draws its strength, and the poet her inspiration.

Physicists talk about light in terms of both particles and waves. We need to become comfortable with a similar set of alternatives to describe the language of West Indian poetry, for it involves both a flowing between points on a linguistic continuum and a set of interactions. Writing about what he called Goodison's "extending of linguistic possibility . . . sliding seamlessly between English and Creole, interweaving erudite literary allusion with the earthiness of traditional Jamaican speech," Edward Baugh used these images of sliding and weaving to describe how this achievement has been part of the process of "perfecting a voice at once personal and anonymous, private and public," a voice that, "personal and unmistakable as it is, is increasingly, and whether she knows it or not, the voice of a people."[61]

This is the voice to which all West Indian poets aspire—a voice uniquely their own and courting the language of their people; soaked in the salt of the sea that surrounds them; connected by the Middle Passage to their African and European inheritances, and by its language to the literary traditions in which they are becoming themselves.

Poets who show us how to see the world in images drawn from our own lives and our own language are educating our imaginations, to use a phrase of Northrop Frye's. This is what Derek Walcott and Kamau Brathwaite and Lorna Goodison and all those who are part of the flowering of contemporary West Indian imaginative expression have been doing, shaping a new literary inheritance—and a new vision of home—for all West Indians. In the next chapter we will look more closely at Walcott, Brathwaite, and Goodison.

5

"Loose now the salt cords
binding our tongues"

 "The ancient concept of the poet," recalls the American writer Adrienne Rich, "is that she is endowed to speak for those who do not have the gift of language, or to see for those who—for whatever reasons—are less conscious of what they are living through."[1]

In the West Indies over the past fifty years, a number of gifted poets have been writing and speaking forth. They have celebrated the desperations and the dreams of West Indians, bringing the legacy of the past into the light of the present and showing the way to a brighter future. As Wordsworth wrote in his sonnet "To Toussaint L'Ouverture," they have written their poems to ensure that "there's not a breathing of the common wind that will forget" the heritage of slavery and the hope of freedom which belongs to the West Indies. And they have spoken to all West Indians with consolation and courage and the self-consciousness of those whose words are acknowledged as representing something beyond their own experience, the character and purpose of their people.

Their ambitions, and their achievements, are larger than life. "To forge a poem is one thing," the Northern Irish poet Seamus Heaney once remarked, recalling words of Stephen Dedalus. "To forge the uncreated conscience of the race . . . is quite another, and places daunting pressures and responsibilities on anyone who would risk the name of poet."[2]

Poetry *is* a risky business, especially when the "conscience of the race" is not so much uncreated as bound and broken by the heritage

of slavery, and when the dominions of hope and hate divide the land.
Heaney had in mind poets whose work founds a new dominion of
possibility for their people. These are the poets who, in Lorna Goodison's words,

> Loose now
> the salt cords
> binding our tongues . . .
> Loose the long knotted hemp
> dragging the old story
> the rotted history.
> Release grace rains, shower
> and water the hope flower.[3]

These are the poets like Lorna Goodison, Edward Kamau Brathwaite,
and Derek Walcott. Except of course that there are none quite like them,
for these three poets have contributed in a special way to the collective
spirit of liberation and independence that has been a central force in
recent West Indian history, and they have done so in ways that are
unmistakably individual.

Walcott and Brathwaite have been prominent both in the West Indies
and abroad in other English-speaking countries. Walcott's reputation,
especially since he received the Nobel Prize for Literature in 1992, is
established across a wide readership in North America, while Brathwaite is well known in the black communities in the United States,
England, and across the English-speaking Commonwealth. Both were
born in 1930, and are of the generation of West Indians who began
writing in the 1940s and 1950s in a period when imitation of imperial
standards was slowly but surely being replaced by local ideals—in education, politics, poetry. It was a time of struggle and determination,
represented in a comment made in 1939 by the Jamaican political leader
Norman Manley that "we can take everything that English education
has to offer us, but ultimately we must reject the domination of her
influence, because we are not English and nor should we ever want to
be. Instead we must dig deep into our own consciousness."[4]

Walcott and Brathwaite come from different islands in the Caribbean, with different histories and different forms of the English language in common use. And they have different visions of the future.
But they share a sense of the connection between the opposing elements
of their heritage—African and European, slavery and freedom, venerable traditions of literary expression and their unique individual talents. Their work has often been contrasted, with Brathwaite described
as representing a radical break from the conventions of European lit-

erature by a return to his African inheritance and its translation over the past five hundred years into the traditions of the West Indian diaspora, while Walcott is said to embody a more conservative acceptance of the possibilities—perhaps indeed the inevitabilities—of his European literary inheritance, along with a deep suspicion of African nostalgia. This opposition between Walcott and Brathwaite has generated considerable melodramatic interest, and it has skewed discussion of each. In fact, both of them are much more complex than these stereotypes would suggest, and both display an intricate and often inconsistent interaction of European and African traditions in their poetry. Walcott does seem more troubled by the determinisms of race and history than by those of literature, while for Brathwaite the opposite seems true. And Brathwaite's work tends to emphasize the possibilities of oral expression, while Walcott's appears to be more committed to the written text. But saying that turns out to be little help when aproaching Brathwaite's *X/Self*, which is intimately involved with written languages, or Walcott's *Omeros*, a poem whose Homeric models have a central place within an oral tradition. Questing and questioning are central to both, and best exemplify their relationship to the inheritances they share.

Goodison is younger than Walcott and Brathwaite, and she has inherited from them a confidence in the possibilities of West Indian poetry. She draws on both African and European inheritances with an imaginative assurance that Brathwaite and Walcott have never had, though it is part of their legacy to her, and part of the legacy of the 1960s in which she began writing. Like Walcott and Brathwaite though, Goodison is one of Adrienne Rich's witnesses, endowed to speak for those who do not have the gift of language and to see for those who are less conscious of what they are living through, a voice of hope and healing. And they each, in company to be sure with many other West Indians, write in what Heaney once called "a language imbued with the climate and love and history of the place," a language celebrating "a marriage between the geographical country and the country of the mind."[5]

Derek Walcott was born in St. Lucia in 1930. His father, who died when he was only a year old, was a civil servant; and his mother was a highly respected primary school teacher. Though certainly not wealthy, the family was part of the middle-class establishment of the island, and so Walcott grew up as a member of what he once called that "high-brown bourgeosie," distanced both from the poor black majority of rural and urban workers, and from the rich white landowners. Furthermore, he was caught in the complicated dynamics of race and class and gender that characterize the West Indies. His grandfathers were from Europe and were well-to-do; his grandmothers were poor and of African heritage.[6]

St. Lucia is mainly Catholic, and Walcott was educated at the Catholic St. Mary's College, though he himself was Protestant. This mixed inheritance gave him a love of the ceremonial language and power of Catholic ritual and of the simple passion of Methodist praise, especially its plain-spoken hymns. Perhaps because an Irish order of priests ran St. Mary's College during his senior years there, Walcott developed a strong sense of the parallels between his country and Ireland, or at least the Ireland of Yeats and Joyce. Recently, this has been brought up to date and reinforced by Walcott's association with Heaney, both of them for the past while living half the year in Boston, both caught in an endless struggle between what Heaney once called "territorial piety and imperial power,"[7] both of them poets of extraordinary talents.

In 1948, a fire swept through Castries, the main town in St. Lucia, destroying most of the heritage of architecture and order that had been built up over centuries of imperial rule, and with it many of the images of that legacy. There was exhilaration in the event, a burning down of Babylon and what Walcott called (in his poem "A City's Death by Fire") a "baptism by fire."[8] But the fire also left Walcott feeling strangely homeless, even though he lived in the part of town that survived. The British Colonial Development and Welfare Organisation, which had come to help with the rebuilding of Castries, awarded him a scholarship; and in 1950 Walcott left to go to the University College of the West Indies in Kingston, Jamaica. He has returned to St. Lucia often, but not to settle, though he now has plans to build a home there once again.

The University College of the West Indies had been established only two years before Walcott's arrival, first of all with a Faculty of Medicine. Walcott was part of the first class in the Faculty of Arts, in which as he later described it "there was a terrific bunch of people from all over the Caribbean, which was a great experience, because I had virtually known only St. Lucia, although I had been to Barbados once or twice. So meeting people from Trinidad, and Jamaicans and so on, was really exciting."[9] Part of this excitement was a sense of the place of the West Indian arts—theatre, music, and painting as well as poetry and fiction—in the development of a new West Indian consciousness, and a sense that the emerging independence of the region was imaginative as well as political.

Walcott and others on the campus at Mona in the early 1950s faced a cultural ideology still firmly attached to European ideals. Rex Nettleford, who was cofounder of the National Dance Theatre Company of Jamaica and has been a cultural leader of exceptional importance over the past forty years, once described his own performance while a youngster at the first Secondary Schools Drama Festival in Jamaica in 1950 as an illustration of this colonial condition. The program consisted, in Nettleford's words, of "excerpts from Shakespearean plays coached and adjudicated by an English actor-director lent by the British Council, whose objective was to transmit British culture."[10] Even Walcott himself had said in the late 1940s that there was no West Indian literature. He and his generation were about to change that.

By the time he went to Jamaica at the age of twenty, Walcott had had a precocious start. He had published two volumes of verse privately, *25 Poems* (1948, in Trinidad; and in Barbados in 1949) and *Epitaph for the Young* (1949). He had held an exhibition of his paintings with his friend the St. Lucian painter Dunstan St. Omer. He had begun the playwriting for which he is almost as well known as he is for his poetry. And he had already directed a production in St. Lucia of his play *Henri Christophe*, about one of the leaders of the Haitian revolution.

Walcott has written well over two dozen plays since then. From the beginning, he incorporated a rich mixture of local folkore, fabulous adventure, and the lives of the poor and dispossessed people of the islands. His subjects and his style were local, but in somewhat the same way Shakespeare's were. For Walcott's ambitions were to combine experiences of West Indian life with possibilities of dramatic expression that were part of a theater tradition going well beyond the Caribbean, and that came to him from Europe and Asia and Africa as well as from Central and South America.

Walcott stayed in the West Indies after he finished university, at a time in the mid-1950s when many of his friends and fellow writers and artists were going abroad to study or live. In 1959, he founded the Trinidad Theatre Workshop, which he directed until 1977. With its powerful sense of collective enterprise providing a source of inspiration and innovation, and its mix of people from across the West Indies bringing a wide range of experiences and traditions together, the Workshop was for Walcott something much more than an experiment in theatrical conventions. It was an attempt to determine the possibilities for cultural expression in the changing times that accompanied the politics of West Indian federation and independence, and to develop new relationships between economic power and social vision by bringing the sometimes desperate realities of Caribbean life into communion with the dreams of Caribbean art.

During this period, Walcott wrote plays for performance in England, Canada, and the United States, as well as in the West Indies. These included *Ti-Jean and His Brothers*, first performed in 1958 at the Little Carib Theatre in Port of Spain, Trinidad, and later at the New York Shakespeare Festival; *Dream on Monkey Mountain*, which was first performed in Toronto in 1967; and an adaption of Tirso de Molina's seventeenth-century play *El Burlador de Sevilla* (which introduced Don Juan to European literature) called *The Joker of Seville*, which was commissioned by the Royal Shakespeare Company in the early 1970s but because of drastic budget cuts in England during that period not performed there. Its first production was in Trinidad in 1974.[11] In 1992, his version of the *Odyssey* was performed by the Royal Shakespeare Company at Stratford.

Playwrights work within a different set of conventions than poets with regard to naturalness and artifice. They draw on the language of speech more directly, though they, too, depend on other forms of language. Walcott worried about the temptation to take language straight from the streets, and merely by framing it with the artifices of the theater to produce nothing more than indulgent novelties or nostalgic entertainments. He was also well aware of how appealing it could be to use the unfamiliarity of local language as colonial polemic. Along with many artists, he was caught by the determinisms of both local circumstances and literary conventions, with engagement or disengagement representing false choices.

Like any committed writer, Walcott wanted to have it both ways, or all ways; and he tried to shape a language that would seem both grounded and heightened. This, for Walcott, was what it meant to forge the uncreated conscience of his people. It was also extraordinarily difficult, as he recounted in an essay called "What the Twilight Says: An Overture," which he wrote as an introduction to a collection of his plays.

> One walks past the gilded hallucinations of poverty with a corrupt resignation touched by details, as if the destitute, in their orange-tinted backyards, under their dusty trees, or climbing to their favelas, were all natural scene-designers and poverty were not a condition but an art. Deprivation is made lyrical, and twilight, with the patience of alchemy, almost transmutes despair into virtue. In the tropics nothing is lovelier than the allotments of the poor, no theatre is as vivid, voluble and cheap.
>
> Years ago, watching them, and suffering as you watched, you proffered silently the charity of a language which they could not speak, until

your suffering, like the language, felt superior, estranged. The dusk was a raucous chaos of curses, gossip and laughter; everything performed in public, but the voice of the inner language was reflective and mannered, as far above its subjects as that sun which would never set until its twilight became a metaphor for the withdrawal of Empire and the beginning of our doubt.

Colonials, we began with this malarial ennervation: that nothing could ever be built among these rotting shacks, barefooted backyards and moulting shingles; that being poor, we already had the theatre of our lives. So the self-inflicted role of martyr came naturally, the melodramatic belief that one was message-bearer for the millennium, that the inflamed ego was enacting their will. In that simple schizophrenic boyhood one could lead two lives: the interior life of poetry, the outward life of action and dialect.[12]

Walcott once said that his "sign was Janus. I saw with twin heads, and everything I say is contradicted."[13] (Janus guarded the gates of heaven in Roman mythology. He was the god of doorways and had two heads to look both ways at once). On another occasion, Walcott recalled how "my generation had looked at life with black skins and blue eyes."[14] He spoke of himself (in his poem "A Far Cry from Africa") as divided to the vein. The notion of a divided self haunted him. In an article written in 1963, he tried to come to terms with this in yet another way, suggesting that "schizoids, in a perverse way, have more personality than the 'normal' person, and it is this conflict of our racial psyche that by irritation and a sense of loss continues to create artists, "most of whom have chosen exile. More than Ireland even, we are deprived of what we cannot remember, of what, when we visit its origins never existed the way we imagined, or where we remain strangers, contemptible cousins, the children of indentured servants and of slaves."[15]

But Walcott turned this disability to his advantage, first of all by going back to what he sensed as the sources of poetic inspiration and redefining the split between the old world and the new, or between outsider and insider, in terms of a poet's necessarily ambivalent desires to make something new and to imitate the old. The contradictions that informed poetry were to Walcott an image of the conflicts that shaped his life, representing the dynamics of difference, strangeness, otherness, artifice, alienation—sometimes debilitating, sometimes empowering.

For Walcott, these defined the condition of the poet, a condition of detachment from reality and dedication to the imagination, with all the ironies and contingencies this involved. As he proposed in an interview with Edward Baugh, the life of the poet begins with imitation. "I think a young person who wants to be a poet, is not excited by his own imagination; he is excited by imitation. That person is excited by the fact that he would like to write with all the discipline and precision of masters, of whatever nationality or epoch, and the warning is to avoid the fact that, because you are a young Jamaican writer, or you are a young Trinidadian writer, you have already been given certain melodramatic privileges. You know, the melodramatic privilege of colour, because the black man is persecuted in the world."[16] In his essay "The Muse of History," Walcott describes how he knew from childhood that he wanted to be a poet, and

> like any colonial child I was taught English literature as my natural inheritance. Forget the snow and the daffodils. They were real, more real than the heat and the oleander, perhaps, because they lived on the page, in imagination, and therefore in memory. There is a memory of imagination in literature which has nothing to do with actual experience, which is, in fact, another life, and that experience of the imagination will continue to make actual the quest of a medieval knight or the bulk of a white whale, because of the power of a shared imagination.[17]

It is this power of a shared imagination—shared with other writers, and with other peoples, and with all West Indians—which has been the legacy of Walcott and Brathwaite and Goodison, and of the others who have been writing West Indian poetry and fiction and history and criticism since the 1940s. It is in this first of all, this forging of a shared imagination, that they have been giving shape and voice to the conscience of their people. In the same way, this was the central achievement of the American writers Whitman and Melville and Hawthorn and Emerson and Thoreau for the United States a century earlier. This is the power that literature provides, educating the imagination through language; and the experience of this shared imagination is what Walcott calls "another life," a life realized through the craft of the writer. The challenge has been to make this a West Indian life, realized by the imaginations of West Indian writers.

In his essay "The Decay of Lying," Oscar Wilde talked about the sense in which we see reality in ways that are determined by our imagination, especially the imaginative representations of art. And he offered characteristically outrageous proof.

> Where, if not from the Impressionists, do we get those wonderful brown fogs that come creeping down our streets, blurring the gas-lamps and changing the houses into monstrous shadows? ... The extraordinary change that has taken place in the climate of London during the last ten years is entirely due to a particular school of Art ... Things are because we see them, and what we see, and how we see it, depends on the arts that have influenced us. To look at a thing is very different from seeing

a thing. One does not see anything until one sees its beauty. Then, and only then, does it come into existence. At present, people see fogs, not because there are fogs, but because poets and painters have taught them the mysterious loveliness of such effects. There may have been fogs for centuries in London. I dare say there were. But no one saw them, and so we do not know anything about them. They did not exist until art had invented them. Now, it must be admitted fogs are carried to excess. They have become the mere mannerism of a clique, and the exaggerated realism of their method gives dull people bronchitis. Where the cultured catch an effect, the uncultured catch cold.[18]

With all the wit, there was wisdom in the argument that Wilde was developing. It has influenced virtually all discussion about the determining power of visual and verbal representation in the century since. It is where we began, with our discussion of the inventions of discovery in the new world, and the power of stereotypes. And it has a special significance here, for its best-known statement, Wilde's famous aphorism "Life imitates Art," was one that Derek Walcott's friend and mentor Harold Simmons used to quote often; and when Walcott heard of Simmons's death in 1966, in the midst of writing the prose draft that eventually became his long autobiographical poem *Another Life*, he recalled this line.

Simmons had been extraordinarily important to Walcott, like another father to him—teaching him to paint, encouraging him to write, and instilling in him a deep affection for their land and its people. As Walcott tried to pay tribute in his notebook to Simmons, prose failed him; and only the artifice of poetry provided an adequate expression for his natural feelings of grief and loss and confusion (for Simmons had committed suicide). Walcott never went back to prose to tell the story that became *Another Life*. And as an epigraph to the first section of the poem, he quoted a passage from André Malraux's *Psychology of Art* (which he had found in Stuart Gilbert's book *James Joyce's Ulysses*): "An old story goes that Cimabue was struck with admiration when he saw the shepherd boy, Giotto, sketching sheep. But, according to the true biographies, it is never the sheep that inspire a Giotto with the love of painting: but, rather, his first sight of the paintings of such a man as Cimabue. What makes the artist is the circumstance that in his youth he was more deeply moved by the sight of works of art than by that of the things which they portray."[19]

Literature as "another life" fascinated Walcott from his early days as a writer. In 1965, he began to write the account of his life that he later turned into *Another Life* (1973). In his prose notes, Walcott recalled two paintings that were reproduced in his primary school reader, and that terrified him. One was of a despairing figure of Hope, by the nine-teenth-century painter G. F. Watt; the other was a painting of Robinson Crusoe.[20] He brought these images together in "Crusoe's Journal," a poem about how to make the imagination more powerful than reality, and how to make something out of nothing. The poem begins with an account of the poet's craft, which is likened both to Crusoe's carpentry and to Biblical creation, and it continues with a description of how creators must first master the art of mimicry, including the God-like art of making something in one's own image.

> Once we have driven past Mundo Nuevo trace
>   safely to this beach house
> perched between ocean and green, churning forest
>   the intellect appraises
> objects surely, even the bare necessities
>   of style are turned to use,
> like those plain iron tools he salvages
>   from shipwreck, hewing a prose
> as odorous as raw wood to the adze,
>   out of such timbers
> came our first book, our profane Genesis
>   whose Adam speaks that prose
> which, blessing some sea-rock, startles itself
>   with poetry's surprise,
> in a green world, one without metaphors;
>   like Christofer he bears
> in speech mnemonic as a missionary's
>   the Word to savages,
> its shape an earthen, water-bearing vessel's
>   whose sprinkling alters us
> into good Fridays who recite His praise,
>   parroting our master's
> style and voice, we make his language ours,
>   converted cannibals
> we learn with him to eat the flesh of Christ.[21]

The beach house "perched between ocean and green, churning forest" is an image for the poem itself, a lyric of the seashore that maps out the territory between all the categories we have conjured with—the natural and the artificial, familiarity and strangeness (including ordi-nary and poetic language), the oral and the written, beginnings and ends, the profane and the sacred, death and life, Them and Us. This is the territory of "poetry's surprise," where words and the Word converge in a language that has recovered its original power of naming, as well as its conflation of sound and sense (in puns and rhymes and rituals). It is a place of translation, conversion, mimicry: the parrot represents not only the archetype of imitation and the dynamics of European invention in the new world beginning with Columbus ("I saw no beast of any kind in this island, except parrots," he said on his arrival),[22] but also Walcott's native St. Lucia (of which it is the national emblem). And the "master's style and voice" recall both the reproductions of RCA Victor and those of the Church victorious.

Having outlined the ironies of both colonial imitation and imperial mastery, Walcott turns to the task of creating a shared imagination for those stranded on their West Indian islands, and of celebrating the hope-in-despair that this everyday imagination offers.

> So from this house
> that faces nothing but the sea, his journals
> assume a household use;
> we learn to shape from them, where nothing was
> the language of a race. [23]

The "nothing" here, of course, is Naipaul's, transformed into the instrument of character and purpose for the West Indies. Walcott has not shied away from the despair that it expresses. (Indeed, a few years later he considered using an epigraph from *The Middle Passage* for *Another Life*.)[24] But for Walcott, the power of difference itself provides some defense against the impoverishments of isolation and some check against the relativities of linguistic and literary traditions by generating the wonder of strangeness and surprise. Although deeply suspicious of easy answers, Walcott sees possibilities for hope in the acknowledgement of a distinct, albeit psychologically difficult, imaginative heritage shared by all West Indians, "another life," which is also a West Indian life. In "What the Twilight Says'," he recalls its legacy.

> We were all strangers here. The claim which we put forward now as Africans is not our inheritance, but a bequest, like that of other races, a bill for the condition of our arrival as slaves. Our own ancestors shared that complicity, and there is no one left on whom we can extract revenge. That is the laceration of our shame. Nor is the land automatically ours because we were made to work it. We have no more proprietorship as a race than have the indentured workers from Asia except the claim is wholly made. By all the races as one race, because the soil was stranger under our own feet than under those of our captors. Before us they knew the names of the forest and the changes of the sea, and theirs were the names we used. We begin again, with the vigour of a curiosity that gave

the old names life, that charged an old language, from the depth of suffering, with awe. To the writers of my generation, then, the word, and
the ritual of the word in print, contained this awe.[25]

Putting revenge aside leaves room for something else, the wonder
of a new way of seeing the new world. And a new way of naming it,
if only to move beyond what Brathwaite once called the "just plain low
down ingorance of not knowing the names of our flowers and trees
and villages and birds and calling them *dat*." Slavery was a nameless
anonymous condition; but it was also the classical pantheon that sur-
vives in the names given to slaves by their masters. In "Names," a
poem dedicated to Brathwaite, Walcott brings us back to the power of
European imperial discovery and invention in the West Indies, shaping
the new world in the image of the old; and to the power of West Indian
poetry to rediscover and reinvent and repossess that world, a world in
which people see things and say things differently . . . with a different
fix on the stars.

> My race began as the sea began,
> with no nouns, and with no horizon,
> with pebbles under my tongue,
> with a different fix on the stars . . .
>
> Have we melted into a mirror,
> leaving our souls behind?
> The goldsmith from Benares,
> the stone-cutter from Canton,
> the bronzesmith from Benin.
>
> A sea-eagle screams from the rock,
> and my race began like the osprey
> with that cry,
> that terrible vowel,
> that I!
>
> Behind us all the sky folded,
> as history folds over a fishline,
> and the foam foreclosed
> with nothing in our hands
>
> but this stick
> to trace our names on the sand
> which the sea erased again, to our indifference.[26]

This poem is about differences and indifferences; about boundaries—
the horizon and the shore and the lines between past and present, here

and hereafter, silence and sound; about mirrorings and makings; and about languages, especially different languages (signaled here in terms of differences between subject and object, singular and plural, vowels and consonants, verbs and nouns) which are the product of environment as much as heredity, and which determine differences in ideas of space and time and matter. Running through all this is the same brutal legacy of the passage across the sea from Africa to the Caribbean that obliterated names and history.

In a poem called "Air," Walcott uses as his epigraph Froude's by now infamous dismissal of the West Indies (which of course was also Naipaul's epigraph to *The Middle Passage*)—"there are no people there in the true sense of the word, with a character and purpose of their own"; and he sets it against the awesome power of the natural world to which the early migrants came from Europe and Africa. The artifice of "discovery"—of civil and religious orderings and European vanity—is overwhelmed by an undiscriminating natural violence of which it is a kind of mirror. The boundaries implied by language and memory and faith are obliterated; and what remains is a silence, a vacancy, an absence. But that, it turns out, is something.

> The unheard, omnivorous
> jaws of this rain forest
> not merely devour all,
> but allow nothing vain;
> they never rest,
> grinding their disavowal
> of human pain.
>
> Long, long before us,
> those hot jaws like an oven
> steaming, were open
> to genocide; they devoured
> two minor yellow races and
> half of a black;
> in the word made flesh of God
> all entered that gross un-
> discriminating stomach;
>
> the forest is unconverted,
> because that shell-like noise
> which roars like silence, or
> ocean's surpliced choirs
> entering its nave, to a censer

of swung mist, is not
the rustling of prayer
but nothing; milling air,
a faith, infested, cannibal,
which eats gods, which devoured
the god-refusing Carib, petal
by golden petal, then forgot,
and the Arawak
who leaves not the lightest fern-trace
of his fossil to be cultured
by black rock,

but only the rusting cries
of a rainbird, like a hoarse
warrior summoning his race
from vaporous air
between this mountain ridge
and the vague sea
where the lost exodus
of corials sunk without trace—

There is too much nothing here.[27]

This "too much nothing," as Walcott said elsewhere, is "like nothing
one has ever seen before." Which is to say, something different. And
making strange precedes making sense in this account of recognizing
difference, beginning with the difference of living in a language that
incorporates this nothingness. The nothingness of being a nigger, a
nobody, living nowhere. When he was asked by Aunt Sally whether
anybody had been hurt by the explosion on the Mississippi river boat,
Huck Finn replied "No. Killed a nigger." "Well, it's lucky," said Aunt
Sally, "because sometimes people do get hurt."[28] As Shabine says in
"The Schooner *Flight*," "we live like our names and you would have
/ to be colonial to know the difference, / to know the pain of history
words contain."[29]

The difference that preoccupies Walcott in his poetry is ultimately
the legacy of slavery, but he celebrates it not in a long lamentation but
in a continuing affirmation of the possibilities for transforming cycles
of suffering into moments of wonder and surprise. This is from "The
Muse as History."

I say to the ancestor who sold me, and to the ancestor who bought me I
have no father, I want no such father, although I can understand you,
black ghost, white ghost, when you both whisper "history," for if I

attempt to forgive you both I am falling into your idea of history which justifies and explains and expiates, and it is not mine to forgive, my memory cannot summon any filial love, since your features are anonymous and erased and I have no wish and no power to pardon. You were when you acted your roles, your given, historical roles of slave seller and slave buyer, men acting as men, and also you, father in the filth-ridden gut of the slave ship, to you they were also men, acting as men, with the cruelty of men, your fellowman and tribesman not moved or hovering with hesitation about your common race any longer than my other bastard ancestor hovered with his whip, but to you, inwardly forgiven grandfathers, I, like the more honest of my race, give a strange thanks. I give the strange and bitter and yet ennobling thanks for the monumental groaning and soldering of two great worlds, like the halves of a fruit seamed by its own bitter juice, that exiled from your own Edens you have placed me in the wonder of another, and that was my inheritance and your gift.[30]

The "strange and bitter and yet ennobling thanks" that Walcott offers is for the heritage of what Eric Roach called "the archipelago hope would mold into dominion . . . (where) economies of hate are soldered with my sweat / Here, everywhere; in hate's dominion." And he shares Roach's sense of the hazards of being preoccupied with this heritage. As the Guyanese poet, novelist, and critic Wilson Harris put it in a lecture on "History, Fable and Myth in the Caribbean and Guianas," "Caribbean man is involved in a civilization-making process (whether he likes it or not), and until this creative authority becomes intimate to his perspective, he will continue to find himself embalmed in his deprivations."[31]

Walcott's poetry draws much of its energy from his uneasiness, his unrest, the hovering and hesitation that he characterizes as the stance of the poet—a detachment from the natural (men acting as men—though there is ambiguity in the word *acting*) and an acceptance of the artifice of another life, another way of seeing the world, a new frame for the familiar. His unease derives partly from his recognition of the ambivalences that define his being, not simply racial and historical but more profoundly imaginative, with allegiances both to piety and power, to the old world and the new, to the condition of insider and outsider, to the particular and the universal, to the world as it is and the world as it might be. But partly also Walcott's unease comes from a deeper contradiction. "Where then is the nigger's home?" asks Brathwaite. Like Odysseus, Walcott might answer—it is where I am going, which is where once I came from; but it is also where I am, for I am a wanderer, and have been one from the start. My cunning and good humor mask a sorrow that I must name; and then I will find peace.

Perhaps. Toward the end of Walcott's epic *Omeros*, a blind old man called Seven Seas, whose "words were not clear. They were Greek . . . or old African babble," discusses how

> there are two journeys
> in every odyssey, one on worried water,
>
> the other crouched and motionless, without noise.
> For both, the "I" is a mast; a desk is a raft
> for one, foaming with paper, and dipping the beak
>
> of a pen in its foam, while an actual craft
> carries the other to cities where people speak
> a different language, or look at him differently,
>
> while the sun rises from the other direction
> with its unsettling shadows, but the right journey
> is motionless; as the sea moves round an island
>
> that appears to be moving, love moves round the heart—
> with encircling salt, and the slowly travelling hand
> knows it returns to the port from which it must start.[32]

The uncertainties of origin and purpose that preoccupy Walcott are shared by many poets, ancient and modern; but the American writer W. S. Merwin is one contemporary of Walcott's who has written of them with the same instinct for the ambivalences of turning away and returning home, and for the ever-present ironies of betrayal. His poem "Odysseus" catches the spirit of Walcott's work.

> Always the setting forth was the same,
> Same sea, same dangers waiting for him
> As though he had got nowhere but older.
> Behind him on the receding shore
> The identical reproaches, and somewhere
> Out before him, the unravelling patience
> He was wedded to. There were the islands
> Each with its woman and twining welcome
> To be navigated, and one to call "home."
> The knowledge of all that he betrayed
> Grew till it was the same whether he stayed
> Or went. Therefore he went. And what wonder
> If sometimes he could not remember
> Which was the one who wished on his departure
> Perils that he could never sail through,

> And which, impossible, remote, and true,
> Was the one he kept sailing home to?[33]

Always the setting forth was the same, just like the arrival. Particulars and universals. The dichotomy of space—the point (of departure and return) and the line (traveled)—is caught here; and the dichotomy of time—as a linear succession of unrepeatable events (for which the flow of the river is a common image), and as the cyclical agency of fundamental and continuing states (the turn of the day, the cycles of the moon, the corn festival and Yom Kippur and Christmas and so forth). Only by bringing these two notions together, as we do in all those moments when things seem both brand new and old as the hills—the birth of a child, say, or reading a great book, or writing a poem, or falling in love—do we realize how intimately they are related to our ways of organizing all our other thoughts and feelings about our world, and about ourselves. And the venerable dichotomy between time's arrow and time's cycle,[34] which generates two concepts of history, in turn generates correspondences both *within* lineages (deriving from some common ancestry) and *across* lineages, correspondences of form and function. For Walcott, these are all interwoven, like another essential dichotomy—the mechanism of origins and sequences and the teleology of purposes and patterns. Or perhaps woven and *un*woven, like Penelope's web ... stitched and unstitched, as Walcott renders it in describing the swift that migrates between Africa and the Americas in *Omeros*—a figure for the story he tells, and for the conscience of his race. Here is Walcott's version of this intricate and perpetually incomplete design from his poem "Sea Grapes," where he traces the borderline between sea and land, ancient and modern, love and war, homeland and frontier, obsession and responsibility.

> That sail which leans on light
> tired of islands,
> a schooner beating up the Caribbean
>
> for home, could be Odysseus,
> home-bound on the Aegean;
> that father and husband's
>
> longing, under gnarled sour grapes, is
> like the adulterer hearing Nausicaa's name
> in every gull's outcry.
>
> This brings nobody peace. The ancient war
> between obsession and responsibility
> will never finish and has been the same

for the sea-wanderer or the one on shore
now wriggling on his sandals to walk home,
since Troy sighed its last flame,

and the blind giant's boulder heaved the trough
from whose ground-swell the great hexameters come
to the conclusions of exhausted surf.

The classics can console. But not enough.[35]

What *is* enough is compassion. This never comes easily. And one of Walcott's great achievements is the way he bears witness to its difficulty, especially for a West Indian whose heritage is slavery—as in his early poem "Ruins of a Great House":

Ablaze with rage I thought,
Some slave is rotting in this manorial lake,
But still the coal of my compassion fought:
That Albion too, was once
A colony like ours[36]

At the end of "The Schooner *Flight*," through Shabine, Walcott voices his ultimate conviction.

Though my *Flight* never pass the incoming tide
of this inland sea beyond the loud reefs
of the final Bahamas, I am satisfied
if my hand gave voice to one people's grief.
Open the map. More islands there, man,
than peas on a tin plate, all different size,
one thousand in the Bahamas alone,
from mountains to low scrub with coral keys,
and from this bowsprit, I bless every town,
the blue smell of smoke in hills behind them,
and the one small road winding down them like twine
to the roofs below; I have only one theme:

The bowsprit, the arrow, the longing, the lunging heart—
the flight to a target whose aim we'll never know,
vain search for one island that heals with its harbor
and a guiltless horizon, where the almond's shadow
doesn't injure the sand. There are so many islands!
As many islands as the stars at night
on that branched tree from which meteors are shaken
like falling fruit around the schooner *Flight*.

But things must fall, and so it always was,
on the one hand Venus, on the other Mars;
fall, and are one, just as this earth is one
island in archipelagoes of stars.
My first friend was the sea. Now, is my last.
I stop talking now. I work, then I read,
cotching under a lantern hooked to the mast.
I try to forget what happiness was,
and when that don't work, I study the stars.
Sometimes is just me, and the soft-scissored foam
as the deck turn white and the moon open
a cloud like a door, and the light over me
is a road in white moonlight taking me home.
Shabine sang to you from the depths of the sea.[37]

From first to last, a vision of home, and of exile. The harbor and the horizon. The spirits of the dead—the drowned slaves of the Middle Passage—haunt the living until a requiem is sung by the duppy conquerors. But sometimes there seems only a cycle of sorrows, and a circle of sufferers. "When one grief afflicts us we choose a sharper grief / in hope that enormity will ease affliction" writes Walcott in *Omeros*, as he tells of the Ghost Dance of the plains Sioux which "tied the tribes into one nation"[38] with breathtaking gestures of faith in the spirits of their dead and in the dances and the dreams and the ghostly shirts that would save them from the horrors (and the bullets) of the enemy—until Wounded Knee, South Dakota, 1890. Walcott has written a play about the Ghost Dance, first performed at Hartwick College in upstate New York in 1989. Both *Omeros* and the play bear witness to a legacy of dreams and dispossession, of broken words and broken spirits, of the exodus of the native people of the new world—the Creek and Choctaw and the Cheyenne and the Sioux—from their homelands into diasporas in the urban and rural slums of agricultural and industrial America, and the exodus of Africans to the Americas. One of Walcott's gifts has been to confirm the enduring witness of story and song to the universal qualities of human experience, and to show its connection to the particulars of West Indian life.

Walcott has written over ten books of poems, not including volumes of selected poems and a *Collected Poems: 1948–1984*. Several of his books have been landmarks in West Indian literature. When it was published in 1962, *In a Green Night* announced Walcott as a major West Indian voice, and established West Indian poetry as a significant presence in contemporary literature. It was followed by books chronicling the ambivalence that has made his poetry so distinctive: *The Castaway* (1965), *The Gulf* (1969), *Another Life* (1973). *Sea Grapes* (1976) confirmed the place of local language in West Indian literary forms with its return to the languages of his native St. Lucia in poems such as "Sainte Lucie."

> Come back to me
> my language.
> Come back . . .
> moi c'est gens Ste. Lucie.
> C'est la moi sorti;
> is there that I born.[39]

And in *The Star-Apple Kingdom* (1979), the voice of Shabine (in the poem "The Schooner *Flight*") showed new possibilities for poetic expression that combined spoken and written language and the imaginative logic of both local and literary inheritances. Through all these years of writing, Walcott has created with diligence and grace a poetry that displays how much of its strength is drawn from the conventions of art, and he has done this as though it all came naturally.

In *The Arkansas Testament*, published in 1987, the poems are divided into two sections nicely called "Here" and "Elsewhere." The title poem is about a trip to the southern United States, and the unease its strange familiarity generated in the poet. Like Seamus Heaney, writing in a poem called "The Tollund Man" of a visit to the ancient site of ritual bog murders in Jutland, Denmark, Walcott feels "lost, unhappy, and at home"[40] in Arkansas. And like Odysseus, he is both engaged and disengaged, tied to the mast so he can listen closely to the sirens of Arkansas (as Shabine was when he sang back to the new-world casuarinas of Barbados, beguiled by their likeness to old-world cypresses). An insider—this is, after all, the history of blacks in the Americas. ("I was still nothing," he says; "this, Sir is . . . my people's predicament.") And an outsider, a traveler, just passing through.

> Hugging walls in my tippler's hop—
> the jive of shuffling bums,
> a beat that comes from the chain—
> I waited for a while by the grass
> of a urinous wall to let
> the revolving red eye on top
> of a cruising police car pass.
> In an all-night garage I saw
> the gums of a toothless sybil
> in garage tires, and she said:

STAY BLACK AND INVISIBLE
TO THE SIRENS OF ARKANSAS . . .

. . . a cafeteria
reminded me of my race.
A soak cursed his vinyl table
steadily, not looking up.
A tall black cook setting glazed
pies, a beehive-blond waitress,
lips like a burst strawberry,
and her "Mornin" like maple syrup.
Four DEERE caps talking deer hunting.
I looked for my own area.
The muttering black decanter
had all I needed; it could sigh for
Sherman's smoking march to Atlanta
or the march to Montgomery.
I was still nothing. A cipher
in its bubbling black zeros, here . . .

this, Sir, is my Office,
my Arkansas Testament,
my two cupfuls of Cowardice,
my sure, unshaven Salvation,
my people's predicament.[41]

What Walcott has been forging is not only the uncreated conscience of his people, but a language in which to put this into words—a language that he has claimed as his heritage and made his own. The extent of this achievement is such that sometimes when you read him he seems to be writing like someone else . . . and you suddenly realize that he is writing like himself . . . that he has become, in a sense, both his own father and his son.

There are risks here, to be sure, mostly of complacency. But Walcott continues to defy these by taking *new* risks and by continuing to write, to use his own phrase, in "a language that goes beyond mimicry, a dialect which has the force of revelation." In his divided consciousness we continue to sense a dream of wholeness for himself and for his people, in a place called home and in a time he wrote about in his book *The Fortunate Traveler* (1981) as "The Season of Phantasmal Peace"— where the compassion that is at the heart of his poetry generates an image of transcendence, a loophole beyond all "the betrayals of falling suns"—in that hovering moment between past and future, within the dichotomies of time and space, around the history of his people.

Then all the nations of birds lifted together
the huge net of the shadows of this earth
in multitudinous dialects, twittering tongues,
stitching and crossing it. They lifted up
the shadows of long pines down trackless slopes,
the shadows of glass-faced towers down evening streets,
the shadow of a frail plant on a city sill—
the net rising soundless as night, the birds' cries soundless, until
there was no longer dusk, or season, decline, or weather,
only this passage of phantasmal light
that not the narrowest shadow dared to sever . . .
                                            . . . it was the light
that you will see at evening on the side of a hill
in yellow October, and no one hearing knew
what change had brought into the raven's cawing,
the killdeer's screech, the ember-circling chough
such an immense, soundless, and high concern
for the fields and cities where the birds belong,
except it was their seasonal passing, Love,
made seasonless, or, from the high privilege of their birth,
something brighter than pity for the wingless ones
below them who shared dark holes in windows and in houses,
and higher they lifted the net with soundless voices
above all change, betrayals of falling suns,
and this season lasted one moment, like the pause
between dusk and darkness, between fury and peace,
but, for such as our earth is now, it lasted long.[42]

Omeros (1990) represents a new kind of achievement, for despite its affiliations with the epic it does not come out the literature and history of Europe; and despite its acceptance of the heritage of slavery it does not come out of Africa either. Rather, it emerges unmistakably from a West Indian literary tradition, one that Walcott has played a major role in shaping but that now has a broad reach and deep roots. Omeros would not be possible outside that tradition.

Set in St. Lucia—called Iounalao, "where the iguana is found," by the Arawaks—it is a story about storytelling, contemplating the relationships between individual and collective histories, invoking figures of fact and fiction, proposing rhymes and half-rhymes across centuries and oceans and peoples and verse forms, a dense weave of metaphors and metonymys . . . and puns, for like all good poems it takes pleasure in its outrageousness and it takes liberties with its readers. Omeros is underwritten by a belief in the power of the imagination, and in real continuities—between the Mediterranean and the Caribbean, between suffering then and now, between all the experiences of men and women, even those that are shadowed by stereotypes. The territory of the poem is, in Walcott's phrase, a "reversible world,"[43] with the pun on verse being one of the least ostentatious in a poem whose exhuberance is sometimes close to overwhelming. One of its most disconcerting extravagances is the number of voices and varieties of language in the poem—not untypical for Walcott, but developed with such irrepressible enthusiasm that ultimately the play becomes the thing and the parts are taken by whoever is next in line. And as so often in West Indian poetry, who is speaking is not nearly as important as who is listening.

There are links here that reinforce associations we have made already: with some of the cities of the African diaspora—London, Boston, New York, Toronto; with Ireland, not just the Ireland of Heaney and Joyce (whose Homeric epic also figures here) but of lesser-known figures too, people such as Joseph Mary Plunkett, a poet and a patriot shot for his part in the Easter Uprising in Dublin in 1916, living on as Walcott's Major Dennis Plunkett, who like one of his ancestors in the poem (a midshipman who spied in the Lowlands and served with Rodney in the Seven Years' War) is caught between two worlds—Africa and Europe, past and present, obsession and responsibility, classical and Caribbean intrigue.

Edward Kamau Brathwaite was born (like Walcott, in 1930) in Barbados. Barbados has always been one of the most English of the Caribbean islands, and Brathwaite's education was modeled very much along English lines. So were his early ambitions and those of many of his contemporaries. He grew up in a comfortably middle-class Barbadian family, and he went to Harrison College, a prestigious school with high standards and high (which was to say essentially English) expectations of its students. In 1950, Brathwaite left Barbados to go to Cambridge University in England.

After graduating, Brathwaite took stock of his situation. He was feeling much like Naipaul in *The Middle Passage*, filled with hopelessness and a sense of loss. In Brathwaite's words, "there was no going back. Accepting my rootlessness, I applied for work in London, Cambridge, Ceylon, New Delhi, Cairo, Kano, Khartoum, Sierra Leone, Carcassone, a monastery in Jerusalem. I was a West Indian, roofless man of the world. I could go, belong everywhere on the worldwide globe. I ended up in a village in Ghana. It was my beginning."[44]

In a sense, Brathwaite was born again in Africa. (Later, while there on another visit, he would accept the African name Kamau. It was given to him by the grandmother of Ngugi wa Thiong'o, a Kenyan novelist and critic whose passionate defense of his African heritage has recently taken the form of saying farewell to the English language as a vehicle for his writing.) Brathwaite served as an education officer in Ghana for eight years, coming as he described it later to an increased "awareness and understanding of community, of cultural wholeness, of the place of the individual within the tribe, in society. Slowly, slowly, ever so slowly, I came to a sense of identification of myself with these people, my living diviners. I came to connect my history with theirs, the bridge of my mind now linking Atlantic and ancestor, homeland and heartland."[45]

Brathwaite came back to the West Indies in 1962 determined to encourage a new respect for indigenous literary traditions based on African as much as European inheritances, and for local language which defied the intimidating authority of standard English. He hoped to create a new kind of commerce between what Rex Nettleford called the rhythm of Africa and the melody of Europe.[46] Brathwaite went to work at the University of the West Indies, first with the extramural department in St. Lucia and then (after completing a doctorate at the University of Sussex on the development of creole society in Jamaica) to teach history on the campus in Kingston.

His heritage of slavery provides a kind of freedom and a kind of determinism that Brathwaite accepts. Much more troubling for him is the determinism of language and the English literary tradition that he also inherits. His unease is reflected in the ways in which he disrupts its conventions, creating a pattern of interference that he has called "tidalectics, which is dialectics with my difference . . . the movement of the water backwards and forwards as a kind of cyclic motion, rather than linear."[47]

It is easy to become infatuated with dichotomies. Several of them have shaped this book, and they certainly condition some of Brathwaite's writing. But one of his contributions has been to resist the most debilitating oppositions, transcending them in ways that have much to do with the resources and possibilities (and, in fairness, with the dichotomies) of language. As a poet, he has been especially interested in words that incorporate the idea of a

> whole new reconstruction of history and possibility. I call that notion "nam" because we have to make words, create words, dream-words, vision-words which make sense to us, although these words are not in the *Concise Oxford Dictionary*. The hurricane does not howl in pentame-

ters, and experience at the crucial areas of the psyche are not to be found in Sigmund Freud. We have our own Freuds, or rather, we ought to recognize that we have them. . . .

"Nam" means so many things for me. "Nam" is "man" spelt backwards, man in disguise, man who has to reverse his consciousness . . . in order to enter the new world in a disguised or altered state of consciousness. "Nam" also suggests "root," or beginning, because of "yam," the African yam, "nyam," to eat, and the whole culture contained in it. It is then able to expand itself back from "nam" to "name," which is another form of "nam": the name that you once had has lost its "e," that fragile part of itself, eaten by Prospero, eaten by the conquistadors, but preserving its essentialness, its alpha, its "a" protected by those two intransigent consonants, "n" and "m." The vibrations "nmnmnm" are what you get before the beginning of the world. And that "nam" can return to "name" and the god "Nyame."[48]

Here is a passage from a poem titled "Nam" in *X/Self* (1987), in which some of these possibilities are presented with characteristic vulnerability. For Brathwaite is a poet who has not been afraid to display the workings of his poems, in the way architects from medieval to modern times have sometimes done with their buildings, exposing the foundations and framing and piping and wiring for all to see.

out of this dust they are coming
our eyes listen out of rhinoceros thunder
darkness of lion

the whale roar stomping in heaven
that black bellied night of hell and helleluia
when all the lights of anger flicker flicker flicker

and we know somewhere there there is real fire
basuto mokhethi namibia azania shaka the zulu kenyatta the shatt
erer the maasai wandering into the everlasting shadow of jah ...

walking back now from the shores of kikuyu water
washing back down now from swahili laughter

zimbabwi kinshasa limpopo
always limpopo the limper the healer

it comes down from the ruins of the north
from the lakes of the luo

from the sunlights and sunrise of the east

as ancient as sheba as wise as the pharoahs
as holy as the early morning mists of ityopia ...

rising

rising

rising

burning

soon

soon

soon

soweto

bongo nam a come

bongo nam a come[49]

The African heritage that Brathwaite embraced early in his career provided relief from what he described as "a famine in the soul of the West Indian artists," and a way of moving from the pathological invisibility of blacks in European eyes to a new visibility in the light of their African heritage.[50] Others have certainly shared Brathwaite's resolve. "Have we melted into a mirror, / leaving our souls behind?"[51] asks Walcott. "Loose now the salt cords binding our tongues. . . . Loose the long knotted hemp / dragging the old story, / the rotted history. / Release grace rains, shower / and water the hope flower,"[52] says Goodison. Brathwaite saw signs that West Indian artists were recovering the importance of African ceremonies and customs not out of hopeless nostalgia (though there was inevitably some of that) but with an instinct for how these might nourish the spirit of new, distinctly West Indian forms of imaginative expression, capable of representing both the different landscape and the different heritage of the West Indies, bringing together the fragments of experience into that dream of wholeness that has inspired Brathwaite and so many other West Indian writers and artists, what Walcott calls a healing "harbour and a guiltless horizon" where "the light over me is a road in white moonlight taking me home."[53]

During the 1950s, there was increased interest in cultural activity that was characteristically West Indian, with dance and theater and painting and sculpture developing across the West Indies in a wide range of local circumstances. Calypso and steel band flourished, as well as older musical forms. And distinctly West Indian traditions of religious expression received more attention and more acknowledgement as important in the lives of West Indians. Political writings of the 1930s and 1940s, including C. L. R. James's *Black Jacobins* (1938) and Eric Williams's *Capitalism and Slavery* (1944), were reinforced by a new generation's revision of colonial history in books such as Elsa Goveia's *A Study of the Historiography of the West Indies* (1956). The heritage of slavery began to shape the consciousness of the West Indies in new and liberating ways.

Brathwaite has often remarked how isolated the anglophone West Indies he grew up in was from Caribbean writing in Spanish and French. For him, it was a book by his fellow Barbadian George Lamming that made a special difference, a novel published in 1953 called *In the Castle of My Skin*. It told the story of a young boy growing up and learning about the world and the color of his skin from the perspective of "Little England," the island of Barbados. One of his friends was very black. "When you asked him why he was so black, he would answer with serious conviction: 'Just as I wus goin' to born the light went out.' Nobody could reply to that. The light, we admitted, had gone out for many of us."[54] The young boys learned in their classroom about slavery . . . or more precisely they were brainwashed into believing that it all happened

> a long, long, long time ago . . . and moreover it had nothing to do with people in Barbados. . . . They had read about the Battle of Hastings and William the Conqueror. That happened so many hundred years ago. And slavery was thousands of years before that. It was really too far back for anyone to worry about teaching it as history. That's really why it wasn't taught. It was too far back. History had to begin somewhere, but not so far back. And nobody knew where this slavery business took place. The teacher had simply said, not here, somewhere else. Probably it never happened at all. . . . It came up like a ghost and soon faded again.

But from time to time it returned to their minds and troubled their spirits. For Brathwaite, Lamming's novel brought him back home. And brought his language back. "Here breathing to me from every pore of line and page, was the Barbados I had lived," he wrote later. "The words, the rhythms, the cadences, the scenes, the people, their predicament. They all came back. They all were possible."[55]

It was this sense of possibility that was most important to Brathwaite, this indication that one could write about the West Indies in a way that was true to the place and its people. The open question was how to do so. Lamming's language of prose fiction (which Brathwaite himself had tried out) was different from the language of poetry. Walcott had mapped out a way that was true to his own sense of his West Indian heritage, insisting that his deepest poetic roots were European because his language was. Brathwaite, while acknowledging this inheritance, returned to the sources of poetry in rhythm and ritual and riddle and charm and found these not only in European literary and religious traditions but also in Atumpan drumming and kumina rituals and the material and spiritual world of African life. He also found them in the developing traditions of the West Indies. As he described it:

> Walking along the beaches of Barbados I had long wanted to write the genesis of those islands, the whole fragmentation, the beauty of it, the movement of them, the belonging and possession of them. Thomas Gray's "Elegy" didn't help. The pentameter didn't help. It was only when I discovered that the calypso (kaiso)—that syncopated traditional music of ours, which was in fact a correlation of fragmented landscapes, that ancient and new musical form which was ours—would help me as a poet to describe the landscape, it was only then that my own poetry began to move, began to take shape. Finally, I was able to describe the islands in this way.

> the stone had skidded arc'd and bloomed into islands:
> Cuba and San Domingo
> Jamaica and Puerto Rico
> Grenada Guadeloupe Bonaire

> curved stone hissed into reef
> wave teeth fanged into clay
> white splash flashed into spray
> Bathsheba Montego Bay

> bloom of the arcing summers . . .[56]

Brathwaite has been an energetic proponent of the transformation of musical expression into literary forms. For him, West Indian musical inheritance includes American jazz, with which he grew up in Barbados and which he celebrates in several poems about notable musicians such as "Basic Basie."

> Hunched, humped backed, gigantic
> the pianist presides above the
> rumpus . . .

> his big feet beat the beat until the whole joint
> rocks . . . till

> brash boogie woogie hordes come burgeoning up from hell[57]

Brathwaite drew on all these resources in the poems that eventually became his trilogy of black presence in the West Indies, *The Arrivants.* The first of the books of the trilogy, *Rights of Passage,* appeared in 1967.

It chronicled the generations from slavery to the years of desperation in the grim factories and slum cities and lonesome roads of freedom in the new world, and on to a time when the question "where then is the nigger's home?" expressed the spirit of restlessness epitomized in what Brathwaite called "the great nigration" of the 1950s, when West Indians went on the move.

Like Walcott, Brathwaite was working to exorcise the spectre of West Indian deficiency and dispossession that Naipaul had conjured up. In one poem in *Rights of Passage*, Brathwaite sings of loss in the voice of Tom, an African in the New World, "father, founder, flounderer" . . . and a sometime uncle. But for now a dreamer, defying the familiar condemnation of his people and his place ("history is built around achievement and creation; and nothing was created in the West Indies"), and instead re-creating the past in a powerful recollection of home . . . here *and* in heaven. And yet his dreaming is circumscribed by a desultory regret and an ennervating despair, exemplified in the ironic echo of Christ's invitation to "suffer the little children to come unto me."

> Drown the screams, shore
> cool the lashed sore,
> keep the dream pure
>
> for we who have achieved nothing
> work
> who have not built
> dream
> who have forgotten all
> dance
> and dare to remember
>
> the paths we shall never remember
> again: Atumpan talking and the harvest branch-
> es, all the tribes of Ashanti dreaming the dream
> of Tutu, Anokye and the Golden Stool, built
> in Heaven for our nation by the work
> of lightning and the brilliant adze: and now nothing
>
> nothing
> nothing
>
> so let me sing
> nothing
> now

> let me remember
> nothing
> now
>
> let me suffer
> nothing
> to remind me now
>
> of my lost children . . .[58]

The dream that follows is expressed in visionary eloquence, but because it reflects the speaker's hopelessness it promises nothing except sorrow. Still, it is enobled by its acknowledgement of the ambiguities of life and language, where the covenant of the rainbow represents both the promise of children and the pain of their loss, both morning and mourning.

> let my children
> rise
> in the path
> of the morning
> up and go forth
> on the road
> of the morning
> run through the fields
> in the sun
> of the morning,
> see the rainbow
> of Heaven:
> God's curved
> mourning
> calling.
>
> But help-
> less my children are
> caught leader-
> less are
> taught fool-
> ishness and use-
> lessness and
> sorrow . . .

The helplessness described here is exemplified by Brathwaite in the bitterness of new-world blacks and the stereotypes with which they live. "I am a fuckin' negro, man," says the speaker in a poem called

'Folkways' (a reference not only to folk traditions but also to Folkways Records, the much praised collecting and recording enterprise of Moses Asch, which in Brathwaite's view contributed, however inadvertently, to the perpetuation and commodification of some of these stereotypes).

> . . . hole
> in my head,
> brains in
> my belly;
> black skin
> red eyes
> broad back
> big you know
> what: not very quick
>
> to take offence
> but once
> offended, watch
> that house
> you livin' in
> an' watch that lit-
> tle sister. . . .
>
> Ever seen
> a man
> travel more
> seen more
> lands
> than this poor
> land-
> less, harbour-
> less spade?[59]

"Yes," said Walcott in a sceptical review. "The Jews, for one."[60] But (as Walcott acknowledged) Brathwaite bound the predicament of blacks into a Jewish tradition of dislocation and dispossession in his epigraph to *Rights of Passage*, which was a passage from Exodus describing the journey of the children of Israel from the land of Egypt to the wilderness of Sin, near Sinai. Brathwaite is as conscious as Walcott of the desperations and the dreamings and the diasporas that are the grim—and shared—inheritances of peoples whose lives are shaped by exodus and exile, binding together the tribes of Israel and the Ashanti and the Celts and the Sioux. In "Wings of a Dove," Brathwaite has a Rastaman pick up the Biblical tradition and the language of

lament in which this has so often been commemorated and transform
it into new-world rhythms of hope rising out of the depths of longing
and despair.

>Brother Man the Rasta
>man, beard full of lichens
>brain full of lice
>watched the mice
>come up through the floor-
>boards of his down-
>town, shanty-town kitchen,
>and smiled. Blessed are the poor
>in health, he mumbled,
>that they should inherit this
>wealth. Blessed are the meek
>hearted, he grumbled,
>for theirs is this stealth.

>Brother Man the Rasta
>man, hair full of lichens
>head hot as ice
>watched the mice
>walk into his poor
>hole, reached for his peace
>and the pipe of his ganja
>and smiled how the mice
>eyes, hot pumice
>pieces, glowed into his room
>like ruby, like rhinestone
>and suddenly startled like
>diamond.

>And I
>Rastafar-I
>in Babylon's boom
>town, crazed by the moon
>and the peace of this chalice, I
>prophet and singer, scourge
>of the gutter, guardian
>Trench Town, Dungle and Young's
>Town, rise and walk through the now silent
>streets of affliction, hawk's eyes
>hard with fear, with

affection, and hear my people
cry, my people
shout . . .

So beat dem drums
dem, spread

dem wings dem,
watch dem fly

dem, soar dem
high dem,

clear in the glory of the Lord.[61]

In the middle book of *The Arrivants* called *Masks,* published in 1968, Brathwaite explores more fully his African heritage. The title refers both to the different voices or masks through which the poet speaks in these poems, and to the importance of ceremonial masks in providing access to a world of spiritual possibilities. In a poem called "The Awakening," Brathwaite recalls a West African creation myth; and he ends the poem—and the book—with Atumpan drumming, at the dawn of a new world and of a new West Indian poetry.

Asase Yaa, Earth,
if I am going away now,

you must help me.
Divine Drummer,

'Kyerema,
if time sends me

walking that dark
path again, you

must help me.
If I sleep,

you must knock me
awake . . .

I will rise
and stand on my feet

like *akoko* the cock
like *akoko* the cock

who cries
who cries in the morning

akoko bon'opa
akoko tua bon

I am learning
let me succeed

I am learning
let me succeed[62]

In *Islands*, the final book of *The Arrivants* published in 1969, Brathwaite returns to the history of blacks in the new world and to its debilitating ironies. His epigraph is from James Baldwin's *Tell Me How Long the Train's Been Gone*. "It was as though, after indescribable, nearly mortal effort, after grim years of fasting and prayer, after the loss of all he had, and after having been promised by the Almighty that he had paid the price and no more would be demanded of his soul, which was harboured now; it was as though in the midst of his joyful feasting and dancing, crowned and robed, a messenger arrived to tell him that a great error had been made, and that it was all to be done again."[63]

Brathwaite begins the book by bringing together old- and new-world inheritances, chronicling both the struggle of West Indian blacks to regain their heritage and the hopelessness that has shadowed this struggle for so long. In a section called "Limbo," he recapitulates the heritage of slavery in the limbo dance itself, a representation of the Middle Passage that recalls the confinement in the narrow space below deck, and the deaths by drowning, and the drumming that came with the slaves and still accompanies the dance. Brathwaite's sense of the psychology of people doomed to live out European fantasies of power is subtle, and includes the demoralizing ironies of seeing and saying things simply to satisfy someone else's dreams. He transforms the familiar image of division, Caliban and Prospero, into that of "a cracked mother," the title of a poem that tells of a Carib girl named Caonoba, who is put in a convent by her mother and told to console herself by imagining she is the great navigator, Columbus. The distraught mother, gone mad with guilt, jibbers a playground jingle.

See?
She saw

the sea
come

up go down
school children

summer-
saulting in the park.

See?
Saw

what on the sea
water?

Some-
thing floating?

See:
here are your

beads: I saw
you take

my children.
Bless

them, mother;
teach

them your
ways.[64]

This passage returns not only to the roots of West Indian experience—the destruction of the aboriginal tribes and their replacement by African slaves and their European masters—but also to the roots of West Indian education. "I see a ship on the sea" is the first sentence of a standard text in West Indian elementary schools, J. O. Cutteridge's primer for beginning readers.[65] It is also Caonoba's first lesson in Caribbean history, and the one her cracked mother cannot get out of her mind. The phrase "see / saw" brings together the present and the past, as well as the roles of the poet as both seer and sayer. It also establishes a grim image of a "divided child," playing on a see-saw.

But there is hope. Brathwaite returns to a biblical inheritance, with its image of the Logos or the creative Word in St. John's gospel, transformed by the heritage of Africans in the West Indies to express this vision of promise and possibility. (The passages are from the poem "Negus," in the section "Rebellion" and from the poem "Vèvè," in the final section "Beginnings.")

it is not
it is not
it is not enough
it is not enough to be free
of the whips, principalities and powers
where is your kingdom of the Word? . . .

I
must be given words to shape my name
to the syllables of trees

I
must be given words to refashion futures
like a healer's hand . . .

. . . the graven Word
carved from Olodumare
from Ogun of Alare, from Ogun of Onire
from Shango broom of thunder and Damballa Grand Chemin.

For on this ground
trampled with the bull's swathe of whips
where the slave at the crossroads was a red anthill
eaten by moonbeams, by the holy ghosts
of his wounds

the Word becomes
again a god and walks among us;
look, here are his rags,
here is his crutch and his satchel
of dreams; here is his hoe and his rude implements

on this ground
on this broken ground.[66]

The final image of "broken ground" is richly ambivalent, with meanings that are equally (and oppositely) appropriate: agricultural, the ground has been harrowed for seeding; and architectural, the old buildings have been torn down and new ones are ready to rise up. In both cases, a new home is coming into being.

Brathwaite's second trilogy—*Mother Poem* (1977), *Sun Poem* (1982), and *X/Self* (1987)—centers around the island of Barbados, where he grew up. Brathwaite begins *Mother Poem* with an epigraph: "We're the first potential parents who can contain the ancestral house."[67] It is from *The Whole Armour* (1962), a novel by Wilson Harris, who was a strong influence on Brathwaite in his early years as a poet. In a book of poems titled *Eternity to Season* (1954), Harris wrote of the exercise of the imagination as a weaving and unweaving of the self (and a convergence of linear and cyclical time), using as epigraph Penelope's account in the *Odyssey:* "In the daytime I would weave the mighty web and in the night unravel the same."[68] Walcott also uses this image, as we have seen; and it catches the indeterminacies of identity that Brathwaite cultivates in his work, usually by embracing the uncertainties and relativities of language. Brathwaite has often written about how West Indians have for so long had no language that derives from the experience of the land and of its people, and instead have had to rely on conventions that create discontinuities between experience and its expression or revelation in language. And so to make the connections possible he has developed strategies derived from the interactions of sound and sense and the patternings of speech and song. For example, in the following poem called "Nametracks" (from *Mother Poem*) he sets the proprieties of one type of language against the potentialities of another, in a voice that says "me" instead of "my," "mud," instead of "mother," and that also speaks the new word "nam." The ancient mother who provides a kind of redemptive subversion here is Sycorax, Caliban's mother and Prospero's real antagonist, whose whispered words finally affirm who he really is ("you nam"), as the catlike images are transformed into "lion eye mane," the icon of Rastafarian pride, the conquering Lion of Judah.[69]

but

muh
muh
mud
me mudda

coo
like she coo
like she cook
an she cumya to me pun de grounn

like she lik mih
like she lik me wid grease like she grease mih
she cum to me years like de yess off a leaf
an she issper
she cum to me years and she purr like a puss and she essssper

she lisper to me dat me name what me name
dat me name is me main an it am is me own an lion eye mane

> dat whinner men tek you an ame, dem is nomminit diff'rent an nan
> so mandingo she yessper you nam[70]

Sun Poem moves from the landscape of Barbados to an account of the island turning around the poet's paternal ancestry. Among other things, it describes the familiar predicament of West Indians growing up in the 1930s and 1940s, "not knowing the names of our flowers and trees / scratchywhist womans tongue hogplum stinkin toe / we could only call our brothers robin hood or barnabas collins."[71]

In the third book of the trilogy, *X/Self*, Brathwaite writes about spiritual discovery. As with many such adventures, this one begins with loss and bewilderment, a dark and negative time. The book opens with a question, posed in the epigraph (from an earlier poem by Brathwaite titled "The Dust," in *Rights of Passage*): "ev'rything look like it comin out wrong. / Why is dat? What it mean?"[72]

X/Self tells of a journey home, a journey both geographical (from Africa and Europe to the West Indies) and psychological (from a diminished and distorted sense of self to a liberated one), and both linear and cyclical. There are accounts, occasionally polemical, about actions and events, causes and effects; and there are images of fulfilment and fatality, occasionally sentimental or melodramatic. All are represented in the journey that is *X/Self*.

The journey also portrays a movement from disbelief to belief in self and in society, as Brathwaite proposes what John Henry Newman once called a "grammar of assent," a way of getting from "no" to "yes," which is to say to an image of self (which for Newman was also an image of God) that can transcend the limitations of our everyday ways of seeing things and of talking about them.

The questing and questioning are obvious in the title itself, and in the use of the letter or prefix "x" in several of the individual poems. "X" has many associations, among them "x" as the unknown in the custom of mathematics. This fits with the riddling quality of the self that is at the center of the book. And there are further connotations, for "x" is routinely used in algebra both as an *unknown*—something you will *discover*; and as a *variable*, a symbol for whatever you want it to be—something you will *invent*, as it were, which makes it a nicely appropriate image for the voices in the poem and the selves they present.

This unknown, or undetermined, quality of "x" is important in another respect, related to the reluctance of many religions to name their God, since naming involves an act of power that is deemed to be the prerogative of God alone. Of course, this is precisely the power that poets sometimes claim, though often in a subordinate capacity; and it is a measure of how Brathwaite—whose namings are legion, and legendary—conceives the subject matter of this poem that he refrains from naming it.

"X" also marks the spot on the map where treasure is to be found, or where someone lives, as on maps we draw to guide a visitor to our home. And "x" was the mark used instead of a European-style signature by Indian chiefs to sign treaties, those oral agreements that only for the convenience of the Europeans were ever written down and that mapped out the dispossession of new-world nations by old-world newcomers.

The importance of exploring the land and the sea as well as the self is identified by Brathwaite right at the beginning of this trilogy, in *Mother Poem*, when he mentions the ancient watercourses, the rivers flowing to the sea. The word *explore*, in which another "x" is sounded, comes from the root word meaning to flow; it is intimately related to influence, and thereby to the continuities this trilogy celebrates. We are surely intended to carry this etymology over into the logic of *X/Self*; just as we are encouraged to link the prefix with the situation of ex-isle that conditions so many West Indian lives.

There are other dimensions to "x." It is one of the least common letters in the English alphabet. But it has a special place in the Greek alphabet, to which our attention is drawn a number of times in Brathwaite's work. And it is prominent in several African languages, as Brathwaite makes apparent in the final poem of *X/Self* about the African god Shango (Xango), the god of thunder. There are also associations in the poem with the Black Muslim leader Malcolm X, and through this with the tradition of black liberation and power that goes back to Marcus Garvey and to Africa.

The particular Greek associations with the letter "x" are both general—most English words beginning with "x" derive from Greek roots—and specific—the letter "x" is often used as an emblem for Christ from the first letter of the Greek spelling (the writing of Christmas as Xmas being the most common instance of this). Furthermore, the Greek associations have to do with the perennial distinction between civilized and barbarian, or Prospero and Caliban. This brutal dichotomy is the element against which the self is protagonist in this book, engaged in the task of finding a language, a word, a letter which will be his own, with which he can identify himself, and by means of which he can transcend the debilitating antagonism that he experiences between the center and the margins, between those gathered within the walls of the city and those huddled or wandering outside.

"Rome burns / and our slavery begins."[73] The Mediterranean and the Caribbean. The story starts with slavery and subjugation and starvation, the barbaric materialism of Europe and the apocalyptic desecration of Africa, the poet's spiritual homeland. Then a vision of the day of judgment, bringing together the heritage of slavery and the suffering of many other peoples and times and places.

> Day of sulphur dreadful day
> when the world shall pass away
> so the priests and shamans say
>
> what gaunt shadows shall affront me
> my lai sharpeville wounded knee
> ho chi marti makandal . . .
>
> day of judgement day of sorrow
> day for which all sufferers pray
> when the sword shall pass away
>
> day of thunder day of hunger
> bring me solace bring me fire
> give me penance bring me power
> grant me vengeance with thy word[74]

Brathwaite transforms European traditions into West Indian terms here. His poem is modeled after the medieval hymn "Dies Irae," which in turn is drawn from a passage in the Old Testament Book of Zephaniah when the end of time is figured in "the great day of the Lord . . . even the voice of the day of the Lord. . . . That day is a day of wrath, a day of trouble and distress, a day of wasteness and desolation, a day of darkness and gloominess, a day of clouds and thick darkness, a day of the trumpet and alarm against the fenced cities, and against the high towers" (Zephaniah 1: 14–16).

But the difference in Brathwaite's poem is crucial, for he is not foretelling the day when time shall end, but instead is writing about a more intense awareness of time, of time's arrow and time's cycle—an awareness of the past and what it has done to his people. This is a poem *about* history, rather than about its obliteration in the apocalypse. Brathwaite signals this in several ways, among them by the title "Dies Irie," a clever turn on "Dies Irae" that picks up the Rastafarian word *irie*, with its strongly positive meanings of powerful or stimulating (Brathwaite glosses it as "high" or "happy"). This change draws our attention both to the difference and to the similarity, for the play on *irie / irae* also confirms the bond between the Old Testament and Rastafarianism.

Brathwaite's vision of this day is terrifying, but it is also filled with the eternal promise of revolution. This is celebrated in another poem in *X/Self* called "The Visibility Trigger," a poem about the poet's African inheritance and its arrival in the consciousness—the ways of seeing and saying—of West Indians with all the violence of surprise and revelation, like Bongo Jerry's Black Powa (Strange Tongue).

> and i beheld the cotton tree
> guardian of graves rise upward from its monument of grass crying
> aloud in its vertical hull calling
> for crashes of branches vibrations of leaves
>
> there was a lull of silver
> and then the great grandfather gnashing upwards from its teeth
> of roots. split down its central thunder
> the stripped violated wood crying aloud in its murder. the leaves
> frontier signals alive with lamentations
>
> and our great odoum
> triggered at last by the ancestors into your visibility
> crashed
>
> into history[75]

There is no lightning to illuminate this thunderous moment. But there is hope, the hope of an inheritance that will come when the unbelievers are cast out. After the "Dies Irie," we see a beginning of belief in judgment and grace that will transform the day of thunder and terror into the day of light and peace described at the end of the book.

> touch
> him
> he will heal
>
> you
>
> word
> and balm
> and water
>
> flow
>
> embrace
> him
> he will shatter outwards to your light and calm and history
>
> your thunder has come home[76]

Whether told about a people or an individual, whether an *Exodus* or a *Pilgrim's Progress*, the story of leaving home and going back is a literary and spiritual inheritance that West Indians share with many others. Brathwaite's question—"where then is the nigger's home?"—both complicates and strengthens this bond, especially with one particular literary heritage. The story of Odysseus and his journey around the Mediterranean on his way home to Penelope from the Trojan Wars, that well-known tale of wandering and return, has a special place for West Indians. The Mediterranean is an African as well as a European sea, and so is the Caribbean; and both present images of home to their peoples, wherever they may be. Like Odysseus, Brathwaite journeys to take back what already belongs to him: his memories, his hopes, his language. Like Odysseus, Walcott is curious about other places too, uneasy about where he belongs but still bound by strong ties to home. Brathwaite and Walcott recognize both sides of that fortunate/unfortunate traveler.

And what of Penelope? Her voice is one that West Indian literature has been waiting for, and one heard now in the poetry of Lorna Goodison. Not that Goodison's poetry is in any sense limited to Penelope's experience, nor that this experience is excluded from the writings of Brathwaite or Walcott, whose cry "come back to me my language" might well be Penelope's. But the poignancy and power of Goodison's voice are drawn from a deep well of sorrow and fortitude and courage of which Penelope is a compelling image. This image—like the narrative for which it stands—is shaped by a literary tradition that reflects certain customary European roles and representations, to be sure; but it also reflects some central aspects of the experience of West Indian women, symbols of patience, resourcefulness, and resistance. At the heart of Goodison's work, as of Brathwaite's and Walcott's, is a profound belief—underlying all the intermittent doubt—in the poet as the voice of one bearing witness, and a belief in the West Indies as a source of strength for its poets and for its people.

Lorna Goodison was born in Jamaica in 1947. After school in Kingston, she studied at the Jamaica School of Art and at the School of the Students' Art League in New York. Nobody seems to have told West Indian writers and artists that they should keep to one form of imaginative expression, and more than most others they have shown the arbitrariness of literary genres. Just as Brathwaite is a historian and critic of considerable importance in West Indian letters, and Walcott is a major playwright and a painter, so Goodison is a painter and a writer of prose fiction. Her paintings have been exhibited in Europe, the

United States, and the West Indies, and she has illustrated several books (including all of her own). Her short stories display a fine instinct for Jamaica, with its hardships and humor, and are included in her collection *Baby Mother and the King of Swords* (1990). But with Brathwaite and Walcott, it is as a poet that Goodison has major stature in contemporary literature.

Goodison grew independent as Jamaica did, in the early 1960s, though probably the same could be said of her as of her country: their spirits were independent from the start. She lived in the United States during the late 1960s, when the ideals of black power were changing some of the realities of black experience in the new world. Her work is conditioned by a sense of the inevitability of freedom and the inevitability of struggle—which is to say, by the determinisms of each, and by a conviction that poetry is both an instrument of liberation and, as Derek Walcott put it, "a life-long sentence."[77]

Goodison's first book, published in 1980, is called *Tamarind Season*, a local phrase synonymous with hard times and referring to the season before the crops have been harvested when food is scarce. In the title poem, Goodison uses the local language and the life of her island to portray a woman waiting for a change of fortune with the restless patience of Penelope, a figure both from many times and places, and from Jamaica. There are several specifically Jamaican references in the poem—to the tamarind fruit, whose pulp is very sour, and to "woman's tongue," the local name for a tree whose seed pods rattle in the wind when they are dry.

> The welcome turns sour
> she finds a woman's tongue
> and clacks curses at the wind
> for taking advantage
>
> box her about this way
> and that is the reason
>
> wait is the reason
>
> Tamarind Season[78]

In another poem, titled "Judges," the poet recounts an experience in court in which a local judge discredited the basis of an application for divorce by saying "unhappiness is not grounds." The poem ends like this.

> And nobody told you I was a poet?
> You who sit in judgement on the ones who come

moved by the nongrounds of unhappiness?
I am lining up these words
holding them behind the barrier of my teeth

biding my time as only a woman can.

I have a poem for you judge man.[79]

The final line is sharply ironic. It is a reminder that the truth of what the poet says is dependent upon the judgement of others. But it is also an assertion of the independence of a woman from a world dominated by men, and of the independence of the poet from doubt and disbelief. The phrase "judge man" echoes in Jamaican speech the earlier word "judgement"; and it also completes the rhyme with "woman can." The cool fury of the line, coming to rest on the word "judge man" and the idea of judgment, undermines any notion of judgment as the monopoly of men, or their institutions . . . including, of course, the institution of literary criticism.

Goodison's is first of all a woman's voice, grounded not just in sorrow but in resolution and independence; the voice of a woman who in her own litany is daughter, sister, mistress, friend, warrior, wife and mother; the voice of a woman for whom home is a place where simple things are central, a place located here and now with pigeons roosting over the door and tomatoes growing in the garden, a place that nourishes the spirit and the imagination.

> At first, we liked to describe them
> as doves,
> the white pigeons who came to live
> at this house.
> Appearing first as a circle with wings,
> then some blessing pulling the circle in,
> so that its centre became our house.
> Now in these eaves
> a benediction of birds.
> Their nervous hearts
> in sync enough
> with our rhythms
> they enter into this house.
> So sometimes in the middle
> of doing some woman's thing
> I look up to find us
> in a new painting.
> House on a rock

with wooden floors
a boy and white pigeons.[80]

Life imitates art. The shaping of reality—or at least, of the ways in which we see and talk about reality—by the conventions of the imagination is a continuing theme in West Indian literature. The experiences of life are realized in the elements and forms of art—circles, centers, patterns, rhythms, rituals—which in turn represent relationships between our ordinary selves and greater powers, part of nature and part of us.

A sense of these powers, immanent and transcendent, is a consistent and compelling feature of Godison's poetry. But it never signals a withdrawal from the ordinariness of life. In his introduction to *The Wisdom of the Desert*, Thomas Merton talks about how the desert fathers

> insisted on remaining human and "ordinary." This may seem to be a paradox, but it is very important. If we reflect a moment, we will see that to fly into the desert in order to be extraordinary is only to carry the world with you as an implicit standard of comparison. The result would be nothing but self-contemplation, and self-comparison with the negative standard of the world one has abandoned. Some of the monks of the Desert did this, as a matter of fact: and the only fruit of their trouble was that they went out of their heads. The simple men who lived their lives out to a good old age among the rocks and sands only did so because they had come into the desert to be themselves, their *ordinary* selves, and to forget a world that divided them from themselves.[81]

It is in Goodison's language as much as in anything else that she combines the ordinary with the uncommon. In one poem, "The Transcendent Song of the Tuareg Woman," she blends the strange and wonderful ("a rising flock of Barbary doves") with the common and familiar (a "fast forward song") in phrasing that in its almost ostentatious precision ("if correctly and effectively done") seems to contradict the magic in which it instructs us ("lift her up to a cool place / above the burning chamber of the sun"). And yet it defies such apparent contradictions, for the poem is about experiences (those "truly unbearable days") known to everyone, everywhere; and it is also about something known only to the poet, or as she says "bought only in the way of the desert."

> A Tuareg woman passing once taught Amber a song.
> It really was a series of intricate notes
> urgently sounded: like the fast forward song
> of a rising flock of Barbary doves.

The song, if correctly and effectively done
could lift her up to a cool place
above the burning chamber of the sun . . .

Amber caught the song and held it.
But somehow she felt it was not wise
to use it frequently, just so.
She learned to save the transcendent Tuareg song
for the truly unbearable days.[82]

Amber herself, the central figure in a sequence of Goodison's poems, represents this paradox of the exceptional and the everyday—as in a poem that takes the form of a letter of "Recommendation for Amber."

With her, you would have a guide
to the small nubians in the garden.
They live only under bushes
that have never known knives . . .

She also knows the secret properties
of gemstones. Take amber itself her name.

Though neither rare, costly nor a gem
but the golden night sweat of a tree
compassionate and resilient, it's special
because it is self healing.

Despite her tendency to wearing her hair
wild and her slow Egyptian eyes which are
fixed always above her employer's head
she has a good hand at plain cooking.[83]

Goodison brings grace and understanding to the plainness of things, and of people. She writes, too, about unusual people and places—about the desert, for example, as a place of wonder and struggle and enlightenment (taking care to include the desert mothers as well as the fathers in her account). But she dignifies all that people do and all the places they live, however humble, by the quality of her attention; and she celebrates the nobility of ordinary things, what she calls "the layered love of our simplest ways."[84] In a poem called "For My Mother (May I Inherit Half Her Strength)" from her second book *I Am Becoming My Mother* (1986), Goodison tells of her mother's life and of her legacy to the poet, a legacy—like Penelope's—of love and loyalty. The poem is filled with the small details of a life dedicated to others, details that take on a new dignity in the telling, and in the unqualified truth of her mother's life and the love to which Goodison bears witness in her poem. The role of universals in countering the contingencies of love and loyalty and belief is central here, and so is the importance of particular details—of remembering *and* forgetting them—in the artifice of truth and beauty.

My mother loved my father
I write this as an absolute
in this my thirtieth year
the year to discard absolutes

he appeared, her fate disguised,
as a sunday player in a cricket match,
he had ridden from a country
one hundred miles south of hers.

She tells me he dressed the part,
visiting dandy, maroon blazer
cream serge pants, seam like razor,
and the beret and the two-tone shoes . . .

My mother was a child of the petite bourgeoisie
studying to be a teacher, she oiled her hands
to hold pens.
My father barely knew his father, his mother died young,
he was a boy who grew with his granny . . .

When I came to know my mother many years later, I knew her as the figure who sat at the first thing I learned to read: "SINGER" . . .

She could work miracles, she would make a garment from a square of cloth in a span that defied time. Or feed twenty people on a stew made from fallen-from-the-head cabbage leaves and a carrot and a cho-cho and a
                                                                                          palmful
of meat.
And she rose early and sent us clean into the world and she went to bed in the dark, for my father came in always last . . .

When he died, she sewed dark dresses for the women amongst us
and she summoned that walk, straight-backed, that she gave to us
and buried him dry-eyed.

Just that morning, weeks after
she stood delivering bananas from their skin
singing in that flat hill country voice

she fell down a note to the realization that she did
not have to be brave, just this once
and she cried.

For her hands grown coarse with raising nine children
for her body for twenty years permanently fat
for the time she pawned her machine for my sister's
Senior Cambridge fees
and for the pain she bore with the eyes of a queen

and she cried also because she loved him.[85]

A recent history of the University of the West Indies by Philip Sherlock and Rex Nettleford begins with a testimony to the women of the
West Indies, "and the mothers especially, (who) stand out for their
courage and resilience in meeting the challenge of deprivation and
change. Any West Indian knows of peasant market women like the
bone-thin elderly woman in the Duncans market in Trelawney, who,
week after week, year after year, out of her meagre earnings sent her
son Amos Foster to Scotland as a medical student and kept him there
until he qualified and returned home; or like Lorna Goodison's
mother."[86] Her poem is then quoted, in tribute to "the chief characters
in our story (who) appear only incidentally. They are the West Indian
folk."

The lives of the folk in Goodison's world are commemorated with
rare and unindulgent sensitivity. In one sequence describing the Kingston streets of her youth, she tells of the man who came to beat and
refill people's mattresses with ticking—or "coir." He is an unlikely
hero, but in Goodison's poem he represents the heritage of his people,
a heritage of violence and suffering and indomitable endurance.
Framed by moments of wonderful tenderness and tranquility, the
poem bears witness not just to his own personal anguish but also to
the history of slavery and its legacy in Jamaica, much of which we have
caught glimpses of already: the Queen's Advice and the Morant Bay
rebellion, Rastafarianism, and the plight of present-day Jamaicans.

Rassy our mattress man was a "beardman" who bore
a resemblance to the monk Rasputin.
He favoured garments in the colours of dust
and if his head was bent over and the light was sloping
towards evening, you could imagine him in a monk's cell
telling beads against the next phase of his life
which would find him in control of a Tzarina.
He had one eye walled off to the public

but I could see through that curtain the worship hidden
there for my mother, but of what use were such feelings?
He was content to receive a meal at noon from her hands
and tremble gratefully at the thought of her pointed fingers
peeling moon-white Lucea yams and seasoning meat
so that you smelled her hand, that is, a benediction
of spices woud rise up to cover you when you entered
through her gates.

His movements are slow, dark molasses in his infrequent
speech. He can sit still for what seems to a fidgety child
like 999 hours but somethings stirs his slow self
into speeded up action when Rassy whips the coir.
First he folds his handkerchief into half, three points
a triangle, a mask. He ties it round the lower half of his face,
pulls down his cap to just above his eyes.
Then he runs his thumb and forefinger along the thick wire of his whip.
The handle too is of wire but padded with cloth over and over.
Ready, he approaches the red unruly mass
spilled from its ripped open ticking case.
He approaches the small red mountain, muttering
some ancient incantation to protect him from fierce fibre.
His arm jerks back and flicks forward he delivers the first
blow, the coir registers receival of whipping
by sending out a cloud of frightened red dust.
When Rassy whips the rebellious coir he whips
all his enemies, exorcizes life pain and causes rain
to fall down red from what he sends up to the
heavens.
The woman who threw the acid that coagulated his eye
first rain of blows.
Then the colonial Government, the Governor and Queen Victoria
for sending that heartless facety letter commending
ex-slaves to hard work and obedience and industry when the people
were just rightly asking for justice work and food.
The first man who had the idea to leave and go
to Africa and interfere with the people who was minding
their own business, a hard rain of blows.
For Mussolini and the Italian Army
on behalf of Haile Selassie, five straight minutes of blows.
To Babylon in general for generic evil, hunger, disease
bad minded people, Rassy rains blows.

He whips them all for a good part of the morning
red clouds about his head flying frightened vapour
from his whip.
And when the coir has been beaten into submission
he walks away triumphant, sweating, removes the mask
and wipes his eyes, it comes away red but his blood
is running free. He asks of my mother, a cool drink
of water which he sips with the air of a victorious warrior
before he settles at the machine to stitch
the big square of new striped ticking
into which he will imprison the chastened coir.[87]

In another of the poems about life on the streets of Kingston when
she was growing up, Goodison tells of a hideously deformed "elephant
man" and of his dream—a memory and a vision of blessing and peace
and his home in Africa, a "wide green space and baobab trees." African
legend tells that the strange appearance of these trees (a few of which
are found in Jamaica) comes from their having been planted upside
down when the world was created.[88] Goodison transforms this image
into a powerful narrative of the orphaned and the outcast, of difference
and dispossession and despair, in which the anguish of a mother looking for her child, and of a child separated from his mother, becomes
one with the heritage of slavery and the hope of freedom.

Memory claims that in a jungle once
a great mother elephant crazed
with grief for her lost son
wrapped her trunk around a baobab tree
and wrenched it free from its upside down
hold in the earth and trumpeted down
the hole in the earth for her vanished one.

Elephant, the lost the cursed one lumbers
up from under the big trees in Queen Victoria's park.
This man more pachyderm than man, skin draped loose,
grey, muddy as tarpaulin over swollen elephantiasis
limbs. He moves bent over weighed by the bag
of crosses over his shoulder, his lips droop tubular.
Small children appear and chant, "elephant, elephant" . . .
till he rears back on his huge hind legs trumpeting
threats of illegal surgery by glass bottle,
death to small children who scatter before him, like antelopes
and elands, skittering across the asphalt heading home.

Elephant, loneliest one in all creation, your friends
the night grazing mules tethered by dark hills of coal
in Mullings grass yard. Poor Elephant always walking
hoping one day he would turn a corner and come upon
a clearing familiar to long memory, wide green space
and baobab trees. For there his mother and the great herds
would be, free.[89]

Goodison's poetic imagination includes both men and women, in Jamaica and elsewhere, with whom she shares a life of struggle and of freedom. But she grounds her imagination at home. In the poem "We Are the Women," she confirms her special bond with other West Indian women, past and present, notable and unknown. Silver coins and cloves of garlic, the precious and the commonplace, come together here in a ritual witnessing whose apocryphal character represents a collective wisdom outside the canon, unauthorized but true, the shared secrets of resistance and restoration.

We are the women
with thread bags
anchored deep in our bosoms
containing blood agreements
silver coins and cloves of garlic
and an apocrypha
of Nanny's secrets.

We've made peace
with want
if it doesn't kill us
we'll live with it.

We ignore promises
of plenty
we know that old sankey.

We are the ones
who are always waiting
mouth corner white
by sepulchres and
bone yards
for the bodies of our men,
waiting under massa
waiting under massa table
for the trickle down of crumbs.

The poem ends with an image of possibility that is Goodison's signature, the sound of her voice.

> We've buried our hope
> too long
> as the anchor to our
> navel strings
> we are rooting at
> the burying spot
> we are uncovering
> our hope.[90]

The complementary images of rooting and burying, and of the land and the sea (the anchor to our navel strings), bring together here the whole history of slavery: the drowning at sea and the death on land and the harrowing legacy of sexual exploitation; the hiding away of secrets and the determination of those entrusted with them to give voice to new hope and to give birth to a new generation of duppy conquerors who will finally set their people free.

"I was sent. Tell that to history." The voice is that of Nanny of the Maroons, one of the inspiring figures of Jamaican resistance and liberation, who legend has it was born in Africa of the Ashanti tribe. She had never been enslaved, and represented the spirit of freedom and independence that the Maroons exemplified. Nanny was a military strategist of extraordinary, some say supernatural, skill; and she gave spiritual as well as military leadership to the Windward Maroons, one of the two main groups in eighteenth-century Jamaica. (The other was the Leeward Maroons, under the leadership of Cudjoe [or Kojo].) For Goodison, Nanny's is the voice of West Indian steadfastness and sacrifice, the voice of West Indian women. It is also, in the way of poetry, Lorna Goodison's voice, surely and paradoxically bound to a destiny of struggle and freedom. "When your sorrow obscures the skies/ other women like me will rise."[91]

This is a central part of the heritage that Goodison celebrates, the heritage that Frederick Douglass identified when he said, "when the true history of the anti-slavery cause shall be written, women will occupy a large space in its pages, for the cause of the slave has been peculiarly women's cause."[92] Some of the burdens that a woman must bear no one else can carry. But Goodison knows that other women have carried these burdens before; and that their experience can give strength and comfort. She recalls this in the poem "Birth Stone," where her ability to bring new life and meaning back into old familiar phrases (such as "no man's land" and "bear down") is evident once again, as artifice and naturalness converge in the wonder and the wisdom that words still hold.

> The older women wise and tell Anna
> first time baby mother,
> "hold a stone upon your head and follow
> a straight line go home."
> For like how Anna was working in the
> field, grassweeder
> right up till the appointed hour
> that the baby was to come.
> Right up till the appointed hour
> when her clear heraldic water
> broke free and washed her down.
> Dry birth for you young mother,
> the distance between field and home
> come in like the Gobi desert now.
> But your first baby must born abed.
> Put the woman stone on your head
> and walk through no man's land
> go home. When you walk, the stone
> and not you yet, will bear down.[93]

The uprisings of women too, like their endurance and devotion, are recognized by Goodison wherever they may take place, from Africa to the West Indies to America, where Rosa Parks quietly said "No" on the bus in Montgomery. This is Goodison's tribute to her, and to what she represents.

> And how was this soft-voiced woman to know
> that this "No"
> in answer to the command to rise
> would signal the beginning
> of the time of walking? . . .
> But the people had walked before
> in yoked formations down to Calabar
> into the belly of close-ribbed whales
> sealed for seasons
> and unloaded to walk again
> alongside cane stalks tall as men.
> No, walking was not new to them . . .
> And the woman who never raised her voice
> never lowered her eyes

just kept walking
leading us towards sunrise.[94]

Goodison brings together the heritages of women from the old and the new world with figures from legend and from life. But she bases her images in the reality of the West Indies and in the actual experience of its women, women like the poet. This identification with the poet herself raises a question we have already touched on, and which we will discuss in more detail in the next chapter. Is the poet herself the speaker of a lyric poem? Or, to put the question differently, is the voice of a lyric poem the poet's voice? The answer, of course, is yes and no . . . or no and yes. Our habit of identifying poetic voices along lines of gender and race as well as along national and historical and other lines invites a simple, sometimes simplistic, link between speaker and poet. And so does our perennial fascination with personal biography. Interviews also present special challenges to contemporary readers, providing quite different kinds of insights from those available, for instance, in the correspondence of writers from earlier periods; and they too often encourage a direct identification of poet and speaker. Goodison, like Walcott and Brathwaite, has given a number of interviews. And much of Goodison's poetry, like much of Walcott's and Brathwaite's, is poised between the authority of the speaker (within the literary tradition) and the autobiography of the poet (living outside that tradition). But it would be a very gullible reader who would assume an identity between them; just as it would take a special sort of naiveté to assume that Goodison *is* Penelope.

And yet . . . here is "The Mulatta as Penelope" . . . speaking in the voice of Lorna Goodison. It is also Lorna Goodison, speaking in the voice of the Mulatta . . . who in turn is speaking as Penelope . . . a voice shuttling between three identifications: one classical, one Caribbean, one personal and contemporary.

Tonight I'll pull your limbs through small
soft garments
your head will part my breasts
and you will hear a different heartbeat.
Today we said the real goodbye, he and I
but this time
I will not sit and spin and spin
the door open to let the madness in
till the sailor finally weary
of the sea
returns with tin souvenirs and a claim

to me.
True, I returned from the quayside
my eyes full of sand
and his salt leaving smell
fresh on my hands.
But, you're my anchor awhile now
and that goes deep,
I'll sit in the sun and dry my hair
while you sleep.[95]

Goodison's figure of Mulatta was at first lightheartedly discounted by the poet in an interview. "I went somewhere in Latin America once and there were these people who kept referring to me as a mulatta, which I found very funny, because I'd never thought of anything like that . . . They told me I was a mulatta and I said all right, I kind of like the sound of that."[96] But Mulatta comes very close to home in this poem, as she does in the poem "Guinea Woman," where Goodison recognizes in her great grandmother—"the first Mulatta / taken into backra's household / and covered with his name"[97]—the heritage of her people, a heritage of oppression and uprising and departure and return. And a heritage of love.

Goodison's inspiration comes from a deep understanding of her experience as a West Indian woman. Images of that inspiration are drawn from the traditions of European literature, but they are transformed by Goodison not only into distinctly West Indian terms but also into her own. Literary tradition has given us the image of a female muse as the source of poetic inspiration. Goodison's muse is not some woman of shadowy power and intermittent presence, as a tradition dominated by men would have it, but is instead the figure of a man, overwhelming and unreliable at times (as muses tend to be), and created as a woman's image of inspiration. She writes about her muse in all the ways that are familiar to readers of European literature . . . except that her muse is different, inspiring her desires and dreams— and occasionally prompting her dismay—as a woman as well as a poet. She finds his image in the peace of God, and His wrath; in the preciousness of her son to her, and the fears she holds for him; in the power of love, her sometime destiny and her despair. Her muse is an image of otherness, a power beyond and within herself, both of her own devising and determined by her literary heritage.

Muses traditionally challenge the balance between detachment and surrender upon which poets depend, for they provide some of our most compelling representations of power and difference. It is in this context that Goodison's muse becomes an especially important figure in her poetry, within a tradition in which love and literature converge. In "Letters to the Egyptian," Goodison displays her special genius for hovering not just between the local and the literary but between the sentimental and the spiritual, as she brings together the actuality of human experience, its private and particular details, with the universal ideals of the poetic imagination, drawn by its muse to a place of peace and light and love.

> In case you do not recognise me
> when I arrive at Alexandria
> I will be wearing a long loose
> jade green dress
> my hair will be hidden
> under a striped fringed headscarf
> and I will smell of roseapples and musk
> O love, forgive my vanity,
> it is also to make sure
> you recognise me
> five pounds lighter
> drawn from the long journey.
> I will bring you a garland
> of search-mi-heart leaves
> on their underside
> I've sewn some woman's tongue seeds.
> You said you loved my chatter.
>
> When the longboat
> drew into Khartoum
> where the White Nile meets the Blue
> I was tempted to abandon ship.
> You see there was this Kushite once
> who . . .
> But how could he ever
> compare to you? . . .
> And am I now nearer to you?
> Does the Nile hold all the world's water?
> How far is Khartoum from you?
>
> Last night there was such
> a storm at sea
> I sought level
> and chained myself with prayers.

(They held)
and in the after
in the soughing of the wind
I'm sure it was you
I heard sing.
Sleep now beloved
fold yourself in softened sails
I wait for you in the Aftergale.
Calm will be our mooring.[98]

In "My Last Poem," Goodison gives a litany of the anxiety her muse brings, and which life brings too; for it is in the realities of life that the knowledge of the poet is located, and it is through this knowledge, with all its uncertainties, that imaginative surrender and salvation occur.

There should be a place for
messages and replies
you are too tightly bound, too whole
he said
I loosened my hair and I bled
now you send conflicting signals they said
divided I turned both ways and fled.
There should be a place for all this
but I'm almost at the end of my last poem
and I'm almost a full woman.
I warm my son's clothes
in this cold time
in the deep of my bosom
and I'm not afraid of love.
In fact, should it be
that these are false signals I'm receiving
and not a real unqualified ending
I'm going to keep the word love
and use it in my next poem.[99]

Through all the divisions and deceptions, there is a deep reserve of hopefulness in Goodison's work, sustained by the links she has forged between the poetic and the personal. There are risks here, mainly of self-conscious ingenuity and sentimental indulgence. But she takes them openly, with almost cavalier disregard for the different conventions of life and literature, in order to challenge our customary distinctions between reality and the imagination, and to bring a spirit of reconciliation back into poetry. In "My Last Poem (Again)," written several years later, she negotiates between images of love to which she has in a sense become hostage, and between the men who are figures of fear and hope to her—as a woman and as a poet.

> When the King of Swords gutted me
> and left me for dead, in my insides were found
> clots of poems, proving that poets are made of poems
> and poems are truth demanding punctutation of light
> and your all, and that makes my head vie with night all day.
> I don't want to live this way anymore.
> Somewhere there is a clean kind man
> with a deep and wide understanding
> of the mercy and the peace and the infinity.
> And we will if we are lucky, live by the sea
> and serve and heal eating of life's salt and bread
> and at night lie close to each other and read poems
> for which somebody else besides me bled . . .
> and that will make me want to write poems.[100]

Goodison often conflates time and space as well as life and literature, generating a kind of magical realism, an oscillating or interweaving of worlds and of languages. But her first and final allegiance is not to figures of fancy but to the here and now. Her attachment to Jamaica runs deep, and much of her poetry is about life there. In "To Us, All Flowers Are Roses," she shapes a meditation around local names. Accompong is the old Maroon settlement in the parish of St. Elizabeth, named after its founder, the brother of Cudjoe. It opens the poem and opens, too, a heritage of slavery, resistance, recovery, and freedom. Come back to me my language, says Goodison, to my places and my people.

> Accompong is Ashanti, root, Nyamekopon
> appropriate name Accompong, meaning
> warrior or lone one. Accompong,
> home to bushmasters, bushmasters being
> maroons, maroons dwell in dense places
> deep mountainous well sealed
> strangers unwelcome. Me No Send You No Come.
>
> I love so the names of this place . . .
>
> There are Angels in St. Catherine somewhere.
> Arawak is a post office in St. Ann.

And if the Spaniards hear of this
will they come again in Caravelles
to a post office (in suits of mail)
to enquire after any remaining Arawaks?
Nice people, so gentle, peaceful and hospitable.

There is everywhere here.
There is Alps and Lapland and Berlin.
Armagh, Carrick Fergus, Malvern,
Rhine and Calabar, Askenish
where freed slaves went to claim
what was left of the Africa within
staging secret woodland ceremonies.

Such ceremonies! such dancing, ai Kumina!
drum sound at Barking Lodge where we hear
a cargo of slaves landed free, because
somebody sign a paper even as they
rode as cargo shackled on the high seas.
So they landed here, were unchained, went free.
So in some places there is almost pure Africa.

Some of it is lost, though, swept away forever,
maybe at Lethe in Hanover, Lethe springs
from the Greek, a river which is the river
of Oblivion. There is Mount Peace here
and Tranquility and Content. May Pen
Dundee Pen, Bamboo Pen and for me,
Faith's Pen, therefore will I write.

There is Blackness here which is sugar land
and they say is named for the ebony of the soil.
At a wedding there once the groom wore cobalt blue
and young bride, cloud white, at Blackness.
But there is blood, red blood in the fields
of our lives, blood the bright banner flowing
over the order of cane and our history . . .[101]

Goodison's language typically combines conversational naturalness with poetic artifice, and her imagery mediates between the wonders of life and of art. She recalls the jazz pianist Keith Jarrett saying that sometimes when he plays he feels like he can make it rain; and she turns this into an image of the water that nourishes both her worlds, real and imagined, local and literary, material and spiritual—the worlds of

those, farmers and artists both, who cultivate the land. The poem is
called "Keith Jarrett—Rainmaker," and begins

> Piano man
> my roots are african
> I dwell in the centre of the sun . . .
>
> So my prayers are usually
> for rain.

Then Goodison speaks of the ways in which these prayers are needed.

> My people are farmers
> and artists
> and sometimes the lines
> blur
> so a painting becomes a
> december of sorrel
> a carving heaps like a yam hill
> or a song of redemption wings
> like the petals of resurrection
> lilies—all these require rain.[102]

As Jarrett plays, he divines water in the dry times, "pull(ing) down . . .
waterfalls of rain." As Goodison sings, she refreshes the spirit that is
in the land and its people.

At the heart of Goodison's poetry is a profoundly religious sensibility, embracing a purpose that both transcends human understanding
and is part of everyday life. There is much pain in her poetry, beginning
with a recognition of the sorrow and suffering that are part of the heritage of all West Indians. But out of this heritage comes the dignity of
a "Survivor," representing all those whom grace has touched . . . which
in some measure should be all of us.

> The strangers passed through here
> for years
> laying waste the countryside . . .
> So, here the wind plays
> mourning notes
> on bones that once were ribs . . .
> That survivor over there
> with bare feet and bound hair
> has some seeds stored
> under her tongue

> and one remaining barrel
> of rain
> She will go indoors
> when her planting is done
> loosen her hair
> and tend to her son,
> and over the bone flute music
> and the dead story it tells
> listen for grace songs
> from her ankle bells.[103]

From ankle chains and slave songs to ankle bells and grace songs. The heritage of slavery and freedom.

There is a passage in Herman Melville's *Moby Dick* where Ishmael talks about how

> that mortal man who hath more of joy than sorrow in him, that mortal man cannot be true—not true, or undeveloped. With books the same. The truest of all men was the Man of Sorrows, and the truest of all books is Solomon's, and Ecclesiastes is the fine hammered steel of woe. "All is vanity." ALL. This wilful world hath not got hold of unchristian Solomon's wisdom yet. But he who dodges hospitals and jails, and walks fast crossing graveyards, and would rather talk of operas than hell . . . not that man is fitted to sit down on tomb-stones, and break the green damp mould with unfathomably wondrous Solomon.[104]

Goodison walks through the streets of Kingston and New York and London, the places of pain and anger and despair, and speaks with a voice of understanding and comfort and wisdom; for she also has what Ishmael calls "a Catskill eagle" in her soul "that can alike dive down into the blackest gorges, and soar out of them again and become invisible in the sunny spaces." And as with Ishmael's figure, when Goodison "flies within the gorge, that gorge is in the mountains"; and she shares Ishmael's profoundly human need to know and understand. This is from Goodison's "Heartease New England 1987," written during a long stay in Boston.

> I see a bird trapped
> under the iron girders of the Ashmont station overpass.
> It is trying to measure the distance between columns
> with its given wing span, and it fails
> for being alone and not having a wing span wide enough.
> I am told that birds travel faster over greater distances
> when they move in chevron formation

a group of birds could measure the width of the Ashmont
station overpass . . . I know how the bird feels . . .
In the fall I search for signs
a pattern in the New England flaming trees
"What is my mission? Speak, leaves"
(for all journeys have hidden missions)
The trees before dying, only flame brighter
maybe that is the answer, live glowing while you can.

That is the only answer, except one evening in November
I see an African in Harvard Square.
He is telling himself a story as he walks
in telling it, he takes all the parts
and I see that he has taken himself home.
And I have stories too, until I tell them
I will not find release, that is my mission.
Some nights though, anxiety assails me
a shroud spinning in the snow . . .
I know how the bird trying to measure the overpass
feels . . .
I reaffirm this knowing one evening, a Wednesday
as I go up Shephard Street. Someone is playing
Bob Marley and the notes are levitating
across the Garden Street end of the street.
They appear first as notes and then feather into birds
pointing their wings, arranging themselves for travelling
long distances.
And birds are the soul's symbol, so I see
that I am only a sojourner here but I came as friend
came to record and sing and then, depart.
For my mission this last life is certainly this
to be the sojourner poet carolling for peace
calling lost souls to the way of Heartease.[105]

The voices in Goodison's poetry are ancient voices, wandering like
Ishmael and waiting like Penelope, bringing together past and present,
personal sorrow and the peace of which everyone dreams and which
no one fully understands. Goodison brings to her poetry a humility
which defies the temptations of despair, and a belief which sustains
her faith that life is a journey from darkness toward light, and toward
home. Most of all Goodison speaks, in Adrienne Rich's words, for those
who do not have the gift of language, and she sees for those who are
less conscious of what they are living through.

Come let your eyes feel
the colours, the landscape
of Heartease
the long day will pass
drawn lightly through rays
of African Star grass
and at night a bed-tranquil
borrowed from rest
and pillows all peaceful
an heart's ease is this.[106]

"I shall light a candle of understanding in thine heart which shall not be put out" is a line from the Book of Esdras, one of the Apocryphal books of the Old Testament. It is also the title of one of Goodison's poems, and opens her book *Heartease* (1988). The poem begins with conscious uncertainty, in a gesture of faith—"I shall light." But by the middle of the poem, Goodison is speaking the full line, in a manner that recalls Gerard Manley Hopkins great poem of faith, "The Wreck of the Deutschland."

The frown of his face
Before me, the hurtle of hell
Behind, where, where was a, where was a place?
I whirled out wings that spell
And fled with a fling of the heart to the heart of the Host.[107]

This is Goodison's poem.

I shall light.
First debts to pay and fences to mend,
lay to rest the wounded past, foes disguised as friends.

I shall light a candle of understanding

Cease the training of impossible hedges round this life
for as fast as you sow them, serendipity's thickets will appear
and outgrow them.

I shall light a candle of understanding in thine heart.

All things in their place then, in this many chambered heart.
For each thing a place and for HIM a place apart.

I shall light a candle of understanding in thine heart
which shall not be put out.

By the hand that lit the candle.
By the never to be extinguished flame.
By the candle-wax which wind-worried drips
into candle wings luminous and rare.
By the illumination of that candle
exit, death and fear and doubt
here love and possibility
within a lit heart, shining out.[108]

Goodison, like Brathwaite and Walcott, writes poems of possibility—the possibility of understanding the past and present experience
of West Indians, the possibility of sharing their heritage of pain, and
the possibility of peace and light and love. Their poetic testaments are
simply and unmistakeably their own, bringing together the old world
of European and African inheritances with the new land and literature
of the West Indies.

Many other West Indian poets have joined their voices to those of
Walcott, Brathwaite, and Goodison, singing (in the words of the Jamaican Anthony McNeill) "out of the dark / the choir of light."[109] The
voices are individual and so are the stories they tell, but the achievement is shared by all. They bear witness to the truth of their experience
as West Indians, as poets, and as participants in a collective enterprise
of chronicling the fears that surround their lives and the hopes that
inspire them, in language that has shaped a new literary tradition. Poets
do not like to think of themselves as singing in a choir; but one way or
another, within the literary or the local tradition, that is what they do.
This, too, is the central heritage of West Indians, a heritage of belief in
what they have said and done together.

6

"i a tell no tale"

"Tell the story in your own words," we often say. It's what we ask of poets, as well as of other people who have something to tell us. We want the plain and simple truth.

But at least for poets, getting it plain is not so simple; and it may not be quite true. "Art is a lie that makes us realize truth,"[1] Pablo Picasso once suggested. Or as Oscar Wilde put it, picking up the paradox we talked about in chapter 4, "truth is entirely and absolutely a matter of style. . . . It is style that makes us believe in a thing—nothing but style."[2]

That is why styles often yearn to be plain as life, with an elemental simplicity. "The household truth, the style past metaphor," Walcott proposed.[3] And elsewhere, he claimed

> I seek
> As climate seeks its style, to write
> Verse crisp as sand, clear as sunlight,
> Cold as the curled wave, ordinary
> As a tumbler of island water.[4]

Artifice and naturalness, craft and candor, the literary and the local, are always in a tense relationship in poetry, and poems that seem casually inevitable are typically (to the poet's private chagrin) those resulting from the most deliberate work.

It is a storyteller's favorite gambit. Sincerity and spontaneity are themselves literary conventions. "i a tell no tale," says the Jamaican poet Oku Onuora.

        i a tell
        of reality . . .
        bout tings
        an time
        i a tell
        of crimes
        gainst humanity
        like poverty
        uh! pain
        an grief . . .[5]

   This, unfortunately, is precisely what the truth is like for many West
Indians. Pain and grief shape their lives, and poets who claim to be
telling their story need to convey the immediacy of this suffering. This
is much more difficult than it sometimes seems. Sympathy with suffering can quickly turn indulgent, with revolution slipping into
romance and the melodrama of fantasy and nostalgia. And poets who
are not careful find themselves merely cashing in. The poet Mutabaruka, also from Jamaica, describes one result.

        revolutionary poets
        'ave become entertainers
        babblin out angry words
        about
                ghetto yout'
        bein shot down
        guns an' bombs
                yes
        revolutionary words bein
        digested with
                bubble gums
                popcorn an
                ice cream[6]

   This is the danger of playing to an appetite for amusement, and the
momentary credibility it gives the entertainer. But there is a more common and more serious danger of not being credible at all. That is why
poets take such care to find the right words. Good poets, in good
poems, make us feel that the words they use are the only ones possible,
and that the words are their own. Handmade and heartfelt. If they
happen to be local words, bit by bit we come to understand the local
world and the poet's attachment to it.
   The simple truth of a poem, then, is first of all the poet's truth. Or
the poem's. It is spoken in the poet's voice, which is to say the voice of

the poem; and heard by the reader, who is expected to believe it. This is where things get more complicated—which is why a lot of attention has focused on the specific situation in which poetic statements are made, which includes the circumstances of publication and distribution as well as of performance; and on readers and audiences, which may contitute anything from what Brathwaite calls a "democracy of witness" to a small elite.

Telling the truth and being believed are two sides of the same coin. Poets make believe; readers suspend their disbelief. And they do so for various reasons. When a poet's language is what Bongo Jerry called a "strange tongue," readers sometimes give a special kind of credit to that strangeness. On the other hand, a familiar idiom has the advantage of . . . well, of familiarity, for a start.

Credit means simply "he or she believes," and ultimately readers have the choice. A poet of course tries to leave them no choice, by making it all seem inevitable. There is a totalitarian streak about assumptions of authority, poetic no less than political. But credibility is not an absolute, nor is it simply located in the text itself. The poet tells the truth . . . sometimes by lying; and readers believe it . . . or not. Credibility hovers between the poet, the poem, and the reader. And in the West Indies it shuttles betwen the prerogatives of European and non-European traditions of expression.

Poets have often been accused of lying. Plato called them untruthful, and therefore immoral. Others have been even less generous. But poets, for the most part, have embraced these accusations, welcoming them as a signal of their freedom from the distorting prerogatives of utility and morality. And yet poets never claim freedom from an obligation to tell the truth, insisting only that they do so in their own way, with the authority that comes from having nothing to gain, and nothing to lose. Of course, that's not quite accurate either, for poets typically are both interested and disinterested parties, claiming at most a special sort of immunity from compromise, a kind of privilege of the imagination, and contending that if they are vulnerable to influence, it is influence of a higher order.

The question of what to believe, and whom, has preoccupied literary criticism for a very long time. In different forms, it preoccupies members of *any* community every time they try to determine the truth. And so they establish some criteria for passing judgment, and develop some consensus (or conspiracy) of sympathetic understandings. In the case of poetry, this question is complicated by an endemic uncertainty about whether we believe the poet or the poem, the teller or the tale. It is an ancient uncertainty, embedded in the language we used to talk about all of this. The word *witness*, for instance, is both a noun and a verb, with the noun referring to the testimony given as well as to the individual giving it. The habit of identifying truth with the teller is encouraged by a variety of associations, some of them linked to the importance of individual testimony in oral traditions. There are other associations, too. In the Bible, the Greek word for which *witness* is the usual translation is the root of our English word *martyr*. On the other hand, the etymology of the English word *witness* centers around notions of memory and knowledge and wisdom, which brings us a bit closer to the authority of texts rather than individuals. The hovering certainties of the Gospel according to St. John, where the concepts both of witness and the word are most prominent, provide a notable example of the contingencies of truth-telling.

The abiding importance of literary criticism is that it focuses our attention on the relationships between the credibility and the conventions of language, relationships that have very wide significance. The balance between spontaneity and style we ask of those bearing witness in church or in court, for example, has close and clear analogues in literature, specifically in the balance between naturalness and artificiality that we admire in the language of a poem. (The Trinidadian educator John Jacob Thomas, who took on James Anthony Froude so passionately in *Froudacity*, wrote his creole grammar specifically to assist those working in local churches and courts, so that they would hear and understand the truth about people's experiences when they told it in their own words.) Poems and witnesses are believable when their language is accepted both as an expression of the tradition within which belief has become customary, and as (in some sense) the poet's or the witness's own words, authentic and authoritative.

Conventions complicate the matter, to be sure, and the conventions of painting provide not only a familiar example of the contingencies of truth in artistic representation but also an instance of how differently art may bear true witness. Let's imagine two painters sitting early one evening across the harbor from a ship at anchor. One, working in a particular tradition, paints the ship according to certain knowledge that she has of it—for instance, that it has twenty-seven portholes, and is gray. The other, working in an equally creditable tradition, paints seven portholes, because that's all he can see in the twilight; and he paints it in unlikely tones of pink and green, because that's what it looks like from where he's sitting at that hour of the day. Which is the true portrait? Both are determined as much by the conventions of artistic style as they are by any supposed certainties of the real thing. And either, taken out of its frame of reference, can be made to seem false, or foolish.

The strategies of hermeneutics, developed especially to deal with problems of authority and authenticity in biblical texts, provide some guidance in dealing with these issues. But only some; for hermeneutical strategies focus on questions of textual meaning, leaving aside the normative or evaluative dimension of critical inquiry. Having understood what has been said, we still need to decide whether to believe it. Biblical interpretation preempts that question, or rather presumes the answer. But it is obviously crucial for determining the truth of poetic discourse, as well as what we could unfashionably call its beauty and intelligence (or what Matthew Arnold called its sweetness and light). Collectively, these determine the significance we attach to a work of art, though they are usually described in more contemporary (but no less arbitrary) terms.

Other critical traditions address aspects of this issue of authority and authenticity, but they all have limitations. The contemporary critical interest in postmodernism and postcolonialism, while certainly interesting, has been narrowly preoccupied with prose. The same is true of recent inquiries into the nature of fictions. The age is not fully chronicled by its prose fictions or by the differently dependent fictions of history. Theories of language, especially those developed from nineteenth-century philology by twentieth-century linguists (such as Benjamin Whorf, on the one hand, and Ramon Jakobson on the other) to describe the conditioning of conceptual as well as cultural norms by linguistic structures, provide another useful dimension, as do current discussions (undertaken by anthropologists as well as literary critics) of the difference between "poetic" and "ordinary" language. There are also useful insights in speech-act theories of discourse, and in discussions of contingent values. But none of these takes full account of the ways in which poetry provides a unique convergence of private confession and public chronicle.

In this chapter we will hear something of how West Indian poets bring together language and place, as well as past and present, to bear witness to their experience. One of the most familiar, not to say old-fashioned, devices for creating authenticity is simple description . . . which may sound simple, but seldom is. Like nearly every other literary strategy, it has become part of the developing tradition of West Indian poetry, especially as it draws on the inheritance of folk customs. We have seen that one of the most obvious techniques is to use local speech to represent local experiences directly—as in the poem "St. Ann Saturday" by the Jamaican Christine Craig. ("Degge, degge" means "only one.")

Saturday afternoon. So many shades
of black swinging down the road.
funeral time.
Nice afternoon she get eh!

If

An so many smady turn out
like a ole days funeral

Dats right.

Imagine her time come
so quick. Well, de Lord giveth
an de Lord taketh away.

Sure ting . . .

Imagine is six pickney Miss Martha
raise, she one bring dem up an
send dem into de world.
Six pickney, she one.
Well as I say she send dem
out an is one degge, degge
daughta come home fe bury her.
Still an all, dem neva come
when she was hearty, no mek sense
dem come when she direckly dead . . .

Nice turn out Miss Martha have.
See Mass Len clear from Topside.
An no Granny Bailey dat from Retreat?
Well I neva. Tink seh she dead
long time. Time passing chile
we all moving down de line weself.

True word.[7]

But there are other strategies, too. In the following poem by the
Trinidadian-born Ian McDonald, who has lived much of his life in Guyana, where the poem is located, "Yusman Ali, Charcoal Seller" comes
alive through language that is more literary than local, and to that
extent represents the voice of the poet as an observer of the world he
describes rather than as a participant in it. The truth of Yusman Ali's
life is in its way as estranged from most of our experience (including
the poet's) as the language of the poem is from local speech. This is not

the only way to bear witness to this reality, of course; but it is a time-honored way, closely related to the often elaborate stylizations of storytellers. This chapter is about poetic storytelling and about poets saying things in their own words, whether these words are literary or local, and whether (as here) they are in the flatter rhythms we often associate with prose, or in the highly defined undulations of some other verse forms. And this chapter is also about the West Indian world of Yusman Ali, and how this world and its people are ennobled and in some (undoubtedly problematic) sense accredited in the accurate images and precise language of poetry, the charcoal-seller's spit shining like an emperor's bracelet.

Some men have lives of sweet and seamless gold.
No dent of dark or harshness mars those men.
Not Yusman Ali though, not that old charcoal man
Whose heart I think has learned to break a hundred times a day.
He rides his cart of embered wood in a long agony.

He grew rice and golden apples years ago
He made an ordinary living by the long mud shore,
Laughed and drank rum like any other man and planned his four sons'
glory
His young eyes watched the white herons rise like flags
And the sun brightening on the morning water in his fields.
His life fell and broke like a brown jug on a stone.
In middle age his four sons drowned in one boat up a pleasant river,
The wife's heart cracked and Yusman Ali was alone, alone, alone.
Madness howled in his head. His green fields died.

He burns the wild wood in his barren yard alone,
Sells the charcoal on the villaged coast and feasts on stars at night.
Thinness makes a thousand bones around his scorched heart.
His moon-scarred skin is sick with boils and warts.
His grey beard stinks with goat-shit, sweat, and coal.
Fire and heated dust have rawed his eyes to redness;
They hit like iron bullets in my guts.
No kindness in him: the long whip smashes on the donkey like on iron.
The black and brittle coal has clogged his chest with dirt,
The black fragrance of the coal is killing him.

He is useful still. I shake with pain to see him pass.
He has not lost his hating yet, there's that sweet thing to say,
He farts at the beauty of the raindipped moon.
The smooth men in their livery of success

He curses in his killing heart
And yearns for thorns to tear their ease.
His spit blazes in the sun. An emperor's bracelet shines.[8]

There is a conversational quality about this poem that masks its artifice, as even its iambic metrical structure merges with the rhythms of
speech. Assumptions about audience become part of the poem's
dynamics, for its detachment from the suffering it describes confirms
a kind of compact between speaker and listener, poet and reader.

In Lorna Goodison's "Bridge Views," another poem of local description, the poet is much more involved as a participant, and so is her
language. She—or more precisely the speaker of the poem—describes
the place and the people she grew up with, beginning with her brothers
and their friends. Her obvious familiarity with her subject gives the
language its immediacy and the poem much of its credibility. But the
poem also enacts its underlying theme, which is about boundaries: not
only between familiarity and strangeness ("ah know yu?"), but also
class lines, allegiances ("little boy loyalty," and "the early locks of
Rasta"), bridges and gullies.

The boys on the gully bridge
Rufus, George, Donkey Knee and
Curriman. My brothers numbering
five, till the little one

grew big enough to represent the half
dozen Goodison on the bridge.

There was the night the masked Indian
transporting the night soil of his
terrible occupation
angered by cries of 'ah know yu?'
turned and flicked his whip.
And the tip marked like snake spit
the red face of Curriman.

In the land of little boy loyalty
their friend became "shit whip."

Knowing no class lines or shoes
they roamed through fields
of police macca.

Played bat-up-and-ketch
and watched Gussie and Lloyd
wrestle with the early locks of
Rasta.

My mother did not forget to tell us
we did not really belong there.

Her family gave their name to rivers
her children should not play in gullies . . .[9]

So they moved, and with the move comes a new distance. It is this distance from which the speaker has been telling her story, of course, and it gives her the detachment of a view from the bridge. It also gives her a language that includes both local and literary dimensions. The strange word *macca*, for example, is familiar to any Jamaican. It comes via Spanish from an Arawak word for the macaw palm and is used in combination with other words to refer to any kind of prickle or thorn. Its use here creates a different effect of naturalness in the description than "the thorns to tear their ease" that Yusman Ali yearns for. On the other hand, there is the artifice of describing the railings on the bridge in highly figurative terms as "really diviner's signs / parallel, they spelt equal." It is this combination that gives the poem its style, both plain as life and convincing as art. It also intensifies the focus on boundaries: the shore, first of all, as well as town and country, power and powerlessness, and the law; and the line between hurt and healing, which is a constant in Goodison's world. As the story continues, the family move to a house near town.

At first the boys would come
to the phenomenon of this house

near the sea with a beach

and proper boundaries.
Unlike the schizoid waters
of the Hunts Bay Power Station
the heated pool of Kingston's poor
children.

And they came.
till Georgie tief some electric wire
from the hardware store.
And Mike discover the healing in white rum
till all his teeth fell out
to make room for more rum
and the neighbourhood was providing
addresses for murder cases.
And One Son shed his fat
and made the front page

of the Star
as the paid stepper of a
political figure
and more than that he broke out
of penitentiary
and shoot a guard as he hurried past.

The relationship between speaker and subject in Goodison's poem lies somewhere between the conscious detachment that characterizes certain descriptive forms, and a deliberate disordering of distinctions. When speaker and subject do converge, as in the poem "No sufferer" by Dennis Scott, the speaker's experience and the language in which it is expressed effectively *become* the subject of the poem, and carry the burden of its credibility. This is what contemporary criticism some-times calls self-reflexivity, which is said to characterize postmodern fiction. Self-reflexivity is not new, of course, though there are new—or at least more insistent—uses of it in prose fiction. One of the reasons poetry has not been a preoccupation of postmodern criticism is that it has been in this business a long time, routinely "problematizing" (to use the jargon) reality and "theorizing" and "thematizing" subjectivity, questioning the privileges of author and text and reader.

In "No sufferer," Scott gives an example of how this works, main-taining a subjective self-consciousness that is as much a style of truth-telling as is supposedly disinterested description. The poem is about the condition of the "sufferers," a word that in Jamaican speech refers to those who are black and poor and mainly live in the wretched slums of Kingston. The speaker bears witness in a voice that calls attention to itself as that of a black West Indian like Scott, one who dreams of "Zion . . . the safe land of my longing" within a framework of Rastafarian belief . . . but at the same time, and also like Scott, one who does not fully share the agony of those about whom he writes. So there is in the voice of the poem both a kind of superiority and a kind of surrender. And in the language of the poem there is the ambivalence of West Indian life and literature—questioning even as it confirms "proper" boundaries, and in that sense very much like Goodison's schizoid waters of the Hunts Bay Power Station.

In its rhythm and phrasing, Scott's poem has affiliations with the conventional English lyric. But it is unmistakeably West Indian in its diction and much of its syntax. "Mabrak," Bongo Jerry's black light-ning, is here; while the "dread time" is what it means to a non–West Indian, a time of fear, but also has its West Indian meanings of Baby-lonian apocalypse and Rastafarian revelation, "the blood's drum." The term *dread* itself plays on the tension between fear and fascination, as well as on the difference between slaver and slave, planter and maroon. "Version" refers to the poet's rendering of the story, his own words, but it has as well a specifically Jamaican reference to the instrumental rendering of a reggae song on the flip side of a 45 rpm record, which is often dubbed by disc jockeys with words of their own. The phrase "acknowledge I" is rich with local associations: to the individual dignity of all who join with Rastafarians in acknowledging the authority of Jah, or God; to His acknowledgment of them in their suffering; and to their collective presence ("I and I" in Rasta talk) and acknowledgment of each other.

> *No sufferer,*
>
> but in
> the sweating gutter of my bone
> Zion seems far
> also. I have my version—
> the blood's drum is
> insistent, comforting.
> Keeps me alive. Like you.
> And there are kinds of poverty we share,
> when the self eats up love
> and the heart smokes
> like the fires behind your fences, when my wit
> ratchets, roaming the hungry streets
> of this small flesh, my city
>
> : in the dread time of my living
> while whatever may be human chains me
> away from the surfeit of light, Mabrak
> and the safe land of my longing,
> acknowledge I.[10]

Scott's poem draws both on the literary authority of the lyric form, with all its engaging artifice, and on the credibility we give to speech that seems plain as life. Saying it in his own words involves using words of "dread talk," which was originally a form of Jamaican speech reflecting the religious, political, and philosophical beliefs of Rastafarianism and restricted to true believers—a secret language of sorts (exemplifying the exclusive codes of a closed community upon which poetry, too, often relies). The currency of dread talk is now much wider, and represents an affirmation of black consciousness and the advocacy of black power, especially by West Indian youth. During the 1960s and

1970s, the use of dread talk in the lyrics of reggae gave it prominence
and popularity. In a nice turnabout, dread talk now has the same place
in the orthodoxy of education as local dialect had a generation earlier.
"The middleclass parent who yesteryear sweated and prayed lest
another son might be 'turning Rasta' when his language suggested it,"
notes the Jamaican linguist, poet, and fiction writer Velma Pollard,
"protests now on aesthetic and pseudo-educational grounds."[11]

In a poem called "Rasta, Me Son," Ann Marie Dewar from Montserrat catches the pathos of this anxiety, once again in a way that
involves the speaker in her subject. The poem's language represents
Rastafarian speech (which extends well beyond Jamaica) and provides
an image of its independence. But representation of speech exemplifies
some of the complications involved in the representation of *anything* in
poetry; and this poem illustrates the irony that dialect in a poem sometimes draws attention to its artificiality rather than to its naturalness.
One of the reasons for this has to do with the representation of nonstandard speech in standard written form, since making our familiar
alphabet work in unfamiliar ways often seems ostentatiously arbitrary.
Dewar's poem has something of this arbitrariness. But it also conveys
in a believable way the feelings of a mother watching her son move
out of reach, and calling to him in a language that binds them to each
other, even—or perhaps especially—at the distance that now separates
them.

> So you tun Rasta now, me son!
> An yu expec dat after eighteen years
> O'callin you Emmanuel
> Ah mus now forget de pride ah did feel
> When you great granpa put ee han pan you head
> An gi you ee's great granpa name!
> Now you say you name Ras Ikido!
> Jesus Christ did name Emmanuel!
> It have any God name Ikido?
>
> An when ah beg you fo comb you head
> An go look fo wuk
> You call you mudda "daughter"
> An tell me fo scant?
> So you locks-up you head, me son!
> An you callin pan Selassie
> An pan Jah, who gi you
> More overstandin dan de res o a-we!

You a dream bout Ithiopia!
While you a dream
Who a go look fo you youths?
Me know mudda milk a ital food!
You a go locks-up dem head!
School children wicked, you know!
Oh! you a go educate dem yourself
An gi dem some o de overstandin
Whey Jah gi you!

You say Jah leadin you to de hills
Fo meditate pan de holy weed
An de Holy Word!
When Ee call you, me son,
Me a go tan up somewhey,
Somewhey you cyan see me,
An me a go say "Son, trod on, wid love"
An den me a go bawl![12]

Dread talk is the language of black power—the strange tongue—to which Bongo Jerry referred, the return to homemade speech after the self-abusive "straightening of the tongue" in imitation of the language of propriety and power. The distinctive character of dread talk is a product of innovations in language that will have a familiar cast to any reader of poetry. Words are made up, such as "spliff" (or "s'liff") for a cone-shaped marijuana cigarette. Familiar words take on unfamiliar meanings, with "bald" being used to describe someone not a Rasta (who at least notionally would have "dreadlocks"), as in "I are di dread, an yu are a bald." There is also a determined use of forms with special significance, such as the prefix "I," which in Rastafarian ideology celebrates both the sanctity of the self and respect for Haile Selassi, after a (probably deliberate) misinterpretation of the Roman numeral I in Haile Selassi I. "We" becomes "I and I" or "iani" or "I-man," with all kinds of puns possible. (Using "iani" as a point of reference, for example, Kamau Brathwaite represents Babylonian egotism and materialism as "mi/ami" (or Miami) in "Poem for Walter Rodney."[13]) And many specific words are changed in the Rastafarian lexicon, such as vital to "I-tal," referring to the presumed goodness (because of the healthy naturalness) of Rasta food. Finally, there is varying use of words that depend upon punning or other meaningful confusions of sound and sense, as we have seen in "downpression" and "overstand."

This serious play with language is part of Rastafarian culture, representing a deliberate expression of difference and a rejection of the conventions of standard West Indian speech. As such, dread talk exemplifies a heightened celebration of black consciousness, an affirmation of Rastafarian defiance and determination. Because of its difference from the standard language, it offers a kind of defense against the seductions of Babylon. It has its own imperatives, of course, as the mother notes when she laments "so you locks-up you head, me son"; but this is part of the paradox of choice that is as old as language, reflecting the necessary surrender of individual freedom in the institutions, including the language, of a community.

In a poem called 'Zoo Story—Ja. '76," the St. Lucian poet Kendel Hippolyte uses the language and the imagery of Rastafarianism, including the Lion of Judah, the red, green and gold colors of Rasta, and local words like "Jamdung" (Jamaica) and "dungle" (a version of dunghill, and the name of a now demolished shantytown in Kingston to which Brathwaite's Rastaman referred in "Wings of a Dove") to create a representation of Rastafarian experience in the dread time of the 1970s, a time of dark troubles and no black lightning.

> dis dungle dread say:
> "Lion!"
> flash de colours
> carry thunder on him head;
> any heart-dead weak-eye
> who try shake him faith
> or break him righteous roots
> him quake dem;
> dis dungle dread roar:
> "Rastafari!"
>
> red-green-gold rainbow
> lif' up from Jamdung
> scatter de white thin clouds of heaven—
> rest in I-tyopia . . .
> but right now, right ya
> earth weird
> creation scared, it turnin' colour . . .
> red-green-gold rainbow
> dis man a-look a swif' way into Zion.
>
> spliff use to take him dere
> before—
> ut wha'?
> spliff turn a white bone in him hand
> rainbow faith bleach down,

city dry him roots to straw.
him still sight, but no lightning . . .[14]

Derek Walcott wrote a play titled *O Babylon*, set in a Rastafarian community near Kingston in 1966 during Emperor Haile Selassie's visit to Jamaica, in which he addressed the difference of dread talk and the challenge of bringing it into the language of literature.

> In trying to seek a combination of the authentic and the universally comprehensible, I found myself at the centre of a language poised between defiance and translation, for pure Jamaican is comprehensible only to Jamaicans. . . . Within that language itself, the Rastafari have created still another for their own nation. . . . If the language of the play remained true to the sect, it would have to use the sect's methods of self-protection and total withdrawal. This would require of the playwright not merely a linguistic but a spiritual conversion, a kind of talking in tongues that is, by its hermeticism and its self-possession, defiantly evasive of Babylonian reason.The Rastafari have created a grammar and a syntax which immure them from the seductions of Babylon, an oral poetry which requires translation into the language of the oppressor. To translate is to betray. My theatre language is, in effect, an adaption and, for clarity's sake, filtered.[15]

Translation as betrayal. Dread talk as nation language. This opens up a very complex question, once again having to do with language and with representation in literary forms. Along with poems, a number of plays and novels have reflected Rastafarian language, one of the most memorable being *The Harder They Come,* by Michael Thelwell. It was inspired by a film with that title written by Perry Henzell and Trevor Rhone and directed and produced by Henzell, which told the story of a legendary reggae songwriter, ganja trader, and gunman named Rhygin. Its use of local language had considerable influence on the development of fiction both in the West Indies and as far away as Australia, where the aboriginal writer Mudrooroo Nyoongah (Colin Johnston) acknowledged Thelwell's inspiration. In an article about the "translation" of the film to the novel form, Thelwell recounts his experiences and his apprehensions. He quotes a particularly revealing conversation that took place when he was about halfway through the writing.

> It was by way of a phone call from Jamaica: quite literally the voice of the audience, and calling about the work too!
> "Breddah Michael, we hear say you writing a book, is true?" The caller was Brother Sam, poet-historian and theologian-in-residence with the Mystic Revelations of Ras Tafari, the very influential cultural ensem-

ble centred around the master drummer and Rasta patriarch Count Ossie, who had recently died. Naturally I was surprised and very pleased—vindicated really—by this unexpected expression of interest from this militant of grass-roots culture. I started to babble on about how very touched I was that he had called all this way and to explain the project, only to be cut off. (The call was, after all, much too expensive for pleasantries.)

"Dass all right Breddah Mike. Soun good, de book, is bout us, right? Den dat mean the Count mus in dere, seen?" The phrasing was a little ambiguous, a question but not a question. It was too early. I wasn't quite sure I understood. So he explained.

"I an I the brederin hear say you doing dis mighty work, seen? Well den, we the brederin checking to mek sure that Count Ossie will get his due and rightful place derein. So long as is about us, the Count supposed to be in dere. True?"

"Wait, is dat you calling me for?" The tone of hurt indignation was not just tactical on my part. "My brother, you really believe say I could write a book about yard, and leave out the Count?"

"Well, not to say you would leave 'im out, but . . ."

"Well, you can tell the brederin that the Count will certainly be in there. Seen, Iyah?"

Then, realizing that I might be making too hasty and sweeping a commitment, I felt compelled to launch into a discussion of the constraints of literary form. I explained at some length, and into a silence that somehow seemed to deepen as I spoke, that were I indeed doing a social or cultural study Count Ossie would inevitably have to be a major figure. Which was quite true. But this was a *novel*. And while I would wish the Count to be in it, and would certainly put him in if it proved possible, it would have to fit the context, and I couldn't categorically guarantee that the opportunity would present itself, or that if it did the Count would be as prominent as the brederin would wish. So much depended on the dictates of form, considerations of narrative structure, historical chronology, and the like.

"Surely you understand, my brother," I implored into the by now unnerving silence, fully aware of how fatuous and arty-farty I sounded as my words echoed back to my own ears. But in Sam there was neither mercy nor absolution.

"Understan?" he mimicked contemptuously. "Understan what? Stan under you mean. Iman must *stan under* say de man *want* to give praises and thanks to the Count, but it depen pon *form*? Pon *narrative struckchah*? Pon *fictional integrity*? Tell me something, mi Lion?"

"Yes?" I asked timidly.

"Tell me dis—is who writing who? *Is you writing de book, or de book writing you?*"

And he did not wait for an answer, a kindness probably not intentional. For a long time after that, I was haunted by a vision of Sam dramatically recounting our conversation to the assembled brederin and concluding with apocalyptic solemnity, "Our brederin gaan. Him laas. For is truly written, 'Many a foolish and heedless Ithiopian shall go down wid Babylon.' "[16]

Films, plays, and prose fiction have all drawn on Rastafarian language for their representation of the West Indies, but within their own conventions of realism. In poetry, as in other forms of imaginative expression, dread talk often merges with less-exclusive dialects of the language. It is an especially important achievement when, as in Lorna Goodison's "The Road of the Dread," we are made to realize that dread talk can be used in literature well beyond the imitation of speech to convey how, as a genuinely creative use of language, it changes the way we see the world, and the way we talk about it. We realize, in other words, that the language of dread talk can make us believe in the same way as any other language of literature, through the possibilities of a kind of artifice that is essentially uncompromised by the privileges and perversions of Babylon, including those of its literary forms. The speaker of Goodison's poem is a Rastafarian journeying on the road of trouble and despair toward a vision of peace.

> That dey road no pave
> like any other black-face road
> it no have no definite colour
> and it fence two side
> with live barbwire.
>
> And no look fi no milepost
> fi measure you walking
> and no tek no stone as
> dead or familiar
>
> for sometime you pass a ting
> you know as . . . call it stone again
> and is a snake ready fi squeeze yu
> kill yu
> or is a dead man tek him
> possessions tease yu
> Then the place dem yu feel
> is resting place because time
> before that yu welcome like rain,
> go dey again?. . .
>
> Some day no have no definite colour
> no beginning and no ending, it just name day
> or night as how you feel fi call it.

Den why I tread it brother?
well mek I tell yu bout the day dem
when the father send some little bird
that swallow flute fi trill me
and when him instruct the sun fi smile pan me first.

And the sky calm like sea when it sleep
and a breeze like a laugh follow mi.
Or a man find a stream that pure like baby mind
and the water ease down yu throat
and quiet yu inside.

And better still when yu meet another traveller
who have flour and yu have water and man and man
make bread together.
And dem time dey the road run straight and sure
like a young horse that cant tire
and yu catch a glimpse of the end
through the water in yu eye
I wont tell yu what I spy
but is fi dat alone I tread this road.[17]

Lines, fences, property and possessions, the boundaries of color, betrayal, the fear and fascination associated with strangeness and difference, beginnings and ends, night and day, life and death, self and other, and the community of brethren and sistren—all of these are represented in this poem, whose literariness is both enhanced by and contributes to the linguistic credibility of dread talk. Stories and songs, after all, do not just come naturally. Their own credibility is a function of conventions of belief as well as of colloquialisms; and they in turn make us believe in the languages they use.

The distinctiveness of West Indian languages, including dread talk, has encouraged the development of distinctively West Indian poetic forms, which have given new opportunities for poets to tell their stories in their own words and their own ways. One of these new forms is "dub poetry," which has been very popular over the past twenty years in the West Indies and in West Indian communities abroad—especially London, Toronto and New York, where it now has strong affinites with (and has had some influence on the development of) "rap," just as it probably took some inspiration itself from scat singing, especially in the ways in which its words shift away from representation. The term *dub*, as we know from Scott's poem, refers to adding or dubbing words to accompany an instrumental rendering of a popular song. Some disc jockeys in Jamaica established their reputations doing this, extending the "toaster" tradition in which DJs talked "smart and silly" before and between the music. Dubbing words over a musical background became common enough that dub poetry came to include any rendition incorporating reggae musical rhythms, and any verse combining reggae rhythms with local speech. Dub poetry is still often performed to the accompaniment of music, maintaining a sense of the influence of reggae musicians such as Bob Marley and Peter Tosh; and the racy style of Jamaican dancehall provides another popular alternative. But musical accompaniment is not as important to dub poetry as hearing the reggae rhythm in the poem, as we do in the madwoman's moving, longing refrain in Jean Binta Breeze's "Riddym Ravings."

> Eh, Eh
> no feel no way
> town is a place dat ah really kean stay
> dem kudda—ribbit mi han
> eh—ribbit mi toe
> mi waan go a country go look mango[18]

The term *dub poetry* itself was popularized by Oku Onuora (formerly Orlando Wong) to characterize the work that he and other Jamaicans such as Noel Walcott, Michael Smith, Jean Breeze, and Mutabaruka (formerly Allan Hope) were performing in public. But the inspiration of Kamau Brathwaite was also very important, for during the 1960s in Marina Ama Omowale Maxwell's Yard Theatre in Jamaica he was reading with Count Ossie on drums; and throughout this period he was bringing the indigenous rhythms of African and West Indian drumming and of jazz into his poetry and performances.

Many other poets outside Jamaica, such as Ras Michael Jeune in Guyana, have picked up this tradition and moved in new directions. Beyond dub poetry, too, is a much wider range of public performance, which for West Indians is linked to their heritage of oral performance and of theater. Telling the story in your own words—and your own rhythms and images—means recognizing them as your own. In Trinidad, Brother Resistance has combined the conventions of dub with those of American rap and Trinidadian calypso to produce a new form called "rapso"; and Delano Abdul Malik DeCoteau, who was born in Grenada but has lived most of his life in Trinidad, has also brought together music (in his case, drum and steel band) and the spoken language in ways that emphasize highly topical, often highly political, themes. Marina Ama Omowale Maxwell has developed a performance poetry that draws on a legacy of song and story in which African and European inheritances merge into what Brathwaite has described as the West Indian creole inheritance of the past five hundred years. Groups such as those led by the Guyanese poet and performer Marc Matthews (Dem Two [with Ken Corsbie], All Ah We, and He and She) and the varied performances of the Popular Theatre movement in the Eastern Caribbean have extended and expanded these traditions.

The performance of poetry, whether live or recorded, has helped poets speak to a wider community than the comparatively elite readership to which written texts often confine them, though like any other form of expression it has its own limitations and determinisms. (It is a nice recognition of the ambivalent character of poetry that some kinds of oral performances are routinely referred to as "readings".) The popularity of these public readings coincides with an unusually talented set of performers among West Indian poets.

One of the most gifted of these was Michael Smith. He has a special status—as martyr and witness—in the contemporary West Indies. In August 1983, just as he began to achieve international renown, he was attacked in Kingston by three men with whom he had had a quarrel after a political gathering, and was fatally injured in the head by a stone thrown at him. Smith belonged to none of the political parties in Jamaica, and he scorned what he called its "partisan politricks." "Me no sectarian inna my view. Me lick out gainst baldhead, PNP, JLP, any one of them P-deh," he said in an interview with Mervyn Morris in 1981.[19] But he had strong opinions, and deplored the general state of affairs in West Indian society. In his poetry he spoke about the suffering experienced by so many West Indians as a sad and constant reminder that they were still not free of the legacy of slavery, nor of the need for voices to cry freedom. His death was for many a symbol of the violence routinely inflicted on those who bear the burden of colonial history. In a grim irony, Smith was killed—stoned to death—at a place in Kingston called Stony Hill.

Although he was an extraordinarily effective performer, he nonetheless thought of himself first of all as a writer: "Me a one writer first, me a one actor second, and me a one director third," he told Mervyn Morris. He became increasingly anxious to see his poems in print, and at the time of his death he was working with Morris to develop written texts for his oral performances. The result of this collaboration was a book *It A Come*, which appeared in 1986 edited by Morris. It gives a powerful illustration of the ways in which the effect of poetry is intensified, and its credibility enhanced, by the development of new relationships between the conditions of literary expression—written and spoken languages, their artifice and their naturalness, their casualness and their deliberateness, their strangeness and their familiarity. It also highlights some of the complicated relationships between text and performance. Do they differ in kind, as well as degree? How does the occasion of a performance affect our response; and how do we compensate for qualities of voice such as tone and rhythm, pitch and phrasing, in a written text. What sort of difference does having heard the poet make in subsequent readings of a poem? What is lost, or gained, in translation between performance and text; and which do we think of as the original? These are questions that bear on all poetry; but once again West Indian poetry provides an unusually clear illustration of them.

Both spoken and written, Smith's poems have a special urgency about them, a sense that the poet is chronicling events with ruthless accuracy because telling the truth—and having it heard—will make a difference. In the title poem, Smith speaks with an apocalyptic voice that picks up the tradition of Biblical prophecy and transforms it through the language of Jamaican speech into a revelation of the reality of West Indian experience, shared with others through the power of its imaginative expression.

> It a come
> fire a go bun
> blood a go run
> No care how yuh teck it
> some haffi regret it
>
> Yuh coulda vex till yuh blue
> I a reveal it to you
> dat cut-eye cut-eye cyaan
> cut dis-ya reality in two
>
> It a come
> fire a go bun
> blood a go run
> it goin go teck you
> it goin go teck you
>
> so Maggie Thatcher
> yuh better watch ya
> yuh goin go meet yuh Waterloo
> yuh can stay deh a screw
> I a subpoena you
> from de little fella

call Nelson Mandela
who goin tun a martyr
fi yuh stop support
de blood-suckin I
call apartheid

for it a come
blood a go run
it goin go teck you
it goin go teck you . . .

not only fi I
but fi you too[20]

This poem has conventional features about it: its refrain; its direct address (from an "I" to a "you," who is at first everyone and then someone [Thatcher] and then back to anyone); its visual imagery centered around the redness of fire and blood; and its voice of authority, hovering on the edge of arrogance, the voice of someone who knows the truth and is telling it. On the other hand, its language is not conventionally literary, but flamboyantly local. This creates a poetic style that sustains both the plain-as-life-like qualities of speech and the heightened sense and highly structured intensity of personal revelation that it is the business of certain forms of poetry, especially lyric poetry, to achieve. Also, there is the convention of poet as participant, not only speaking *for* the sufferers but also as one of them. The martyrdom of Michael Smith has enhanced this role, fitting in with that sad but venerable etymology of witnessing.

Smith's poem "Me Cyaan Believe It" carries this a step further, directly involving the speaker and his language in a tension between doubt and belief that becomes the poem's real subject, reinforced by the image of the poet as outcast ("Madhouse!"). In a sense, a West Indian poet comes into that role naturally, representing a marginal society. But there is also a longstanding literary convention here, strongly developed during the nineteenth century but with deep roots in an earlier European tradition, of the poet as either recluse or prisoner, in one way or another inside a cell. The important element was always the power that forced him there or forced him to make that choice. As the seventeenth-century playwright Nathaniel Lee said when he was sent to an insane asylum: "they said I was mad and I said they were mad; and damn them, they outvoted me."[21] Smith's poem sets the conditions of contemporary Jamaican life and its coercions against the poet's claim on us. Both in different ways require a suspension of disbelief; for the conditions and coercions are fantastic (the way a night-mare is), and the claim is fiercely personal. ("Cyaan" means "can't" in Jamaican speech—with the pitch creating the difference between "can" and "cannot," and sometimes also generating a significant ambiva-lence.)[22]

Me seh me cyann believe it
me seh me cyaan believe it

Room dem a rent
me apply widin
but as me go een
cockroach rat an scorpion
also come een

Waan go
nose haffi run
but me naw go siddung pon high wall
like Humpty Dumpty
me a face me reality

One little bwoy come blow im horn
an me look pon im wid scorn
an me realize now me five bwoy-picni
was a victim of de trick
dem call partisan politricks

an me ban me belly
an me bawl
an me ban me belly
an me bawl
Lawd
me cyaan believe it
me seh me cyann believe it

Me daughter bwoy-frien name Sailor
an im pass through de port like a ship
more gran-picni fi feed
an de whole a we in need
what a night what a plight
an we cyaan get a bite
me life is a stiff fight
an me cyaan believe it
me seh me cyaan believe it . . .

Teck a trip from Kingston
to Jamaica
Teck twelve from a dozen
an me see me mumma in heaven
Madhouse!   Madhouse!

Me seh me cyaan believe it
me seh me cyaan believe it

Yuh believe it?
How yuh fi believe it
when yuh laugh
an yuh blind yuh eye to it?

But me know yuh believe it
Lawwwwwwwwd
me know yuh believe it[23]

The power of Smith's witness to contemporary Jamaican life recalls
something we touched earlier in our discussion of the *Savacou* anthology. Is there some canon (or anticanon) of correctness governing poetic
subjects and styles, some things poets should or should not do, perhaps
depending on who they are and where they are? Edward Baugh reflects
on this in "Truth and Consequences."

When the mob swerved
at him
he screamed
"I'm not the man you're after.
I'm Cinna the poet.
I never meddled in politics!"

The mob knew better. "Then tear him,"
it screamed back, "tear him
for his bad verses!"

It was then he learned
too late
there's no such thing as *"only* literature."
Every line commits you.
Those you thought dead will rise,
accusing. And if you plead
you never meant them,
then feel responsibility

break on you in a sudden sweat
as the beast bears down.[24]

Saying it in your own words is one side of this coin; what to talk about is the other—and trouble. Something false on either side can produce counterfeit currency. So poets must pay attention to both when they make their poetic transactions. Medium and message, form and content, are not separable. Hardly a new insight; and we have seen its import from the beginning of this story about poetry in the West Indies and its negotiation between particulars and universals. In "Two Poems On: What I Can Write" Mutabaruka gives an account of the predicament.

can i write poems
about:
tall green grass
shadin the tough
earth,
about:
dew drops on beautiful
spreadin lilies?

can i write
of lovers
makin love
in parks
with moon shine caressin
their faces?
. . . of rainbow coloured birds
singin their nature songs
in tall lush trees?

all of this i can write.

but now,
i write; . . .
i write of tall trees
shadin black skins
from
hot death
of:
guns   and
bombs
hidden under spreadin white sheets

                    i write
                    of people
                    bein shot down in parks
                    with blood washin their faces
                    . . . of negroes and
                              coloureds
                    shoutin freedom songs
                    in tall anti-freedom
                    buildins

                              all this i write.[25]

Poets are not about to be told what to do—not by communities, and
not by critics. Only by their own instincts; and these are sometimes
very troublesome. There are times, plenty of times, when a poet's
thoughts and feelings are not in concert with those of the society, and
when he or she chooses the imperialisms of literary convention over
those of the community. In a poem titled "Cold Comfort," Baugh
describes how after reading the poem "Aubade" by the English poet
Philip Larkin he

                              had
                    the authentic shivers, gooseflesh.
                    Then started worrying about how
                    supposedly death poems and
                    love poems are luxuries
                    we in the third world
                    cannot afford . . .[26]

But as Baugh knows well, poetry is a luxury in the way falling in
love is a luxury . . . the way moments of peace and hope are luxuries
in a life of trouble and despair. The way death is a luxury in some
people's lives. And Baugh knows, too, and has eloquently conveyed in
his poetry and criticism, that neither a poem's subject nor its style necessarily certifies the poet's allegiance or guarantees the poem's credibility. As the Argentinian writer Edward Galeano insisted in an essay
on "The Imagination and the Will to Change,"

> the literature that is most political, most deeply committed to the political
> process of change, can be the one that least needs to name its politics, in
> the same sense that the crudest political violence is not necessarily dem-
> onstrated by bombs and gunshots. . . . Those who approach the people
> as if they were hard of hearing and incapable of imagination confirm the
> image of them cultivated by their oppressors. . . . Literature that shrinks
> the soul instead of expanding it, as much as it might call itself militant,

objectively speaking is serving a social order, which daily nibbles away
at the variety and richness of the human condition. . . . I believe that
literature can recover a political, revolutionary path every time it contributes to the revelation of reality. . . . From this point of view, a love
poem can be more fertile than a novel dealing with the exploitation of
miners in the tin mines or workers on the banana plantations.[27]

A poem by the Guyanese poet and critic Mark McWatt (from his
book *Interiors* [1987]) provides a good example of how a poet's
intensely private feelings—in this case his sorrow at the passing of a
peaceful time—can convey something of public consequence. The
poem is called "Morawhanna" after a town on the north coast of Guyana, and it is about the poet's love for his father and his memories of
travels through the country with him. But better than any polemic
about the condition of a society, and simply by speaking in a quiet
voice about love and loss, the poet tells a compelling story of the land
and its people—people who are turned into beasts of burden descending with their dreams into the swamp.

> Morawhanna names all moments of morning mist,
> of desperate tranquility violated
> by structures of wood and steel—
> coffin of night, nail of light—
> one feels old wounds again
> and the heart's vain hesitation
> at the approach and rhythm of painful words:
> "morning," "destination."
>
> Even within that last dim peace, you know
> there are bent bodies on the stelling
> shouldering the foreday like beasts
> of burden, while others wait
> with lost whistles
> and branches of fire and smoke
> that ape the sun.
> The ship's bow ripple is now discerned,
> stark, curling to the dark trees:
> morning's life-line or the last tail of metal
> from the lathe of night?
>
> The world's eye opens
> on vendors of fruit and crabs
> and morning, full of gold teeth
> and the oldest appetites,

is loud and heroic
on the shop-bridges of Morawhanna.

"Where does that road go?"
(you hear someone, squinting, say)—
"it goes into muffled laughter,
points the way to all foundered dreams,
like back-stairs
descending to the swamp."

Nothing on this river knows
that, as the hawser stiffens
in your tide of pain, tying you
to earth and light again,
Morawhanna names that love for a dead father
and these mornings can never know peace again.[28]

The painful words "morning" and "destination" catch the two notions
of time (linear and cyclical) and the two explanations of events (according to origins and ends) which shape the poet's memories of the lost
and the found, fathers and founderers, and which confirm his ambivalent heritage of pain and a peace that is both rhetorically denied and
imaginatively confirmed in the poem's lovely closing. The feelings in
"Morawhanna"—private, public, deliberately "poetic"—are layered
and interwoven in ways that illuminate the character and credibility of
poetic representation. Truth as a matter of style.

The *making* of a work of art is as much a part of bearing witness to
the West Indies as the *mirroring* of West Indian life. This is an obvious
statement. But we sometimes forget its implications; and indeed poets
sometimes work hard to make us forget. All good poets pay attention
to their craft. A dub poet such as Michael Smith, no less than Mark
McWatt, put together his poems (and in the case of Smith, his performances) with painstaking care. For Smith, the illusion of spontaneity and
inevitability was part of this craft, part of the deliberate effect of making
a poetic line which (to quote W. B. Yeats) "might take an hour maybe,
but if it does not seem a moment's thought, the stitching and unstitch-
ing have been nought."[29]

The way in which the naturalness of a good poem is balanced by its
artifice corresponds to the equilibrium a poem achieves between
engagement with the realities of life and detachment as a work of the
imagination. Yeats once talked about literature as "the disinterested
contemplation of life," echoing Wordsworth's description of poetry as
"emotion recollected in tranquility." For all poets, the challenge is to

write poems in which the confusions of life are transformed into the coherence of art (which may of course provide a new *representation* of those confusions), taking the trouble to make the voice of experience into a credible poetic voice. The Jamaican poet Anthony McNeill wrote in 1970 that "I don't think I could write if my first concern weren't for the aesthetic, a concern that would be immoral / Uncle Tom here," here being the United States, where McNeill was living in the late sixties and early seventies. For McNeill, the key was to get the poem "together so inevitably harmonious and *right* that the caught energy *stays.*"[30] At the same time, he was conscious of the limitations of appealing only to an elite audience of fellow poets; and he praised what he called the eccentric and untidy voice of Walt Whitman, a voice that maintained its integrity while extending its audience.

McNeill was well aware of the intimidating pressures that the experiences of life place on art, and of the temptation to write in ways determined exclusively by reality. He recognized that the imagination is not *un*determined but *differently* determined, and that it is one of the most powerful instruments of resistance to the intimidations of reality. McNeill's resistance in his poetry becomes an image of the struggle of all West Indian artists, and indeed of all West Indians, to affirm the authority of their own imaginations in forms that express the immediacy of the world in which they live and the possibilities of liberation from its imperious demands. In his poem "Ode to Brother Joe" (from *Reel from "The Life-Movie"* [1975]) McNeill presents an account of the Rastafarian rejection of contemporary West Indian life and the ironies of that rejection. The poem includes words, such as "s'liff" and "the Babylon" (the police), which are in dread talk; and the rhythms, too, are distinctly Jamaican, though in a subtler way. On the other hand, the energy of the poem is maintained by a lyric structure that owes little to Rastafarianism and is not exclusively West Indian. Odes, after all, are a literary form going back a very long way, and McNeill's poem becomes part of a literary tradition to which readers from well beyond the West Indies are accustomed. Its conversational language merges with highly literary phrases (albeit ones shaped by Rastafarian imagery) such as "head swollen with certainties," "the door gives in a rainbow gust," and "a furnace of optimism." As a result, West Indian experience comes alive in a voice whose credibility is equally the product of its local authenticity and its literary authority, the words those of a West Indian and a poet.

> Nothing can soak
> Brother Joe's tough sermon,

his head swollen
with certainties.

When he lights up a s'liff
you can't stop him,
and the door to God, usually shut,
gives in a rainbow gust.

Then it's time for the pipe,
which is filled with its water base
and handed to him for his blessing.
He bends over the stem,
goes into the long grace,
and the drums start

the drums start
Hail Selassie I
Jah Rastafari,
and the room fills with the power
and beauty of blackness,
a furnace of optimism.

But the law thinks different.
This evening the Babyon catch
Brother Joe in his act of praise
and carry him off to the workhouse.[31]

"The law thinks different." Colloquial syntax highlights both the local idiom and the various dimensions of this statement. The laws governing Brother Joe have a fair bit in common with the laws governing poems about him. Both endorse good behavior. But according to whose standards: those represented by Rastafarian drumming; or by the authority of Babylon? Brother Joe and the law think differently on these matters. Haile Selassie, in the words of the poem, "is far away / and couldn't care less;" and Brother Joe "has become a martyr; / But still in jail."

The workhouse to which Brother Joe is taken is an institution out of Thomas Carlyle's time, and carries with it all that legacy of incarceration. West Indian poets are determined that the creative imaginations of West Indians, not of Europeans or Africans or anyone else, will legislate new laws governing West Indian life and literature. In literary terms, this means reevaluating criteria of meaning and value. The mirrored phrasing of that last sentence—"this means reevaluating . . . meaning and value"—indicates the irony, and the circularity, of such exercises. But they *can* generate new freedoms as well as new determinisms, and at the very least create a heightened sensitivity to the ways in which West Indian poetry meets normative standards shared with others elsewhere. To the extent that new standards are developed and *are* genuinely different, they may simply replace one authoritarianism with another, of course, as the categories of critical approbation become instruments of appropriation.

But there are other checks and balances. In the case of West Indian literature, its variety has been the surest. Another is what might be called the competitive judgment of the wide community of readers—wider, at least, than the circle of critics. Literary critics have been loath to accept competition as having anything to do with critical judgment . . . but in fact it goes back to the origins of literary criticism. The first truly official—which may be to say, the first truly officious—literary critics in European literary affairs were the judges appointed in early Greek times to decide between rival rhapsodists. The footrace and the wrestling mat provided the more permanent ancient pleasures, perhaps, but they also provided an early pattern for critical as well as rhetorical enterprise. Many of the terms of rhetoric came from the sports arena, and so did much of its exhilaration. (The Guyanese critic Gordon Rohlehr has added another element by occasionally shouting terms of challenge from stick fighting and other indigenous West Indian sports at the beginning and end of his lectures.) West Indian literature has maintained this element in calypso, where competition and judgment are accepted principles. And of course the varied responses of different readers and audiences to *any* poem or poet provides a check against the exclusive judgment of critics. Not that critics should necessarily defer to the opinions of others; but neither should they dismiss them.

Some poetry, of course, does not fall into the tidy classifications necessary for competitive judgment. We need to know whether it is a footrace or a wrestling match in order to decide the winner (though professional wrestling may be an exception here). Any poem must be placed, at least provisonally, within some tradition, if only so that its defiance may be acknowledged. That's one of the ways in which good literary criticism can be crucial. McNeill's defiance has been unmistakable, but unpredictable. He is sometimes difficult to categorize and therefore sometimes difficult to read. I do not mean this in a trivial way. But whether we like it, or indeed whether we know it, we always read according to conventions. That's why the framing we talked about earlier is so important to recognize, so that as readers and critics we don't become like that dog in the *New Yorker* cartoon, barking (as it were) up the wrong tree.

McNeill's latest work moves to new relationships with a distinctly American literary tradition, one that complements an older British literary inheritance and includes poets such as Walt Whitman and William Carlos Williams and W. S. Merwin. And yet the voice is still recognizably McNeill's, telling his own story in his own words. These are some passages from his book *Credences at The Altar of Cloud* (1979).

> I asked   the voice answered
> I wept   the voice bled
> I drank   the voice thundered
> I kissed   the voice fell
>
> The bell
>
> in the clearing . . .
>
> fell   word of great beauty
> I write you down
>
> the lovers have kissed
> you the high cliffs
>
> hollow you back
> with your feet dragging
>
> and the soul is a lit
> candle in space . . .
>
> turn   I am dizzy
> the world turns
>
> out of the cradle
> endlessly rocking
>
> out of the valley
> endlessly speaking
>
> out of the dark
> the choir of light[32]

Contemporary West Indian poetry includes both singers and storytellers, with no tidy distinction between the ways in which they bear witness to their experience as West Indians and to the past and future of the West Indies. The range of these experiences is very wide, as are their perspectives, and the languages and forms in which they write.

Diversity is one of the most significant features of contemporary West Indian poetry, in fact, and has helped ensure that these experiences become part of the present heritage of West Indians and (almost as importantly) are not appropriated as part of someone else's.

This heritage, the heritage of slavery, is founded in loss—or what Edward Baugh once described as "the one grief of the world." For Baugh, West Indians are connected by the difficult grace that brought them together, and by the persistent, patient love that holds them together. At the heart of his own work is a love of language, and of his land and its people; and a conviction that literature can be both its most powerful expression and what Michael Smith called "a vehicle of giving hope."[33] This is Baugh's poem "Lignum Vitae."

> When the final carry-down artist lock down
> this town and scorch the earth till not
> even lizard don't crawl, those who still living
> next morning will see me surviving still
> wood of life, salvation tree
> I renew my phases of lilac-blue
> and gold and always green, I am
> a shady place . . .
> And to think, so many people born
> and grow and dead and never feel
> the rainbreeze blowing cool across
> Cinchona from Catherine's Peak at middle
> day. Sometimes I feel my heart
> harden, but I not going nowhere, my root
> sink too deep, and when the 8 o'clock sun
> wake up the generations of stale pee and puke
> that stain the sidewalk by Parade, I weep
> I bloom choirs of small butterflies.[34]

Poets such as the Jamaican Olive Senior also write from the center of their people's lives, with a sure sense of the struggle that has shaped them. Senior grew up in rural Jamaica near the Cockpit Country, the refuge of the Maroons. She is best known as a writer of short stories, including *Summer Lightning* (1986) and *Arrival of the Snake Woman* (1989), though she has also written social and historical studies. For several years she was editor of the magazine *Jamaica Journal*, in which capacity she drew from her own heritage to bring lively attention to all aspects of Jamaican life, landscape, and language. "Ancestral Poem," from her book *Talking of Trees* (1985), tells of this heritage, the poet's hard-won freedom from its rituals and rigors, and its continuing hold on her imagination. This is a complex poem, its juxtapositions at first relatively untroubled but quickly becoming very disturbing, as thoughts and emotions are intersected by the menace of ingrained ritual and encased memory, and then by the violence and betrayal that are their legacy. The second stanza, in parenthesis, portrays one of those moments outside any frame of resolution—a moment of fierce and indelible irrationality, represented by the confusing of her father on earth with the Father in heaven, a confusion that intensifies the disabling bewilderment of the moment and of her memory. The irony of the final line of this whole passage, where the deeply ambivalent ritual of religious confirmation provides a gesture of freedom in a language that accumulates betrayal and abstraction, is hauntingly reminiscent of one of the themes of this book, for the ambiguous syntax is generated by the local use of the word *me* in a literary context. And the final word *freedom*, with its rhetorical flourish, is as much a gesture of ill-fated defiance of her heritage as a description of any new liberation.

> When my father planted
> his thoughts took flight.
> He did not need to think.
> The ritual was ingrained
> in the blood, embedded
> in the centuries of dirt
> beneath his fingernails
> encased in the memories
> of his race.
>
> (Yet the whiplash of my
> father's wrath rever-
> berated days in my
> mind with the inten-
> sity of tuning forks.
> He did not think.
> My mother stunned wept
> and prayed Father
> Forgive Them knowing not
> what she prayed for.)
>
> One day I did not pray.
>
> A gloss of sunlight through
> the leaves betrayed me so
> abstracted me from rituals.
> And discarded prayers and

disproven myths
confirmed me freedom.[35]

The voices in "The Mother," another of Senior's poems, speak of the life of the West Indian poor, for whom the legacy of slavery has produced new forms of disgust and despair, and whose only hope may be in bearing witness to their own lives in their own words—words full of suffering and self-hatred and the sad ironies of self-conscious pretense and pathos. ("Crosses," in the final line, means particular bad fortune or adversity.)

Muma mi belly soon
grow bed so small
last night Uncle Paul
bizniz with me
didn't know till he done—

Hush yu mout little gal
have no right
talk such nonsense
how come yu so shurance
and force ripe. Uncle Paul
help with school fees
and dress say he like

—what go on
under cover

girls look nice when they go
off to school

Muma no school today
mi body a hot me. Mi
head dis a grow muma
beg yu no lash me

One night you even say
yu own father did try
O god pickney nowadays
so wicked and lie

Study books dem not story.
If you get heddication dont
have to be like me

As for that lazy bitch there the
one Mistress Marshall she going
get her comeuppance as soon as a done

she think I dont know when she
think I round back who she entertain
round front say is insurance they selling
dont know where she gone in her
prison-pon-wheel. Say I tief out
the rice. Say black people not nice

Who dont know it will feel.

And where Bobby eh? A just know seh is trouble
that boy done get into. Do nutten but walk
street keep company. Toyota have no right
pull up door at night call the boy out say is
business he gone on. What right boy that age
have with business and firearm (that he swear he dont have).

O God but this town is a crosses.[36]

Other poets whose work deserves attention also write from the center of their people's lives—poets of several generations, including Jan Carew and Abdur-Rahman Slade Hopkinson from Guyana, and Howard Fergus and E. A. Markham, both from Montserrat, all of whom were born in the 1920s and 1930s. These kinds of lists of names and dates do not tell a lot; but perhaps they continue the process of recognition that this book is all about. Poets such as Pamela Mordecai, Rachel Manley, and Velma Pollard (from Jamaica), Wayne Brown, Roger McTair, Faustin Charles, Cynthia James, and Dionyse McTair (from Trinidad), Wordsworth McAndrew (from Guyana), and John Robert Lee (from St. Lucia) represent a tradition of West Indian poetry that is being shaped by a wide range of personal experiences, regional and national heritages, and literary ambitions. This tradition includes East Indian voices, which (except for Vidia Naipaul) have not been prominent in this account, as indeed they have not been (until quite recently) in contemporary West Indian poetry. The Guyanese writers Mahadai Das, Sasenarine Persaud, and Cyril Dabydeen, who now lives in Canada, deserve mention, along with the Trinidadian Ramabai Espinet. And the poems of Rajandaye Ramkissoon-Chen, also from Trinidad, present images of East Indian life that convey the differences with compelling authority. There are some especially interesting uses of the languages, forms, and rhythms of Hindu chants, Muslim calls to prayer, and the curses and cow-calls of the Indian communities in Trinidad and Guyana in contemporary Indo-Caribbean poetry, offering a new dimension to the discussion of relationships between local and literary language.

One of the most notable poets of East Indian descent is David Dabydeen, a Guyanese now living in England. His first book was called *Slave Song* (1984), a testimony to the central heritage of all West Indians. In the title poem of his second book *Coolie Odyssey* (1988), Dabydeen picks up his own East Indian inheritance, describing his return home for his mother's funeral and his determination to tell her story. His poem is a catalog of images of the new world and the old, of things of value and things deemed worthless, and finally of the dreams of a better world that make men and women leave home and go elsewhere . . . and then sometimes return. The poem uses literary conventions to highlight the language of conversation, and it illuminates how the complementary elements of strangeness and familiarity work together to establish the credibility of both the poet's and his mother's words.

> I have come back late and missed the funeral.
> You will understand the connections were difficult.
> Three airplanes boarded and many changes
> Of machines and landscapes like reincarnations
> To bring me to this library of graves,
> This small clearing of scrubland.
> There are no headstones, epitaphs, dates.
> The ancestors curl and dry to scrolls of parchment.
> They lie like texts
> Waiting to be written by the children
> For whom they hacked and ploughed and saved
> To send to faraway schools.
> *Is foolishness fill your head.*
> *Me dead.*
> *Dog-bone and dry-well*
> *Got no story to tell.*
> *Just how me born stupid is so me gone.*
> Still we persist before the grave
> Seeking fables.
> We plunder for the maps of El Dorado
> To make bountiful our minds in an England
> Starved of gold.[37]

There have been other innovations in West Indian poetry, as new voices make older literary forms over in their own image and find

different possibilities for the imaginative representation of local realities. Other forms of artistic expression, such as painting and music,
have of course been part of the development of a distinctive artistic
tradition in the West Indies, and West Indian poetry has taken some
of its character from these. In the European literary tradition both painting and music have a long association with poetry, and both are part
of a West Indian inheritance from Africa as well as Europe. As we have
noted, a variety of forms of music have had special significance in the
West Indies, from African drumming and nonconformist church music
to calypso and the steel band. West Indian painting too has developed
its own styles, and two of the major contemporary poets—Walcott and
Goodison—are notable painters. But it has been music, with its unique
importance in the cultural and political history of the West Indies,
which has had a particularly strong influence on West Indian poetry.
Poets such as Anthony Kellman from Barbados, along with a new generation of writers from the eastern Caribbean, have taken up the complex mix of European and African elements in unique local traditions
such as Barbadian Landship—a parade in which the imitation of English naval uniforms and ships is combined with dancing that has clear
African origins. Music is provided by the so-called Tuk bands (which
are also found separately from Landship parades) that bring together
instruments that owe something to the eighteenth-century British fife
and drum bands with dancing and entertainment that reflects an African (and creolized West Indian) heritage. Kellman picks up these elements in the title poem of his book *Watercourse* (1990), using the place
names of Barbados to locate his inheritance and to lament its debase-
ment in the corruptions of neocolonialism.

> Island
> is the water of my name
> coasting round St. Lucy
> down through them St. John hills,
> coursing through to St. Peter
> ruk-a-tukking to St. Michael . . .
>
> I see I
> I see islands building and breaking
> churning like wild tides
> rukking around a round rock
> and tukking around a rock . . .
> and the neo-colonial stench is everywhere,
> My choiceless navel-string buried there

ruk-a-ruk-a-rock, ruk
tuk a-tuk-a-talk, tuk
Porous rock, a rock that can talk
water talking around your flesh of stone.[38]

One of the earliest poets to move in this direction, incorporating indigenous musical forms and local traditions of secular and sacred celebration, was Elsworth McGranaham (Shake) Keane, a jazz musician and poet from St. Vincent. Among his best-known poems is "Shaker Funeral," first published in 1950.

Sorrow sin-
bound, pelting din
big chorusclash
o' the mourners;
eyes red
with a shout for the dead,
yelling crash-
ing sadness in
the dusty tread
o' the mourners.

    Sweet Mother gone
    to the by and by,
    follow her to the brink o' Zion . . .

And heads were white
in starched cloth . . . Bright
was the blood from the eyes
o' the candles;
and the 'horn of the Ram
of the great I Am'
spoke hoarse in cries . . .
and crowned with the light
o' the Judah Lamb
were the candles.

    Lord delivered Daniel
    from shame's mouth,
    (o strong, o strong roll Jordan).
    Lord deliver our Mother
    gone to the Glory Home
    gone to the Glory Home, gone to Zion.[39]

Drawing on the traditions of Carnival and the music of the steel drums has also been an important part of West Indian literary expression, often in ways that convey the spirit of independence that both drumming and street celebrations have represented—sometimes to the consternation of the authorities. This goes back to the early days of slavery and of chronic imperial concern with law and order in the West Indies. After emancipation, this anxiety became acute. For example, the colonial government in Trinidad banned drum processions in the 1880s because of its worries about troubles both at carnival time leading up to Lent and at carnivals such as the August celebration of emancipation. A law in St. Lucia forbade the beating of a drum after 10 o'clock at night within a mile of any town or village well into this century; and Derek Walcott's friend Harold Simmons told the story of the Governor of the Windward Islands, Sir Arthur Grimble, receiving a summons to appear before a St. Lucia court to answer a charge of dancing to the tune of drums at the Castries Social Club in 1943.[40] From the nineteenth century, this kind of prohibition had provoked both anger and invention, as people improvised other instruments for carnival music, from the shak-shak or calabash gourd to old boxes and kettles. During the decades up to the 1930s, parades in Trinidad often included both string bands (with violins, mandolins, and guitars) and bamboo percussion groups known as "tamboo bamboo" bands (from the French *tambour*, for "drum"). John Agard has a poem about this in his book *Man to Pan*, a cycle of poems published in 1982 to be performed with drums and steel band. ("Canboulay" in the poem refers to the torchlight procession on the first of August (Emancipation Day), the word itself coming from the French *cannes brulées*, meaning "burning cane.")

They mean to licence we tongue,
yes, that's why they ban we drum.
They don't have to find reason
to throw people in prison

But if they think we go stay dumb
since they decide to ban we drum
then they got to think again
cause we go rage like burning cane

CANBOULAY CANBOULAY
we celebrating today . . .

Well, too bad, they don't have a clue
they forget nature give we bamboo
growing wild and growing free,

bamboo band belong to you and me.
Is part of we ancestry . . .

If they think we go stay dumb
since they decide to ban we drum
then they got to think again
cause we go rage like burning cane[41]

During the 1930s, biscuit tins and dust bins came to be played during the carnival processions. It was just after the Second World War that steel pans beaten into shapes to produce different tones were first used, and the steel drum bands that are now so widely associated with Trinidad came into being. The tradition of steel band and calypso, as well as of carnival parades and other processions, has its roots in the collective heritage of the West Indies, and it is not surprising that the central elements of that heritage shape these forms of expression. More particularly, various African melodies and rhythms have strongly influenced calypso, and some of its common modes of provocation and satire have come directly from Yoruba songs.[42] Specifically *political* dissatisfaction and dissent has sometimes been part of carnival events, though often inseparable from the exhuberance of celebration when restraints of all kinds are removed; and calypso (or "kaiso," as it is also called, from an African [Hausa] word meaning "bravo") depends for its appeal on a balance between criticism of the existing order and a playful cleverness. The fusion of these elements is what is distinctly West Indian; though the energy of resistance and rebellion is there at the center, the deepest expression of the heritage of slavery and freedom shared by all West Indians. Those who celebrate contemporary West Indian music as a call to "lively up," in Bob Marley's words, are missing, deliberately or otherwise, the call to uprising that is also there at the heart of it all.

The Trinidadian poet Victor Questel wrote a poem called "Pan Drama" which catches the element of struggle that has been a key to the tradition of drumming from the beginning in the West Indies. This is the opening of Questel's poem, which first appeared in Brathwaite's *Savacou* anthology in 1971.

Ex-
it
mas' man
push on
pan man,
a man
attuned, trapped

caught (like me)
making
subtle inden-
tations
in his
spider web

(now)
limbo-
ing from flambeau-
pan-yard
to
flying Pan Am

a-
massing cultural
missions

(then)
bombing down
the town
down

Frederick Street.[43]

Lorna Goodison's "Jah Music" illustrates in a final example how musical traditions, along with other traditions of imaginative expression, can merge in a way that is centered in the language of the West Indies and in the writing of its poets. "Red and yellow and dark green," mentioned in the poem, are the colors of Rastafari, a tradition from another arena of symbolic expression that has also been a part of West Indian independence, and of West Indian art.

The sound bubbled up
through a cistern one night
and piped its way into
the atmosphere
and decent people wanted
to know
"What kind of ole nayga music is that
playing on the Government's radio?"
But this red and yellow and dark green
sound
stained from travelling underground
smelling of poor people's dinners

"i a tell no tale" 259

from a yard dense as Belgium
has the healing
more than weed and white rum healing
more than bush tea and fever grass cooling
and it pulses without a symphony conductor
all it need is a dub organiser.[44]

The heritage of the West Indies follows West Indians around the world. The sense of dispossession, which is still the bitter legacy of slavery, has merged with the experience of exile to produce poetry embodying complex feelings of loss and a longing for home. A favorite device has been to cast poems in the form of letters, in which the conventions of written and spoken language, and the categories of naturalness and artifice, are purposefully confused. Letters also focus attention on the ironic predicament of a people whose tradition once was oral being confined now by the conditions of exile to written expression. But most of all letters provide a vehicle for exploring what Philip Larkin once called "the experience of elsewhere," an experience that has been a predominant part of life for many English-speaking West Indians. This experience goes back to slavery; but it has been given new significance with the dramatic increase in emigration since the late 1940s and early 1950s to England, the United States and Canada.

James Berry, who was born in Jamaica in 1924 but has lived in England for over forty years and provided encouragement and inspiration to a couple of generations of expatriate West Indians, has a sequence of letter poems (published in *Lucy's Letters and Loving* [1975]) in which the voice is that of Lucy, a West Indian living in London. In one of the poems she reflects on a holiday home. Her language is local, while the figures of speech she writes have literary currency. In the Jamaican proverb at the end, these local and literary qualities converge. Between them, woven out of their separate logics, the pathos of the situation takes shape.

I'm here an not here. Me head's
too full of mornin sun
an sea soun' an voices
echoin words this long long
time I never have.

Seeing home again, Leela chile,
I bring back a mind to Englan
tha's not enough to share . . .

> I glad you don't grow bitter.
> I glad how the sun still ripen
> evenin, so strong in colour.
> An there, where I did go
> to school with one piece of book,
> I came, I walked in darkness,
> an it was a soothin blot.
>
> Too many sea waves passed between
> us, chile. Let us remind the other,
> "Length of time gets rope buried."[45]

Fred D'Aguiar's "Letter from Mama Dot" reverses this relationship between local and literary language, with the letter conveying the artifice of literature in its language, while the proverb with which it closes is ostentatiously in dialect, underlining the authenticity of the narrator in the naturalness of the language. And yet the truth of the account depends equally on its literary style. Born in 1960 in England of Guyanese parents, D'Aguiar lived in the West Indies until he was twelve, when he returned to England. His poem (from his book *Mama Dot* [1985]) conveys the wisdom of a grandmother writing about the experience of coming from the margins of the empire to live on the margins in England, a fringe dweller.

> You are a traveller to them.
> *A West Indian working in England;*
> *A Friday, Tonto or Punkawallah;*
> *Sponging off the state.* Our languages
> Remain pidgin like our *dark, third,*
> *Underdeveloped,* world. I mean their need
> To see our children cow-eyed and pot-bellied . . .
>
> You know England, born there, you live
> To die there, roots put down once
> And for all. Drop me a line soon,
> You know me. *Neva see come fo see.*[46]

"One's origin lies in a huge disappointment," Mark McWatt once said about the myth of El Dorado, that failed dream of gold and a golden age.[47] Coming to terms with this disappointment has been part of the witness of West Indian literature, especially in the context of a magical realism that has such appeal for many contemporary authors, but such challenge for those whose lives already seem like a bad dream. Fred D'Aguiar has written about returning to his native Guyana with

a special sense of the surreal bewilderment of it all. In *Airy Hall*, he
gives an "El Dorado Update."

> *Riddle me, riddle me, riddle.*
> One people, one nation, one destiny?
> Let's take a walk
> not to stay, just to see . . .
>
> You think it's easy?
> You walk down the middle
> of the road with your head
> in the air.
>
> Crowd on the left-hand side shout,
> "Shop for something to eat, no?
> Wheat-flour scarce,
> rice-flour is eye-pass,
> we got cassava bread,
> mauby and class."
>
> Crowd on the right side
> play a different tune,
> they point smoking guns,
> they say, "All eat rice,
> that is revolutionary food,
> don't bother with wheat import,
> imperialist food;
> we're the proprietor of this country,
> not the administrator" . . .
>
> Lord, what to do in this fowl-coop
> republic, risk my neck on a demo
> or in a food queue? . . .
>
> *Riddle me, riddle me, riddle.*[48]

Other West Indians living in England have mapped out a literary
landscape in which the grim realities of life for blacks in the inner cities
of England are given powerful expression. "Inglan is a bitch," says
Linton Kwesi Johnson in the title of one of his poems (and one of his
books); but the English language is still (as Walcott puts it in "The
Schooner *Flight*") "all them bastards have left us." Along with others
such as Jean Binta Breeze, Valerie Bloom, Levi Tafari, and Benjamin
Zephaniah, Johnson has led the way toward new possibilities for using
a West Indian's mother tongue to transform literary traditions inherited
from the Mother Country.

Poetry is first and last a matter of language. Poets pride themselves on uses of language that are somehow different from others—clearer, purer, closer to the ground, nearer collapse . . . whatever. This difference determines the relationship of the poem to both local and other literary discourses, and it also determines a particular balance between making art and mirroring life. Since the subject of black writers in England *begins* with their difference, and especially the difference in their language, this takes us back to where we began and to a very close connection between style and subject.

There are many other differences, of course: differences of color, of being black in a country that is—or that thinks of itself as—predominantly white; and differences of heritage, with parents or family having come to England from somewhere else, and bringing with them a legacy of colonial imposition to a land so accustomed to dominion that it wonders what all the fuss is about. But the starting point is that West Indian poets in England are different because they speak differently— more or less, but identifiably. This variance in speech is important in two ways: it separates the speaker from others; and, more positively, it defines an area of imaginative authority that is in some sense immune from the impositions of the majority tongue. Being on the margins, after all, is what poets have often insisted upon, and it is what many contemporary critics define as *the* condition of poetic language. Recalling this does not discount the political and social and economic consequences of marginality, but it does draw attention to the sense in which language that is marginal in social terms may be central in literary terms, simply by being different.

And yet the difference in language that characterizes West Indian speech is routinely denounced by the purveyors of the imperial tongue as degenerate, and despised by those who think literature is in the business of high imperial fashion or of instruction in the decorums of speech. As we have seen, the idea that a particular form of language is inferior seems to encourage the equally warped view that those who use it are too. Many people still assume that those who speak—and perhaps if they are really pushy, even write—in dialect cannot possibly have thoughts and feelings that are very deep, and in any case that such expression is unlikely to achieve any great height. The special risk for West Indian poets in England is that because of their proximity to the notional linguistic "standard," the Greenwich mean time of the English language, their work will be looked upon more than ever as a kind of curiosity, generating imperial condescension, perhaps some sympathy, and a set of parliamentary resolutions to improve their education so that the next generation of blacks will be able to speak properly.

Nonetheless, poets of West Indian heritage in England have taken the opportunity that their situation gives them to intensify our understanding of how, in the words of Derek Walcott, "no language is neutral." No one holds on to language quite as fiercely as the person who has nothing else. And that, while it is in one sense the condition of all poets, is the immediate condition of many black writers, and many black people, in England today. If their language does not work for them, it seems nothing else will. That is why their poetry is so important—important to them, and to the rest of us who are trying, in our less-desperate ways perhaps, to say who we are and where we belong. In "It Dread Inna Inglan," Johnson claims his place and that of his people and their language. The defiance of the message—we are here, and we will not and cannot become other than who we are—is matched by the resistance of the language to assimilation or translation. Its style embodies the obstinacy, the intransigence, of its statement.

> Maggi Tatcha on di go
> wid a racist show
> but a she haffi go
> kaw,
> rite now,
> African
> Asian
> West Indian
> an' British Black
> stan firm inna Inglan
> inna disya time yah
>
> far noh mattah wat dey say,
> come wat may,
> we are here to stay
> inna Inglan
> inna disya time yah . . .[49]

Writing by West Indians in England moves along a continuum from oral performance that only barely holds its place on the page to carefully crafted written texts. And its audience represents a corresponding continuum—or discontinuum, some would say. Johnson is one of the most prominent exponents of a poetry in which rhythm and sound are central, a poetry of performance. Of course, rhythm and sound are always important in poetry, just as language is. And performance is not something confined to the stage. Poetry always shows off language. Some poetic forms, however, bring rhythm and sound into the foreground on center stage, drawing attention to the fact that certain ways of seeing are only possible through certain ways of saying. In his moving tribute to his father, "Reggae Fi Dada," Johnson shows that his people's ways are capable of extraordinary power and sensitivity, incorporating a style and language that are a unique fusion of traditions, and of private and public witness—for like all great elegies, this poem is about both a person's and a people's grief.

> galang dada . . .

> di lan is like a rack
> slowly shattahrin to san
> sinkin in a sea of calamity
> where fear breed shadows
> dat lurks in di daak
> where people fraid fi waak
> fraid fi tink fraid fi taak
> where di present is haunted by di paas . . .

> a deh soh mi bawn
> get fi know bout staam
> learn fi cling to di dawn
> an wen di news reach mi
> seh mi wan daddy ded
> mi ketch a plane quick . . .

> galang dada
> galang gwaan yaw sah
> yu nevah ad noh life fi live
> jus di wan life fi give
> yu did yu time pan ert
> yu nevah get yu jus dizert
> galang goh smile inna di sun
> galang goh satta inna di palace af peace[50]

John Agard and Grace Nichols, both from Guyana and now living in England, have taken their language and their poetry in other directions, bearing different witness to their lives in England, though their sense of their heritage as West Indians is as sure as Johnson's. Agard has a strong interest in the West Indian musical inheritance, which he has displayed in *Man to Pan* (1982) and *Limbo Dancer in Dark Glasses* (1983), with his later books (*Mangoes and Bullets* [1985] and *Lovelines for a Goat-born Lady* [1990]) expanding his range. And he has a fine sense of humor, displayed for example in "Palm Tree King" where he comments on the expectations that condition West Indian life in England.

> Because I come from the West Indies
> certain people in England seem to think
> I is an expert on palm trees
>
> So not wanting to sever dis link
> with me native roots (know what ah mean?)
> or to disappoint dese culture vulture
> I does smile cool as seabreeze
>
> and say to dem
> which specimen
> you interested in
> cause you talking
> to the right man
> I is palm tree king
> I know palm tree history
> like de palm o me hand . . .[51]

Grace Nichols has written of women's experiences in books such as *i is a long memoried woman* (1983), *The Fat Black Woman's Poems* (1984) and *Lazy Thoughts of a Lazy Woman* (1989). Her work contains a sensitive irony and a voice of self-deprecating humor, and her poems collectively have a subtlety that is not easily conveyed in selections. In one, "Wherever I Hang," she shows the perplexity and pathos of exile, all the while playing with its stereotypes.

> I leave me people, me land, me home
> For reasons, I not too sure
> I forsake de sun
> And de humming-bird splendour
> Had big rats in de floorboard
> So I picked up me new-world-self
> And come, to this place call England
> At first I feeling like I in dream—
> De misty greyness
> I touching de walls to see if they real
> They solid to de seam
> And de people pouring from de underground system
> Like beans
> And when I look up to de sky
> I see Lord Nelson high—too high to lie

And is so I sending home photos of myself
Among de pigeons and de snow
And is so I warding off de cold
And is so, little by little
I begin to change my calypso ways
Never visiting nobody
Before giving them clear warning
And waiting me turn in queue
Now, after all this time
I get accustom to de English life
But I still miss back-home side
To tell you de truth
I don't know really where I belaang

> Yes, divided to de ocean
> Divided to de bone

Wherever I hang me knickers—that's my home.[52]

Somehow, in all her poetry Nichols conveys the impression that the language she uses is no one else's, incorporating her own experiences and her own literary instincts both old and new and saying it all in her own words.

> I have crossed an ocean
> I have lost my tongue
> from the root of the old one
> a new one has sprung[53]

It is an epilogue for all those who went on the Middle Passage, as well as those who have been traveling since.

Many other poets of West Indian heritage are living abroad, especially in England, the United States, and Canada. Among those in Canada are Claire Harris, Arnold Itwaru, Marlene Nourbese Philip, and Afua Cooper, each of whom has brought the issues we have been discussing into clearer view in a unique way. Harris's work displays her restless sense of the limits and the possibilities of language; and Philip's *She Tries Her Tongue, Her Silence Softly Breaks* (1989) tells of the journey from the uneasy privileges of an imperial language to the uneasy embrace of a mother tongue.

Canada, or more particularly Toronto, has also seen the development of a lively tradition of dub poetry, with Lillian Allen and Clifton Joseph among its best-known proponents. And as a final witness to the experience of migration and exile, and to the challenge of finding a

language and a literary inheritance in which being a West Indian will
converge with being a poet, there is the Trinidadian-born writer Dionne
Brand, who now lives in Toronto. The range of her work is exceptional.
She is a short-story writer (*Sans Souci* [1988]) and a filmmaker of considerable prominence. She has written in a form as old as European
literature, using the epigram (which Greek writers made popular) in a
book titled *Winter Epigrams and Epigrams to Ernesto Cardenal In Defense
of Claudia (1983)*. And she too has written letters, such as one about her
time in Grenada just before the American invasion in 1983, entitled
"P.P.S. Grenada" (in *Chronicles of the Hostile Sun* [1984]), in which the
tradition of the poetic catalog, the naming of places and people,
becomes a means of making sense of a reality that would otherwise
defy the imagination.

> I have never missed a place either
> except now
> there was a house
> there was a harbour, some lights
> on the water, a hammock
> there was a road . . .
> there was a boat,
> I made friends
> with its owner and he called
> me on his way to work each morning
> there was another road, the one to Goave,
> all the way up looking back
> the rainy season greened the hills
> dry spells reddened the flambouyant
> there was a river
> at concord
> seeing it the first time surprised me
> big smooth stones, brown and ashen
> and women standing in its water
> with washing
> there was a farm
> on a hillside
> as most are, forty acres with a
> river deep inside, Jason and Brother-
> man picked coconuts . . .
> there was a wall of rock which sank into the street
> in the trees and vine and lizards
> it cooled the walk from town . . .

once I lay down on the edge
afraid to stand
past the cactus and the prickly shrub
at point salines' most eastern tip
the sharpened cliff, the dark blue water
the first meeting of the atlantic and the caribbean
gave me vertigo,
that was the last time I went there
before the war . . .[54]

In a set of lesbian love poems, Brand has also shifted the paradigms of love in a way that sustains and extends the heritage with which we began this book: the heritage of dispossession, resistance, and recovery; of love and literature; of difference; of another life. The heritage of roses and onions, of the ordinary and the extraordinary . . . or, as Brand says, the "unordinary."

Then it is this simple. I felt the unordinary romance of
women who love women for the first time. It burst in
my mouth. Someone said this is your first lover, you
will never want to leave her. I had it in mind that I
would be an old woman with you. But perhaps I
always had it in mind simply to be an old woman,
darkening, somewhere, with another old woman . . .

I have become myself. A woman who looks
at a woman and says, here, I have found you,
in this, I am blackening in my way. You ripped the
world raw. It was as if another life exploded in my
face, brightening, so easily the brow of a wing
touching the surf, so easily I saw my own body, that
is, my eyes followed me to myself, touched myself
as a place, another life, terra. They say this place
does not exist, then, my tongue is mythic. I was here
before.[55]

In her book *No Language is Neutral* (1990), Brand has taken inspiration from lines by Derek Walcott, in *Midsummer* (1984).

Have we changed sides . . .
because we serve English, like a two-headed sentry
guarding its borders? No language is neutral;
the green oak of English is a murmurous cathedral
where some took umbrage, some peace, but every shade, all,
helped widen its shadow. I used to haunt the arches
of the British barracks at Vigie[56]

In the title sequence of poems, Brand recalls her native land and comes to terms with her new home. She does so in language that represents a heritage to which she bears witness from the distance that both geography and literature afford. But now, for Brand's generation, the literary inheritance is in some genuine measure West Indian, a legacy of Walcott and Brathwaite and others. A West Indian inheritance, like the life she describes from old memories and a new language. Which is to say from the heart of poetry.

> No language is neutral. I used to haunt the beach at
> Guaya, two rivers sentinel the country sand, not
> backra white but nigger brown sand, one river dead
> and teeming from waste and alligators, the other
> rumbling to the ocean in a tumult, the swift undertow
> blocking the crossing of little girls except on the tied
> up dress hips of big women, then, the taste of leaving
> was already on my tongue and cut deep into my
> skinny pigeon toed way, language here was strict
> description and teeth edging truth. Here was beauty
> and here was nowhere. The smell of hurrying passed
> my nostrils with the smell of sea water and fresh fish
> wind, there was history which had taught my eyes to
> look for escape even beneath the almond leaves fat
> as women, the conch shell tiny as sand, the rock
> stone old like water. I learned to read this from a
> woman whose hand trembled at the past, then even
> being born to her was temporary, wet and thrown half
> dressed among the dozens of brown legs itching to
> run. It was as if a signal burning like a fer de lance's
> sting turned my eyes against the water even as love
> for this nigger beach became resolute.[57]

Brand once said that the language of a poem is made up specially for the occasion. This is the language we have talked about through this book: the language in which West Indian poets are bearing witness to the truth of their lives and their West Indian heritage; the language in which they are giving expression to their own defiance of Naipaul's disbelief and giving their own answers to Brathwaite's question, "where then is the nigger's home?" This is the language that is now shaping a distinctly West Indian poetic tradition, inspiring West Indian poets, and illuminating the West Indies.

The Irish Language Board recently used an advertisement to encourage people to speak Irish Gaelic: "You never know how well something suits you until you try it. A new fashion . . . a different colour . . . your own language." Language is where this business begin for the poets of the West Indies. Language both rooted in the land and rising into song. Language that is their own, as poets and as West Indians: so that when they write, each phrase go be soaked in salt; and when we read their poetry, its language go be the wind.

Epilogue

The liberation of the West Indies is rooted not in laws and institutions, though these may be the basis of political independence, but in the imaginations of West Indians and in their determination to be free. When slavery began, their words were taken from them. Freedom meant taking them back. This freedom, along with the love and language of their islands, has been nourished by West Indian poets.

Language has been the key. It is where poetry is always centered and where the everyday and the remarkable come together. But for West Indians, language also connects their past and their present, along with their old worlds of Africa and Europe and the new world in which they now live. And it gives them their surest sense of what it is to be West Indian.

For those of us who are neither black nor West Indian, this concentration on language has significance too. I grew up shadowed in a kindly way by the great cedars and Douglas firs and Sitka spruces of the coastal rain forests of the west coast of Canada, and surrounded by the sea. But there were other shadows, and other surroundings. Neither the forests nor the sea nor the arid lands of the interior of the province where my relatives lived, nor the mountains where I worked for some of each year, were part of the imaginative inheritance that surrounded me. They were not named in the books that I read as I was growing up, for I also grew up shadowed by British literary traditions and a British language. Few of the towns and cities in that tradition were known to me, and the names never included Squamish or Sicamous or

Horsefly or Telegraph Creek or other places in my life; and the Windermere I knew well, high in the Rocky Mountains, was nothing like the place that Wordsworth wrote about, and certainly had never seen a daffodil. All of the institutions that influenced me, from the schools I attended to the radio programs I listened to, were part of a language located somewhere else: in southern England, for my teachers; somewhere in the middle of the Atlantic, for the announcers on the Canadian Broadcasting Corporation, who spoke a language never heard elsewhere, or since; and somewhere in middle America, from New York to Nashville to Los Angeles, on the popular radio stations. Some of these languages did not exactly belong to anybody. None belonged to me.

West Indian poets have done what many others have tried, especially in the past half century. They have taken back what belongs to them—not only their own language, but the freedom to use it. And they have used this freedom to give new meaning and purpose to their lives. This achievement is not a marginal one. It recalls the great enterprises in art and literature during the Renaissance, when Europeans defined their heritage through the language of imaginative expression, and in doing so both discovered and invented themselves as people for whom certain values and traditions were precious. It recalls the years after the American revolution, when a newly recognized language gave form to the thoughts and feelings of a new nation, and gave its people a way to see themselves and look at others. And it recalls the struggle of every one of us who has tried to tell our own story in our own words.

The nations of the English-speaking West Indies have gone their own ways, and political federation has eluded them. But they have shared one common enterprise, a federation of the arts, and a vision of the West Indies that accepts the prismatic variety of local lives and their surroundings. This vision has had its most powerful expression in contemporary West Indian poetry. It provides a unique way of understanding the West Indies, and thereby a way of understanding what has happened in much of the world in the last while—as people have searched for ways to be different, and to be free of the expectations of others, and to share their aspirations and achievements. In times when the West Indies has been more than ever beseiged by troubles and tensions, its poetry has conveyed the unconquerable mind that has sustained its people over the past five hundred years, and the spirit of freedom and power that inspires them now.

West Indian poets have brought all of us closer to what Seamus Heaney once called "that moment when the bird sings very close / To the music of what happens."[1] Close to the ground; but lifted up too, so that we do not become overwhelmed by events or overcome by despair. The poets of the West Indies have brought courage and hope to the world, as well as the honesty of those who bear true witness. And they have given us a way of bringing together the wide range of West Indian realities.

The first time I went to the West Indies, I saw the mountains and villages of St Lucia, a place of extraordinary beauty where people live difficult lives at the end of difficult roads and speak a language that contains the complicated history of the island. I was there on the day St. Lucia became independent, one of the last of the English-speaking islands to be free of European imperial authority, and there was celebration. On another occasion, I was in Jamaica when nobody was celebrating, during a time of violent unrest when the guns were out and people who had a place stayed indoors. I saw fear and hatred in the streets of Kingston; and I saw too the rain washing the world clean in the peaceful Blue Mountains above the grim city. But in Kingston that time I also saw the annual Christmas pantomime, full of fun and a fine edge of satire; and a powerful play about Alexander Bedward and his West Indian heritage of slavery and freedom; and a workshop production about the hard lives of women on the islands. At other times I have been in Trinidad for Carnival; and watched cricket in Barbados, and seen the breakers roll in from Africa at Bathsheba on its turbulent east coast. All of this, and much more, makes up the West Indies. It is a place bound to its past by a heritage that holds its people together. And it is a place that is looking to its future.

A while ago I was in Jamaica at a gathering of writers and critics, with Derek Walcott and Edward Brathwaite and Lorna Goodison and many of the other poets whom we have heard in this book. Walcott gave an opening address, in which he talked about how "the imagination is a territory as subject to invasion and seizure as any far province of Empire."[2] Goodison spoke of "the half that's never been told . . . and some of us going to tell it."[3] And Brathwaite read a poem called "Stone for Mikey Smith: stoned to death on Stony Hill 1954—1983."

> When the stone fall that morning out of the johncrow sky
> it was not dark at first, that opening on to the red sea humming
> but something in my mouth like feathers, blue like bubbles
> carrying signals and planets and the sliding curve of the world . . .
>   was a bad bad dream . . .
> and not a soul on stony hill to even say amen
> and yet it was happening happening happening . . .[4]

West Indians have needed faith and fortitude and a special kind of language and music to survive what sometimes happens in the West Indies. As Michael Smith said a few years before his tragic death,

> well, you see, anytime you dead, you dead. There is work to be done and the living have fi do it, so the living have fi carry on. So although it is good to mention those that is past—right?—me can't get bogged down into lamentation all day long. You know. So you have work fi go on, so me just deal with it. People deh really a feel the pinch, so you deal with it. . . . Love inna my work, still. All a my works-dem have love inna it; because the love fi a people, that's what me a write about.[5]

West Indian poets have spoken of the dead and of their heritage of slavery. But they have also written with a faith that life goes on, held together in language and in the things that language makes possible— hope, and humor, and healing. If we want to know what is happening in the West Indies, we should listen to their poets, giving in their own words the message chalked up on a wall in Grenada. "We freedom is ours."

In the period during the late 1940s and early 1950s when West Indian literature was in the making, and so were the nations of the West Indies, the Jamaican poet and critic J. E. Clare McFarlane wrote in the Guyanese literary magazine *Kyk-Over-Al* about what he called "The Prospect of West Indian Poetry." He was worried about a crisis of confidence in the West Indies. People "will not read poetry that is lacking in faith, and therefore lacking in courage," he wrote, for men and women "need courage by which to live."[6] That is what their poets have given to West Indians; and to the rest of us, courage and understanding too. And a new faith in the power of language.

Notes

Chapter 1: "A black apostrophe to pain"

1. Dennis Scott, "Epitaph," *Uncle Time* (Pittsburgh: University of Pittsburgh Press, 1973), p. 41. Excerpts reprinted by permission of Joy R. Scott.

2. Martin Carter, "I Come from the Nigger Yard," *Poems of Succession* (London: New Beacon, 1977), p. 38.

3. John Agard, "Go Spread Wings," *Lovelines for a Goat-Born Lady* (London: Serpent's Tail, 1990), p. 10. Excerpt reprinted by permission of John Agard.

4. Lorna Goodison, "Guinea Woman," *I Am Becoming My Mother* (London: New Beacon, 1986), pp. 39–40. Excerpts reprinted by permission of Lorna Goodison.

5. Derek Walcott, *Omeros* (New York: Farrar, Straus and Giroux, 1990), p. 19. © 1990 by Derek Walcott. Excerpts reprinted by permission of Farrar, Straus and Giroux, Inc., and Faber and Faber, Ltd.

6. Ibid., p. 3.

7. Ibid., p. 325.

8. *The Voyages of Christopher Columbus*, trans. Cecil Jane (London: Argonaut Press, 1930), p. 149. The date was October 12, 1492. See also Gerald Sider, "When Parrots Learn to Talk, and Why They Can't: Domination, Deception, and Self-deception in Indian-White Relations," *Comparative Study of Society and History* 1 (1987), 3–23.

9. Quoted in F. R. Augier, S. C. Gordon, D. G. Hall, and M. Reckord, *The Making of the West Indies* (London: Longman, 1960), p. 22. For a full acount of the dispute between Las Casas and Sepulveda, see Lewis Hanke, *All Mankind Is One: A Study of the Disputation between Bartoleme de Las Casas and Juan Gines de Sepulveda in 1550 on the Intellectual and Religious Capacity of the American*

Indians (DeKalb, Ill.: 1974); and Sylvia Wynter, "New Seville and the Conversion Experience of Bartoleme de Las Casas," Parts 1 and 2, *Jamaica Journal* 17:2 (1984), 25–31, and 17:3 (1984), 46–55.

10. See Elsa Goveia, *The West Indian Slave Laws of the 18th Century* (London: Ginn and Company, 1970).

11. Quoted in ibid., p. 35. Edwards was the author of a *History, Civil and Commercial, of the British Colonies in the West Indies*, first published in 1793 and expanded in 1801 and 1819.

12. Quoted in Goveia, *West Indian Slave Laws*, p. 33.

13. Quoted in ibid., p. 44.

14. Quoted in ibid., p. 52.

15. Dick Hebdige, *Cut 'N' Mix: Culture, Identity and Caribbean Music* (London: Methuen, 1987), p. 23.

16. John H. Parry and Philip M Sherlock, *A Short History of the West Indies*, 3d ed. (London: Macmillan, 1971), p. 188.

17. Anthony Trollope, *The West Indies and the Spanish Main* (New York: Harper and Brothers, 1860), pp. 58, 94.

18. Ibid., p. 58.

19. Ibid., p. 65.

20. Ibid., pp. 111–12.

21. Thomas Carlyle, *The Nigger Question* and John Stuart Mill, *The Negro Question*, ed. Eugene R. August (New York: Appleton-Century-Crofts, 1971), pp. 9, 10, 29. See also Eric Williams, *British Historians and the West Indies* (London: Andre Deutsch, 1966) and Hugh A. MacDougall, *Racial Myth in English History: Trojans, Teutons and Anglo-Saxons* (Hanover, N.H.: University Press of New England, 1982).

22. Testimony before the Royal Commission set up by the British Government to investigate the Morant Bay uprising. Quoted in Williams, *British Historians and the West Indies*, p. 122.

23. Quoted in ibid., p. 116.

24. Lorna Goodison, "Name Change: Morant Bay Uprising," *Saturday Night* 105:7 (1990), 53. Excerpt reprinted by permission of Lorna Goodison.

25. Edward Baugh "Nigger Sweat," *A Tale from the Rainforest* (Kingston, Jamaica: Sandberry, 1988), pp. 50–51. Excerpts reprinted by permission of Edward Baugh.

26. Edward Kamau Brathwaite, "Postlude/Home," *The Arrivants: A New World Trilogy* (London: Oxford University Press, 1973), p. 77. © 1967, 1968, 1969, 1973 by Edward Brathwaite. Excerpts reprinted by permission of Oxford University Press.

Chapter 2: "Where then is the nigger's home?"

1. Edward Kamau Brathwaite, "Postlude/Home," *The Arrivants*, p. 79.

2. Paul Theroux, *Sunrise with Seamonsters: Travels and Discoveries, 1964–1984* (Boston: Houghton Mifflin, 1985), p. 95.

3. V. S. Naipaul, *The Middle Passage* (Harmondsworth: Penguin, 1969), p. 209.

4. Ibid., p. 29.

5. Walt Whitman, "Starting from Paumanok," in *Leaves of Grass*, ed. Sculley Bradley and Harold W. Blodgett (New York: Norton, 1973), p. 19.

6. William Wordsworth, "To Toussaint L'Ouverture," in *William Wordsworth*, ed. Stephen Gill (Oxford: Oxford University Press, 1984), p. 282.

7. Philip Sherlock, "The Land of Look Behind," in *Caribbean Poetry Now*, ed. Stewart Brown (London: Hodder and Stoughton, 1984), pp. 7–10. Excerpt reprinted by permission of Philip Sherlock.

8. Ansel Wong, "Creole as a Language of Power and Solidarity," in *The Language of the Black Experience: Cultural Expression through Word and Sound in the Caribbean and Black Britain*, ed. David Sutcliffe and Ansel Wong (Oxford: Basil Blackwell, 1986), p. 121.

9. See Edward Kamau Brathwaite, *History of the Voice: The Development of Nation Language in Anglophone Caribbean Poetry* (London: New Beacon, 1984).

10. See Hubert Devonish, *Language and Liberation: Creole Language Politics in the Caribbean* (London: Karia Press, 1986), pp. 44–48.

11. Edward Baugh, "Sometimes in the Middle of the Story," *A Tale from the Rainforest*, p. 52.

12. Quoted in Naipaul, *The Middle Passage*, p. 7.

13. Quoted in Hugh A. MacDougall, *Racial Myth in English History*, p. 101.

14. Samuel Taylor Coleridge, *Essays on His Times*, Vol II, ed. D. V. Erdman (Princeton: Princeton University Press, 1978), p. 411. See also Seamus Deane, *Civilians and Barbarians* (Derry: Field Day, 1983).

15. Quoted in MacDougall, *Racial Myth in English History*, p. 112.

16. In a letter written in 1887. Quoted by Donald Wood in his Biographical Note to J. J. Thomas's *Froudacity* (with an Introduction by C. L. R. James) (London: New Beacon, 1969), p. 19.

17. Quoted in Elsa Goveia, *A Study of the Historiography of the British West Indies* (Mexico: Instituto Panamericano de Geografia e Historia, 1956), p. 155.

18. Quoted in Eric Williams, *British Historians and the West Indies*, p. 178.

19. Repeated by John Tyndall in testimony before the Eyre Defence Aid Fund Committee in 1866. Quoted in Eric Williams, *British Historians and the West Indies*, p. 137.

20. Quoted in ibid., p. 179.

21. Thomas Gray, letter to Richard West, April, 1742. Correspondence of Thomas Gray, ed. P. Toynbee and L. Whibley, vol. 1 (Oxford: Clarendon Press, 1971), p. 192.

22. *Kyk-Over-Al* 5:15 (1952).

23. Derek Walcott. The prose version, begun in April 1965 with some passages in verse beginning early in 1966, is contained in two exercise books, written in longhand, in the Library of the University of the West Indies, Mona Campus, Kingston, Jamaica. It will be referred to hereafter as Holograph MS (*Another Life*).

24. Derek Walcott, "The Schooner Flight," *The Star Apple Kindgom* (New York: Farrar, Straus and Giroux, 1979), p. 4. © 1979 by Derek Walcott. Excerpts reprinted by permission of Farrar, Straus and Giroux, Inc. and Faber and Faber, Ltd.

25. Ibid., p. 8.

26. Naipaul, *The Middle Passage*, p. 6.

27. Ernest Renan, "Qu'est-ce qu'une nation?" *Oeuvres Completes*, Vol. I (Paris: Calmann-Levy, 1947–61), p. 892. Quoted in Benedict Anderson, *Imagined Communities: Reflections on the Origin and Spread of Nationalism* (London: Verso, 1983), p. 15.

28. See William H. McNeill, *Polyethnicity and National Unity in World History* (Toronto: University of Toronto Press, 1986).

29. Samuel Smith, *To Shoot Hard Labour: The Life and Times of Samuel Smith, an Antiguan Workingman, 1877–1982*, ed. Keithlyn B. Smith and Fernando C. Smith (Toronto: Edan's Publishers, 1986), p. 38.

30. Hugh L. Shearer, Prime Minister of Jamaica in 1968; quoted in Rex M. Nettleford, *Identity, Race and Protest in Jamaica* (New York: William Morrow, 1972), p. 116.

31. Quoted in Abiola Irele, *The African Experience in Literature and Ideology* (London: Heinemann, 1981), pp. 67–68. See also Aimé Césaire, *Collected Poetry of Aimé Césaire*, trans, with intro. and notes by Clayton Eshelman and Annette Smith (Berkeley: University of California Press, 1983).

32. Jean Paul Sartre, *Black Orpheus*, trans. Samuel W. Allen (Paris: Presence Africaine, 1963), pp. 22–23.; originally published as the preface to *Anthologie de la nouvelle poèsie nègre et malgache de langue française*, ed. L. S. Senghor (Paris: Presses Universitaires de France, 1948).

33. Quoted in Barbara Harlow, *Resistance Literature* (London; Methuen, 1987), pp. 5–6.

34. See *The Writer in Modern Africa: Proceedings of the Afro-Scandinavian Writer's Conference*, Stockholm, 1967, ed. Per Wastberg (Uppsala, 1968). Soyinka recast his comment as "the tiger does not go about proclaiming its tigritude. It just pounces"; and in this form it has widespread currency. The Guyanese poet Abdur-Rahman Slade Hopkinson used it as the epigraph for his poem "The Jaguar and the Theorist of Negritude" (*Bim* 44 [1967], 274).

35. Quoted in Harlow, *Resistance Literature*, p. 6.

36. Philip Sherlock, in an address in London at the Commonwealth Institute, 1975. Quoted in Rex Nettleford, *Cultural Action and Social Change: The Case of Jamaica* (Kingston, Jamaica: Institute of Jamaica, 1978), pp. 42–43.

37. Quoted in Rex Nettleford, *Identity, Race and Protest in Jamaica*, p. 118. See also *Jamaica Journal* 20:3 (1987), which includes articles on Garvey and a comprehensive bibliography of works by and about him.

38. Quoted in Velma Pollard, "The Social History of Dread Talk," *Caribbean Quarterly* 28:4 (1982), 17.

39. See Mervyn Alleyne, *Roots of Jamaican Culture* (London: Pluto Press, 1988), pp. 76–105.

40. Herman Melville, *Moby Dick*, ed. Harrison Hayford and Herschel Parker (New York: Norton, 1967), p. 56.

41. See *Caribbean Quarterly* 26:4 (1980), a special issue on Rastafari.

42. Quoted in Keith Q. Warner, *The Trinidad Calypso: A Study of the Calypso as Oral Literature* (London: Heinemann, 1982), p. 84.

43. M. G. Smith, Roy Augier, and Rex Nettleford, *The Rastafari Movement in Kingston, Jamaica* (Kingston, Jamaica: Institute of Social and Economic Research, University of the West Indies, 1960), p. 27.

44. Lee "Scratch" Perry. Quoted in Dick Hebdige, *Cut 'N' Mix*, p. 75.

45. Linton Kwesi Johnson, "Reggae Sounds," *Dread Beat and Blood* (London: Bogle-L'Ouverture, 1975), p. 56. Excerpt reprinted by permission of Linton Kwesi Johnson.

46. See Carolyn Cooper, "Chanting Down Babylon: Bob Marley's Song as Literary Text," *Jamaica Journal* 19:4 (November 1986–January 1987), 2–8.

47. Brother Resistance, "Book So Deep," in *Voiceprint: An Anthology of Oral and Related Poetry from the Caribbean*, ed. Stewart Brown, Mervyn Morris, and Gordon Rohlehr (London: Longman, 1989), pp. 168–72.

48. See Philip Sherlock and Rex Nettleford, *The University of the West Indies: A Caribbean Response to the Challenge of Change* (London: Macmillan, 1990).

49. Bruce St. John, "West Indian Litany," *Bumbatuk I* (Bridgetown, Barbados: Cedar Press, 1982), p. 2.

50. Quoted in Gordon Rohlehr, *Pathfinder: Black Awakening in the Arrivants of Edward Kamau Brathwaite* (Tunapuna: Gordon Rohlehr, 1981), p. 46; from "Timehri," *Savacou* 2 (1970), 35–44. See also Anne Walmsley, *The Caribbean Artists Movement, 1966–1972: A Literary and Cultural History* (London: New Beacon, 1992).

51. Walcott, "The Hotel Normandie Pool," *The Fortunate Traveller* (New York: Farrar, Straus and Giroux, 1981), p. 69. © 1980, 1981 by Derek Walcott. Excerpts reprinted by permission of Farrar, Straus and Giroux, Inc. and Faber and Faber, Ltd.

52. *Breaklight: The Poetry of the Caribbean*, ed. Andrew Salkey (London: Hamish Hamilton, 1971).

53. Brathwaite, "Forward," *Savacou* 3/4 (December 1970-March 1971), 5–9.

54. Bongo Jerry, "Mabrak," *Savacou* 3/4, 13–16. Excerpt reprinted by permission of Bongo Jerry (Robin Small).

55. See, for example, Gordon Rohlehr, "West Indian Poetry: Some Problems of Assessment," *Bim* 14: 54 and 55 (1972), 80–88 and 134–44; "Afterthoughts," *Bim* 56 (1973), 227–32; and "A Carrion Time," *Bim* 58 (1975), 92–109.

Chapter 3: "Come back to me my language"

1. Derek Walcott, *The Voice of St. Lucia*, May 2, 1973.

2. Edward Kamau Brathwaite, *The Development of Creole Society in Jamaica* (Oxford: Clarendon Press, 1971), p. 237.

3. John Agard, "Listen Mr Oxford don" *Mangoes and Bullets* (London: Pluto Press, 1985), p. 44. Excerpt reprinted by permission of John Agard.

4. Quoted in Frederic Cassidy, *Jamaica Talk: Three Hundred Years of the English Language in Jamaica* (London: Macmillan, 1971), p. 23.

5. Quoted in Peter Hulme, *Colonial Encounters: Europe and the Native Caribbean, 1492–1797* (London: Methuen, 1986), p. 1.

6. Thomas Pickering quoted in Bernard W. Sheehan, *Seeds of Extinction: Jeffersonian Philanthropy and the American Indian* (Chapel Hill: University of North Carolina Press, 1973), p. 36. See also J. Edward Chamberlin, *The Harrowing of Eden: White Attitudes Towards Native Americans* (New York: Seabury, 1975).

7. George Manuel and Michael Posluns, *The Fourth World: An Indian Reality* (Don Mills, 1974), p. 63.

8. See Benjamin Lee Whorf, *Language, Thought and Reality: Selected Writings,* ed. John B. Carroll (Cambridge, Mass.: M.I.T. Press, 1956). Whorf acknowledged his debt to Edward Sapir, whose book *Language: An Introduction to the Study of Speech* (New York: Harcourt, Brace and World, 1921) had considerable influence and whose name is often linked with Whorf's in the discussion of this hypothesis. See also Emily A. Schultz, *Dialogue at the Margins: Whorf, Bakhtin and Linguistic Relativity* (Madison: University of Wisconsin Press, 1990).

9. See Frederic Jameson, *The Prison-House of Language: A Critical Account of Structuralism and Formalism* (Princeton: Princeton University Press, 1972), p. i.

10. Frantz Fanon, *Black Skins: White Masks* (New York: Grove Press, 1967), p. 188. Quoted in Sander L. Gilman, *Jewish Self-Hatred: Anti-Semitism and the Hidden Language of the Jews* (Baltimore: Johns Hopkins University Press, 1986), p. 17.

11. Quoted in Rohlehr, *Pathfinder,* p. 9.

12. Quoted in Anne Walmsley, "A Far-Reaching Voice," in *Hinterland: Caribbean Poetry from the West Indies and Britain,* ed. E. A. Markham (London: Bloodaxe Books, 1989), p. 232.

13. Merle Hodge, *Crick Crack, Monkey* (London: Heinemann, 1970), p. 30.

14. Henry Reeve quoted in Linda Dowling, *Language and Decadence in the Victorian Fin de Siècle* (Princeton: Princeton University Press, 1986), pp. 87, 36.

15. Charles Mackay quoted in Dowling, *Language and Decadence,* p. 67.

16. Thomas Hardy, *The Mayor of Casterbridge,* ed. Dale Kramer (Oxford: Oxford University Press, 1987), p. 130.

17. J. H. Marsden quoted in Dowling, *Language and Decadence,* p. 100.

18. Quoted in Margaret Cruikshank, *Thomas Babinton Macaulay* (Boston: Twayne, 1978), p. 43.

19. Thomas Babington Macaulay, "Minute on Indian Education," in *Selected Writings,* ed. John Clive and Thomas Pinney (Chicago: University of Chicago Press, 1972), pp. 241–42.

20. Philip Sherlock and Rex Nettleford, *The University of the West Indies,* pp. 5–6. (The first twelve chapters were written by Philip Sherlock).

21. Merle Collins, "The Lesson," *Because the Dawn Breaks!* (London: Karia Press, 1985), pp. 15–22. Excerpt reprinted by permission of Merle Collins.

22. A. J. Seymour, *Edgar Mittelholzer: The Man and His Work* (Georgetown, Guyana: National History and Arts Council, 1968), pp. 48–49. Quoted in Edward Baugh, *West Indian Poetry, 1900–1970: A Study in Cultural Decolonisation* (Kingston, Jamaica: Savacou, 1971), p. 4.

23. Seamus Deane quoted in Declan Kiberd, *Anglo-Irish Attitudes* (Derry: Field Day, 1984), p. 11.

24. Samuel Selvon, *The Lonely Londoners* (London: Longman, 1976), p. 72.

25. See Peter Roberts, *West Indians and Their Language* (Cambridge: Cambridge University Press, 1988).

26. Quoted in Loreto Todd, *Pidgins and Creoles* (London: Methuen, 1974), p. 26.

27. Bruce St. John, "Introduction" to *Bumbatuk: Poems in Barbadian Dialect, Revista de Letras (Universidad de Puerto Rico en Mayaguez)*, 4:16 (1972), 540–53.

28. The phrase is Seamus Heaney's. (See Seamus Heaney, *The Government of the Tongue* [London: Faber, 1988]).

29. A. C. Brook, *Times Literary Supplement*, January 23, 1937.

30. Thomas Hardy, *The Well-Beloved*, ed. Tom Hetherington (Oxford: Oxford University Press, 1986), p. 19.

31. Max Muller quoted in Dowling, *Language and Decadence*, pp. 66–67.

32. See K. M. Elisabeth Murray, *Caught in the Web of Words: James A. H. Murray and the Oxford English Dictionary* (Oxford: Oxford University Press, 1979).

33. Charles Mackay quoted in Dowling, *Language and Decadence*, p. 96.

34. Noah Webster, *Dissertations on the English Language* (Boston, 1789). Quoted in H. L. Mencken, *The American Language: An Inquiry into the Development of English in the United States* (New York: Knopf, 1937), p. 10.

35. Quoted in Mencken, ibid., p. 12.

36. D. H. Lawrence, "Whitman," *Studies in Classic American Literature* (New York: Viking Press, 1964), p. 173.

37. Whitman, in conversation with Horace Traubel, quoted in Mencken, *American Language*, p. 73.

38. From a lecture titled "An American Primer" which Whitman wrote but never delivered, quoted in Mencken, ibid., pp. 73–74.

39. Quoted by Mervyn Morris in *Louise Bennett: Selected Poems*, ed. Mervyn Morris (Kingston, Jamaica: Sangster's, 1983), pp. xii–xiii.

40. Selvon, *The Lonely Londoners*, pp. 125–26.

41. Quoted by John Wickham in an article on "West Indian Writing" in *Bim* 50 (1969), 68. For a recapitulation of early twentieth-century West Indian poetry, see Edward Baugh, *West Indian Poetry, 1900–1970*.

42. Claude McKay, "Fetchin' Water," in *The Penguin Book of Caribbean Verse in English*, ed. Paula Burnett (Harmondsworth: Penguin, 1986), p. 142.

43. Philip Sherlock, "Pocomania," in *The Penguin Book of Caribbean Verse*, ed. Paula Burnett, pp. 154–155. Excerpt reprinted by permission of Philip Sherlock.

44. Martin Carter, "University of Hunger," *Poems of Succession*, p. 34.

45. Louise Bennett, "No Lickle Twang," in *Selected Poems*, ed. Mervyn Morris, pp. 2–4. Excerpts reprinted by permission of Louise Bennett.

46. Bennett, "Dry-Foot Bwoy," ibid., pp. 1–2.

47. Evan Jones, "The Song of the Banana Man," in *The Penguin Book of Caribbean Verse in English*, ed. Paula Burnett, p. 222.

48. Walcott, Holograph MS (*Another Life*), book 1, p. 42.

49. St. John, "Education," *Bumbatuk I*, pp. 3–4.

50. Walcott, "Ste. Lucie," *Sea Grapes* (New York: Farrar, Straus and Giroux, 1976), pp. 35–39. © 1976 by Derek Walcott. Excerpts reprinted by permission of Farrar, Straus and Giroux, Inc. and Faber and Faber, Ltd.

51. Northrop Frye, *The Great Code: The Bible and Literature* (Toronto: Academic Press, 1982) p. 18.

52. Mervyn Morris, "Valley Prince," *Savacou* 3/4 (1971), 38. Also published in *The Pond* (London: New Beacon, 1973), p. 7. Excerpts reprinted by permission of Mervyn Morris.

53. Morris, "The Pond," *Savacou* 3/4 (1971), 37–38. Also published in *The Pond*, p. 42.

54. Eric Roach, "Growing Up in Tobago," *David Frost Introduces Trinidad and Tobago* (London: Deutsch, 1975), p. 157. Quoted in Rohlehr, *Pathfinder*, p. 7.

55. Roach, "Letter to Lamming in England," *Bim* 17: 36–37. Excerpts reprinted by permission of Peepal Tree Press.

56. Roach, in a review of Savacou 3/4 in the *Trinidad Guardian*, July 14, 1971. Quoted in Gordon Rohlehr, "West Indian Poetry: Some Problems of Assessment," *Bim* 14:54, and 55 (1972), esp. 82–85 and 141. See also Rohlehr, "Introduction," *Voiceprint*, ed. Stewart Brown, Mervyn Morris, and Gordon Rohlehr, pp. 1–23.

57. George Lamming, *Season of Adventure* (London: Allison and Busby, 1979), p. 363.

58. Roach, "I am the archipelago," in *Voiceprint*, ed. Stewart Brown, Mervyn Morris, and Gordon Rohlehr, pp. 196–97.

Chapter 4: "To court the language of my people"

1. Derek Walcott, "The Gulf," *The Gulf* (London: Jonathan Cape, 1969), p. 28. © 1969, 1970 by Derek Walcott. Excerpts reprinted by permission of Farrar, Straus and Giroux, Inc. and Faber and Faber, Ltd.

2. Walcott, "The Muse of History," *Carifesta Forum*, ed. John Hearne (Kingston: Institute of Jamaica, 1976), p. 126. This essay was also published in *Is Massa Day Dead*, ed. Orde Coombs (New York: Anchor, 1974), pp. 1–27.

3. Walcott, Holograph MS (*Another Life*), book 2, p. 82.

4. See Hubert Devonish, *Language and Liberation: Creole Language Politics in the Caribbean* (London: Karia Press, 1986).

5. Walcott, "What the Twilight Says: An Overture," *Dream on Monkey Mountain and Other Plays* (New York: Farrar, Straus and Giroux, 1970), p. 27. © 1970 by Derek Walcott. Excerpts reprinted by permission of Farrar, Straus and Giroux, Inc. and Faber and Faber, Ltd.

6. Walcott, "Ruins of a Great House," *In a Green Night* (London: Jonathan Cape, 1962), pp. 19–20. Also published in *Collected Poems: 1948–1984* (New York: Farrar, Straus and Giroux, 1986). © 1962, 1986 by Derek Walcott. Excerpts reprinted by permission of Farrar, Straus and Giroux, Inc. and Faber and Faber, Ltd.

7. William Wordsworth, "London 1802," in *William Wordsworth*, ed. Stephen Gill, p. 286.

8. e. e. cummings, "next to of course god america i," *Complete Poems, 1904–1962*, ed. George James Firmage (New York: Liveright, 1991), p. 267. © 1926 by Horace Liveright; © 1954 by E. E. Cummings; © 1991 by E.E. Cummings Trust and George James Firmage. Excerpt reprinted by permission of Liveright Publishing Corp. and HarperCollins Publishers.

9. Tony Harrison, *V.* (Newcastle: Bloodaxe Books, 1985), n.p.

10. Harrison, "On Not being Milton," *Selected Poems* (Harmondsworth: Penguin, 1984), p. 112.

11. Claude McKay, "The White House," in *The Penguin Book of Caribbean Verse*, ed. Paula Burnett, p. 144.

12. Walcott, *Bim* 7:26 (1958), 6.

13. Walcott, "Chapter VI" of "Tales of the Islands: A Sonnet Sequence," ibid., p. 69.

14. Walcott, "Tales of the Islands: Chapter VI," *In a Green Night*, p. 28.

15. Philip Levine, "Looking for an Opening," in *Naked Poetry: Recent American Poetry in Open Forms*, ed. Stephen Berg and Robert Mezey (Indianapolis: Bobbs-Merrill, 1969), p. 392.

16. James Joyce, *Portrait of the Artist as a Young Man* (Harmondsworth: Penguin, 1960), pp. 187–89.

17. Ibid., p. 251.

18. Walcott, "The Muse of History," *Carifesta Forum*, p. 112.

19. Walcott, "What the Twilight Says," *Dream on Monkey Mountain*, p. 9.

20. Quoted in Walcott, ibid., p. 10. See also Aimé Césaire, "Cahier d'un retour au pays natal," *Collected Poems*, trans. Clayton Eshelman and Annette Smith, pp. 42–43.

21. Walcott, "The Schooner Flight," *The Star-Apple Kingdom*, p. 5.

22. Ibid., pp. 3–4.

23. Seamus Heaney, 'The Murmur of Malvern," *The Government of the Tongue*, p. 25. See also Edward Kamau Brathwaite, *History of the Voice*, pp. 9–10.

24. Walcott, "The Muse of History," *Carifesta Forum*, p. 112.

25. Walcott, *Omeros*, pp. 73–76.

26. Walcott, "A Far Cry from Africa," *In a Green Night*, p. 18.

27. William Butler Yeats, "A General Introduction for My Work," *Essays and Introductions* (New York, 1968), p. 519.

28. "Mikey Smith: Dub Poet," interviewed by Mervyn Morris, *Jamaica Journal* 18:2 (May–July, 1985), 39.

29. Michael Hartnett, *Collected Poems, Vol. I* (Dublin: Raven Arts Press, 1984), p. 157.

30. Ibid., p. 162.
31. Ibid., p. 163.
32. See Gordon Rohlehr, "Introduction: The Shape of That Hurt," in *Voiceprint*, ed. Stewart Brown, Mervyn Morris, and Gordon Rohlehr, p. 12, for a useful discussion of the relationship between oral and folk traditions in the West Indies.
33. William Wordsworth, *Lyrical Ballads*, ed. R. L. Brett and A. R. Jones (London: Methuen, 1965), pp. 241–47, 253–65.
34. William Wordsworth, "The Thorn," in *William Wordsworth*, ed. Stephen Gill, p. 59.
35. Edward Kamau Brathwaite, "Rites," *Islands, The Arrivants*, pp. 199–201.
36. Lorna Goodison, "My Will," *I Am Becoming My Mother*, p. 19.
37. Henry Vaughan, "The World," *Complete Poetry of Henry Vaughan*, ed. French Fogle (New York: New York University Press, 1965), p. 231.
38. Don McKay, "March Snow," *Birding, or Desire* (Toronto: McClelland and Stewart, 1983), p. 63. Excerpt reprinted by permission of McClelland and Stewart.
39. Seamus Heaney, "Nerthus," *Wintering Out* (New York: Oxford University Press, 1973), p. 49. Heaney has not included this poem in either volume of his selected poems.
40. Levi Tafari, "Black Sufferation," *Polygon* (Birmingham), 147 (December 1984).
41. Paul Keens-Douglas, "When Moon Shine," *When Moon Shine* (Port of Spain: Keensdee, 1979), p. 9.
42. Owen Barfield, *Poetic Diction: A Study in Meaning*, 3d ed. (Middletown, Conn.: Wesleyan University Press, 1973), p. 43.
43. Ibid., pp. 48–49.
44. Ibid., p. 49.
45. Ibid.
46. See Frederick Cassidy, *Jamaica Talk*, pp. 86, 400.
47. Winnifred Nowottny, *The Language Poets Use* (London: Athlone Press, 1965), pp. 9–10.
48. See Northrop Frye, *The Great Code: The Bible and Literature* (Toronto: Academic Press, 1982) and *Words with Power* (New York: Viking, 1990); and Stephen Prickett, *Words and the Word: Language, Poetics and Biblical Interpretation* (Cambridge: Cambridge University Press, 1986).
49. George Orwell, "Politics and the English Language," *Inside the Whale and Other Essays* (Harmondsworth: Penguin, 1962), p. 149.
50. Oscar Wilde, "The Critic as Artist," in *Plays, Prose Writings and Poems*, ed. Isobel Murray (London: Dent, 1975), p. 57.
51. George Campbell, *First Poems: A New Edition with Additional Poems* (New York: Garland, 1981), p. 42.
52. Walcott, *Another Life* (New York: Farrar, Straus and Giroux), pp. 143. © 1972, 1973 by Derek Walcott. Excerpts reprinted by permission of Farrar, Straus and Giroux, Inc. and Faber and Faber, Ltd.
53. Ibid., p. 147.

54. See Velma Pollard, "Dread Talk—The Speech of the Rastafari in Jamaica," *Caribbean Quarterly* 26:4 (1980), 32–41; "Social History of Dread Talk," *Caribbean Quarterly* 28:4 (1982), 17–40; "Words Sounds: the Language of the Rastafari in Barbados and St. Lucia," *Jamaica Journal* 17:1 (1984), 57–62.

55. Quoted in Pollard, "Word Sounds: The Language of Rastafari in Barbados and St. Lucia," *Jamaica Journal* 17:1 (1984), 57.

56. Linton Kwesi Johnson, "Youtman," in *Caribbean Poetry Now*, ed. Stewart Brown, p. 20. Excerpts reprinted by permission of Linton Kwesi Johnson.

57. Mervyn Morris, *On Holy Week* (Brown's Town, Jamaica: Earle Publishers, 1976), pp. 20–21. Excerpt reprinted by permission of Mervyn Morris.

58. Brathwaite, "Sam Lord," *Mother Poem* (Oxford: Oxford University Press, 1977), pp. 8–9. © 1977 by Edward Kamau Brathwaite. Excerpts reprinted by permission of Oxford University Press.

59. Goodison, "Heartease II," *Heartease* (London: New Beacon, 1988), pp. 34–35. Excerpts reprinted by permission of Lorna Goodison.

60. Wilde, "The Critic as Artist," in *Plays, Prose Writings and Poems*, p. 40.

61. Edward Baugh, "Goodison on the Road to Heartease," *Journal of West Indian Literature* 1:1 (1986), 20–21.

Chapter 5: "Loose now the salt cords binding our tongues"

1. Adrienne Rich, "Vesuvius at Home: The Power of Emily Dickinson," *On Lies, Secrets and Silence* (New York: Norton, 1979), p. 181.

2. Seamus Heaney, "Feeling Into Words," *Preoccupations: Selected Prose, 1968–1978* (New York: Farrar, Straus and Giroux, 1980), p. 60.

3. Lorna Goodison, "Songs of Release II," *Heartease*, p. 13.

4. Norman Manley, quoted in Rex Nettleford, *Cultural Action and Social Change: The Case of Jamaica* (Kingston: Institute of Jamaica, 1978), pp. 67–68.

5. Heaney, "Place, Pastness, Poems: A Triptych," *Salmagundi* 68–69 Fall 1985–Winter 1986), 41; and "The Sense of Place," *Preoccupations*, p. 132.

6. See Edward Baugh, *Derek Walcott. Memory as Vision: Another Life* (London: Longman, 1978), esp. pp. 1–18.

7. Heaney, "Feeling into Words," *Preoccupations*, p. 57.

8. Derek Walcott, "A City's Death by Fire," *In a Green Night*, p. 14.

9. Baugh, "Derek Walcott on West Indian Literature and Theatre: An Interview," *Jamaica Journal* 21:2 (1988), 50.

10. Nettleford, *Cultural Action and Social Change*, p. 33.

11. See "Derek Walcott Talks About *The Joker of Seville*," *Carib* 4, 1–15.

12. Walcott, "What the Twilight Says: An Overture," *Dream on Monkey Mountain*, pp. 3–4.

13. Walcott, *Another Life*, p. 139.

14. Walcott, "What the Twilight Says: An Overture," *Dream on Monkey Mountain*, p. 9.

15. Walcott, "His is the Pivotal One About Race," *Sunday Guardian*, Dec 1, 1963, p. 23; quoted in Gordon Rohlehr, *Pathfinder*, p. 111.

16. Baugh, "Derek Walcott on West Indian Literature and Theatre: An Interview," *Jamaica Journal* 21:2 (1988), 52.

17. Walcott, "The Muse of History," *Carifesta Forum*, p. 126.

18. Oscar Wilde, "The Decay of Lying," in *The Soul of Man Under Socialism and Other Essays*, ed. Philip Rieff (New York : Harper and Row, 1970), pp. 61–62.

19. Walcott, *Another Life*, p. 1.

20. Walcott, Holograph MS (*Another Life*), book 1, p. 23.

21. Walcott, "Crusoe's Journal," *The Castaway* (London: Jonathan Cape, 1965), p. 51. Also published in *Collected Poems: 1948–1984*. © 1965, 1986 by Derek Walcott. Excerpts reprinted by permission of Farrar, Straus and Giroux, Inc. and Faber and Faber, Ltd.

22. *The Voyages of Christopher Columbus*, trans. Cecil Jane, p. 149.

23. Walcott, ibid., p. 52.

24. Walcott, Holograph MS (*Another Life*), book 1.

25. Walcott, "What the Twilight Says: An Overture," *Dream on Monkey Mountain*, pp. 10–11.

26. Walcott, "Names," *Sea Grapes*, pp. 32–34.

27. Walcott, "Air," *The Gulf*, pp. 36–37.

28. Mark Twain, *The Adventures of Huckleberry Finn* (New York: Harper and Row, 1987), p. 280.

29. Walcott, "The Schooner *Flight*," *The Star-Apple Kingdom*, p. 12.

30. Walcott, "The Muse of History," *Carifesta Forum*, p. 128.

31. Wilson Harris, *History, Fable and Myth in the Caribbean and Guianas: Edgar Mittelholzer Memorial Lecture* (Georgetown, Guyana: National History and Arts Council, 1970), p. 29.

32. Walcott, *Omeros*, p. 291.

33. W. S. Merwin, "Odysseus," *The Drunk in the Furnace, The First Four Books of Poems* (New York: Atheneum, 1975), p. 201. © 1956, 1957, 1958, 1959, 1960, 1975 by W. S. Merwin. Excerpts reprinted by permission of W. S. Merwin.

34. See Stephen Jay Gould, *Time's Arrow, Time's Cycle: Myth and Metaphor in the Discovery of Geological Time* (Cambridge, Mass.: Harvard University Press, 1987).

35. Walcott, "Sea Grapes," *Sea Grapes*, p. 3.

36. Walcott, "Ruins of a Great House," *In A Green Night*, p. 20.

37. Walcott, "The Schooner Flight," *The Star-Apple Kingdom*, pp. 19–20.

38. Walcott, *Omeros*, pp. 181, 217.

39. Walcott, "Sainte Lucie," *Sea Grapes*, pp. 36, 39.

40. Seamus Heaney, "The Tollund Man," *Wintering Out*, pp. 47–48.

41. Walcott, "The Arkansas Testament," *The Arkansas Testament* (New York: Farrar, Straus and Giroux, 1987), pp. 109–10, 116. © 1987 by Derek Walcott. Excerpts reprinted by permission of Farrar, Straus and Giroux, Inc. and Faber and Faber, Ltd.

42. Walcott, "Season of Phantasmal Peace," *The Fortunate Traveller* (New York: Farrar, Straus and Giroux, 1981), pp. 98–99. © 1980, 1981 by Derek Wal-

cott. Excerpts reprinted by permission of Farrar, Straus and Giroux, Inc. and Faber and Faber, Ltd.

43. Walcott, *Omeros;* the quotations are from pp. 4, 207.

44. Brathwaite, "Timehri," *Savacou* 2 (1970), 38; quoted in Rohlehr, *Pathfinder,* p. 3. An excerpt from this article is published in *Hinterland: Caribbean Poetry from the West Indies and Britain,* ed. E. A. Markham, pp. 117–19.

45. Brathwaite, ibid., p. 38.

46. See Nettleford, *Identity, Race and Protest in Jamaica,* where a chapter (pp. 171–211) has this title.

47. Brathwaite. Interview (April 1990) with Nathaniel Mackey, *Hambone,* pp. 42–59.

48. Brathwaite, "History, the Caribbean Writer and X/Self," in *Crisis and Creativity in the New Literatures in English,* ed. Geoffrey V. Davis and Hena Maes-Jelinek (Atlanta, Ga.: Rodopi, 1990), pp. 33–34.

49. Brathwaite, "Nam," in *X/Self* (Oxford: Oxford University Press, 1987), pp. 73–79. © 1987 by Edward Kamau Brathwaite. Excerpts reprinted by permission of Oxford University Press.

50. See Rohlehr, *Pathfinder,* pp. 24–28.

51. Walcott, "Names," *Sea Grapes,* p. 32.

52. Goodison, "Songs of Release II," *Heartease,* p. 13.

53. Walcott, "The Schooner *Flight,*" *The Star-Apple Kingdom,* pp. 19–20.

54. George Lamming, *In the Castle of My Skin* (London: Longman, 1979), pp. 128 and 57–58.

55. Brathwaite, "Timehri," *Savacou* 2 (1970), 37.

56. Brathwaite, "History, the Caribbean Writer and X/Self," in *Crisis and Creativity in the New Literatures in English,* ed. Geoffrey V. Davis and Hena Maes-Jelinek, pp. 27–28.

57. Brathwaite, "Basic Basie," *Jah Music* (Kingston, Jamaica: Savacou, 1986), p. 9. Excerpts reprinted by permission of Edward Kamau Brathwaite.

58. Brathwaite, "Tom," *Rights of Passage, The Arrivants,* pp. 13–14.

59. Brathwaite, "Folkways," *Rights of Passage, The Arrivants,* pp. 30, 34.

60. Walcott, "Tribal Flutes: Review of *Rights of Passage,*" *Sunday Guardian,* March 19, 1967; quoted in Rohlehr, *Pathfinders,* p. 31.

61. Brathwaite, "Wings of a Dove," *Rights of Passage, The Arrivants,* pp. 42–45.

62. Brathwaite, "The Awakening," *Masks, The Arrivants,* pp. 156–57.

63. James Baldwin, quoted in Brathwaite, *Islands, The Arrivants,* p. 160.

64. Brathwaite, "The Cracked Mother," *Islands, The Arrivants,* pp. 180–81.

65. See Rohlehr, *Pathfinder,* pp. 207–13.

66. Brathwaite, "Negus" and "Vèvè," *Islands, The Arrivants,* pp. 222–24 and 265–66.

67. Wilson Harris, *The Whole Armour, The Guyana Quartet* (London: Faber, 1985), p. 335.

68. Harris, *Eternity to Season* (London: New Beacon, 1978), p. 7.

69. See Maureen Warner-Lewis, "Image and Idiom in Nationalist Literature: Achebe, Ngugi and Brathwaite," in *Studies in Commonwealth Literature,* ed.

Eckhard Breitinger and Reinhard Sander (Tübingen: Gunter Narr Verlag, 1985), pp. 111–13.

70. Brathwaite, "Nametracks," *Mother Poem*, pp. 61–62.

71. Brathwaite, "Yellow Minnim," *Sun Poem* (Oxford: Oxford University Press, 1982), p. 20. © 1982 by Edward Kamau Brathwaite. Excerpts reprinted by permission of Oxford University Press.

72. Brathwaite, "The Dust," *Rights of Passage, The Arrivants,* pp. 68–69; and *X/Self,* p. vi. See also J. Edward Chamberlin, "Myself Made Otherwise: Edward Kamau Brathwaite's *X/Self,*" *Carib: Journal of the West Indian Association for Commonwealth Literature and Language Studies* 5 (1989), 19–32.

73. Brathwaite, "Salt," *X/Self,* p. 5.

74. Brathwaite, "Dies Irie," *X/Self,* pp. 37–39.

75. Brathwaite, "The Visibility Trigger," *X/Self,* pp. 49–50.

76. Brathwaite, "Xango," *X/Self,* p. 111.

77. Derek Walcott, from "Caligula's Horse," his keynote address to a conference on "Biography/Autobiography in West Indian Literature" hosted by the English Department, University of the West Indies, Mona Campus, Kingston, Jamaica in May, 1988. This address is published in *After Europe: Critical Theory and Post-Colonial Writing,* ed. Stephen Slemon and Helen Tiffin (Mundelstrup, Denmark: Dangaroo Press, 1989), pp. 138–42.

78. Lorna Goodison, "Tamarind Season," *Tamarind Season* (Kingston, Jamaica: Institute of Jamaica, 1980), p. 73. Excerpts repinted by permission of Lorna Goodison.

79. Goodison, "Judges," *Tamarind Season,* p. 55.

80. Goodison, "White Birds." Unpublished. Excerpt printed by permission of Lorna Goodison.

81. Thomas Merton, *The Wisdom of the Desert: Sayings from the Desert Fathers of the Fourth Century* (New York: New Directions, 1960), pp. 22–23.

82. Lorna Goodison, "The Transcendent Song of the Tuareg Woman." Unpublished. Excerpt printed by permission of Lorna Goodison.

83. Goodison, "Recommendation for Amber," *The Hudson Review* 43:4 (Winter 1991), 617–18. Excerpts reprinted by permission of Lorna Goodison.

84. Goodison, "My Will," *I Am Becoming My Mother,* p. 19.

85. Goodison, "For My Mother (May I Inherit Half her Strength)," *I Am Becoming My Mother,* pp. 46–48.

86. Philip Sherlock and Rex Nettleford, *The University of the West Indies,* pp, 1–3.

87. Goodison, "Coir," *Jamaica Journal* 22:1 (1989), 38–39. Excerpts reprinted by permission of Lorna Goodison.

88. See John Rashford, "The Search for Africa's Baobab Tree in Jamaica," *Jamaica Journal* 20:2 (May–July, 1987), 2–11.

89. Goodison, "Elephant," *Jamaica Journal* 22:1 (1989), 39.

90. Goodison, "We Are the Women," *I Am Becoming My Mother,* pp. 12–13.

91. Goodison, "Nanny," *I Am Becoming My Mother,* p. 45.

92. Quoted in Philip Sherlock and Rex Nettleford, *The University of the West Indies,* p. 2.

93. Goodison, "Birth Stone," *The Hudson Review* 43:4 (Winter 1991), 618–19.

94. Goodison, "For Rosa Parks," *I Am Becoming My Mother*, p. 41.

95. Goodison, "The Mulatta as Penelope," *I Am Becoming My Mother*, p. 25.

96. Edward Baugh, interview with Lorna Goodison (December 1984). Quoted in Baugh, "Lorna Goodison on the Road to Heartease," *Journal of West Indian Literature* 1:1 (1986), 20.

97. Goodison, "Guinea Woman," *I Am Becoming My Mother*, p. 39.

98. Goodison, "Letters to the Egyptian," *I Am Becoming My Mother*, pp. 49–50.

99. Goodison, "My Last Poem," *I Am Becoming My Mother*, pp. 7–8.

100. Goodison, "My Last Poem (Again)," *Heartease*, p. 14.

101. Goodison, "To Us, All Flowers Are Roses." Unpublished. Excerpt printed by permission of Lorna Goodison.

102. Goodison, "Keith Jarrett—Rainmaker," *I Am Becoming My Mother*, p. 33.

103. Goodison, "Survivor," *Heartease*, p. 16.

104. Herman Melville, *Moby Dick*, ed. Harrison Hayford and Herschel Parker (New York: Norton, 1967), p. 355.

105. Goodison, "Heartease New England 1987," *Heartease*, pp. 40–41.

106. Goodison, "Come Let Your Eyes Feel," *Heartease*, p. 42.

107. Gerard Manley Hopkins, "The Wreck of the Deutschland," *Poems*, ed. W. H. Gardner and N. H. Mackenzie (Oxford: Oxford University Press, 1970), p. 52.

108. Goodison, "I Shall Light A Candle," *Heartease*, p. 7.

109. Anthony McNeill, "if i had meant this," *Credences at The Altar of Cloud* (Kingston, Jamaica: Institute of Jamaica, 1979), p. 48. Excerpts reprinted by permission of Anthony McNeill.

Chapter 6: "i a tell no tale"

1. Pablo Picasso, "Picasso Speaks," *The Arts* (New York), May 1923, pp. 315–26. This idea has been expressed by a wide range of writers and artists over the past hundred years, from Robert Browning to Roland Barthes.

2. Oscar Wilde, "The Decay of Lying," in *The Soul of Man Under Socialism and Other Essays*, ed. Philip Rieff (New York: Harper and Row, 1970), pp. 53 and 67.

3. Derek Walcott, "Nearing Forty," *The Gulf*, p. 67.

4. Walcott, "Island," *In a Green Night*, p. 77.

5. Oku Onuora, "i a tell," in *Focus 1983: An Anthology of Contemporary Jamaican Writing*, ed. Mervyn Morris (Kingston: Jamaica: Caribbean Authors Publishing, 1983), p. 105. Excerpt reprinted by permission of Oku Onuora.

6. Mutabaruka, "Revolutionary Poets," in *Penguin Book of Caribbean Verse in English*, ed. Paula Burnett, p. 80. Excerpt reprinted by permission of Mutabaruka.

7. Christine Craig, "St. Ann Saturday," in *Creation Fire: A Cafra Anthology of Caribbean Women's Poetry*, ed. Ramabai Espinet (Toronto: Sister Vision, 1990), pp. 159–161. Excerpt reprinted by permission of Christine Craig.

8. Ian McDonald, "Yusman Ali," in *Caribbean Poetry Now*, ed. Stewart Brown, p. 36. Excerpt reprinted by permission of Ian McDonald.

9. Lorna Goodison, "Bridge Views," *Tamarind Season*, pp. 46–48.

10. Dennis Scott, "No sufferer," *Uncle Time*, p. 53.

11. Velma Pollard, "Social History of Dread Talk," *Caribbean Quarterly* 28:4 (1982), 25.

12. Ann Marie Dewar, "Rasta, Me Son," in *One People's Grief: New Writing from the Caribbean*, ed. Robert Bensen, *Pacific Quarterly Moana* 8:3 (1983), 70–71. Also published in *Flowers Blooming Late: Poems from Montserrat*, ed. Howard Fergus (Montserrat: University of the West Indies, 1984), pp. 69–70. Excerpt reprinted by permission of Ann Marie Dewar.

13. Edward Kamau Brathwaite, "Poem for Walter Rodney," *Third World Poems* (London: Longman, 1983), pp. 62–68.

14. Kendel Hippolyte, "Zoo Story—Ja. '76," in *Voiceprint*, ed. Stewart Brown, Mervyn Morris, and Gordon Rohlehr, pp. 50–51. Excerpt reprinted by permission of Kendel Hippolyte.

15. Walcott, *The Joker of Seville and O Babylon!* (New York: Farrar, Straus and Giroux, 1978), pp. 155–56. Sam Selvon has said almost exactly the same thing about his use of dialect in *Lonely Londoners*. (See "Sam Selvon Talking: a Conversation with Kenneth Ramchand," *Canadian Literature* 95 (1982), 60–61.)

16. Michael Thelwell, "*The Harder They Come*: From Film to Novel. How questions of technique, form, language, craft, and the marketplace conceal issues of politics, audience, culture, and purpose," *Grand Street* 37 (New York, 1991), pp. 150–51.

17. Goodison, "The Road of the Dread," *Tamarind Season*, pp. 22–23.

18. Jean Binta Breeze, "Riddym Ravings (The Mad Woman's Poem)," in *Riddym Ravings and Other Poems*, ed. Mervyn Morris (London: Race Today, 1988), pp. 58–61.

19. "Mikey Smith: Dub Poet." Interview with Mervyn Morris, *Jamaica Journal* 18:2 (1985), 39 and 40. PNP refers to the People's National Party, then led by Michael Manley; and JLP to the Jamaica Labour Party, led by Edward Seaga. See also Mervyn Morris, "The Poetry of Mikey Smith," in *West Indian Literature and its Social Context*, ed. Mark McWatt (Bridgetown, Barbados: Department of English, University of the West Indies, 1985), pp. 48–54; and "Printing the Performance," *Jamaica Journal* 23:1 (1990), 21–26.

20. Michael Smith, "It A Come," in *It A Come: Poems by Michael Smith*, ed. Mervyn Morris (London: Race Today, 1988), pp. 19–20. Excerpts reprinted by permission of Race Today Publications.

21. Northrop Frye, "The Imaginative and the Imaginary," *Fables of Identity* (New York: Harcourt, Brace and World, 1963), p. 163.

22. See Rex Nettleford, "Introduction" to *Jamaica Labrish: Jamaica Dialect Poems by Louise Bennett* (Kingston, Jamaica: Sangster's, 1966), p. 13.

23. Smith, "Me Cyaan Believe It," *It A Come: Poems by Michael Smith*, ed. Mervyn Morris, pp. 13–15.

24. Edward Baugh, "Truth and Consequences," *A Tale from the Rainforest*, p. 12.

25. Mutabaruka, "Two Poems On: What I Can Write," in *From Our Yard: Jamaican Poetry Since Independence*, ed. Pamela Mordecai (Kingston, Jamaica: Institute of Jamaica, 1987), pp. 180–81. Excerpt reprinted by permission of Mutabaruka.

26. Baugh, "Cold Comfort," *A Tale from the Rainforest*, p. 33.

27. Edward Galeano, "The Imagination and the Will to Change," trans. Mariana Valverde, *The Writer and Human Rights* (Toronto: Lester and Orpen Dennys, 1983), pp. 121–22.

28. Mark McWatt, "Morawhanna," *Interiors* (Mundelstrup: Dangaroo Press, 1987), pp. 32–33. Excerpt reprinted by permission of Mark McWatt.

29. Willliam Butler Yeats, "Adam's Curse," *Collected Poems* (London: Macmillan, 1967), p. 88.

30. Dennis Scott, "Notes on a Correspondence"; Anthony McNeill, *Reel from "The Life-Movie"* (Kingston, Jamaica: Savacou, 1975), pp. 1–5.

31. Anthony McNeill, "Brother Joe," *Reel from "The Life-Movie,"* pp. 29–30. Excerpt reprinted by permission of Anthony McNeill.

32. McNeill, *Credences at The Altar of Cloud*, pp. 1, 18 and 48.

33. "Mikey Smith: Dub Poet." Interview with Mervyn Morris, *Jamaica Journal* 18:2 (1985), 40.

34. Baugh, "Lignum Vitae," *A Tale from the Rainforest*, p. 53.

35. Olive Senior, "Ancestral Poem," *Talking of Trees* (Kingston, Jamaica: Calabash, 1985), pp. 9–10. Excerpts reprinted by permission of Olive Senior.

36. Senior, "The Mother," *Talking of Trees*, pp. 68–69.

37. David Dabydeen, "Coolie Odyssey," *Coolie Odyssey* (Coventry: Dangaroo, 1988), p. 12. Excerpt reprinted by permission of David Dabydeen.

38. Anthony Kellman, "Watercourse," *Watercourse* (Leeds: Peepal Tree Press, 1990), p. 59. Excerpt reprinted by permission of Peepal Tree Press.

39. Shake Keane, "Shaker Funeral," *Penguin Book of Caribbean Verse in English*, ed. Paula Burnett, pp. 226–27.

40. Walcott, Holograph MS (*Another Life*), book 1, p. 36.

41. John Agard, *Man to Pan* (Habana: Casa de Las Américas, 1982), pp. 18–19. Excerpt reprinted by permission of John Agard.

42. See Gordon Rohlehr, *Calypso and Society in Pre-Independence Trinidad* (Port of Spain: Gordon Rohlehr, 1990), especially pp. 1–42.

43. Victor Questel, "Pan Drama," *Near Mourning Ground* (Port of Spain: New Voices, 1979), pp. 4–5.

44. Lorna Goodison, "Jah Music," *I Am Becoming My Mother*, p. 36.

45. James Berry, "From Lucy: Holiday Reflections," in *Penguin Book of Caribbean Verse in English*, ed. Paula Burnett, pp. 207–8.

46. Fred D'Aguiar, "Letter from Mama Dot," *Mama Dot* (London: Chatto and Windus, 1985), p. 21. Excerpt reprinted by permission of Fred D'Aguiar.

47. Mark McWatt, "The Two Faces of Eldorado: Contrasting Attitudes Towards History and Identity in West Indian Literature," in *West Indian Literature and its Social Context*, ed. Mark McWatt, p. 33.

48. D'Aguiar, "El Dorado Update," *Airy Hall* (London: Chatto and Windus, 1989), pp. 32–35. Excerpt reprinted by permission of Fred D'Aguiar.

49. Linton Kwesi Johnson, "It Dread Inna Inglan," *Inglan is a bitch* (London: Race Today, 1980), pp. 14–15. Excerpt reprinted by permission of Linton Kwesi Johnson.

50. Johnson, "Reggae Fi Dada," in *From Our Yard: Jamaican Poetry Since Independence*, ed. Pamela Mordecai, pp. 124–26. Excerpt reprinted by permission of Linton Kwesi Johnson.

51. John Agard, "Palm Tree King," *Limbo Dancer in Dark Glasses* (Islington: Greenheart, 1983), pp. 37–38. Excerpt reprinted by permission of John Agard.

52. Grace Nichols, "Wherever I Hang," *Lazy Thoughts of a Lazy Woman* (London: Virago, 1989), p. 10. Excerpt reprinted by permission of Grace Nichols.

53. Nichols, "Epilogue," *The Fat Black Woman's Poems* (London: Virago, 1984), p. 64. This poem was also the epigraph for the *Penguin Book of Caribbean Verse in English*, ed. Paula Burnett. Excerpt reprinted by permission of Grace Nichols.

54. Dionne Brand, "P.P.S. Grenada," *Chronicles of the Hostile Sun* (Toronto: Williams-Wallace, 1984), pp. 52, 56. Excerpt reprinted by permission of Dionne Brand.

55. Brand, "hard against my soul," X, *No Language is Neutral* (Toronto: Coach House, 1990), pp. 46, 51. Excerpts reprinted by permission of Dionne Brand.

56. Derek Walcott, "I heard them marching the leaf-wet roads of my head," LII, *Midsummer* (New York: Farrar, Straus and Giroux, 1984). © 1984 by Derek Walcott. Excerpt reprinted by permission of Farrar, Straus and Giroux, Inc. and Faber and Faber, Ltd.

57. Brand, "No language is neutral," *No Language is Neutral*, p. 22.

Epilogue

1. Seamus Heaney, "Song," *Field Work* (London: Faber, 1982), p. 56. © 1982 by Seamus Heaney. Excerpt reprinted by permission of Faber and Faber, Ltd. and Farrar, Straus and Giroux, Inc.

2. Derek Walcott, "Caligula's Horse." Keynote address to the conference on "The Written Life: Biography/Autobiography in West Indian Literature," University of the West Indies, Kingston, Jamaica, May 1988.

3. Lorna Goodison, reading at the conference on "The Written Life" at the University of the West Indies, Kingston, Jamaica, May, 1988. See also Lorna Goodison, "Mother the Great Stones Got to Move," in *Voiceprint*, ed. Stewart Brown, Mervyn Morris and Gordon Rohlehr, pp. 219–20.

4. Edward Kamau Brathwaite, "Stone for Mikey Smith," *Jah Music* (Kingston, Jamaica: Savacou Cooperative, 1986), p. 24.

5. "Mikey Smith: Dub Poet." Interview with Mervyn Morris, *Jamaica Journal* 18:2 (1985), 41.

6. J. E. Clare MacFarlane, "The Prospect of West Indian Poetry," *Kyk-Over-Al* 16 (1953).

Selected Bibliography

Contemporary West Indian Poetry in English

Agard, John
    Shoot Me with Flowers. Georgetown, Guyana, 1973.
    Man to Pan. Habana: Casa de las Americas, 1982.
    Limbo Dancer in Dark Glasses. Islington, England: Greenheart Press, 1983.
    Mangoes and Bullets: Selected and New Poems 1972–1984. London: Pluto Press, 1985.
    Lovelines for a Goat-born Lady. London: Serpent's Tail, 1990.
Allen, Lillian
    Rhythm an' Hardtimes. Toronto: Domestic Bliss, 1982.
Baugh, Edward
    A Tale from the Rainforest. Kingston, Jamaica: Sandberry Press, 1988.
Bennett, Louise
    Jamaica Labrish: Jamaica Dialect Poems, ed. Rex Nettleford. Kingston, Jamaica: Sangster's, 1966.
    Selected Poems, ed. Mervyn Morris. Kingston, Jamaica: Sangster's, 1983.
Berry, James
    Fractured Circles. London: New Beacon, 1979.
    Lucy's Letters and Loving. London: New Beacon, 1982.
    Chain of Days. Oxford: Oxford University Press, 1985.
Bloom, Valerie
    Touch mi; Tell mi. London: Bogle-L'Ouverture, 1983.
Brand, Dionne
    Fore Day Morning. Toronto: Williams-Wallace, 1979.
    Primitive Offensive. Toronto: Williams-Wallace, 1982.

Winter Epigrams. Toronto: Williams-Wallace, 1983.
Chronicles of the Hostile Sun. Toronto: Williams-Wallace, 1984.
No Language is Neutral. Toronto: Coach House Press, 1990.
Brathwaite, Edward Kamau
The Arrivants: A New World Trilogy. London: Oxford University Press, 1973.
Other Exiles. London: Oxford University Press, 1975.
Mother Poem. Oxford: Oxford University Press, 1977.
Sun Poem. Oxford: Oxford University Press, 1982.
Third World Poems. London: Longman, 1983.
Jah Music. Kingston, Jamaica: Savacou Cooperative, 1986.
X/Self. Oxford: Oxford University Press, 1987.
Sappho Sakyi's Meditations. Kingston, Jamaica: Savacou Cooperative, 1989.
Middle Passages. Newcastle: Bloodaxe, 1992.
Breeze, Jean Binta
Riddym Ravings and Other Poems, ed. Mervyn Morris. London: Race Today Publications, 1988.
Spring Cleaning. London: Virago, 1992.
Brother Resistance
Rapso Explosion. London: Karia Press, 1986.
Brown, Beverly
Dream Diary. Kingston, Jamaica: Savacou Cooperative, 1982.
Brown, Wayne
On the Coast. London: Andre Deutsch, 1972.
Voyages. Port of Spain, 1989.
Campbell, George
First Poems. Kingston, Jamaica, 1945; New York: Garland Publishing, 1981.
Earth Testament. Kingston, Jamaica, 1983.
Carew, Jan
Streets of Eternity. Georgetown, Guyana, 1952.
Sea Drums in My Blood. Port of Spain: The New Voices, 1980.
Carter, Martin
Poems of Resistance. Georgetown, Guyana,1954.
Poems of Succession. London: New Beacon, 1977.
Poems of Affinity. Georgetown, Guyana: Release, 1980.
Selected Poems. Georgetown, Guyana: Demerara Publishers, 1989.
Charles, Faustin
The Expatriate. London: Brookside Press, 1969.
Crab Track. London: Brookside Press, 1973.
Days and Nights in the Magic Forest. London: Bogle L'Ouverture, 1986.
Collins, Merle
Because the Dawn Breaks! London: Karia Press, 1985.
Collymore, Frank
Collected Poems. Bridgetown, Barbados, 1959.
Selected Poems. Bridgetown, Barbados, 1971.
Cooper, Afua
Breaking Chains. Toronto: Weelahs Publications, 1984.

Memories Have Tongues. Toronto: Sister Vision, 1992.
Craig, Christine
Quadrille for Tigers. Berkeley, Calif.: Mina Press, 1984.
Dabydeen, Cyril
Distances. Vancouver: Fiddlehead, 1977.
Goatsong. Ottawa: Mosaic, 1977.
Coastland: New and Selected Poems, 1973–1987. Oakville: Mosaic Press, 1989.
Islands Lovier Than a Vision. Leeds: Peepal Tree Press, 1986.
Dabydeen, David
Slave Song. Mundelstrup, Denmark: Dangaroo Press, 1984.
Coolie Odyssey. Coventry: Dangaroo Press, 1988.
D'Aguiar, Fred
Mama Dot. London: Chatto and Windus, 1985.
Airy Hall. London: Chatto and Windus, 1989.
Das, Mahadai.
Bones. Leeds: Peepal Tree Press, 1989.
DeCoteau, Delano Abdul Malik
Black-Up. Port of Spain: Kairi, 1972.
Revo. Port of Spain: Kairi, 1975.
The Whirlwind. London: Panrun Collective, 1988.
Escoffery, Gloria
Loggerhead. Kingston, Jamaica: Sandberry Press, 1988.
Espinet, Ramabai
Nuclear Seasons. Toronto: Sister Vision, 1991.
Fergus, Howard
Green Innocence. Montserrat, 1978.
Figueroa, John
Blue Mountain Peak. Kingston, Jamaica, 1943.
Love Leaps Here. Liverpool, 1962.
Ignoring Hurts. Washington, D.C., 1976.
The Chose: A Collection of Poems, 1941–1989. Leeds: Peepal Tree Press, 1991.
Gonzales, Anson
Collected Poems. Diego Martin, Trinidad: The New Voices, 1979.
Moksha: Poems of Light and Sound. Port of Spain: New Voices, 1988.
Goodison, Lorna
Tamarind Season. Kingston, Jamaica: Institute of Jamaica, 1980.
I Am Becoming My Mother. London: New Beacon, 1986.
Heartease. London: New Beacon, 1988.
Selected Poems. Ann Arbor: University of Michigan Press, 1992.
Goulbourne, Jean.
Actors in the Arena. Kingston, Jamaica: Savacou Cooperative, 1977.
Under the Sun. Port of Spain: New Voices, 1988.
Harris, Claire
Fables from the Women's Quarter. Toronto: Williams-Wallace, 1984.
Translations into Fiction. Fredericton, New Brunswick: Fiddlehead, 1984.
Travelling to Find a Remedy. Fredericton, New Brunswick: Goose Lane, 1986.

The Conception of Winter. Toronto: Williams-Wallace, 1988.
Drawing Down a Daughter. Fredericton, New Brunswick: Goose Lane, 1992.
Harris, Wilson
Eternity to Season. London: New Beacon, 1978.
Hendricks, A. L.
On This Mountain. London: Andre Deutsch, 1965.
These Green Islands. Kingston, Jamaica: Bolivar Press, 1971.
Madonna of the Unknown Nation. London: Workshop Press, 1974.
The Islanders. Kingston, Jamaica: Savacou Cooperative, 1983.
To Speak Simply: Selected Poems, 1961–1986. Sutton: Hippopotamus Press, 1988.
Herbert, Cecil
Poems, ed. Danielle Gianetti. Port of Spain: Eric Roach Trust, 1979.
Hippolyte, Kendel
Island in the Sun, Side Two. St. Lucia: The Morne, 1980.
bearings. St. Lucia, 1986.
Hopkinson, Abdur-Rahman Slade
The Four, and Other Poems. Bridgetown, Barbados, 1955.
The Madwoman of Papine. Georgetown, Guyana, 1976.
The Friend. Georgetown, Guyana, 1976.
Itwaru, Arnold.
Shattered Songs. Toronto: Aya Press, 1982.
Entombed Survivals. Toronto: Williams-Wallace, 1987.
body rites (beyond the darkening). Toronto: Tsar Press, 1991.
James, Cynthia.
Iere, My Love. Port of Spain, 1990.
Johnson, Amry L. *Long Road to Nowhere.* London: Virago, 1985.
Gorgons. Country: Cofa Press, 1992.
Johnson, Linton Kwesi
Voices of the Living and the Dead. London: Race Today Publications, 1974.
Dread Beat and Blood. London: Bogle—L'Ouverture, 1975.
Inglan Is a Bitch. London: Race Today Publications, 1980.
Tings and Times. Newcastle: Bloodaxe, 1991.
Keane, Shake
One a Week with Water. Habana: Casa de las Americas, 1979.
The Volcano Suite. St. Vincent, 1979.
Keens-Douglas, Paul
When Moon Shine. Port of Spain: Keensdee Productions, 1975.
Tim Tim. Port of Spain: Keensdee Productions, 1976.
Tell Me Again. Port of Spain: Keensdee Productions, 1979.
Is Town Say So. Port of Spain: Keensdee Productions, 1982.
Bobots. Port of Spain: Keensdee Productions, 1984.
Kellman, Anthony
The Black Madonna. Bridgetown, Barbados, 1975.
In Depths of Burning Light. Bridgetown, Barbados, 1982.
The Broken Sun. Bridgetown, Barbados, 1984.
Watercourse. Leeds: Peepal Tree Press, 1990.

Lee, John Robert
  Vocation. St. Lucia, 1975.
  Dread Season. St. Lucia, 1978.
  The Prodigal. St. Lucia,1983.
  Possessions. St. Lucia, 1984.
  Clearing Ground. Boston: New Life Fellowship, 1991.
MacKenzie, Earl.
  Against Linearity. Leeds. Peepal Press, 1992.
Manley, Rachel
  Prisms. Kingston, Jamaica, 1972.
  Poems 2. Bridgetown, Barbados, 1978.
  A Light Left On. Leeds: Peepal Tree Press, 1992.
Markham, E. A.
  Human Rites: Selected Poems, 1970–1982. London: Anvil Press, 1984.
  Living in Disguise. London: Anvil Press, 1986.
  Towards the End of a Century. London: Anvil Press, 1989.
Marson, Una
  Tropic Reveries. Kingston, Jamaica, 1930.
  Heights and Depths. Kingston, Jamaica, 1932.
  The Moth and the Star. Kingston, Jamaica, 1937.
Matthews, Marc
  Guyana My Altar. London: Karnak Press, 1987.
McDonald, Ian
  Selected Poems. Georgetown, Guyana, 1984.
  Mercy Ward. Manchester: Peterloo Poets, 1988.
  Essequibo. Calstock: Peterloo Poets, 1992.
McFarlane, Basil
  Jacob and the Angels and Other Poems. Georgetown, Guyana, 1952; Kraus
    Reprint, 1970.
McFarlane, J. E. Clare
  Selected Shorter Poems. Kingston, Jamaica, 1954.
McKay, Claude
  Selected Poems. New York, 1953.
McNeill, Anthony
  Hello Ungod. Baltimore, 1971.
  Reel from "The Life-Movie." Kingston, Jamaica: Savacou Publications, 1975.
  Credences at The Altar of Cloud. Kingston, Jamaica: Institute of Jamaica, 1979.
McTair, Dionyse.
  Notes Towards an Escape from Death. London: New Beacon, 1987.
McWatt, Mark
  Interiors. Coventry: Dangaroo Press, 1987.
Monar, Rooplall.
  Koker. Leeds: Peepal Tree Press, 1987.
Mordecai, Pamela
  Journey Poem. Kingston, Jamaica: Sandberry Press, 1989.
Morris, Mervyn

The Pond. London: New Beacon, 1973.
On Holy Week. St. Ann, Jamaica: Earle Publishers, 1976; rev ed. Kingston: Pathways, 1988.
Shadowboxing. London: New Beacon, 1979.
Mutabaruka (formerly Allan Hope)
First Poems, 1970–1979. Kingston, Jamaica: Paul Issa, 1980.
Nichols, Grace
i is a long-memoried woman. London: Karnak House, 1983.
The Fat Black Woman's Poems. London: Virago Press, 1984.
Lazy Thoughts of a Lazy Woman. London: Virago Press, 1989.
Onuora, Oku (formerly Orlando Wong)
Echo. Kingston, Jamaica: Sangster's, 1977.
Oku. Kingston, Jamaica, 1979.
Palmer, Opal Adisa.
Tamarind and Mango Women. Toronto: Sister Vision, 1992.
Persaud, Sasenarine
Demerary Telepathy. Leeds: Peepal Tree Press, 1989.
Philip, Marlene Nourbese
Looking for Livingstone: An Odyssey of Silence. Stratford: Mercury Press, 1991.
Salmon Courage. Toronto: Williams-Wallace, 1983.
She Tries Her Tongue: Her Silence Softly Breaks. Charlottetown: Ragweed, 1989.
Thorns. Toronto: Williams-Wallace, 1980.
Pollard, Velma
Crown Point. Leeds: Peepal Tree Press, 1988.
Shame Trees Don't Grow Here, but poincianas bloom. Leeds: Peepal Tree Press, 1992.
Questel, Victor D
Near Mourning Ground. Diego Martin, Trinidad: New Voices, 1979.
Hard Stares. Diego Martin, Trinidad: New Voices, 1982.
Roach, Eric
The Flowering Rock: Collected Poems, 1938–1974. Leeds: Peepal Tree Press, 1992.
Roy, Lucinda
Wailing the Dead to Sleep. London: Bogle L'Ouverture, 1988.
St. John, Bruce
Joyce and Eros and Varia. Bridgetown, Barbados: Yoruba, 1976.
Bumbatuk I. Bridgetown, Barbados: Cedar Press, 1982.
Salkey, Andrew
Jamaica. London: Hutchinson, 1974.
In the Hills Where Her Dreams Live. Habana: Casa de las Americas, 1979.
Away. London: Allison and Busby, 1980.
Scott, Dennis
Uncle Time. Pittsburgh: University of Pittsburgh Press, 1973.
Dreadwalk. London: New Beacon, 1982.
Strategies. Kingston, Jamaica: Sandberry Press, 1990.
Senior, Olive
Talking of Trees. Kingston, Jamaica: Calabash, 1985.

Seymour, A. J.
  The Guiana Book. Georgetown, Guyana, 1948.
  Images of Majority. Georgetown, Guyana, 1978.
  Selected Poems. Georgetown, Guyana, 1983.
Sherlock, Philip
  Ten Poems. Georgetown, Guyana, 1953.
Smith, Michael
  It A Come, ed. Mervyn Morris. London: Race Today Publications, 1986.
Thompson, Ralph.
  The Denting of a Wave. Leeds: Peepal Tree Press, 1992.
Walcott, Derek
  In a Green Night: Poems 1948–1960. London: Jonathan Cape, 1962.
  The Castaway and Other Poems. London: Jonathan Cape, 1965.
  The Gulf and Other Poems. London: Jonathan Cape, 1969.
  Another Life. New York: Farrar, Straus and Giroux, 1973.
  Sea Grapes. New York: Farrar, Straus and Giroux, 1976.
  The Star-Apple Kingdom. New York: Farrar, Straus and Giroux, 1979.
  Selected Poetry, ed. Wayne Brown. London: Heinemann, 1981.
  The Fortunate Traveller. New York, Farrar, Straus and Giroux, 1981.
  Midsummer. New York: Farrar, Straus and Giroux, 1984.
  Collected Poems: 1948–1984. New York: Farrar, Straus and Giroux, 1986.
  The Arkansas Testament. New York: Farrar, Straus and Giroux, 1987.
  Omeros. New York: Farrar, Straus and Giroux, 1990.

Anthologies of West Indian Poetry

Selected General Anthologies

Caribbean Voices, 1 (Dreams and Visions) and 2 (The Blue Horizons), ed. John Figueroa. London, 1966, 1971.
Caribbean Verse, ed. O. R. Dathorne. London: Heinemann, 1967.
Savacou: A Journal of the Caribbean Artists Movement. Kingston, Jamaica: No. 3/4: December 1970–March 1971.
Breaklight: The Poetry of the Caribbean, ed. Andrew Salkey. London, 1971.
Caribbean Rhythms: The Emerging English Literature of the West Indies, ed. J. T. Livingstone. New York, 1974.
The Caribbean Poem: An Anthology of Fifty Caribbean Voices, ed. Neville Dawes and Anthony McNeill. Kingston, 1976.
Malanthika: An Anthology of Pan-Caribbean Writing, ed. Nick Toczek, Philip Nanton, and Yann Lovelock. Birmingham, 1977.
New Planet: Anthology of Modern Caribbean Writing, ed. Sebastian Clarke. London: Karnak House, 1978.
Bluefoot Traveller, ed. James Berry. London: Harrap, 1981.
One People's Grief: New Writing from the Caribbean, ed. Robert Bensen. *Pacific Quarterly Moana* 8:3. Hamilton, New Zealand, 1983.

Caribbean Poetry Now, ed. Stewart Brown. London: Hodder and Stoughton, 1984, 1992.

News For Babylon: The Chatto Book of Westindian-British Poetry, ed. James Berry. London: Chatto and Windus, 1984.

New Poetry from the West Indies, ed. Edward Baugh. *The Greenfield Review* 12:3–4 (1985).

Other Voices: Writings by Blacks in Canada, ed. Lorris Elliott. Toronto: Williams-Wallace, 1985.

Facing the Sea: A New Anthology from the Caribbean Region, ed. Anne Walmsley and Nick Caistor. London: Heinemann, 1986.

Dub Poetry, ed. Christian Habekost. Neustadt: Michael Schwinn, 1986.

The Penguin Book of Caribbean Verse, ed. Paul Burnett. Harmondsworth: Penguin, 1986.

Watchers and Seekers: Creative Writing by Black Women in Britain, ed. Rhonda Cobham and Merle Collins. London: The Women's Press, 1987.

A Shapely Fire: Changing the Literary Landscape, ed. Cyril Dabydeen. Oakville: Mosaic Press, 1987.

Hinterland: Caribbean Poetry from the West Indies and Britain, ed. E. A. Markham. Newcastle: Bloodaxe, 1989.

Voiceprint: An Anthology of Oral and Related Poetry from the Caribbean, ed. Stewart Brown, Mervyn Morris, and Gordon Rohlehr. London: Longman, 1989.

Creation Fire: A Cafra Anthology of Caribbean Women's Poetry, ed. Ramabai Espinet. Toronto: Sister Vision, 1990.

So Much Poetry in We People: An Anthology of Performance Poetry, ed. Kendel Hippolyte. Eastern Caribbean Popular Theatre Organization, 1990.

New Poetry from the West Indies, ed. Kenneth Ramchand. *Graham House Review*, 14 (Spring 1991).

Crossing Water, ed. Anthony Kellman. Greenfield Center, N.Y.: Greenfield Review Press, 1992.

Women Poets of the Caribbean, ed. Pamela Mordicai and Betty Wilson. *The Literary Review*, 35:4 (September 1992).

The Heinemann Book of Caribbean, ed. Ian McDonald and Stewart Brown. London: Heinemann, 1992.

Selected Regional and National Anthologies

Focus, ed. Edna Manley (1943, 1948, 1956, 1960); ed. Mervyn Morris (1983). Kingston, Jamaica.

Independence Anthology of Jamaican Literature, ed. A. L. Hendricks and Cedric Lindo. Kingston, Jamaica, 1962.

Seven Jamaican Poets: An Anthology of Recent Poetry, ed. Mervyn Morris. Kingston, Jamaica, 1971.

New Poets from Jamaica, ed. Edward Kamau Brathwaite, *Savacou* 14–15. Kingston, Jamaica, 1979.

Jamaica Woman: An Anthology of Poems, ed. Pamela Mordecai and Mervyn Morris. Kingston, Jamaica: Heinemann, 1980.

From Our Yard: Jamaican Poetry Since Independence, ed. Pamela Mordecai. Kingston, Jamaica: Institute of Jamaica, 1987.
Independence 10: Guyanese Writing, 1966–1976, ed. A. J. Seymour. Georgetown: National History and Arts Council, 1976.
Confluence: Nine St. Lucian Poets, ed. Kendel Hippolyte. Castrics, St. Lucia: The Source, 1988.
Bahamian Anthology. Introduction Marcella Taylor. London: Macmillan, 1983.
Flowers Blooming Late: Poems from Montserrat, ed. Howard Fergus. Montserrat, 1984.
Washer Woman Hangs Her Poems in the Sun: Poems by Women of Trinidad and Tobago, ed. Margaret Watts. Tunapuna, Trinidad, 1990.

Secondary Sources

Aarsleff, Hans. *From Locke to Saussure.* Minneapolis, 1982.
Abrahams, Roger D. *The Man of Words in the West Indies: Performance and the Emergence of Creole Culture.* Baltimore, 1983.
Alleyne, Mervyn. *Roots of Jamaican Culture.* London, 1989.
Anderson, Benedict. *Imagined Communities: Reflections on the Origin and Spread of Nationalism.* London, 1983.
Anozie, Sunday O. *Structural Models and African Poetics: Towards a Pragmatic View of Literature.* London, 1981.
Arnold, Matthew. *Culture and Anarchy,* ed. J. Dover Wilson. Cambridge, 1963.
Auerbach, Eric. *Mimesis: The Representation of Reality in Western Culture,* trans. W. R. Trask. Princeton, 1953.
Augier, F. R., S. C. Gordon, D. G. Hall, and M. Reckord. *The Making of the West Indies.* London, 1960.
Bailey, Richard W. *Images of English: A Cultural History of the Language.* Ann Arbor, 1991.
Bailyn, Bernard. *The Peopling of British North America: An Introduction.* New York, 1986.
Baker, Houston A. Jr. *Reading Black: Essays in the Criticism of African, Caribbean and Black American Literature.* Ithaca, 1976.
———. *The Journey Back: Issues in Black Literature and Criticism.* Chicago, 1980.
Bakhtin, Mikhail. *The Dialogic Imagination,* trans. Caryl Emerson and Michael Holquist. Austin, Tex., 1981.
Barber, Karin, and Paulo Fernando de Moraes Farias, ed. *Discourse and its Disguises: The Interpretation of African Oral Texts.* Birmingham, 1989.
Barfield, Owen. *Poetic Diction: A Study in Meaning.* London, 1928.
Barrett, L. *The Rastafarians: The Dreadlocks of Jamaica.* London, 1977.
Batsleer, Janet, Tony Davies, Rebecca O'Rourke, and Chris Weedon. *Rewriting English: Cultural Politics of Gender and Class.* London, 1985.
Baugh, Edward. "Metaphor and Plainness in the Poetry of Derek Walcott." *The Literary Half-Yearly* 11 (July 1970), 47–58.

————. *West Indian Poetry, 1900–1970: A Study in Cultural Decolonisation.* Kingston, Jamaica, 1971.

————, ed. *Critics on Caribbean Literature.* London, 1978.

————. *Derek Walcott. Memory as Vision: Another Life.* London, 1978.

————. "Edward Brathwaite as Critic: Some Preliminary Observations." *Caribbean Quarterly* 28:1–2 (1982), 66–75.

————. "Goodison on the Road to Heartease," *Journal of West Indian Literature* 1:1 (1986), 13–22.

————. "Derek Walcott on West Indian Literature and Theatre." *Jamaica Journal* 21:2 (1988), 50–52.

————. "Lorna Goodison in the Context of Feminist Criticism." *Journal of West Indian Literature* 4:1 (1990), 1–13.

Baugh, Edward, and Mervyn Morris, eds. *Progressions: West Indian Literature in the 1970s.* Kingston, Jamaica, 1991.

Beckles, Hilary. *Black Rebellion in Barbados: The Struggle Against Slavery, 1627–1838.* Bridgetown, Barbados, 1987.

————. *Natural Rebels: A Social History of Women in Barbados.* New Brunswick, N.J., 1989.

Bell, Roseann P., Bettye J. Parker, and Beverly Guy-Sheftall, eds. *Sturdy Black Bridges: Visions of Black Women in Literature.* New York, 1979.

Berger, John. *Ways of Seeing.* London, 1972.

Bhabha, Homi K. "Signs Taken for Wonders: Questions of Ambivalence and Authority under a Tree Outside Delhi, May, 1817." *Critical Inquiry* 12:1 (1982), 144–65.

————. "Difference, discrimination and the discourse of colonialism." in *The Politics of Theory,* ed. Francis Barker, Peter Hulme, Margaret Iversen, and Diana Loxley. Colchester, 1983, pp. 194–211.

————. "Representation and the Colonial Text: A Critical Exploration of Some Forms of Mimeticism." *The Theory of Reading,* ed. Frank Gloversmith. Brighton, 1984, pp. 93–122.

————. *Nation and Narration.* New York, 1990.

Birbalsingh, Frank, ed. *Indenture and Exile: The Indo-Caribbean Experience.* Toronto, 1989.

Black, Max. *Models and Metaphors.* Ithaca, 1962.

Blackburn, Robin. *The Overthrow of Colonial Slavery, 1776–1848.* London, 1988.

Blackman, Margot. *Bajan Proverbs.* Montreal, 1982.

Blake, N. F. *Non-Standard Language in English Literature.* London, 1981.

Blonsky, Marshall. *On Signs.* Baltimore, 1985.

Boon, James A. *Other Tribes, Other Scribes.* Cambridge, 1982.

Brathwaite, Edward Kamau. *The Development of Creole Society in Jamaica, 1770–1820.* Oxford, 1971.

————. *Contradictory Omens: Cultural Diversity and Integration in the Caribbean.* Kingston, Jamaica, 1974.

————. *The Folk Culture of the Slaves in Jamaica.* London, 1981.

————. "Sir Galahad and the Islands." *Bim* 25 (1957), 8–16.

———. "The African Presence in Caribbean Literature," *Dedalus*103:2 (1974), 73–109.

———. *Wars of Respect: Nanny and Sam Sharpe*. Kingston, Jamaica, 1977.

———. "The Love Axe/1: Developing a Caribbean Aesthetic, 1962-1974." *Bim* 16:61 (1977), 53–65; 16:62 (1977), 100–106; 16:63 (1978), 181–92.

———. *History of the Voice: The Development of Nation Language in Anglophone Caribbean Poetry*. London, 1984.

Breiner, Laurence A. "Lyric and Autobiography in West Indian Literature." *Journal of West Indian Literature* 3:1 (1989), 3–15.

Breitinger Eckhard, and Reinhard Sander, eds. *Studies in Commonwealth Literature*. Tübingen, 1985.

Brereton, Bridget. *Colonial Trinidad, 1870–1900*. Cambridge, 1979.

Brodber, Erna. *Myal*. London, 1988.

Brodsky, Joseph. "The Sound of the Tide," *Less Than One*. New York, 1986, pp. 164–75.

Brown, Lloyd. *West Indian Poetry*. Boston, 1978.

Brown, Stewart, ed. *The Art of Derek Walcott*. Mid Glamorgan, 1991.

Bürger, Peter, *Theory of the Avant-Garde*, trans. Michael Shaw. Minneapolis, 1984.

Bush, Barbara. *Slave Women in Caribbean Society, 1650–1838*. London, 1990.

Campbell, Mavis C. *The Maroons of Jamaica, 1655–1796*. Trenton, New Jersey, 1990.

Carlyle, Thomas. *The Nigger Question* and John Stuart Mill, *The Negro Question*, ed. Eugene R. August. New York, 1971.

Carrington, L. D., ed. *Studies in Caribbean Language*. Port of Spain, 1983.

Cassidy, Frederic. *Jamaica Talk: Three Hundred Years of the English Language in Jamaica*. London, 1971.

Cassidy, Frederic, and R. B. LePage. *Dictionary of Jamaican English*. Cambridge, 1980.

Cassirer, Ernst. *Language and Myth*, trans Suzanne K. Langer. New York, 1946

———. *The Philosophy of Symbolic Forms: Language,* trans. Ralph Mannheim. New Haven, 1953.

Caws, Mary Ann. *The Eye in the Text: Essays on Perception, Mannerist to Modern*. Princeton, 1981.

Césaire, Aimé. *Collected Poetry*, trans. Clayton Eshelman and Annette Smith. Berkeley, 1983.

Chamberlin, J. Edward. *The Harrowing of Eden: White Attitude Towards Native Americans*. New York, 1975.

———. "Speaking in Tongues: The Languages of West Indian Poetry." *Brick* 26 (Winter 1986), 14–20.

———. "Myself Made Otherwise: Edward Kamau Brathwaite's *X/Self*." *Carib* 5 (1989), 19–32.

———. "Bury the Dead and Pay the Rent: Blacks and Whites in Australia." *Descant* 20, 3–4 (1989), 87–110.

Chamberlin, J. Edward, and Sander L. Gilman, eds. *Degeneration: The Dark Side of Progress*. New York, 1985.

Chatman, Seymour, ed. *Literary Styles.* London, 1971.

Chinweizu, Onwuchekwa Jemie, and Ihechukwu Madubuike. *Toward the Decolonization of African Literature: African Fiction and Poetry and their Critics.* Enugu, Nigeria, 1980.

Christian, Barbara. *Black Feminist Criticism: Perspectives on Black Women Writers.* New York, 1985.

Clifford, James. *The Predicament of Culture: Twentieth-Century Ethnography, Literature and Art.* Cambridge, 1988.

Collymore, Frank A. "Notebook—a letter from Derek Walcott." *Bim* 7:26 (1958), 65.

———. *Barbadian Dialect.* Bridgetown, Barbados, 1970.

Columbus, Christopher. *The Voyages of Christopher Columbus,* trans. Cecil Jane. London, 1930.

Coombs, Orde, ed. *Is Massa Day Dead?* New York, 1974.

Cooper, Carolyn. "Proverb as Metaphor in the Poetry of Louise Bennett." *Jamaica Journal* 17:2 (1984), 21–24.

———. "'That Cunny Jamma Oman': the Female Sensibility in the Poetry of Louise Bennett." *Jamaica Journal* 18:4 (November 1985-January 1986), 2–9.

———. "Chanting Down Babylon: Bob Marley's Song as Literary Text." *Jamaica Journal* 19:4 (1986–87), 2–8.

———. "Words Unbroken by the Beat: The Performance Poetry of Jean Binta Breeze and Mikey Smith." *Wasafiri* 11 (1990), 7–13.

Corsbie, Ken. *Theatre in the Caribbean.* London, 1984.

Cottom, Daniel. *Text and Culture: The Politics of Interpretation.* Minneapolis, 1989.

Crahan, Margaret E., and Franklin W. Knight, eds. *Africa and the Caribbean: The Legacies of a Link.* Baltimore, 1979.

Craton, Michael. *Testing the Chains: Resistance to Slavery in the British West Indies.* Ithaca, 1982.

Craton, Michael, and James Walvin. *A Jamaican Plantation: the History of Worthy Park, 1670–1970.* London, 1970.

Crawford, Robert. *Devolving English Literature.* Oxford, 1992.

Crowley, Tony. *The Politics of Discourse: The Standard Language Question in British Cultural Debates.* London, 1989.

Cudjoe, Selwyn R., ed. *Caribbean Women Writers: Essays from the First International Conference.* Wellesley, Mass., 1990.

Culler, Jonathan. *Structuralist Poetics: Structuralism, Linguistics and the Study of Literature.* London, 1975.

Curtin, Philip. *The Atlantic Slave Trade.* Madison, Wis., 1969.

Dabydeen, David, and Nana Wilson-Tagoe. *A Reader's Guide to West Indian and Black British Literature.* London, 1988.

Dalphinis, Morgan. *Caribbean and African Languages: Social History, Language, Literature and Education.* London, 1985.

Dance, Daryl, ed. *Fifty Caribbean Writers: A Bio-bibliographical and Critical Source Book.* Westport, Conn., 1986.

Dash, Michael J. *Haiti and the United States: National Stereotypes and the Literary Imagination.* London, 1988.

Dathorne, O. R. *Dark Ancestor: The Literature of the Black Man in the Caribbean.* Baton Rouge, 1981.

Davidson, Basil. *Black Mother: The Years of the African Slave Trade.* Boston, 1961.

Davies, Carol Boyce, and Elaine Savory Fido, eds. *Out of the Kumbla: Caribbean Women and Literature.* Trenton, N.J., 1990.

Davis, David Brian. *The Problem of Slavery in Western Culture.* Ithaca, N.Y., 1966.

Davis, Geoffrey B., and Hena Maes-Jelinek, eds. *Crisis and Creativity in the New Literatures in English.* Amsterdam, 1990.

Dawes, Neville. *Prolegomena to Caribbean Literature.* Kingston, Jamaica, 1977.

D'Costa, Jean, and Barbara Lalla, eds. *Voices in Exile: Jamaican Texts of the 18th and 19th Centuries.* Tuscaloosa, Ala., 1989.

———, eds. *Language in Exile: Three Hundred Years of Jamaican Creole.* Tuscaloosa, Ala., 1990.

Deane, Seamus. *Civilians and Barbarians.* Derry, 1983.

———. *Heroic Styles: The Tradition of an Idea.* Derry, 1984.

———, ed. *Nationalism, Colonialism and Literature.* Minneapolis, 1990.

DeCerteau, Michel. *Heterologies: Discourse on the Other,* trans. Brian Massumi. Minneapolis, 1986.

Derrida, Jacques. *Writing and Difference,* trans. Alan Bass. Chicago, 1978.

Devonish, Hubert. *Language and Liberation: Creole Language Politics in the Caribbean.* London, 1986.

———. *Talking in Tones: A Study of Tone in Afro-European Creole Languages.* London, 1989.

Dillard, J. L. *Lexicon of Black English.* New York, 1977.

Diop, Cheikh Anta. *Civilization or Barbarism: An Authentic Anthropology,* trans. Yaa-Lengi Meema Ngemi. Edited by Harold J. Salemson and Marjolijn de Jager. Brooklyn, 1991.

Dowling, Linda. *Language and Decadence in the Victorian Fin de Siècle.* Princeton, 1986.

Dunn, Richard S. *Sugar and Slaves: The Rise of the Planter Class in the English West Indies, 1624–1713.* New York, 1973.

Eagleton, Terry. *Marxism and Literary Criticism.* London, 1976.

Edwards, Viv, and Thomas J. Sienkewicz. *Oral Cultures Past and Present: Rappin' and Homer.* Oxford, 1990.

Ellis, Keith. *Cuba's Nicolas Guillen: Poetry and Ideology.* Toronto, 1983.

Fanon, Frantz. *Black Skin: White Masks.* New York, 1967; first published, 1952.

———. *The Wretched of the Earth.* Harmondsworth, 1982; first published, 1961.

Fiedler, Leslie, and Houston Baker Jr., eds. *English Literature: Opening Up the Canon.* Baltimore, 1981.

Fiet, Lowell, ed. *West Indian Literature and its Political Context.* Rio Piedras, Puerto Rico, 1988.

Finnegan, Ruth. *Oral Literature in Africa.* Oxford, 1970.

5

———. *Oral Poetry; Its Nature, Significance, and Social Context.* Cambridge, 1977

Fish, Stanley. *Is There a Text in This Class? The Authority of Interpretive Communities.* Cambridge, Mass., 1980.

Fisher, Lawrence E. *Colonial Madness: Mental Health in the Barbadian Social Order.* New Brunswick, N.J., 1985.

Foucault, Michel. *Power/Knowledge,* ed. Colin Gordon. London, 1980.

Fraser, Henry, and Sean Carrington, Addington Forde, John Gilmore. *A-Z of Barbadian Heritage.* Kingston, Jamaica, 1990.

Fraser, Robert. *West African Poetry: A Critical History.* Cambridge, 1986.

Friedrich, Paul. *Language, Context and Imagination.* Stanford, 1979.

———. *The Language Parallax: Linguistic Relativism and Poetic Indeterminacy.* Austin, Tex., 1986.

Froude, J. A. *The English in the West Indies; or, The Bow of Ulysses.* London, 1888.

Frye, Northrop. *The Educated Imagination.* Toronto, 1963.

———. *Anatomy of Criticism.* Princeton, 1957.

———. *Fables of Identity.* New York, 1963.

———. *The Great Code.* New York, 1982.

———. *Words with Power.* New York, 1990.

Galeano, Eduardo, "The Imagination and the Will to Change," *The Writer and Human Rights.* Toronto, 1983.

Gates, Henry L., ed. *Black Literature and Literary Theory.* New York, 1984.

———. *The Signifying Monkey: A Theory of Afro-American Literary Criticism.* New York, 1988.

———, ed. *Reading Black, Reading Feminist.* New York, 1990.

Genovese, Eugene. *The World the Slave Holders Made.* New York, 1969.

———. *Roll, Jordan, Roll: The World the Slaves Made.* New York, 1972.

Gilman, Sander L. *On Blackness without Blacks: Essays on the Image of the Black in Germany.* Boston, 1982.

———. *Difference and Pathology: Stereotypes of Sexuality, Race and Madness.* Ithaca, 1985.

———. *Jewish Self-Hatred: Anti-Semitism and the Hidden Language of the Jews.* Baltimore, 1986.

———. *Inscribing the Other.* Lincoln, Nebraska, 1991.

Goffman, Erving. *Frame Analysis: An Essay on the Organization of Experience.* Cambridge, Mass., 1974.

Gombrich, *Art and Illusion.* London, 1962.

Goodman, Nelson. *Ways of Worldmaking.* Indianapolis, 1978.

Goody, J. *The Interface between the Written and the Oral.* Cambridge, 1987.

Goveia, Elsa V. *A Study of the Historiography of the West Indies.* Mexico City, 1956.

———. *Slave Society in the British Leeward Islands at the End of the Eighteenth Century.* New Haven, 1965.

———. *The West Indian Slave Laws of the Eighteenth Century.* London, 1970.

Greenbaum, Sidney, ed. *The English Language Today.* Oxford, 1985.

Gregory, Michael, and Susanne Carroll. *Language Varieties and Their Social Contexts.* London, 1978.

Griffiths, Gareth. *A Double Exile: African and West Indian Writing Between Two Cultures.* London, 1978.

Hamner, Robert. *Derek Walcott.* Boston, 1981.

Hanke, Lewis. *All Mankind is One: A Study of the Disputation between Bartoleme de Las Casas and Juan Gines de Sepulveda in 1550 on the Intellectual and Religious Capacity of the American Indians.* De Kalb, Ill., 1974.

Harlow, Barbara. *Resistance Literature.* London, 1987.

Harper, Michael S., and Robert B. Stepto, eds. *A Chant of Saints: A Gathering of Afro-American Literature, Art and Scholarship.* Urbana, Ill., 1979.

Harris, Wilson. *Tradition, the Writer and Society.* London, 1967.

———. *History, Fable and Myth in the Caribbean and Guianas.* Edgar Mittelholzer Memorial Lecture. Georgetown, Guyana, 1970.

———. *A Selection of Talks and Articles, 1966–1981,* ed. Hena Maes-Jelinek. Mundelstrup, 1981.

———. *The Guyana Quartet.* London, 1985.

Havelock, E. *The Muse Learns to Write: Reflections on Orality and Literacy from Antiquity to the Present.* New Haven, 1986.

Heaney, Seamus. "Feeling into Words" and "The Sense of Place." *Preoccupations.* London, 1980, pp. 41–60, 131–149.

———. "Place, Pastness, Poems: A Triptych." *Salmagundi* 68–69 (Fall 1985-Winter 1986), 30–47.

———. "The Murmur of Malvern." *The Government of the Tongue.* London, 1988, 23–29

Hebdige, Dick. *Cut 'N' Mix.* London, 1987.

Herskovits, M. J. *The Myth of the Negro Past.* New York, 1938.

Hill, Robert. "Leonard P. Howell and Millenarian Visions in Early Rastafari." *Jamaica Journal* 16:1 (February 1983), 24–39.

Hirsch, Edward. Interview with Derek Walcott. *The Paris Review* 101 (1986), 196–230.

Hobsbawm, Eric, and Terence Ranger, eds. *The Invention of Tradition.* Cambridge, 1983.

Hodge, Merle. *Crick Crack, Monkey.* London, 1970.

Hollander, John. *Vision and Resonance: Two Senses of Poetic Form.* New York, 1975.

Holm, John. *Pidgins and Creoles: Theory and Structure.* Cambridge, 1988.

hooks, bell. *Feminist Theory: From Margin to Centre.* Boston, 1984.

Hulme, Peter. *Colonial Encounters: Europe and the Native Caribbean 1492–1797.* London, 1986.

Hulme, T. E. *Speculations: Essays on Humanism and the Philosophy of Art.* London, 1924.

Hymes, D. L., ed. *Pidginization and Creolization of Languages.* Cambridge, 1971.

Inikori, J. E., ed. *Forced Exile: The Impact of the Forced Slave Trade on African Societies.* New York, 1982.

Irele, Abiola. *The African Experience in Literature and Ideology.* London, 1981.

Irigaray, Lucy. *Speculum of the Other Woman,* trans. Gillian C. Gill. Ithaca, 1985.

Ismond, Patricia. "Walcott vs. Brathwaite." *Caribbean Quarterly* 17 (1971), 54–71.

Jackson, J., and J. Allis. *West Indian Poetry.* St. Thomas, U.S. Virgin Islands, 1986.

Jakobson, Roman. *Language in Literature,* ed. Krystyna Pomorska and Stephen Rudy. Cambridge, Mass., 1987.

James, C. L. R. *Black Jacobins.* New York, 1963; first published, 1938.

——. *Beyond a Boundary.* London, 1963.

James, Louis. *The Island in Between: Essays on West Indian Literature.* London, 1968.

Jameson, Frederic. *Marxism and Form.* Princeton, 1971.

——. *The Prison-House of Language.* Princeton, 1972.

Jan Mohamed, Abdul. *The Politics of Literature in Colonial Africa.* Amherst, Mass., 1983.

Johnson, Barbara. *A World of Difference.* Baltimore, 1987.

Joyce, James. *Portrait of the Artist as a Young Man.* Harmondsworth, 1960.

Kachru, Braj, ed. *The Other Tongue: English Across Cultures.* Urbana, Ill., 1982.

Kiberd, Declan. *Anglo-Irish Attitudes.* Derry, 1984.

King, Bruce, ed. *West Indian Literature.* London, 1979.

Klein, Herbert S. *The Middle Passage: Comparative Studies of the Atlantic Slave Trade.* Princeton, 1978.

Knight, Franklin W. *The Caribbean: The Genesis of a Fragmented Nationalism.* New York, 1990.

Kochman, T., ed. *Rappin' and Stylin' Out: Communication in Black Urban America.* Urbana, Ill., 1972.

——. *Black and White Styles in Conflict.* Chicago, 1981.

Kristeva, Julia. *Desire in Language: A Semiotic Approach to Literature and Art,* trans. Thomas Gora, Alice Jardine, and Leon S. Roudiez. New York, 1980.

Kuhn, Thomas. *The Structure of Scientific Revolutions,* 2d ed. Chicago, 1970.

Lamming, George. "The Negro Writer and His World." *Caribbean Quarterly* 5:2 (1958), 115–119.

——. *In the Castle of My Skin.* London, 1953.

——. *The Pleasures of Exile.* London, 1960.

Lawler, Justus George. *Celestial Pantomime: Poetic Structures of Transcendence.* New Haven, 1979.

Leech, Geoffrey N. *A Linguistic Guide to English Poetry.* London, 1969.

Lentricchia, Frank. *After the New Criticism.* Chicago, 1980.

LePage, R. B., and Andree Tabouret-Keller. *Acts of Identity: Creole-based Approaches to Language and Ethnicity.* Cambridge, 1985.

Levin, Samuel. *The Semantics of Metaphor.* Baltimore, 1977.

Lewis, Gordon K. *The Growth of the Modern West Indies.* London, 1983.

——. *Mainstreams of Caribbean Thought.* Baltimore, 1985.

Lewis, Rupert. *Marcus Garvey: Anti-Colonial Champion.* London, 1987.

Lewis, Rupert, and Maureen Warner-Lewis, eds. *Garvey—Africa, Europe, the Americas*. Kingston, Jamaica, 1986.

Lieberman, Laurence, "New Poetry: the Muse of History." *Yale Review* 43 (1973), 113–36.

Macauley, T. B. *Life and Letters*, by G. O. Trevelyan. London, 1889.

MacDougall, Hugh A. *Racial Myth in English History: Trojans, Teutons and Anglo-Saxons*. London, 1982.

Macksey, Richard, and Eugenio Donato, eds. *The Languages of Criticism and the Sciences of Man: The Structuralist Controversy*. Baltimore, 1970.

Mannoni, O. *Prospero and Caliban: The Psychology of Colonization*. New York, 1956.

Maine, Henry, *Ancient Law*. London, 1859.

Mais, Roger. *Brother Man*. Introduction by Edward Brathwaite. London, 1974.

Malcolm X. *Autobiography*. New York, 1966.

Manuel, George, and Michael Posluns. *The Fourth World: An Indian Reality*. Toronto, 1974.

Martin, G. D. *Language, Truth and Poetry*. Edinburgh, 1975.

Martin, Tony. *Race First: The Ideological and Organizational Struggles of Marcus Garvey and the Universal Negro Improvement Association*. Westport, Conn., 1976.

Martini, Jurgen, ed. *Missile and Capsule*. Bremen, 1983.

Mathurin, Lucille. *The Rebel Woman in the British West Indies during Slavery*. Kingston, Jamaica, 1975.

————. *Women Field Workers in Jamaica during Slavery*. Kingston, Jamaica, 1986.

McFarlane, J. E. Clare. *A Literature in the Making*. Kingston, Jamaica, 1956.

————. "The Prospect of West Indian Poetry." *Kyk-Over-Al* 16 (1953).

McNeill, William H. *Polyethnicity and National Unity in World History*. Toronto, 1986.

McWatt, Mark, ed. *West Indian Literature and its Social Context*. Cave Hill, Barbados, 1985.

Memmi, Albert. *The Colonizer and the Colonized*, trans. Howard Greenfeld. New York, 1965.

Mencken, H. L. *The American Language: An Inquiry into the Development of English in the United States*. New York, 1936.

Miller, Christopher L. *Theories of Africans: Francophone Literature and Anthropology in Africa*. Chicago, 1990.

Mintz, Sidney W., ed. *Slavery, Colonialism, and Racism*. New York, 1974.

————. *Sweetness and Power: The Place of Sugar in Modern History*. Harmondsworth, 1985.

Mintz, Sidney W., and Sally Price, eds. *Caribbean Contours*. Baltimore, 1985.

Moore, Gerald. *The Chosen Tongue*. London, 1969.

Moore, Terence, and Chris Carling. *The Limitations of Language*. London, 1988.

Morris, Mervyn. "Mikey Smith; Dub Poet." *Jamaica Journal* 18:2 (1985), 38–45.

―――. "The Poetry of Mikey Smith." In *West Indian Literature and its Social Context*, ed. Mark McWatt. Bridgetown, Barbados: Department of English, University of the West Indies, 1985, pp. 48–54.

―――. "Linton Kwesi Johnson: An Interview." *Jamaica Journal* 20:1 (1987), 17–28.

―――. "Printing the Performance," *Jamaica Journal* 23:1 (1990), 21–26.

Mudimbe, V. Y. *The Invention of Africa: Gnosis, Philosophy and the Order of Knowledge*. Bloomington, Ind., 1988.

Murray, K. M. Elisabeth. *Caught in the Web of Words: James A. H. Murray and the Oxford English Dictionary*. Oxford, 1979.

Naipaul, V. S. *The Middle Passage*. London, 1962.

Nelson, Cary. *The Incarnate Word: Literature as Verbal Space*. Chicago, 1973.

Nettleford, Rex. *Identity, Race and Protest in Jamaica*. New York, 1972.

―――. *Cultural Action and Social Change: The Case of Jamaica*. Kingston, Jamaica, 1978.

―――. "The Spirit of Garvey: Lessons of the Legacy." *Jamaica Journal* 20:3 (1987), 2–9.

―――. *Dance Jamaica: Cultural Definition and Artistic Discovery*. New York, 1985.

Ngugi wa Thiong'o. *Homecoming: Essays on African and Caribbean Literature, Culture and Politics*. London, 1972.

―――. *Decolonising the Mind: The Politics of Language in African Literature*. Harare, 1987.

Nowottny, Winifred. *The Language Poets Use*. London, 1962.

Omotoso, Kole. *The Theatrical Into Theatre: A Study of the Drama and Theatre of the English-speaking Caribbean*. London, 1982.

Ong, Walter. *The Barbarian Within*. New York, 1962.

―――. *The Presence of the Word*. New Haven, 1967.

―――. *Interfaces of the Word: Studies in the Evolution of Consciousness and Culture*. Ithaca, 1977.

―――. *Orality and Literacy*. London, 1982.

Ortony, Andrew, ed. *Metaphor and Thought*. Cambridge, 1979.

Orwell, George. "Politics and the English Language." *Inside the Whale and Other Essays*. Harmondsworth, 1962.

Owens, J. *Dread: The Rastafarians of Jamaica*. Kingston, Jamaica, 1976.

Parker, Andrew, Mary Russo, Doris Sommer, and Patricia Yaeger, eds. *Nationalisms and Sexualities*. New York, 1992.

Parry, John H., Philip Sherlock, and Anthony Maingot. *A Short History of the West Indies*, 4th ed. London, 1987.

Paterson, Orlando. *The Sociology of Slavery: An Analysis of the Origins, Development and Structure of Negro Slave Society in Jamaica*. London, 1967.

―――. *The Children of Sisyphus*. London, 1964.

Paulin, Tom. "A New Look at the Language Question." *Ireland and the English Crisis*. Newcastle, 1984.

Pereira, J. R., ed. *Caribbean Literature in Comparison*. Kingston, Jamaica, 1990.

Petersen, Kirsten Holst, and Anna Rutherford, eds. *A Double Colonization: Colonial and Post-Colonial Women's Writing.* Mundelstrup, Denmark, 1986.

Petrey, Sandy. *Speech Acts and Literary Theory.* New York, 1990.

Philip, M. Nourbese. *Frontiers and Writings in Racism and Culture.* Toronto, 1992.

Poggioli, Renato. *Theory of the Avant-Garde,* trans. Gerald Fitzgerald. Cambridge, 1968.

Poirier, Richard. *The Performing Self: Compositions and Decompositions in the Languages of Contemporary Life.* New York, 1971.

Pollard, Velma. "Dread Talk—The Speech of the Rastafari in Jamaica." *Caribbean Quarterly* 26:4 (1980), 32–41.

———. "Figurative Language in Jamaican Creole." *Carib* 3 (1983), 24–36.

———. "Word Sounds; the Language of Rastafari in Barbados and St. Lucia," *Jamaica Journal* 17,1 (1984), pp. 57–62.

———. "Social History of Dread Talk." *Caribbean Quarterly* 28:4 (1982), 17–40.

———. "Overlapping Systems: Language in the Poetry of Lorna Goodison." *Carib* 5 (1989), 33–47.

Poynting, Jeremy. *The Second Shipwreck: Indo-Caribbean Literature.* London, 1988.

Pratt, Mary Louise. *Toward a Speech Act Theory of Literary Discourse.* Bloomington, Ind., 1977.

Price, Richard, ed. *Maroon Societies: Rebel Slave Communities in the Americas.* Baltimore, 1979.

Prickett, Stephen. *Words and the Word: Language, Poetics and Biblical Interpretation.* Cambridge, 1986.

Ramchand, Kenneth. *The West Indian Novel and Its Background.* London, 1970.

———. *Introduction to the Study of West Indian Literature.* London, 1976.

———. "Parades, Parades: Modern West Indian Poetry." *Sewanee Review* 87 (1979), 96–118.

———. "The Fate of Writing." *Caribbean Quarterly* 28:1–2 (1982), 76–84.

Ramchand, Kenneth, and Cecil Gray, eds. *West Indian Poetry: New Edition.* London, 1989.

Reckord, Verena. "Reggae, Rastafarianism and Cultural Identity." *Jamaica Journal* 46 (1982), 70–79.

Reid, V. S. *New Day.* London, 1949.

———. "A Daunting Prospect." *Progressions: West Indian Literature in the 1970s,* ed. Edward Baugh and Mervyn Morris. Kingston, Jamaica, 1991, pp. 258–63.

Rickford, John R. *Dimensions of a Creole Continuum.* Stanford, 1987.

Ricks, Christopher, and Leonard Michaels, eds. *The State of the Language.* Berkeley, 1990.

Ricoeur, Paul. *The Rule of Metaphor: Multi-disciplinary Studies of the Creation of Meaning in Language,* trans. Robert Czerny. Toronto, 1977.

Roberts, Peter A. *West Indians and Their Language.* Cambridge, 1988.

Rodney, Walter. *How Europe Underdeveloped Africa.* Washington, D. C., 1974.

————. *The Groundings with My Brothers*. London, 1975.

Rohlehr, Gordon. "West Indian Poetry: Some Problems of Assessment." *Bim* 14:54 (1972), 80–88 and 14:55 (1972), 134–44.

————. "Afterthoughts." *Bim* 56 (1973), 227–32.

————. "A Carrion Time." *Bim* 58 (1975), 92–109.

————. "My Strangled City: Poetry in Trinidad, 1964–1975." *Caliban* 2:1 (1976), 50–122.

————. *Pathfinder: Black Awakening in The Arrivants of Edward Kamau Brathwaite*. Port of Spain, 1981.

————. *Calypso and Society in Pre-Independence Trinidad*. Port of Spain, 1990.

Rubin, Vera, and A. Tuden, eds. *Comparative Perspectives on Slavery in New World Plantation Societies*. New York, 1977.

Saakana, Amon Saba. *The Colonial Legacy in Caribbean Literature*. Trenton, N.J., 1987.

Said, Edward. *Orientalism*. New York, 1978.

————. *The World, The Text and the Critic*. Cambridge, Mass., 1983.

————. *Nationalism, Colonialism and Literature: Yeats and Decolonization*. Derry, 1988.

St. John, Bruce. "Poems in Barbadian Dialect." *Revista de Letras* (Universdad de Puerto Rico en Mayaguez), 4:16 (1972), 540–85.

Sale, Kirkpatrick. *The Conquest of Paradise: Christopher Columbus and the Columbian Legacy*. New York, 1990.

Sampietro, Luigi. Interview with Derek Walcott. *Caribana* 2 (1991), 24–360.

Sansom, Basil. *The Camp at Wallaby Cross: Aboriginal Fringe Dwellers in Darwin*. Canberra, 1980.

Sapir, Edward. *Language: An Introduction to the Study of Speech*. New York, 1921.

Sartre, Jean-Paul. *Black Orpheus*, trans. S. W. Allen. Paris, 1948.

Schechner, Richard. *Between Theatre and Anthropology*. Philadelphia, 1985.

————. *Performance Theory*. London, 1988.

Schechner, Richard, and Willa Appel, eds. *By Means of Performance: Intercultural Studies of Theatre and Ritual*. Cambridge, 1990.

Schultz, Emily A. *Dialogue at the Margins: Whorf, Bakhtin and Linguistic Relativity*. Madison, Wis., 1990.

Scott, Dennis. "Walcott on Walcott: Interview with Derek Walcott." *Caribbean Quarterly* 14 (1968), 77–82.

Sealey, John, and Krister Malm. *Music in the Caribbean*. London, 1982.

Searle, J. R. *Speech Acts*. Cambridge, 1975.

Sebeok, Thomas A., ed. *Style and Language*. Cambridge, Mass., 1960.

Senior, Olive. *A-Z of Jamaican Heritage*. Kingston, Jamaica, 1987.

————. *Working Miracles: Women's Lives in the English-speaking Caribbean*. Bloomington, Ind., 1991.

Selvon, Samuel. *The Lonely Londoners*. London, 1956.

Sherlock, Philip. *West Indian Nations: A New History*. New York, 1973.

Sherlock, Philip, and Rex Nettleford. *The University of the West Indies: A Caribbean Response to the Challenge of Change*. London, 1990.

Shoemaker, Adam. *Black Words, White Page: Aboriginal Literature, 1929–1988.* St. Lucia, Queensland, 1989.

Sider, Gerald. "When Parrots Learn to Talk, and Why They Can't: Domination, Deception and Self-deception in Indian-White Relations." *Comparative Study of Society and History* 1, (1987), 3–23.

Sistren, with Honor Ford-Smith. *Lionheart Gal: Life Stories of Jamaican Women.* London, 1986.

Sjoberg, Leif. Interview with Derek Walcott. *Greenfield Review* 12:1–2 (1984), 9–15.

Slemon, Stephen, and Helen Tiffin, eds. *After Europe: Critical Theory and Post-Colonial Writing.* Mundelstrup, Denmark, 1989.

Smilowitz, Erika Sollish, and Roberta Quarles Knowles, eds. *Critical Issues in West Indian Literature.* Parkersburg, Iowa, 1984.

Smith, Barbara Herrnstein. *On the Margins of Discourse: The Relation of Literature to Language.* Chicago, 1978.

———. *Contingencies of Value: Alternative Perspectives for Critical Theory.* Cambridge, Mass., 1988.

Smith, Keithlyn B., and Fernando C. Smith, eds. *To Shoot Hard Labour: The Life and Times of Samuel Smith, an Antiguan Workingman, 1877–1982.* Toronto, 1986.

Smith, Michael G. *The Plural Society of the British West Indies.* Los Angeles, 1967.

Smith, Michael G., Roy Augier, and Rex Nettleford. *The Rastafari Movement in Kingston, Jamaica.* Kingston, Jamaica, 1960.

Smith, Paul. *Discerning the Subject.* Minneapolis, 1988.

Smitherman, G. *Talkin and Testifyin: The Language of Black America.* Boston, 1977.

Soyinka, Wole. *Myth, Literature and the African World.* Cambridge, 1976.

Steiner, George. *After Babel: Aspects of a Theory of Translation.* New York, 1975.

———. *Real Presences.* Chicago, 1989.

Sutcliffe, David, and Ansel Wong, eds. *The Language of the Black Experience.* Oxford, 1986.

Tanna, Laura. *Jamaican Folk Tales and Oral Histories.* Kingston, Jamaica, 1984.

Tannen, D., ed. *Coherence in Spoken and Written Discourse.* Norwood, N.J., 1984.

Taylor, Patrick. *The Narrative of Liberation: Perspectives on Afro-Caribbean Literature, Popular Culture and Politics.* Ithaca, 1989.

Terada, Rei. *The Poetry of Derek Walcott: American Mimicry.* Boston, 1992.

Thelwell, Michael. *The Harder They Come.* New York, 1980.

———. "*The Harder They Come*: From Film to Novel. How questions of technique, form, language, craft, and the marketplace conceal issues of politicis, audience, culture, and purpose," *Grand Street* 37 (1990), 134–65.

Thomas, J. J. *Froudacity.* Introduction by C. L. R. James. London, 1969.

Thomas, Ned. *Derek Walcott.* Cardiff, 1980.

Todd, Loreto. *Pidgins and Creoles.* London, 1974.

Todorov, Tzvetan. *The Conquest of America: The Question of the Other*, trans. Richard Howard. New York, 1984.

Trollope, Anthony. *The West Indies and the Spanish Main*. London, 1860.

Turner, Victor. *Dramas, Fields and Metaphors: Symbolic Action in Human Society*. Ithaca, 1974.

Walcott, Clyde. *Island Cricketers*. London, 1958.

Walcott, Derek. "Tales of the Islands: A Sonnet Sequence." *Bim* 7:26 (1958), 67–70.

———. "The Muse of History." In *Carifesta Forum*, ed. John Hearne. Kingston, Jamaica, 1976, 111–28.

———. "What the Twilight Says: An Overture." *Dream on Monkey Mountain and Other Plays*. New York, 1970, 3–40.

———. "Caligula's Horse." In *After Europe: Critical Theory and Post-Colonial Writing*, eds. Stephen Slemon and Helen Tiffin. Mundelstrup, Denmark, 1989, pp. 138–42.

Walmsley, Anne. "Dimensions of Song." *Bim* 13:51 (1970), 152–66.

———. *The Caribbean Artist Movement, 1966–1972: A Literary and Cultural History*. London, 1992.

Warner, Keith Q. *The Trinidad Calypso: A Study of the Capypso as Oral Literature*. London, 1982.

Warner-Lewis, Maureen. *The Nkuyu: Spirit Messengers of the Kumina*. Kingston, Jamaica, 1977.

———. *Guinea's Other Suns: The African Dynamic in Trinidad Culture*. Dover, Mass., 1991.

Wastberg, Per, ed. *The Writer in Modern Africa. Proceedings of the Afro-Scandinavian Writer's Conference*, Stockholm, 1967. Uppsala, 1968.

Welsh, Andrew. *Roots of Lyric: Primitive Poetry and Modern Poetics*. Princeton, 1978.

Whalley, George. *Poetic Process: A Study in Poetics*. London, 1953.

Wheelwright, Philip. *The Burning Fountain: A Study in the Language of Symbolism*. Bloomington, Ind., 1954.

White, Hayden. *Metahistory: The Historical Imagination in 19th Century Europe*. Baltimore, 1973.

———. *Tropics of Discourse: Essays in Cultural Criticism*. Baltimore, 1978.

White, J. P. Interview with Derek Walcott. *Green Mountain Review* 4:1 (1990), 11–37.

Whorf, Benjamin Lee. *Language, Thought and Reality*, ed. John Carroll. Cambridge, Mass., 1964.

Wilde, Oscar. "The Critic as Artist." In *Plays, Prose Writings and Poems*, ed. Isobel Murray. London, 1975, pp. 1–65.

Williams, Eric. *Capitalism and Slavery*. Chapel Hill, N.C., 1944.

———. *Documents of West Indian History, 1492–1655*. Port of Spain, 1963.

———. *History of the People of Trinidad and Tobago*. London, 1964.

———. *British Historians and the West Indies*. London, 1966.

Williams, Raymond. *Culture and Society, 1780–1950*. London, 1960.

Williams, Robert A. *The American Indian in Western Legal Thought: The Discourses of Conquest.* New York, 1990.

Woodson, Carter G. *The Mis-Education of the Negro.* Trenton, N.J., 1990; first published 1933.

Wordsworth, William. "Preface" to the Lyrical Ballads (1800). In *Wordworth and Coleridge's Lyrical Ballads,* ed. R. L. Brett and A. R. Jones. London, 1978.

Wynter, Sylvia. "New Seville and the Conversion Experience of Bartolome de Las Casas." Parts 1 and 2, *Jamaica Journal* 17:2 (1984), 25–32 and 17:3 (1984), 46–55.

Index

Aboriginal peoples, 5–10, 14, 16, 32, 38, 39, 45, 50, 57, 69, 70, 86–87, 106, 109, 129–30, 163, 165–66, 171, 174, 183, 187, 190–91, 210, 225, 231

Accompong (Maroon leader), 210

Acton, John, 39

Adams Grantley, 59

Africa, heritage of, 1, 4–5, 16, 18–19, 21, 34, 45, 47–48, 49–59, 60, 62–66, 67, 73, 77, 81, 82, 90, 94, 98, 106, 112, 124–25, 134, 138, 145, 149, 151, 157, 167, 169, 175–78, 179, 181, 185, 187–88, 191, 202, 204, 207, 210–11, 235, 236, 254, 257

Agard, John, 123, 264–65; "Go Spread Wings," 4; "Listen Mr. Oxford don," 67–68; "Man to Pan," 256–57; "Palm Tree King," 265

Allen, Lillian, 266

Alleyne, Mervyn: *Roots of Jamaican Culture,* 56

Aristotle, 8, 139

Arnold, Matthew, 41, 51; *Culture and Anarchy,* 40, 105–6, 221

Asch, Moses, 183

Augier, F. Roy, 58

Bakhtin, Mikhail, 72

Baldwin, James, 52; *Tell Me How Long the Train's Been Gone,* 186

Barfield, Owen: *Poetic Diction,* 139–41

Basie, Count. *See* Count Basie

Baudelaire, Charles, 112

Baugh, Edward, 151, 155–56, 159; "Cold Comfort," 242; "Lignum Vitae," 249; "Nigger Sweat," 27–28; "Sometimes in the Middle of the Story," 37–38; "Truth and Consequences," 240–41

Bedward, Alexander, 56, 273

Bennett, Louise, 88–89, 95–97; "Dry-Foot Bwoy," 96–97; "No Lickle Twang," 96

Berry, James: "From Lucy: Holiday Reflections," 259–60

Bible, 76, 139, 141–51, 162, 181, 183, 187–88, 192, 193, 215, 220, 221, 237, 255

Bim, 89, 117–19

Black Power, 45, 48, 49, 51–55, 57, 59–60, 64–66, 101, 137, 194–95, 228–29

Black Stalin (Leroy Calliste): "Caribbean Man," 57–58

Blackman, Margot, 89

Blake, William: "The Little Black Boy," 143

Bloom, Valerie, 261

Boas, Franz, 70

Boethius, Anicius Manlius Severinus: *The Consolation of Philosophy,* 42

Bogle, Paul, 26–27

Bongo Jerry (Robin Small), 64, 105; "Mabrak," 64–66, 100–101, 137, 192, 219, 226, 229

Brand, Dionne, 268–69; "Hard Against My Soul, X," 268; "No Language is Neutral," 268–69; "P.P.S. Grenada," 267–68

Brathwaite, Edward Kamau, 36, 50, 54–55, 61–64, 83, 88, 100, 101, 120, 126, 151, 154–55, 160, 164, 176–94, 206, 216, 219, 235, 236, 257, 269, 270; "Basic Basie,"180; "Dies Irie," 192, 193; "Folkways," 182–83; "Nam," 177–78; "Nametracks," 189–90; "Negus," 187–88; "Poem for Walter Rodney," 229; "Postlude/Home," 28–29, 30, 44, 49, 56, 81, 148, 166, 180, 192, 269; "Rites," 132–33; "Salt," 192; "Sam Lord," 147–49; "Stone for Mikey Smith," 273; "The Awakening," 185–86; "The Cracked Mother," 186–87; "The Dust," 190; "The Visibility Trigger," 193; "Tom," 181–82; "Vèvè," 187–88; "Wings of a Dove," 183–85, 230; "Xango," 193; "Yellow Minnim," 189; *The Development of Creole Society in Jamaica*, 67, 70; *History of the Voice*, 35, 70–71, 89, 95, 231

Breeze, Jean Binta, 261; "Riddym Ravings," 233

Bridgetown Players, 91

Brontë, Emily, 91

Brook, A. C., 84

Brother Resistance, 235–36; "Book So Deep," 60–61

Brother Sam, 231–33

Brown, H. Rap, 54

Brown, Wayne, 106, 252

Bunyan, John: *The Pilgrim's Progress*, 194

Burns, Robert, 3, 93, 123

Bustamante, Alexander, 59

Butler, Tubal Uriah Buzz, 80

Calliste, Leroy. *See* Black Stalin

Calypso, 57–58, 178, 180, 233, 247, 254, 256–58, 266, 273

Campbell, George: "Holy," 143

Carew, Jan, 252

Carlyle, Thomas, 106, 246; *Occasional Discourse on the Nigger Question*, 23–24

Carmichael, Stokely, 49, 54, 61–62

Carpentier, Alejo, 53

Carter, Martin: "I Come from the Nigger Yard, 3, 23; "University of Hunger," 95

Cassidy, Frederic: *Dictionary of Jamaican English*, 89; *Jamaica Talk*, 89, 140

Césaire, Aimé, 49–53, 93; "Cahier d'un retour au pays natal" ("Notebook of a Return to the Native Land"), 49, 52, 116–17, 122

Charles, Faustin, 252

Chaucer, Geoffrey, 90–91, 102

Christophe, Henri, 35, 157

Cimabue, 161

Clemens, Samuel. *See* Mark Twain

Coleridge, Samuel Taylor, 38–39

Collins, Merle: "The Lesson," 78–81

Collymore, Frank, 89, 117–18

Columbus, Christopher, 5, 6–7, 8, 28, 68, 163, 186–87

Cooper, Afua, 266

Cooper, Carolyn, 59

Corsbie, Ken, 236

Count Basie, 180

Count Ossie, 232, 235

Craig, Christine: "St. Ann Saturday," 221–22

Cudjoe [Kojo] (Maroon leader), 34, 204, 210

cummings, e. e.: "next to of course god america i," 115, 118

Cutteridge, J. O., 187

D'Aguiar, Fred: "Letter from Mama Dot," 260; "El Dorado Update," 261

Dabydeen, Cyril, 252

Dabydeen, David: "Coolie Odyssey," 253

Damas, Léon, 50

Dante Alighieri, 90

Das, Mahadai, 252

Deane, Seamus, 81

Debray, Régis, 52

Defoe, Daniel, *Robinson Crusoe*, 161–63

Dessalines, 35

Devonish, Hubert: *Language and Liberation*, 35, 89, 105

Dewar, Ann-Marie: "Rasta, Me Son," 228–29

Dickens, Charles, 91

Dictionaries, 85–90
Dilke, Charles Wentworth, 38
Diop, Cheikh Anta: *Civilization or Barbarism*, 50
Donne, John, 115
Douglass, Frederick, 204
Drake, Francis, 14, 114
Drumming, 34, 64, 104–5, 179, 185, 186, 227, 235, 246, 254, 256–58
Drummond, Don, 101–4
Dub, 217–18, 227, 234–41, 244
DuBois, W. E. B.: *The Souls of Black Folk*, 50

Education, 19, 41, 55, 66, 69, 73–81, 98, 104, 106–7, 145, 154, 156, 175–76, 194, 228, 262–63
Edwards, Bryan: *History, Civil and Commercial, of the British Colonies in the West Indies*, 12
Eliot, T. S., 117, 124; "Little Gidding," 87; "The Waste Land," 113–14
Emerson, Ralph Waldo, 43, 140, 160
Espinet, Ramabai, 252
Eyre, E. J., 25–27, 40

Fanon, Frantz, 51, 53, 71
Fedon, Julien, 80
Fergus, Howard, 252
Freeman, Edward A., 38
Freud, Sigmund, 177
Froude, James Anthony, 106; *The English in the West Indies*, 38–41, 76, 106, 165
Frye, Northrop, 100, 151

Galeano, Edward: "The Imagination and the Will to Change," 242–43
Garvey, Marcus Mosiah, 53–54, 55, 56, 149, 191
Gilbert, Stuart: *James Joyce's Ulysses*, 161
Giotto, 161
Goodison, Lorna, 55, 73, 113, 120, 155, 160, 194–216, 254, 273; "Birth Stone," 204–5; "Bridge Views," 224–26; "Coir," 200–202; "Come Let Your Eyes Feel," 214–15; "Elephant," 202–3; "For My Mother (May I Inherit Half Her Strength)," 199–200; "For Rosa Parks," 205–6; "Guinea Woman," 4–5, 34, 101, 207; "Heartease II," 149–52;
"Heartease New England 1987," 213–14; "I Shall Light A Candle," 215–16; "Jah Music," 258–59; "Judges," 195–96; "Keith Jarrett—Rainmaker," 211–12; "Letters to the Egyptian," 208–9; "My Last Poem," 209; "My Last Poem (Again)," 210; "My Will," 133–34, 137, 141, 198; "Nanny," 204; "Recommendation for Amber," 198; "The Road of the Dread," 233–34; "Songs of Release II," 154, 178; "Survivor," 212–13; "Tamarind Season," 195; "The Mulatta as Penelope," 206–7; "The Transcendent Song of the Tuareg Woman," 197–98; "To Us, All Flowers Are Roses," 210–11; "We Are the Women," 203–4; "White Birds," 196–97
Gordon, George William, 26
Gould, Stephen Jay, 169
Goveia, Elsa: *The West Indian Slave Laws of the Eighteenth Century*, 11–14; *A Study of the Historiography of the West Indies*, 40, 178–79
Gray, Thomas, 43; "Elegy Written in a Country Churchyard," 43, 116, 180
Grimble, Arthur, 256
Guillén, Nicholás, 53

Hardy, Thomas, 91; *The Mayor of Casterbridge*, 75; *The Well-Beloved*, 84
Harris, Claire, 266
Harris, Wilson, 50, 167; *Eternity to Season*, 189; *The Whole Armour*, 188
Harrison, Tony: "On Not Being Milton," 116–17; *V*, 116
Hartnett, Michael: "A Farewell to English," 126–28, 151
Hawkins, John, 14, 114
Hawthorne, Nathaniel, 160
Hayakawa, Samuel: *Language in Action*, 70
Heaney, Seamus, 84, 115, 120, 123–24, 153–54, 155, 156, 175; "Nerthus," 136; "Song," 272; "The Tollund Man," 172
Henzell, Perry, 231
Hill, Errol, 91
Hill, Geoffrey, 115
Hippolyte, Kendel: "Zoo Story—Ja. '76," 230–31

Hodge, Merle: *Crick Crack, Monkey*, 73–74
Homer, 5–6, 36, 124, 155, 158, 167–69, 174–75, 188, 193–94, 195, 198, 206–7
Hooker, William, 40
Hope, Allan. *See* Mutabaruka
Hopkins, Gerard Manley, 117; "The Wreck of the Deutschland," 215
Hopkinson, Abdur-Rahman Slade, 52, 252
Humboldt, Wilhelm von, 70

Indenture, 17, 48, 57, 77, 159, 163
Isabella, Queen (of Spain), 68
Itwaru, Arnold, 266

Jakobson, Roman, 71–72, 221
James, C. L. R.: *Black Jacobins*, 178–79
James, Cynthia, 252
Jarrett, Keith, 211–12
Jerry, Bongo. *See* Bongo Jerry
Jeune, Ras Michael. *See* Ras Michael Jeune
Johnson, Colin. *See* Mudrooroo Nyoongah
Johnson, Linton Kwesi, 261–64; "Inglan is a bitch," 261; "It Dread Inna Inglan," 263; "Reggae Fi Dada," 264; "Reggae Sounds," 59; "Youtman," 144–45
Johnson, Samuel, 85
Jones, Evan: "The Song of the Banana Man," 97–98, 101
Joseph, Clifton, 266
Joyce, James, 84, 156, 161, 175; *Portrait of the Artist as a Young Man*, 120–21, 125

Keane, Elsworth McGranaham (Shake): "Shaker Funeral," 255
Keans-Douglas, Paul: "When Moon Shine," 137–38
Keats, John, 118
Kellman, Anthony: "Watercourse," 254–55
Khalkhali, Ayatollah, 36
King, Martin Luther, Jr., 42, 55
Kunene, Mazisi, 126
Kyk-Over-Al, 44, 81, 89, 274

Lamming, George, 105, 120; *In the Castle of My Skin*, 179
Levine, Philip, 120
Langland, William: *Piers Plowman*, 123–24

Language: African influence, 18–19, 34–35, 73, 82–83, 90, 98, 106, 134, 154–55, 176–78, 181, 185, 187–88, 191, 257; and difference, 3–9, 21, 28, 67–73, 81–85, 91, 101–102, 104–6, 109–13, 121–22, 126–28, 138–39, 146, 159, 164, 166, 262, 271; and poetic voice, 45, 61, 104, 113–14, 117–19, 120, 123, 124, 134, 205–6, 218–21, 222–34; dread talk, 35, 64–66, 144–45, 226–40, 245–47; local and literary, 26, 35, 37, 42, 43, 46, 64–66, 72–73, 75, 85–102, 111–13, 116, 117–20, 122–24, 130–32, 134–36, 138–39, 151, 158, 171–72, 207, 210–12, 221, 223, 225–27, 233–34, 250, 259–64, 271–72; naturalness and artifice of, 8, 19, 40, 46, 72, 74, 88, 92–93, 104, 109–13, 119, 123, 128–38, 140, 141–43, 145, 151, 158, 162, 197, 204, 225, 227, 228, 237, 259; spoken and written, 2, 60–61, 72, 85–101, 103, 109–11, 112–13, 114, 119, 130–33, 134–36, 141–42, 151, 155, 227, 234–40, 244, 259; standard, 8, 25, 42, 64–66, 68, 74–75, 83–87, 92–93, 105–7, 111, 136, 228, 262; strangeness and familiarity of, 8, 63, 64–66, 68, 72–73, 84–85, 95–97, 100, 112–13, 119, 135–41, 142, 151, 158, 162, 163–64, 192, 219, 228–29, 237; West Indian, 18–20, 81, 82–84, 90, 101–106, 120
Larkin, Philip, 242, 259
LaRose, John, 61
Las Casas, Bartoleme de, 8–10, 38
Lawrence, D. H., 87
Lee, John Robert, 252
Lee, Nathaniel, 238
LePage, R. B.: *Dictionary of Jamaican English*, 89
Levi Tafari, 261; "Black Sufferation," 137
Lewis, C. S., 4
Literature: and collective identity, 35, 39, 43, 46, 62–64, 75–76, 86–90, 95, 102–3, 114–15, 124, 137, 151, 153–55, 160, 163, 173, 174, 176–77, 179–80, 216, 269–70, 272, 274
Little Carib Theatre (Trinidad), 91
Little Theatre movement (Jamaica), 91

Macaulay, T. B., 76–77
Mackay, Charles, 75, 85

Maine, Henry: *Ancient Law*, 128–30
Mais, Roger, *Brother Man*, 92
Malcolm X, 54, 191
Malik, Delano Abdul DeCoteau, 235
Mallarmé, Stephane, 87
Malraux, André: *Psychology of Art*, 161
Manley, Norman, 154
Manley, Rachel, 252
Manuel, George, 69
Markham, E. A., 252
Marley, Bob, 59, 101, 214, 235, 257;
    "Chant Down Babylon," 59, 66, 145,
    149; "Duppy Conqueror," 36
Maroons, 33–35, 204, 249
Marryshow, T. A., 80
Marsden, J. H., 76
Marti, Jose, 53
Matthews, Marc, 236
Maxwell, Marina Ama Omowale, 235, 236
McAndrew, Wordsworth, 252
McDonald, Ian: "Yusman Ali, Charcoal
    Seller," 222–24
McFarlane, J. E. Clare: "The Prospect of
    West Indian Poetry," 274
McKay, Claude, 97; "Fetchin Water," 93–
    94; "The White House," 117
McKay, Don: "March Snow," 135
McNeill, Anthony, 245–48; "Credences at
    The Altar of Cloud," 216, 248; "Ode to
    Brother Joe," 245–47
McNeill, William T.: *Polyethnicity and
    National Unity in World History*, 48
McTair, Dionyse, 252
McTair, Roger, 252
McWatt, Mark, 260; "Morawhanna," 243–
    44
Melville, Hermann, 160; *Moby Dick*, 57,
    213–15
Mencken, H. L.: *The American Language*,
    89
Meredith, George: *Modern Love*, 116
Meredith, James, 54
Merton Thomas: *The Wisdom of the Desert*,
    197
Merwin, W. S., 248; "Odysseus," 168–69
Mill, John Stuart, 128
Milton, John, 76, 115, 116–17
Montesinos, Fray Antonio de, 8–9
Montessori, Maria, 74
Mordecai, Pamela, 252

Morris, Mervyn, 101–4, 105, 107, 236–37;
    "On Holy Week," 145–46; "The
    Pond," 102–3; "Valley Prince," 101–3
Mudrooroo Nyoongah (Colin Johnson),
    231
Muller, Max, 85
Murray, James: *Oxford English Dictionary*,
    85–86
Mutabaruka (Allan Hope), 235;
    "Revolutionary Poets," 218; "Two
    Poems On: What I Can Write," 241–42

Naipaul, V. S., 30–32, 252; *The Middle
    Passage*, 31–32, 38, 44, 47–48, 67, 76,
    105, 120, 143, 163, 165, 175, 181, 269
Nanny (Maroon leader), 34, 203, 204
National Dance Theater Company
    (Jamaica), 91, 157–58
Negritude, 49–52, 93
Nehru, Jawaharlal, 52
Neruda, Pablo, 124
Nettleford, Rex, 58, 89, 200, 239; *Cultural
    Action and Social Change: The Case of
    Jamaica*, 157; *Identity, Race and Protest
    in Jamaica*, 176
Newman, John Henry, 120, 190
Ngugi wa Thiong'o, 176
Nichols, Grace: "Epilogue," 266;
    "Wherever I Hang," 265–66
Nietzsche, Friedrich, 70

Okot p'Bitek, 126
Oku Onuora (Orlando Wong), 235; "i a
    tell," 217–18
Orwell, George: "Politics and the English
    Language," 142
Ossie, Count. *See* Count Ossie

Parks, Rosa, 54, 205
Parry, John, 17–18
Perry, Lee "Scratch," 59
Persaud, Sasenarine, 252
Philip, Marlene Nourbese, 266
Picasso, Pablo, 217
Pickering, Thomas, 69
Plato, 149, 219
Poe, Edgar Allan, 87
Pollard, Velma, 144–45, 228, 252
Pope, Alexander, 69
Popular Theatre movement (Eastern
    Caribbean), 236

Queen's Advice (Jamaica, 1865), 25–26, 106, 142, 200–201

Questel, Victor: "Pan Drama," 257–58

Raleigh, Walter, 14, 114

Ramkissoon-Chen, Rajandaye, 253

Ras Michael Jeune, 233

Rastafarianism, 35, 55–59, 60–61, 62, 64–66, 91, 144–45, 183–85, 189, 192, 200–201, 224–25, 226–34, 245–47, 258–59

Reckord, Barry, 91

Reeve, Henry, 75

Reggae, 36, 58–59, 227, 228, 231, 235, 264

Reid, V. S.: *New Day*, 92

Renan, Ernst, 47

Representation, 5–8, 11, 21–24, 27–28, 32–33, 44, 54, 70–72, 73, 78, 81, 83, 87, 89, 91–93, 94–104, 106, 108, 160–61, 182–83, 194, 220, 228, 233, 244, 245

Resistance, Brother. *See* Brother Resistance

Rhone, Trevor, 91, 231

Rich, Adrienne, 153, 155, 214

Roach, Eric, 104–8; "I am the archipelago," 107–8, 125, 167; "Letter to Lamming in England," 105

Roberts, Peter: *West Indians and their Language*, 89

Rodney, Walter, 59–60, 229

Rohlehr, Gordon, 66, 105, 178, 187, 247, 257

Salkey, Andrew, 61, 63

Salmon, C. S., 40

Sam, Brother. *See* Brother Sam

Sapir, Edward, 70

Sartre, Jean-Paul: *Black Orpheus*, 50–51, 53

Saussure, Frederick de, 91, 92

Sauvy, Alfred, 52

Scott, Dennis, 105; "Epitaph," 2; "No sufferer," 226–27, 234

Scott, Walter, 91

Selassie, Haile, 55–56, 201, 229, 231, 246

Selvon, Samuel: *Lonely Londoners*, 81–82, 92–93, 231

Senghor, Leopold, 50, 52

Senior, Olive, 249–52; "Ancestral Poem," 249–19; "The Mother," 251–52

Sepulveda, Juan Gines de, 8, 38

Sewell, W. G.: *The Ordeal of Free Labour in the West Indies*, 25

Seymour, A. J., 44, 81

Shakespeare, William, 76, 139, 157

Shearer, Hugh L., 49

Shelley, Percy Bysshe, 119

Sherlock, Philip, 17–18, 54, 78, 200; "Land of Look Behind," 34; "Pocomania," 94–95

Simmons, Harold, 160, 256

Slavery, 1–28, 33, 37–38, 40–41, 44–44, 47–50, 53, 55–56, 58, 60–61, 62–66, 81, 102, 105, 108, 111, 124–25, 143–44, 153–54, 159, 163–65, 166–67, 170, 176, 178–81, 186–88, 191, 200–201, 203–4, 205, 210, 213, 236, 249, 256–57, 259

Small, Robin. *See* Bongo Jerry

Smith, A. J. M., 44, 81

Smith, Michael, 126, 235, 236–40, 244, 249, 274; "It A Come," 237–38; "Me Cyaan Believe It," 238–40

Smith, Michael, G., 58

Smith, Samuel: *To Shoot Hard Labour*, 48–49

Soyinka, Wole, 52, 126

Spenser, Edmund, 115

St. John, Bruce, 83–84; "Education," 98–99; "West Indian Litany," 61

St. Omer, Dunstan, 157

Steiner, Rudolf, 74

Stevens, Wallace, 134

Tafari, Levi. *See* Levi Tafari

Thatcher, Margaret, 238, 263

Thelwell, Michael: *The Harder They Come*, 231–33

Theroux, Paul, 31

Thomas, John Jacob: *Froudacity*, 41, 220; *The Theory and Practice of Creole Grammar*, 41, 220

Thoreau, Henry David, 160

Tosh, Peter, 235

Toussaint, L'Ouverture, 33, 35, 37, 38, 40, 48, 79–80

Trinidad Theatre Workshop, 91, 157–58

Trollope, Anthony, *The West Indies and the Spanish Main*, 22–23

Truman, Harold, 52

Tuk bands, 254–55

Twain, Mark: *The Adventures of Huckleberry Finn*, 166

University of the West Indies, 59–61, 62, 77–78, 89, 111, 156–57, 176, 200

Vaughan, Henry: "The World," 135

Walcott, Clyde, 132–33
Walcott, Derek, 54–55, 67, 88, 90, 91, 98, 101, 103, 104, 105, 110, 113, 121–26, 140, 149, 152, 154, 155–75, 183, 194, 195, 206, 216, 231, 254, 256, 273; "A City's Death By Fire," 156; "A Far Cry from Africa," 125–26, 159; "Air," 165–66; *Another Life*, 44, 98, 110, 143–44, 159, 160–61, 163; "Arkansas Testament," 172–73; "Crusoe's Journal," 161–63; "Island," 217; "Midsummer, LII," 263, 268–69; "Names," 164–65, 178; "Nearing Forty," 217; *Omeros*, 6, 36, 124, 167–69, 171, 174–75; "Ruins of a Great House," 114, 170; "Sainte Lucie," 99–100, 126, 172, 194; "Sea Grapes," 169; "The Gulf," 109, 131, 141, 217; "The Hotel Normandie Pool," 63; "The Schooner Flight," 44–46, 122–24, 166, 170–71, 172, 178, 261, 270; "The Season of Phantasmal Peace," 173–74; "Tales of the Islands, VI," 117–20, 124; "Note" to *O Babylon!* 231; "Caligula's Horse," 195, 273; "The Muse of History," 110, 121, 124, 160, 166–67; "What the Twilight Says," 112–13, 121, 157–59, 163–64
Walcott, Noel, 235

Walcott, Roderick, 91
Wardle, John, 132–33
Warner-Lewis, Maureen, 189
Washington, Booker T., 53
Watt, G. F., 162
Webster, Noah: *American Dictionary of the English Language*, 86–87, 90
Weekes, Everton, 132
Whitman, Walt, 32, 43, 87–88, 110, 124, 160, 245, 248
Whorf, Benjamin Lee, 70–72, 140, 221
Wilberforce, William, 16
Wilde, Oscar: "The Critic as Artist," 143, 149–50; "The Decay of Lying," 160–61, 196, 217
Williams, Eric, 47; *British Historians and the West Indies*, 24–25, 40; *Capitalism and Slavery*, 178–79
Williams, William Carlos, 3, 123, 248
Wittgenstein, Ludwig, 70
Wong, Ansel, 35
Wong, Orlando. *See* Oku Onuora
Wordsworth, William, 97, 101, 130–32, 244; "London, 1802," 115; "The Thorn," 131; "To Toussaint L'Ouverture," 33, 153
Worrell, Frank, 132
Wright, Richard, 52

Yard Theatre (Jamaica), 235
Yeats, William Butler, 123, 125, 156, 244; "Adam's Curse," 244

Zephaniah, Benjamin, 261

J. EDWARD CHAMBERLIN was born in Vancouver and educated at the universities of British Columbia, Oxford, and Toronto. Since 1970, he has been on the faculty of the University of Toronto, where he is now professor of English and comparative literature. He has published and lectured widely on late nineteenth- and early twentieth-century literature, contemporary poetry, and aboriginal rights. He is a member of several editorial boards, a senior research associate with the Royal Commission on Aboriginal Peoples in Canada, and the poetry editor of *Saturday Night* magazine. His books include *The Harrowing of Eden: White Attitudes towards Native Americans* (1975), *Ripe Was the Drowsy Hour: The Age of Oscar Wilde* (1977), *Degeneration: The Dark Side of Progress* (1985), and *Oscar Wilde's London* (1987).